CONSENSUS AND CONTROVERSY

Defending Pope Pius XII

Pope Pius XII

Consensus and Controversy

Defending Pope Pius XII

Margherita Marchione

PAULIST PRESS
New York / Mahwah, N.J.

Acknowledgments: The author is indebted to the following: Barbara and Peter Bye for their computer assistance; Sisters Filomena DiCarlo, Josephine Cucuzzella, and Helen Sholander for secretarial help; historians Ronald Rychlak, William Doino, Jr., Rudolph Faller, and Karol Jozef Gajewski for reading the manuscript; the staff of *Inside the Vatican* and Reverend Lawrence Boadt for offering valuable suggestions. She also expresses gratitude for a grant from the Ralph M. Cestone Foundation.

Quotations from the eleven volumes of Vatican documents are from *Actes et Documents du Saint-Siège relatifs à la Seconde Guerre Mondiale,* edited by Pierre Blet, Angelo Martini, Burkhart Schneider, and Robert A. Graham (Città del Vaticano: Editrice Vaticana, 1965–81).

We are grateful to Religion News Service for permission to use its syndicated series of six unforgettable articles (copyright 1942) that appeared in the *New York Times* from June 8 to June 13, 1942.

Book design by Theresa M. Sparacio

Cover design by Valerie Petro

Library of Congress Cataloging-in-Publication Data

Marchione, Margherita.
    Consensus and controversy : defending Pope Pius XII / Margherita Marchione.
      p. cm
    Includes bibliographical references and index.
    ISBN 0-8091-4083-7 (alk. paper)
    1. Pius XII, Pope, 1876–1958—Relations with Jews. 2. Holocaust, Jewish (1939–1945). 3. Judaism—Relations—Christianity. 4. Catholic Church—Relations—Judaism. 5. Christianity and antisemitism—History—20th century. 6. World War, 1939–1945—Religious aspects—Catholic Church. I. Title.
BX1378 .M26 2002
282′.092—dc21

                                       2002001920

Published by Paulist Press
997 Macarthur Boulevard
Mahwah, New Jersey 07430

www.paulistpress.com

Printed and bound in the
United States of America

To Ralph M. Cestone,
my very dear friend and benefactor,
whose generosity has made possible
this book on Pope Pius XII

Contents

Chapter IV
Church Leaders versus Tyrant

Chapter V
Survivors' Testimonials

Chapter VI
Meeting the Challenge

Part III: The Media

Chapter VII
The New York Times

Chapter VIII
The Vatican Radio

Chapter IX
L'Osservatore Romano

Part IV: The Discussion Continues

Chapter X
Feeding the Controversy

Chapter XI
The New Commission and Its Questions

Chapter XII
Pope John Paul II

Part V: Conclusion

Chapter XIII
The Catholic Church

Part VI: Appendices

Part VII: Notes

Part VIII: Index

Foreword

---

*T*he work of Sister Margherita Marchione, *Consensus and Contro-versy: Defending Pope Pius XII,* has a special importance today. Her dedicated scholarship in defense of Pope Pius XII is much needed in response to the careless innuendoes and unfounded accusations that have been leveled against his good name and his reputation as a coura-geous and holy pastor of souls.

To the Catholic world, which knew him as a saintly man, a scholar, a man of peace and a committed defender and protector of the victims of the war and hatred that drenched Europe in blood, these attacks are hard to understand.

At the end of World War II, Western nations paid tribute to Pope Pius XII's efforts on behalf of the oppressed. This was especially true in the case of the Jewish communities of Europe. When he died in 1958, Jews everywhere praised him for his help and were among the first to express sorrow and gratitude for his solicitude during the Holocaust.

In the 1960s, however, a campaign of vilification began against Pope Pius XII. His detractors claimed that he lacked courage, human compassion, and a sense of moral rectitude. Today, this revisionist his-tory has even persuaded some Catholics, academicians, and editorial commentators that these alleged claims are unquestionably true. The hostile attacks by the media, characterizing Pius as a weak, cold, Church bureaucrat, replaced the historical record that showed him as an uncommonly good man confronted by a monstrous evil.

The continuation of the smear campaign of innuendo against the memory of Pius XII, that began in 1963 with Rolf Hochhuth's play, *The Deputy,* has created this "black legend" that accuses the Pope of refusing

1

to speak out about the Holocaust in spite of his detailed knowledge of Jewish suffering.

In her effort to set the record straight, Sister Margherita has contributed to the history of Jewish-Catholic relations by recording the witness of Jews and Catholics and by reproducing Vatican documentary records. In this book, *Consensus and Controversy: Defending Pope Pius XII,* and in her two earlier studies on the history of the pontificate of Pius XII—*Yours Is a Precious Witness: Memoirs of Jews and Catholics in Wartime Italy* (1997), and *Pope Pius XII: Architect for Peace* (2000)—Sister Margherita presents strong evidence to counter the "black legend" of an uncaring Pope.

As the President of the United States Conference of Catholic Bishops, Bishop Joseph Fiorenza, wrote recently "Whatever standard is used, Pius XII prevented Hitler from succeeding with his demonic plan to eliminate all European Jews, and for that he deserves admiration." It is this historic truth that Sister Margherita proclaims loud and clear in her most recent work.

All of us who long for the truth to prevail and the reputation of a good man to be restored commend the truly heroic dedication of this scholarly religious not only to set the record straight, but indeed to show Pius XII to be a leader of heroic virtue at a brutal and fear-filled time. Her work is a work of simple justice on behalf of a great religious leader, and I enthusiastically recommend it to scholars and the general public alike.

Theodore Cardinal McCarrick, Ph.D.

Presentation

Sister Margherita Marchione, Ph.D., made significant contributions to both the history and culture of America and Italy. As an international scholar she continues to inspire others with forty books and over one hundred magazine and newspaper articles. Several years ago she launched a crusade in defense of Pope Pius XII. Word that she has completed another powerful book to such purpose is no surprise.

Sister Margherita now offers a definitive and conclusive volume—*Consensus and Controversy: Defending Pope Pius XII.* This new book successfully counters the current procession of books that ignore the historic truth about the Holocaust.

Before, during, and after World War II, Jews and Catholics applauded Pius XII for having saved the lives of so many victims of Nazism. On the death of the Pontiff in 1958, Golda Meir, Foreign Minister and later the Prime Minister of the State of Israel, sent this message: "We share in the grief of humanity....When fearful martyrdom came to our people, the voice of the Pope was raised for its victims. The life of our times was enriched by a voice speaking out about great moral truths above the tumult of daily conflict. We mourn a great servant of peace."

It is my hope that readers will benefit by the documentation Sister Margherita provides in her new book, *Consensus and Controversy: Defending Pope Pius XII,* gaining insight into the truth about the actions of the saintly and courageous Eugenio Pacelli, who served as Supreme Pontiff of the Catholic Church from 1939 to 1958.

Ralph M. Cestone

3

Part I
Prologue

Chapter I
The Consensus and the Controversy

1. Education Needed

" A full exploration of Pope Pius XII's conduct is needed. He did *not* encourage Catholics to defy Nazi orders." Such was the March 18, 1998 *New York Times* editorial statement. And, three days later, Peter Steinfels wrote, "The Vatican Document skirts the issue of the Pope's *silence.*" The allegations that followed on April 26, 1998, in the *New York Times* magazine article, "John Paul's Jewish Dilemma," maligned the character of both Pius XII and John Paul II, offended Catholics, and denigrated the Catholic faith.

I have been called a crusader for the truth, as well as defender of Pope Pius XII, who was unjustly criticized for "silence" during the Holocaust. However, German bishops had warned the Vatican about Hitler's unpredictable and irrational fury: Open defiance would only lead to greater brutality. By not attacking the Nazis directly, he was able to protect those threatened and to provide shelter in church buildings.

Seeing it is the duty of every Catholic to defend the truth, I challenge readers to recall Saint Paul in fighting "the good fight" (Tim 4:7), and to take a strong stand in defense of Pius XII. However, I pray you will be more successful than I have been. In fact, I had the honor in the above-mentioned article of being singled out as "a faithful remnant." Why? Because I had written many "pro-Pius letters to the editor" of the *New York Times*—none of which were ever published? Indeed, I felt honored to be mentioned, because, at times, remnants are useful!

The negative propaganda about Pope Pius XII misleads many. After refuting the allegations made by John Cornwell in his book, *Hitler's Pope,* on several radio and TV programs, I received a multitude of letters and telephone calls encouraging me to continue my efforts. I see the need to summarize the present controversy in order to help people recognize the truth about Pius XII.

If history is to reflect the true account of Pius XII's efforts, it will have to be taught to Catholic children. Recently, in an address to the members of a diocesan Pastoral Council, I stated: "As Christians, we are called to turn the other cheek. But when we are defending the Church, we must stand for the truth." I called for the formation of a diocesan Holocaust curriculum and a concerted effort on the part of Catholic educators to familiarize themselves with the subject and to impart that knowledge to today's youngsters. I further explained that the state's curriculum for Holocaust education (New Jersey) is lacking in information about the Pope's efforts and about the many Catholic rescuers who saved the lives of Jews and others. Pope Pius XII was not "silent," and his courageous acts during World War II are incontestable. Through public discourses, appeals to governments, and secret diplomacy, he was engaged more than any other individual or agency combined in the effort to curb the excesses of war and to rebuild the peace.

I recounted how I had written to the Catholic superintendents of schools in the United States enlisting their help to increase awareness of Pius XII's role. I also sent a questionnaire for teachers, which would indicate their awareness of the subject. A significant number of respondents welcomed the idea of teaching about Pius XII but admitted their own lack of knowledge. The place to begin to pass on "the truth" to the next generation is in Catholic schools and in religious education programs, where Holocaust education must be included in the regular curriculum.

Objectives should identify "promoting respect, freedom, and opportunity for all, regardless of nationality, religion, or race"; teaching about the work of "rescuers whose extraordinary acts of courage" saved many Jews from death; explaining that Pope Pius XII was not "silent" during the war; demonstrating that "Pius XII's humanitarianism was a new and effective method of fighting anti-Semitism"; emphasizing "American Jewry's appreciation for Pope Pius XII's extraordinary accomplishments during the Holocaust." The charges claiming "silence," "moral culpability," or "anti-Semitism" can be refuted by anyone who examines evidence carefully. These charges derive from a wide spectrum of political and ideological attacks on Christianity.

I also shared Rabbi Harold Schulweis's statement published in *America* magazine: "I am chagrined in speaking to Catholic audiences that there is no awareness of their own heroes." In the article, the Rabbi estimated that there were at least fifty thousand people in Europe who risked their own lives trying to help persecuted Jews.

Perhaps an examination of conscience is in order during this millennium. I was pleased to read about Rabbi Meir Lau's rejection of some Israelis' call for a boycott of the papal pilgrimage to Jerusalem. "Judaism has taught us to turn an enemy into a lover," he said. "But to take a friend and turn him into an enemy is not sensible and not just." His reference to Pope John Paul II in this last sentence can and should also be applied to Pope Pius XII.

2. The Unknown Story

Revisionists, whose strategy is to rewrite the history of the Holocaust, ignore the truth. During the late nineteenth and early twentieth centuries, the world was plagued with racism, nationalism, and militarism long before Eugenio Pacelli became a priest, papal diplomat, and finally Pope. As Vatican Secretary of State, Cardinal Pacelli, who sent sixty protests to Germany between 1933 and 1939, did not have the power to make Adolph Hitler obey him. Nor did he have this power as Pope Pius XII. How can one ignore these facts?

Hitler despised Christianity and saw the Catholic Church as an opponent. He targeted, isolated, and destroyed Jews, Communists, Social Democrats, and members of the Catholic Center party. As early as January 1934, the Berlin government complained about the unusually antagonistic tone of the Vatican. Statements against Cardinal Pacelli also appeared in the Nazi *Voelkischer Beobachter,* along with photographs of him and other Church dignitaries beneath the heading: "Agitators in the Vatican against Fascism and National Socialism."[1]

When news was released that, on January 30, 1933, Adolf Hitler had been appointed Chancellor of Germany, the Vatican's first official step was a defense of the Jews by Secretary of State Eugenio Cardinal Pacelli, who six years later would be elected Pope. An article by historian Robert Leiber, S.J., who became Pius XII's private secretary, clearly indicates that the Holy See ordered the Apostolic Nuncio at Berlin to make an official representation to the German government in defense of the Jews and to warn the Nazi government against the dangers of an anti-Semitic policy.[2]

Thus, when dictatorial emergency powers were granted to Hitler only ten days after the Empowerment Law of January 30, 1933, the Vatican requested that the Apostolic Nuncio in Berlin point out to the Reich government all the dangers of an anti-Semitic policy and speak out in favor of the Jews. In his correspondence with the German archbishops and bishops (1939–45), Pope Pius XII insisted that peaceful arrangements must be preserved, but without abandoning the principles of natural law and of revelation.

Despite the multiplication of punitive measures against the Church, the Pope stressed the importance of the Peace Conference and the need for the bishops to continue efforts toward a compromise with the State. Later, on April 1, 1933, the Holy See lodged a forceful protest to Berlin, warning the Nazis not to proceed with the anti-Jewish boycott. [3]

Difficulties arose between the Vatican and Hitler. On April 30, 1937, Cardinal Pacelli asked the German Ambassador to send the following response to the government in Berlin: "Your Excellency, Responding to the German Government's protest against the encyclical *Mit brennender Sorge,* based on the assumption that the Holy See has a hostile attitude against the German government, I ask you to note that, if you read the encyclical carefully, Pope Pius XI is saying the truth, giving full support of morality and showing the extent of today's crisis. The Holy See has no other aim but the speedy healing among all peoples. An honest clarification does not mean we do not recognize one's accomplishments. A careful reading of the encyclical will show that there are no political aims. The Church is not willing to have any other point of view. It wishes to avoid damage to the German people; to overcome disturbances of present-day Germany that aim to destroy the Church. The government has not stopped this dangerous, anti-Christian, tragic situation. The encyclical describes the danger of Bolshevism. The Holy See knows that the use of force and a systematic coalition against Bolshevism is important. But it also recognizes that the Germans are using the same methods of the Bolshevists against the Catholic Church. The authority of the Church cannot tolerate such treatment. We are solely interested in the well-being of souls."[4]

When I began the research for *Consensus and Controversy: Defending Pius XII,* I was unaware of the above-cited crucial information, which contradicts the statement that Eugenio Cardinal Pacelli did not defend the Jews. Further research not only confirmed my conviction that the Vatican Secretary of State's policy toward the Jews was one of deep sensitivity and brotherhood but also assured me that throughout his life Pope Pius XII was not anti-Semitic.

During World War II, Pius XII believed that, had he publicly confronted Hitler, thousands more would have been exterminated. In an article, "Pius XII as Scapegoat," Michael Novak refers to some critics who "demand in retrospect an open, no-holds-barred papal condemnation of unprecedented evil. They offer nothing but speculation…and must concede to the papacy far greater rhetorical power than modern theories of the advanced secularization of Europe permit. Do such historians pledge that they, for instance, would heed the solemn words of a pope today, even when those words go against their own beliefs and interests? And if they wouldn't today, why would others then?"[5]

3. Seeking the Sources

As I contemplated this new book, I was undecided about the format. My previous books cited specific quotes from hundreds of news reports of the *New York Times* and other World War II media in support of the rational conclusion that Pius XII was not "silent." This book, *Consensus and Controversy: Defending Pope Pius XII,* is a sequel to the two books published by Paulist Press: *Yours Is a Precious Witness: Memoirs of Jews and Catholics in Wartime Italy* (1997) and *Pius XII: Architect for Peace* (2000).[6] In these publications, scholarly evidence vindicates the reputation of Pope Pius XII.

Eugenio Pacelli held the office of Nuncio in Germany (1917–29), then rose to Vatican Secretary of State (1930–39), and finally was elected Pope (1939–58). Besides the collection of books preceding his pontificate—*Gesammelte Reden*[7] and *Discorsi e panegirici* (1931–39)[8]—I found the following collections most important from a religious and a political point of view: *Discorsi e radiomessaggi* (twenty volumes)[9]; *Atti e discorsi di Pio XII* (twenty volumes).[10] Besides these fifty volumes, one must add the monumental work *Actes et Documents du Saint-Siège relatifs à la Seconde Guerre Mondiale* [sometimes referred to in the text as *Actes, Actes et documents,* or *ADSS*],[11] edited by Pierre Blet, Robert A. Graham, Angelo Martini, and Burkhart Schneider.

No one can deny that, during the period of the Holocaust, Pius XII spoke out against Nazism! His voice was heard. There is documentation available in the archives of the Vatican Radio, *L'Osservatore Romano,* the London *Times,* as well as *The Tablet* of London and, of course, the *New York Times.* Throughout World War II, Pius XII continually attacked Nazi policies. He so provoked the Nazis that they called him "a mouthpiece of the Jewish war criminals."

Numerous examples of Germany's policies in the period 1933–39 and of the attitude of the Nazi hierarchy toward the Vatican are found in *The Persecution of the Catholic Church in the Third Reich.*[12] This volume, a compilation of primary source material from Nazi Germany, was translated into English. Its documentary evidence proves that Nazis held Pius XII in contempt and even ridiculed him when he was Secretary of State. Indeed, cartoons appearing in propaganda articles depict Pius as a coconspirator with Jewish and Communist elements, acting to destroy National Socialism. He is drawn with grotesque "Jewish" features. Hideous caricatures of this type appeared regularly in publications such as *Der Sturmer,* produced by Julius Streicher, later sentenced to death at Nuremberg for his vile war crimes. If the Nazis could have cited the Pope as their secret sympathizer, they would have gained an immense propaganda coup. With the combined forces of the USA, USSR, and Great Britain being ranged against Germany, their need to boost morale was desperate!

4. Speaking Out

Among the first historians to "speak out" on the Holocaust was the Jewish scholar Jenö Levai, who insisted that the bishops of the Catholic Church "intervened again and again on the instructions of the Pope," adding that "the one person who did more than anyone else to halt the dreadful crime and alleviate its consequences, is today made the scapegoat for the failures of others."[13]

Pope Pius XII's experience before the outbreak of war in September 1939 conditioned his responses to the excesses of the Nazi regime. Speaking out against the atrocities effected no relief. He sent dozens of protests when the Nazis began destroying Catholic societies, schools, and parish organizations. Instead of stopping these measures, the Nazi leaders whipped up anti-Catholic hysteria to an even more hysterical degree. Had Pius XII stridently protested, more lives would have been lost.

Before the 1933 concordat with Germany, the SS and Gestapo had rounded up and incarcerated thousands of supporters and activists of the leading Catholic Center party and were threatening thousands more. The former Chancellor, Heinrich Brüning, stated that Catholic youth leaders had already been tortured to death and there was a ghastly fate hanging over others. By signing a concordat, which might give legal protection and accord a semblance of civil rights to those already imprisoned, Pius XII was following the most admirable principles of Christian charity. He could not foresee the horrors that Nazism employed in the following years.

In the spring of 1933 the German government asked the Holy See to conclude a concordat with the Reich: The proposal had the approval of the Episcopate and of at least the majority of the German Catholics. In fact, the bishops and this German majority thought that neither the concordats previously negotiated with some individual German states nor the Weimar Constitution provided adequate guarantees or assurances, of respect for their convictions, for their faith, rights, or their liberty of action. In such volatile conditions the guarantees would not be secure unless they were legalized by a concordat entered into with the contemporary Central Government of the Reich.[14]

Since it was the government that made the proposal, the responsibility for all regrettable consequences would have fallen on the Holy See had that office refused the proposed concordat. It was not that the Church, for her part, had any illusions of excessive optimism or that, in concluding the concordat, she had the intention of approving the teachings or positions of National Socialism; this was expressly declared and explained at the time.[15] It must, however, be recognized that the concordat in the years that followed brought some advantages or at least prevented greater evils. In fact, in spite of all the times the provisions of the concordat had been violated, the concordat itself gave Catholics a juridical basis for their defense, a stronghold behind which to shield themselves in their opposition—as long as this was possible—to the ever growing campaign of religious persecution.

The bitter struggle against the Church did, in fact, escalate in intensity; there was the dissolution of Catholic organizations; the gradual suppression of the flourishing Catholic schools, both public and private, forced eventually to kneel to the pressure of a clever, closely organized propaganda effort. Next came the closing, dissolution, and confiscation of religious houses and other ecclesiastical institutions as well as the complete suppression of the Catholic press and publishing houses.

Long before any major voice in Europe condemned the Nazis, Pacelli helped prepare a decree condemning anti-Semitism, issued March 25, 1928: "Moved by Christian charity, the Holy See is obligated to protect the Jewish people against unjust vexations and, just as it reprobates all rancour and conflicts between peoples, it particularly condemns unreservedly hatred against the people once chosen by God; the hatred that commonly goes by the name of anti-Semitism."

Eugenio Cardinal Pacelli never swerved from his principles and spoke out repeatedly against the outrages of Nazism. He strongly disapproved of German politics and always objected to the Nazis. On becoming Pope, he was no different. My books will help enlighten all who seek the truth.

5. Giovanni Miccoli

Professor Giovanni Miccoli is a Church History professor at the University of Trieste. His book *I dilemmi e i silenzi di Pio XII* (Rizzoli, 2000) attempts to assess the so-called "silence" of Pius XII. Recently he stated: "It is not a case of condemning or absolving Pius XII, or of asking what Pius XII should have done. Rather, the fundamental point is to illustrate what he and his collaborators did, how they operated and why they did what they did."[16]

The author further explains that the approach should be that of a historian who researches the documents, understands the facts, reconstructs the material, and does not seek sensationalism. According to Miccoli, the motivation for the Pope's silence may be found in the Vatican's interpretation of the war, in the rapport between German Catholicism and Nazism, in the Vatican's attitude regarding the dangers of Communism, in the occupation of Rome, as well as in the Vatican's position on anti-Semitism and the racial laws. The Vatican remained impartial for three reasons: to be able to mediate among the parties and attain peace; to supervise the humanitarian organizations on all fronts during the conflict; and to represent a sign of unity among all Christians at the conclusion of the war. Regarding information reporting the extermination of

Jews, what was the Church to do? The choice was to remain impartial and to risk appearing indifferent.

Records show that the Catholic Church consistently assisted many Jewish victims of Nazi anti-Semitism, even before the outbreak of World War II. Proof is supported by news reports, testimony at the Nuremberg trials, documents in foreign archives, and research of reputable Jewish, Catholic, and other historians who were witnesses to these events.

6. Conclusion

Catholics and Jews can no longer continue to condone statements by those who defame Pope Pius XII, ignore the facts, take information out-of-context, or limit themselves to the opinion of prejudiced writers. Nowhere is the lack of truth and accuracy more evident than in the many recent attacks on Pope Pius XII. I believe that my book offers significant, incontrovertible proof of the historic truth: It effectively refutes the "big lie" regarding the role of Pius XII toward the Jewish victims of the Nazi terror, a role which, strangely and unfortunately, certain elements of the secular media have continued to broadcast and enhance.

During the April 26–28, 1998, Conference on "Humanity at the Limit: The Impact of the Holocaust on Jews and Christians," Dr. Hoeckman, Secretary of the Holy See's Commission for Religious Relations with the Jews, observed: "A growing number of Catholic people...are fed up with unrelenting pressure in matters and issues that not only pertain to Jewish concerns, but that also deeply touch *their* concerns, convictions, and sensitivities....They resent the fact that informed Jewish leaders refer to *their* leader, Pope John Paul II, as 'the very best friend of the Jews'[17] one day, but more or less accusing him of 'historical distortion'[18] the next. In fact, I feel insulted when I read a Jewish paper in which the director of interreligious affairs of a Jewish organization is reported to have referred to Catholic positions as 'a charade of self-righteous responses.'"[19]

In a paper entitled, "Catholics and Jews: Confronting the Holocaust Together," Judith Banki, Associate National Director for Interreligious Affairs of the American Jewish Committee, stated (December 1987): "Let us resolve to pursue [our efforts] toward the goal of understanding and combating the pathology of group hatred and persecution in an atmosphere free of polemics. We are not responsible for the prejudices of the world into which we were born, but we are responsible for fighting them. We are not accountable for past events over which we had no control, but we are accountable for the future. We are jointly responsible for facing history and for forging new traditions of human and spiritual solidarity—for the sake of our children, our world, and the sanctification of the One who is Holy to all of us."

In his "Message to the Jews" on the occasion of the fiftieth anniversary of the "Uprising of the Warsaw Ghetto" (April 6, 1993), Pope John Paul II stated: "As Christians and Jews, following the example of the faith of Abraham, we are called to be a blessing for the world (Gen 12:2 ff.). This is the common task awaiting us. It is therefore necessary for us, Christians and Jews, to be first a blessing to one another. This will effectively occur if we are united in the face of the evils which are still threatening: indifference and prejudice, as well as displays of anti-Semitism."

This volume, *Consensus and Controversy: Defending Pope Pius XII,* provides information and documentation for the general public. It not only responds to the criticisms against this Pope, but endeavors to place the arguments in the context of World War II.

Part 1, the prologue, follows the foreword by Theodore Cardinal McCarrick and the presentation by Ralph Cestone. Chapter 1 serves as an introduction to the book and chapter 2 deals with the life of Eugenio Pacelli.

Part 2, "Remembering the Truth," is clearly a defense of Pope Pius XII. I point out the significance of a syndicated series of articles that appeared in the *New York Times* as written by feature writer Henry Smith Leiper (Copyright by Religion News Service: *Six Churchmen Who Defied Hitler,* June 8, 1942–June 13, 1942).

This section also directly responds to the media's later accusations that churchmen did not defy Nazism. The religious leaders who defied Hitler are: two Protestants, Bishop Eivand Berggrav (Lutheran Bishop of Oslo) and Professor Karl Barth; Greek Orthodox Patriarch Gavrilo of Yugoslavia; and three Catholics: Bishop Clemens August von Galen (Bishop of Müenster), Archbishop Johann de Jong (Archbishop of Utrecht), and Cardinal Ernest van Roey (Archbishop of Malines).

Part 3, "The Media," is an important source of information. It examines significant contemporary documentation from the *New York Times* and *L'Osservatore Romano,* as well as information from the Vatican Radio archives.

Part 4, "The Discussion Continues," consists of the following three chapters: "Feeding the Controversy," "The New Commission and Its Questions," and "John Paul II."

Part 5, "Conclusion," is followed by part 6, the appendix, that includes valuable summaries of selected *ADSS* documents[20] and a bibliography. Part 7, the notes, is followed by part 8, the index.

I have deliberately chosen to involve myself in this contemporary issue affecting the Magisterium of the Catholic Church. Speaking in St. Louis, Missouri, January 27, 1999, Pope John Paul II stated: "If you want Peace, work for Justice. If you want Justice, defend Life. If you want Life, embrace the Truth—the Truth revealed by God."

It is my fervent prayer that as people are informed about the truth, misunderstandings will cease and that genuine reconciliation and regard for the sanctity of life, to which Pope Pius XII and Pope John Paul II each have dedicated a lifetime of saintly efforts, will motivate Jews and Christians. Only then will all members of the human family promote the truth about the Holocaust.

The Jubilee Year of grace proclaimed by Jesus of Nazareth continues in the life of the Church and in the personal life of each believer. The millennium Holy Year concluded on January 6, 2001, as television cameras "sculpted" the sixteen panels of the Holy Door of the Vatican Basilica as testimony to the Jubilee experience. These panels spoke of the history of salvation and, in particular, of a gracious God filled with love for mankind. The scenes remind us that, in Christ who is like us in all things except sin, God has become our traveling companion, to make our pilgrimage a journey of conversion and of return home to the Father.

In the synagogue of Nazareth, Jesus proclaimed "a year of grace from the Lord" and "the eyes of all were fixed on him" (Luke 4:20). So too, my eyes joined those of the pilgrims who passed through the Holy Door as we celebrated the mysteries of salvation in union with Pope John Paul II. He exhorted all to look beyond space and time for a goal that lies beyond the limits of this world. May we continue to keep our eyes fixed on Christ and, in communion with John Paul II and Pius XII, share the Gospel message of hope.

Chapter II
The Career of Pope Pius XII

---

1. Early Years

*E*ugenio Maria Giuseppe Giovanni Pacelli, son of Filippo Pacelli and Virginia Graziosi, was born in Rome, March 2, 1876, and baptized two days later. After kindergarten and elementary school, he began his studies at the Ennio Quirino Visconti Lyceum. In 1894, he entered the Capranica Seminary and enrolled at the Gregorian University. Owing to poor health, Eugenio continued his education at home and registered in the Sapienza School of Philosophy and Letters, as well as at the Papal Athenaum of St. Apollinaris for Theology. He received the Baccalaureate and Licentiate degrees summa cum laude. He was ordained a priest April 2, 1899.

Father Eugenio Pacelli was assigned to serve as curate to the Chiesa Nuova while continuing studies for a doctorate in Canon Law and Civil Law at the Apollinaris. The young priest also served as a research aide in the Office of the Congregation of Extraordinary Ecclesiastical Affairs and, from 1904 to 1916, as assistant to Pietro Cardinal Gasparri in the codifying of canon law.

In 1904, Father Pacelli became a Papal Chamberlain with the title of Monsignor and one year later a Domestic Prelate. In 1910, Monsignor Pacelli represented the Holy See at the Coronation of King George V in London. He was appointed Assistant Secretary of the Congregation of Extraordinary Ecclesiastical Affairs and, in 1912, became Pro-Secretary of State. In 1914, he became Secretary of the Congregation of Extraordinary Ecclesiastical Affairs.

2. Diplomatic Service

On April 20, 1917, Pacelli was appointed Nuncio to Bavaria, Germany. Soon after (May 13), he was consecrated Bishop and elevated to the rank of Archbishop. He presented his credentials to Ludwig III, King of Bavaria, May 28, 1917. Pope Benedict XV, who had undertaken a peace initiative, sent Pacelli to Kaiser Wilhelm II. Unfortunately, when the morale in the Russian army collapsed, the Germans felt that victory was assured, but they were not ready for peace.

In 1918, after Germany was defeated, the papacy turned the attention of the Allied powers to the great dangers that would arise "unless a peace which Germans can accept and which is not humiliating for them is…reached." Most Germans found it difficult to live with the Treaty of Versailles of 1919, which, if not accepted, the Allies stated, would mean the resumption of their military operations. Among those who objected most indignantly to the rebirth of Poland was General Von Seeckt, a power in the rebirth of the vanquished German army, who stated in 1922: "Poland's existence is intolerable and incompatible with the essential conditions of Germany's life. Poland must go and will go.…The obliteration of Poland must be one of the fundamental drives of German policy."[1]

On June 22, 1920, Pacelli became the first Apostolic Nuncio to Germany. Four years later, March 29, 1924, he signed a concordat with Bavaria, ratified by its Parliament on January 15, 1925. Pope Benedict XV sent Pacelli to Munich. Later the Nuncio's residence was transferred to Berlin. Again, unfortunately, the Germans were not ready for peace.

For two decades Pacelli confronted world problems. He was able to conclude concordats with Bavaria, Prussia, and Baden, but had no success with either the Reich or the Soviet Union. As Nuncio and then as Vatican Secretary of State, he faced and feared the rise of the National Socialists.

The Lateran Treaty of 1929 established formal relations between Italy and the papacy. After concluding a concordat with Prussia, Pacelli was recalled to Rome and received a Cardinal's hat on December 16. Soon after, February 7, 1930, he was appointed Secretary of State (succeeding his former mentor Pietro Cardinal Gasparri) and became archpriest of the Vatican Basilica.

3. Secretary of State

Following the example of Mussolini, who had established formal relations between Italy and the Vatican in 1929, Hitler initiated a concordat. The Holy See agreed especially with this move since the new German regime was determined to tamper with the existing concordats. Cardinal Pacelli negotiated with the Germans to protect the rights of Catholics. The official Protestant Church soon came under Nazi influence and a Reichsbischof was appointed. As long as the German government guaranteed freedom of religion, the Catholic Church could express its point of view. Opposed to Nazi ideology, the Church could yet register protests and keep its independence in Nazi Germany. However, the Holy See had to make concessions, for only party members were allowed to engage in politics. The clergy could no longer participate.

The National Socialist party exploited all the problems and fears of Germans to their own purpose, promising to achieve national unity, to undo the "shame" of Versailles, and to make Germany great again. The party vowed to fight Communism and any form of Marxism and to deprive all Jewish descendants, even if baptized, of their German citizenship. President Paul von Hindenburg, who for many years had refused to appoint Adolf Hitler as Chancellor, succumbed to the opposition on January 30, 1933. In replacing Franz von Papen, a Catholic Center party member of the Prussian legislature, Hitler became the leader of the largest party in the Reichstag.

In 1934, after the Nazi persecution of Jews in Germany, Cardinal Pacelli published three articles in the Vatican newspaper proclaiming that National Socialism better deserved the name of "national terrorism." Like all movements that resort to terrorism, the offending group "sprang from a gang rather than from a party," according to Charles Pichon, a French wartime correspondent. In his book, *The Vatican and Its Role in World Affairs,* Pichon testified that Pius XII's speeches on behalf of victims of Nazi terrorism were clear. Pichon explained that the Nazis were hostile to Catholics and Jews. In fact, Hitler's principal collaborator, Martin Borman, declared: "We Germans are the first to be appointed by destiny to break with Christianity. It will be an honor for us. A thousand ties link us to the Christian faith; they will be broken at a single blow. Our intention is not to raze the cathedrals to the ground, but to fill them with a new ideology and with proclamations of a new faith." [2]

Nonetheless, the Catholic Church did not surrender into silence, and numerous protests and interventions were made through the nuncios and the ambassadors. On page 167, Charles Pichon states: "The pontifical texts condemned most strongly the antisemitic persecutions, the oppression of invaded lands, the inhuman conduct of the war, and also the deification of earthly things which were made into idols: the Land and the Race, the State and the Class. In the positive order, these documents urged the Christian restoration of family life and education, the harmonious reconstruction of society, the admittance of the working man to common and private property, the equality of nations, small and large, the participation of impoverished peoples in the natural resources of the globe, the suppression of hate propaganda and, finally, an international organization for disarmament and the maintenance of peace."

Cardinal Pacelli presided as Papal Legate at the International Eucharistic Congress in Buenos Aires, Argentina, October 10–14, 1934. He was Pope Pius XI's delegate to France for the closing days of the Jubilee Year honoring the nineteenth centenary of Redemption.

In an open letter dated March 12, 1935, to Cardinal Schulte of Cologne, Pacelli attacked the Nazis as "false prophets with the pride of Lucifer," labeling them "bearers of a new faith and a new gospel" who were attempting to create a "mendacious antimony between faithfulness to the Church and to the Fatherland."[3]

The following month, Cardinal Pacelli delivered an address before a quarter of a million people at Lourdes, April 25–28, 1935, where he described the Nazis as "possessed by the superstition of race and blood" and declared that "the Church does not consent to form a compact with them at any price." Describing the speech, the *New York Times* headlined its story (April 29, 1935): "Nazis Warned at Lourdes."

Representing the Vatican, Cardinal Pacelli arrived in the United States on the *Conte di Savoia,* October 8, 1936, for an "unofficial" trip covering some eight thousand miles, to be covered chiefly by plane. As Vatican Secretary of State, he made an in-depth study of the American Church and appealed to the United States to throw open its doors to Jewish refugees, but his request went unheeded. The day after President Franklin D. Roosevelt's reelection, Pacelli was invited to a luncheon at Hyde Park.

The following year Pacelli returned to France as Cardinal-Legate to consecrate and dedicate the new basilica in Lisieux during the

Eucharistic Congress and made another anti-Nazi statement. He again presided on May 25–30, 1938, at the International Eucharistic Congress in Budapest.

4. Papal Election

On February 28, 1939, the *New York Times* reported that "the Jewish issue in Italy is growing more intense and is one of the gravest of the many serious problems being considered by the cardinals who will enter the conclave...to elect a new Pope."[4]

The cardinals elected Eugenio Pacelli March 2, 1939. He selected the name of his predecessor—Pope Pius XII. The bells of St. Peter's pealed on March 12, 1939, as the eyes of a million people turned toward the balcony. Dressed in a white cope and wearing a silver, gem-studded mitre on his head Pope Pius XII appeared. Cardinal Canali removed the mitre. Cardinal Caccia-Dominioni replaced it with the papal tiara and prayed: "Receive the tiara adorned with the three crowns and know that you are the Father of princes and kings, the Sovereign of the world, and the Vicar on earth of our Savior Jesus Christ, to Whom is honor and glory, now and forever. Amen."

Pope Pius XII's coat of arms showed the symbol of peace: a dove with an olive branch. His motto indicated peace to be a fruit of justice: *Opus justitiae pax* (Isa 34:17). His first radio message to the world was, "Peace, gift of God, desired by all upright men, the fruit of love and justice." He was a man of peace.

Immediately after his election, Pius XII issued a call for a peace conference of European leaders. His request went unheeded. He then met with the German cardinals who had been present in the recent conclave, in order to ascertain the real situation of the Church in Nazi Germany.

These meetings provided him with direct proof and information that motivated the content of his first encyclical, *Summi Pontificatus.* Dated October 20, 1939, it was a strong attack on totalitarianism. In it, Pius XII singled out those governments, which by their deification of the state, imperiled the spirit of humanity. He spoke about restoring the foundation of human society to its origin in natural law, to its source in Christ, the only true ruler of all men and women of all nations and races.

In this encyclical Pius XII reprimanded his audience: "What age has been, for all its technical and purely civic progress, more tormented than ours by spiritual emptiness and deep-felt interior poverty?" (par. 5). The world had abandoned Christ's cross for another (the Swastika) that brings only death. The consecration of the world to Christ the King celebrates "a penetrating wisdom which sets itself to restore and to ennoble all human society and to promote its true welfare" (par. 6). Indeed, Pius XII's encyclicals, discourses, and radio messages clearly assert that the only solid foundation for social order is the law of God.

5. World War II

In view of the plight of the Jewish people of Europe, resolutions emerged and were adopted at the January 1939 meeting of the Jewish Congress in Geneva. Dr. Nahum Goldmann, chairman, stated: "We record the Jewish people's deep appreciation of the stand taken by the Vatican against the advance of resurgent paganism which challenges all traditional values of religion as well as inalienable human rights upon which alone enduring civilization can be found. The Congress salutes the Supreme Pontiff, symbol of the spiritual forces which under many names are fighting for the re-establishment of the rule of moral law in human society."[5]

World leaders were not aware that Hitler's movement included the "final solution" of the Jews and the elimination of the Polish nation. After World War I, Germany refused to pay war debts; she rebuilt her military power, annexed the Sudetenland and the whole of Czechoslovakia, and on September 1, 1939, Nazi tanks crossed the Polish border. Thus began World War II.

Pope Pius XII acted as a link to the British government for a number of German dissidents desiring to overthrow Hitler. He went beyond his usual caution and maintained these contacts until the German invasion of Denmark and Norway in April 1940.

When the Germans invaded the Low Countries in May 1940, the Pope sent telegrams with his prayers for their deliverance to the leaders of these besieged nations. The following month Mussolini joined Hitler, and the Vatican was now engulfed in territory at war. Everywhere in Europe, persecuted people, the Jews especially, appealed to Pius XII. When some five hundred Jews embarked at Bratislava on a steamer for Palestine, their ship tried to enter the seaport of Istanbul but was refused permission to land. Captured by an Italian patrol boat, the

Jews were imprisoned in a camp at Rhodes. During an audience one of the prisoners managed to appeal to the Pope for help.

Thanks to Pope Pius XII's intervention, unknown to the Axis, the refugees were transferred to an improvised camp in Southern Italy, where they were found safe three years later, in December 1943. The papacy had rescued Jews by channeling money to those in need, issuing baptismal certificates to Jews for their protection, negotiating with Latin American countries to grant them visas, and keeping in touch with their relatives through the Vatican Information Service.

The Nazis occupied Rome in September 1943. The Pope saved as many Jews as possible and issued directives to all convents and monasteries to open their doors to protect Jews. The Swiss Guards increased from four hundred to four thousand to incorporate many Jews and other refugees among their numbers. Could Pope Pius XII have done more than he did?

The charge of Pius XII's "silence" with regard to the Nazis is simply not true. Recently a review of the biography of John Paul II further brought to light several facts that will oblige critics to rewrite the story of the presumed "silence" of Pius XII during the Holocaust. On August 17, 2000, reporter Salvatore Giannella explained the "silence" of Pius XII in the Italian magazine *Oggi*. He credits Cardinal Adamo Stefan Sapieha, the Archbishop of Cracow during World War II, for having saved the life of Karol Wojtyla, the future John Paul II, by burning the anti-Hitler letter sent to him by Pius XII. In it the Pope denounced the horrors of the Holocaust and the Nazi regime and asked Sapieha to have it published in Poland. Instead, the Archbishop destroyed it in the presence of witnesses for fear of reprisals against the Polish Church.

Giannella explains that Pius XII's scathing statement against Hitler was burned by Sapieha, a prince and the only Polish Cardinal in the country who, in 1942, acted as though he had a divine mandate. To avoid reprisals, not only did he silence one Pope, but he discovered another. He recognized the gifts of the young actor Karol Wojtyla, and his intuition saved Wojtyla from the Nazi raid against the Resistance. He also encouraged him to become a priest and to enter the underground seminary.

Further enlightening readers about the role of Pius XII with regard to Nazi atrocities, Cardinal Ersilio Tonini of Ravenna highlighted this unknown episode: "They reproach Pius XII with an act of cowardice for his silence. But that is not the case. When he had to speak out, the Pope was not afraid. He condemned Hitler's invasion of Belgium, defining it a crime against every human and divine right. In Rome he ordered that the doors of all buildings belonging to the Vatican be opened for Jews and other political refugees. Jewish students were forbidden by Fascist law to continue their studies. The Pope arranged for the pontifical universities to accept them." [6]

During World War II, when the Nazi persecution began in Poland, Pope Pius XII was deeply troubled. One of his classmates, Monsignor Quirino Paganucci, was appointed Chaplain of the Supreme Military Order of Malta. His assignment was to accompany the trains that brought help directly to Poland. On one of these occasions, Pius XII asked him to bring a message to Archbishop Sapieha. The Pope intended to denounce the crimes that were being committed and wanted the Polish Bishop's opinion. Archbishop Sapieha implored the Holy Father not to act. The Polish people would have to pay dearly in terms of reprisals.

Reporter Giannella found another testimonial regarding this episode in the writings of the well-known Church historian and priest, Rosario F. Esposito, author of the book *Processo al Vicario*[7] and collaborator of the monthly magazine *Vita pastorale*.

From his office at the Generalate of the Society of Saint Paul in the Portuense Quarter of Rome, Father Esposito confirmed his 1965 statements: Monsignor Quirino Paganuzzi was born in 1914 in Varsi, Diocese of Piacenza. He and Cardinal Ersilio Tonini had been classmates. For years after his ordination to the priesthood, April 18, 1937, Paganuzzi worked in the Office of the Papal Maestro di Camera. He was also the ambassador for secret missions to countries occupied by the Axis. On the afternoon of August 14, 1942, Father Joseph Kaul, who had been drafted by the Wehrmacht (the German Army), accompanied Monsignor Quirino Paganuzzi in a military car, from the station of Cracow to the archbishopric, opposite the SS headquarters.

In his *Diary,* published in the '70s, four years before his death, and reprinted recently by the Italian magazine, *30 giorni,* Paganuzzi writes: "Six meters separated the two entrances. I experienced the agitation and violence of those inflexible men in front of the Archbishop's residence. The Reverend Kaul jumped out of the car with the typical naturalness of one of the *leaders* of the period and rang the doorbell that opened the door with difficulty. I don't know why, but of all that scene what attracted my attention was the entrance of the SS. With smiles, and pointing to the bottles of wine we were carrying, we tried to distract the attention of the guards on duty who scrutinized us with penetrating glances. I don't think the guards appreciated our familiarity....They were not aware that Pius XII's documents were camouflaged and packed with spaghetti labels inserted in bottles labeled *Chianti*. As always, Archbishop Sapieha greeted us affectionately and particularly enjoyed the packaged *Fiaschi*."

What happened in those decisive moments proves the truth of the account related by both Kaul and Paganuzzi. Kaul states: "Midst tears of joy the Archbishop read the Holy Father's handwriting. Then he broke the seal of the large package given to him by Monsignor Quirino and opened it. I saw that it was a printed encyclical in Polish, the work of Pius XII. The title of the encyclical: *Ideological Differences and Opposition to National Socialism*. The Cardinal began to read it. Suddenly he hit his head with his hand, dropped the sheet and exclaimed: 'For the love of God! It is absolutely impossible for me to share His Holiness' letter with my clergy, and much less can I communicate it to the people of Poland. It would be sufficient for only one copy to reach the hand of the SD and all our heads would fall. In this case, the Church in Poland would be lost. But doesn't the Holy Father know the terrible position we are in? This letter must be burned immediately.' And without thinking further, the entire package was thrown into the fire."

Monsignor Paganuzzi confirms this in writing with the following version: "Archbishop Sapieha opened the package, read several pages and commented in a very understanding manner. Then he opened the door of the stove in the wall, applied more wood to the fire, and threw the correspondence into the fire....Finally, when he noticed my astonishment, to justify his action, he said: 'Thank the Holy Father very much, dear Monsignor. No one is more grateful to the Holy Father for his interest than the Poles. It is not necessary for us to have an external demonstration of the love and interest of Pope Pius XII regarding our troubles, when that would only serve to increase our sufferings. This is precisely the case, Monsignor.' 'Your Excellency, have I been too bold, too irresponsible?' I asked. 'That I shall not be, dear Monsignor,' Sapieha answered. 'But don't you know that if I publicize these words or if they are found in this house by the Nazi *gauleiter* Franck, all the heads of the Poles will not suffice as a reprisal? Come, come, Monsignor, it is better not to speak of this. Why, yes, the Jews! But here they kill everyone. What is the purpose of saying what everyone knows? We know that the Pope is with us. But why speak about the sorrow and the condemnation of the Pope, if it serves only to augment our troubles?' Thus the astonished Vatican prelate listened to Archbishop Sapieha describe the apocalyptic spectacle of the horrors of the ghetto of Cracow: 'Do you see, Monsignor Paganuzzi, what we have been reduced to? But the saddest fact is that we have to leave those unfortunate people without help, isolated by the entire world. They are people dying for whom even a word of comfort is lacking. In order not to abbreviate their days we cannot, we must not speak. We live the tragedy of those unfortunate people and no one more than the Poles would like to help them; no one is in such an impossible situation of trying to help the Jews. Between Jews and Poles there is no difference. The Nazis have taken from us our bread, our freedom. At least, let us keep our life and the hope of seeing the end of our Calvary.' " Even though the text of that Polish letter may no longer be found in the Vatican, we have the testimony of those who were present in 1942.

In this same period, the well-established information services of the SS in Cracow lengthened their list of the intelligentsia to be decapitated, beginning with Wojtyla, who was to be captured in his underground house-theater at Number 10 Tyniecka Street. In the archives of the Stary Theater in Cracow, one can examine a map belonging to the Gestapo where that apartment is targeted as a den of opposition leaders in which the name of Karol Wojtyla is listed. But the future Pope, responding to the invitation of Archbishop Sapieha, moved to the Archbishop's house with six other seminarians and remained there until the end of the war. Wojtyla was later ordained to the priesthood, became a Bishop, received the Cardinal's hat, and was elected Pope, taking the name of his predecessor, John Paul II.

No doubt Archbishop Sapieha's letter to Pope Pius XII, dated October 28, 1942, made reference to the above-mentioned episode: "It displeases us greatly that we cannot communicate Your Holiness' letters to our faithful, but it would furnish a pretext for further persecution and we have already had victims suspected of communicating with the Holy See."

Later the Pope would cite this experience in a letter to Bishop Preysing of Berlin: "We leave it to the local bishops to weigh the circumstances in deciding whether or not to exercise restraint, *ad maiora mala vitanda* [to avoid greater evil]. This would be advisable if the danger of retaliatory and coercive measures would be imminent in cases of public statements by the Bishop. Here lies one of the reasons We Ourselves restrict Our public statements. The experience we had in 1942 with documents which We released for distribution to the faithful gives justification, as far as We can see, for Our attitude." Certain Polish bishops, exiled in London, called for stronger statements by the Pontiff, while those who remained in Poland and had to deal with the Nazis cautioned the Pope to refrain from "speaking out" against Hitler, lest his words be used as a pretext for savage reprisals.

Frank Eyck wrote: "I believe that Pius XII took his responsibilities seriously, that he tried to guard against any misstep that might endanger his flock and the potential victims he was trying to save, and that therefore he felt that he could not do more publicly. This may well have been the lesson he learned from the deportation and killing of Jewish descendants in Dutch monasteries, including the Carmelite nun Edith Stein, which followed the public protest of the Catholic Bishop of Utrecht, Johann de Jong, made in July 1942 against the deportation of Dutch non-Aryans. It is believed that Jewish Protestants in the Netherlands were reprieved at that time, because the Protestant Church under threats omitted its protest....Did Pius XII strive to do the best he could for those who were being persecuted? This is a judgment call which everyone of us has to make. In the light of my reading and of my experience of those terrible times I have tried to do justice to Pius XII." [8]

6. Detractors

Throughout his papacy, Pope Pius XII was almost universally regarded as a saintly man, a scholar, a man of peace, a tower of strength, and a compassionate defender and protector of all victims of the war and genocide that had drenched Europe in blood for six years. At the end of the war Western nations paid tribute to his efforts on behalf of the oppressed. When Pius XII died on October 9, 1958, Jews praised him for his help and were among the first to express sorrow and gratitude for his solicitude during the Holocaust.

In the 1960s, however, a campaign of vilification began against the Pope. His detractors claimed that he had lacked courage, human compassion, and a deep sense of moral rectitude. Today some in the media, uninformed Catholics, academicians, and some editorial commentators accept these claims as unquestionably true. The hostile attacks contending that he was a weak, cold, church bureaucrat replace the praise accorded Pius XII as a great and good man. It is a smear campaign against the memory of Pius XII that began with Rolf Hochhuth's play, *The Deputy,* staged for the first time in 1963 in Germany. This "black legend," accusing the Pope of refusing to speak out about the Holocaust in spite of his detailed knowledge of Jewish suffering, was devoid of any factual basis.

It is claimed that, during the war, either due to political calculation or faintheartedness, Pius XII remained unmoved and silent before the crimes against humanity that his intervention would have prevented. In view of the neutrality of the Vatican, how could the Pope have intervened? If he had openly condemned the Nazis, he would have also had to openly condemn the Fascists and the Communists. He was a prisoner of the Germans and of the Italians. Nazi and Fascist intelligence organizations invaded the Vatican. Services were entirely controlled by the Italian government: food, water, electricity, sewage. Communication was censored: mail, telephone, and telegraph too.

Information appeared in the Milan newspaper *Il Giornale* on July 5, 1998, confirming what some historians have always believed—Hitler intended to kidnap the Pope. In fact, Hitler gave orders to occupy the Vatican. However, his plans did not materialize. The Allies wanted Pius XII to condemn the Nazis, and they did not want him to criticize the Communists. Certainly they knew that Pius XII could not violate neutrality. He could not make partial public condemnations.

Nonetheless, the Pope's voice was heard on the Vatican Radio and in *L'Osservatore Romano.* Although the world had not listened to his pleas for peace and justice in 1939, he tried now to help alleviate the suffering of thousands of victims. In fact, when American bombers dropped hundreds of tons of explosives on Rome, July 19, 1943, Pius XII comforted the injured, administered the Last Rites, and distributed money to those in need of food and clothing.

Unfortunately, many critics cite evidence out of context. The record shows that the Catholic Church consistently assisted many Jewish victims of Nazi anti-Semitism, even before the outbreak of World War II. Critics ignore documents describing the incomparable and unrelenting efforts of Pius XII, through his nuncios' assistance as well, toward many thousands of Jewish victims. In some instances, when confronted with frustration, Catholic appeals were made on behalf of baptized Jews, as Catholics, in the hope that they might be respected as such, or on the basis of their civil rights as specified in the concordats. These appeals should not detract from the singular efforts of the Catholic Church on behalf of all Jewish victims of the Nazis. Documents reveal Pius XII's constant, untiring steps and appeals, on behalf of peace, before the outbreak and during the war. His efforts can only be characterized as extraordinary.

The persecution of the Catholic Church by the Nazis was evidenced by the incarceration of thousands of priests, sisters, and brothers. Both Protestant and Catholic clergy sent an open letter about the treatment of Jews and other minorities to Arthur Seyss-Inquart, the Reich Commissar, who then threatened that, unless they were silent, he would round up baptized Jews. Catholic bishops refused to obey and, on July 20, 1942, sent a pastoral letter that was read from all Catholic pulpits in the Netherlands.

The National Socialist Mayor of Rotterdam responded: "When the terrorism of the Church widens its scope and calls for sabotage, as it did in these letters, the time has come for the party to react in an appropriate manner."[9] Consequently, Jewish converts to Catholicism, including Edith Stein, were rounded up and sent to the concentration camps; Jewish converts to Protestantism were left unharmed.

Edith Stein had appealed to Pius XI in 1933, asking him to condemn anti-Semitism. In his encyclical *Mit brennender Sorge* the Pope wrote: "None but superficial minds could stumble into concepts of a national God, of a national religion; or attempt to lock within the frontiers of a single people, within the narrow limits of a single race, God, the Creator of the universe, King and Legislator of all nations before whose immensity they are 'as a drop of a bucket' (Isaiah 11, 15)."

The encyclical, prepared under the direction of Cardinal Pacelli, then Secretary of State, was written in German for wider dissemination in that country. It was smuggled out of Italy, copied and distributed to parish priests to be read from all of the pulpits on Palm Sunday, March 14, 1937. It concluded that "enemies of the church, who think that their time has come, will see that their joy was premature." No one who heard the pontifical document had any illusion about the gravity of these statements or their significance. Certainly the Nazis understood their important message. An internal German memorandum dated March 23, 1937 stated that it was "almost a call to do battle against the Reich government." The encyclical was confiscated, printers arrested, and presses seized. The following day *Das Schwarze Korps* called it "the most incredible of Pius XI's pastoral letters: every sentence in it was an insult to the new Germany."

The German ambassador to the Holy See was instructed not to take part in the solemn Easter ceremonies, and German missions throughout Europe were informed by the Nazi Foreign Office of the "Reich's profound indignation." Hitler not only dictated a letter of protest to the Pope, complaining that the Vatican had gone to the people instead of coming to him, but he also verbally attacked the German bishops at a rally in Berlin.

7. The Jewish Community

When Pius XII died, October 9, 1958, he was the object of unanimous admiration and sincere gratitude. "The world," President Eisenhower declared, "is now poorer following the death of Pope Pius XII."

In contrast to the esteem Pius XII enjoyed until his death in 1958, his reputation today suffers many unjust attacks. Some say that a theological condemnation of the Holocaust would have made a difference. Others want to weaken the moral authority of the papacy. However, according to Michael Novak, these critics "are deflecting attention from themselves.... Today's charges against Pope Pius XII cannot stand scrutiny."[10]

What Pius XII did for the Jews directly and indirectly through his diplomatic representatives and the bishops is well documented. At the end of World War II, Dr. Joseph Nathan, representing the Hebrew Commission, addressed the Jewish community, expressing heartfelt gratitude to those who protected and saved Jews during the Nazi-Fascist persecutions. "Above all," he stated, "we acknowledge the Supreme Pontiff and the religious men and women who, executing the directives of the Holy Father, recognized the persecuted as their brothers and, with great abnegation, hastened to help them, disregarding the terrible dangers to which they were exposed."

Reuben Resnick, American Director of the Committee to Help Jews in Italy, declared that "all the members of the Catholic hierarchy in Italy, from Cardinals to Priests, saved the lives of thousands of Jews, men, women, and children who were hosted and hidden in convents, churches, and other religious institutions."[11]

Chief Rabbi Alexander Safran, of Bucharest, Rumania, made the following statement on April 7, 1944, to Monsignor Andrea Cassulo, Papal Nuncio to Rumania: "In the most difficult hours which we Jews of Rumania have passed through, the generous assistance of the Holy See was decisive and salutary. It is not easy for us to find the right words to express the warmth and consolation we experience because of the concern of the Supreme Pontiff who offered a large sum to relieve the sufferings of deported Jews—sufferings which had been pointed out to him by you after your visit to Transnistria. The Jews of Rumania will never forget these facts of historic importance."

The following petition was presented to Pope Pius XII in the summer of 1945 by twenty thousand Jewish refugees from Central Europe: "Allow us to ask the great honor of being able to thank, personally, His Holiness for the generosity he has shown us when we were being persecuted during the terrible period of Nazi-Fascism."

There was a story in an American newspaper (January 1946) about a special Thanksgiving service in Rome's Jewish Temple that was heard over the radio. The Jewish chaplain of the Fifth American Army gave a discourse in which, among other things, he said: "If it had not been for the truly substantial assistance and the help given to Jews by the Vatican and by Rome's ecclesiastical authorities, hundreds of refugees and thousands of Jewish refugees would have undoubtedly perished before Rome was liberated."[12]

The Italian Jewish community on April 5, 1946, sent the following message to His Holiness, Pius XII: "The delegates of the Congress of the Italian Jewish Communities, held in Rome for the first time after the Liberation, feel that it is imperative to extend reverent homage to Your Holiness, and to express the most profound gratitude that animates all Jews for your fraternal humanity toward them during the years of persecution when their lives were endangered by Nazi-Fascist barbarism. Many times priests suffered imprisonment and were sent to concentration camps, and offered their lives to assist Jews in every way. This demonstration of goodness and charity that still animates the just, has served to lessen the shame and torture and sadness that afflicted millions of human beings."

8. Documents of the Holy See

Indeed, historians must base the written history of events on documents, and not only on testimonies. But there are rules: Documents that concern people still alive or which, once revealed, could hinder negotiations in process cannot be published. This criterion was followed in the publication of the Holy See's documents.

Did Pius XII give instructions during the Holocaust? Indeed he did. Is documentation available to confirm this statement? Yes. One need only consult the eleven volumes (vol. 2 is in two tomes) of Vatican documents. To provide this documentation, Pope Paul VI in 1963 ordered the opening of the Vatican archives. He selected Jesuit Church historians Pierre Blet, Angelo Martini, Burkhart Schneider, and Robert A. Graham. Their combined scholarship produced *Actes et Documents du Saint-Siège relatifs à la Seconde Guerre Mondiale,* published between 1965 and 1981 by Città del Vaticano. Historian Eamon Duffy stated that the *Acts and Documents of the Holy See Relative to the Second World War,* "decisively established the falsehood of Hochhuth's specific allegations."

Historians may now study the role and activity of the Holy See during the war. The documents show the groundlessness of the attacks on Pius XII regarding his so-called silence and establish once and for all times the action of the Holy See in sympathy with the victims of the war, in opposition especially to the racial persecutions. Of course, historians should also consult other documents related to the war, such as: *Documenti diplomatici italiani, Documents on British Foreign Policy: 1919–1939, Foreign Relations of the United States, Diplomatic Papers, Akten zur deutschen auswärtigen Politik 1918–1945.*

With regard to sources for the situation of the Catholic Church in Germany on the eve of World War II, a July 10, 1939, Vatican document described the opposition and protests of the Holy See toward the Nazis. These notes are entitled: "Some of the main dispositions and acts against the Catholic Church that took place in Germany during the last few months." *Il Nazionalsocialismo e la Santa Sede,* by historian Michele Maccarrone[13] provides this firsthand information about the

Concordat agreed to with Hitler and the Nazi oppression against the clergy in Germany prior to and during the war, as well as does an analysis of the papal encyclical *Mit brennender Sorge* and the work of the Holy See during the war years. In a letter dated August 25, 2000, the Vatican Secretariat of State[14] confirmed that the document in *Il Nazionalsocialismo e la Santa Sede*[15] corresponds to the original text conserved in the Vatican Archives.[16]

During the winter of 1965, Father Robert Leiber, who had been for more than thirty years the Private Secretary of Eugenio Pacelli, disclosed the existence of drafts of the letters of Pius XII to the German bishops. These personal letters best explain the Pope's instructions. They show objectively the true attitude and behavior of Pius XII during the conflict and, consequently, the groundlessness of the accusations against his memory.

There is no evidence that the attitude Pacelli is said to have absorbed during his years as Nuncio to that country was in any way favorable to the Hitler Government. Of forty-four major addresses in Germany, forty condemned some aspect of Nazism. Pacelli also comforted the Catholic Church in Germany, which was being persecuted by the German government. His efforts—joining President Roosevelt to keep Italy out of the conflict; sending the May 10, 1940, telegrams to the sovereigns of Belgium, Holland, and Luxemburg after the invasion by the *Wehrmacht;* courageously advising Mussolini and King Vittorio Emanuele III to explore a separate peace—surely do not suggest such a pro-Nazi attitude.

Neither does the accusation of "silence" hold up. What appears to be silence was, in fact, a concealment of action conducted through the nunciatures and the bishops to avoid or, at least, limit the deportations and persecutions. In many speeches Pope Pius XII clearly explained that discretion was exercised in his letters to the German bishops. Documents show he constantly opposed the deportation of the Holocaust victims.

Father Pierre Blet, one of the four editors of the *Actes,* stated that "a public declaration would not have been of any help; it would have accomplished nothing except to aggravate the situation of the victims and multiply their number....Without Father Leiber, we would not have been aware of the existence of the drafts of Pius XII's letters to the German bishops and the collection would have been deprived of perhaps the most precious texts to understand the Pope's mind. But all of those texts taken together do not contradict at all what we learn from the diplomatic notes and correspondence."

In these documents we learn that Pius XII emphasized to the bishops the need to warn German Catholics against National Socialism as an enemy of the Church—a risky move on his part, even more so in a time of war. This correspondence, published in the second volume of *Actes et Documents,* confirms, then, the stern opposition of the Church to National Socialism and the Church's compassion for the victims. Already there had been warnings—disseminated by Bishops Faulhaber and von Galen, and by many religious and clergymen in Germany— that culminated with the encyclical *Mit brennender Sorge,* read in all the German churches on Palm Sunday 1937.

9. Letters to the Bishops

Volume 2 of the Vatican documents, *Actes et Documents du Saint-Siège relatifs à la Seconde Guerre Mondiale 1965–1982,* is entitled *Lettres de Pie XII aux Évêques Allemands.*[17] Preceded by a sixty-page Introduction in French, there are 124 autographed letters addressed to the German bishops during World War II. Of these, 103 are in German; the others in Latin.

Each letter in volume 2 is preceded by a summary in French. (See Appendix, "Documents," pp. 331–41.) The letters are not limited to a particular topic. They do not constitute a systematic exposé. They treat of contemporary problems and focus on particular situations. They reflect the current situation of the Church in Germany. The Pope gives counsel to his correspondents on the attitude they should adopt during their conflict with the regime, explains the difficulties and the anguish of the Holy See, describes how he must safeguard its neutrality, offers reflections on what must be accomplished, or informs the bishops of his efforts toward peace.

Attached to Letter 42, addressed to the Cardinal-Archbishop of Breslau, dated March 17, 1940, are two pages of Italian notes used by Pius XII that summarize actions committed against the Catholic Church in Germany. I have translated six paragraphs[18] that were to be brought to the attention of German Foreign Minister von Ribbentrop:

1. "In most of Germany, contrary to the dispositions of the Concordat, the civil authorities have suppressed private Catholic schools.

The same has happened in all of Austria. In various regions, religious instruction in elementary and professional schools is curtailed and, in some localities, entirely suppressed. Efforts have been made by the authorities to eliminate every form of religious education, substituting the catechism with the so-called National Socialist "Weltanschauung." The Crucifix has been removed in classrooms, and ecclesiastics have been dismissed.

2. "Many Minor Seminaries have been closed. This has happened to not a few Major Seminaries and various Departments of Theology, closed during the war period without the consent of the Holy See as stated in the Concordat.

3. "Numerous are the Catholic boarding schools that were suppressed, while conditions imposed on others are such that either they must subscribe to norms not conforming to Christian education, or they must cease to exist. Besides all this, ancient abbeys, some of world fame, religious houses, associations and charitable Catholic institutions, particularly in Austria, are systematically suppressed. One religious house after the other is mandated to other purposes, the Church patrimony is confiscated, a large number of Religious are dispersed, their works and many apostolic missions obstructed.

4. "Apart from the suppression ordered by the State there are financial burdens on the Catholic Church in Bavaria, with the Law of April 30, 1939. It seriously violates the rights and the liberty of the Church itself, which were abolished in a unilateral way; the obligations (Paragraph 5) that State Funds in the municipalities, etc....to be used by the Church are no longer available. The same dispositions of this Law, enforced on May 1, were adopted in other territories.

5. "It must be noted also that, unfortunately, sacrilegious vandalism continues to be perpetrated here and there and these people are not discovered and punished; the serious offenses to religion, to the clergy and to the pontiffs, at times with public manifestations as, for example, the sacrilegious parody on the streets of Paderborn of June 15; the arbitrary limitation of religious functions often ordered by the authorities; the prohibition, in some cases, of pastoral letters, and the prohibition to publish and spread among the faithful the very pontifical documents; the repeated difficulties imposed at the return of His Excellency, the Bishop of Rottemburg to his diocese; the frequent

arrests of ecclesiastics particularly in Austria and in the Protectorates of Bohemia and Moravia.

6. "One must add to all this the anti-Christian propaganda that takes place during conferences, days of study and more frequently in the media, especially in the weekly papers distributed by the organizations and in the party camps, and in books that do not even spare the Holy Pontiffs replete with accusations contrary to historical truth, while civil authorities exercise the strictist and severest censure of Church activities. The Church cannot even refute these calumnious and offensive attacks because under various pretexts the circulation of only a few weeklies are permitted by the authorities."

Among the documents in volume 2, one is dated September 8, 1941. Pope Pius XII responded to the German bishops who, during their annual Episcopal Conference in Fulda, had sent him a report describing the terrible Nazi oppression. He thanked them for their attestation of strong faith and devotion and for informing him of the present sad conditions of the Church in Germany. Profoundly moved by their communication, the Pope reminded them that, throughout the centuries, persecutions were never lacking in the Church. He referred to the insidiousness of the situation and to their brave martyrdom:

"Thus the Catholic Church in Germany is oppressed by serious difficulties, as are clearly demonstrated by the many violences you mentioned: men, especially those who hold civic responsibilities, are forced to deny their Christian religion; limits are placed on your care for souls; young people are taught doctrines contrary to Christian dogma and are kept away from the clergy; almost all Catholic newspapers and magazines have been suppressed; Religious Houses are gradually closed and their property confiscated....While you are afflicted by these unjust dispositions, you are concerned about the greater ones that are feared imminent. You foresee indications of a turbulent tempest that will fall upon our beloved sons and daughters of Germany.

"You ask us, beloved children and venerable brothers: 'What should be our defense? The arms of our adversary are numerous, the Church seems to be almost defenseless.' But then you immediately add: 'And yet, it is not permitted to despair' and you promise to be faithful to God and to Christ at any cost....You have expressed your resolutions with clarity and seriousness in your Pastoral Letter of last June 26, the reading of which moved me deeply....We do not doubt but that you will implement, with constancy and valor, the proposals you so courageously established, unhesitatingly. Your faith and that of your priests and faithful is worthy of admiration. May the indomitable fidelity that from the beginning of our pontificate has given us such comfort continue to shine in the midst of adversity...." The letter concludes with hope in the future of the German Church and with the prayer that "the enemies of the Church may finally understand that there is nothing so wicked as hurting one's mother and, recognizing their errors, they will soon repent."

Later, in his message of June 2, 1945, Pius XII addressed the cardinals on the condition of the Church after the surrender of Germany. It was an earnest appeal for World Peace: "...Today, after six years, the fratricidal struggle has ended in one section of this war-torn world. It is a peace—if you can call it such—as yet very fragile, which cannot endure or be consolidated except by expending on it the most assiduous care; a peace whose maintenance imposes on the whole church, both pastor and faithful, grave and very delicate duties: patient prudence, courageous fidelity, the spirit of sacrifice!

"All are called upon to devote themselves to it, each in his own office and at his own place. Nobody can bring to this task too much anxiety or zeal. As to us and our apostolic ministry, we well know, venerable brethren, that we can safely count on your sage collaboration, your unceasing prayers, your steadfast devotion....Would it then have been possible, by opportune and timely political action, to block once and for all the outbreak of brutal violence and to put the German people in the position to shake off the tentacles that were strangling them? Would it have been possible thus to have saved Europe and the world from this immense inundation of blood? Nobody would dare to give an unqualified judgment....But in any case nobody could accuse the Church of not having denounced and exposed in time the true nature of the National Socialist movement and the danger to which it exposed Christian civilization: 'Whoever sets up race or the people or the state or a particular form of state or the depositaries' power or any other fundamental value of the human community to be the supreme norm of all, even of religious values, and divinizes them to an idolatrous level distorts and perverts an order of the world planned and created by God.'

Pacelli was ordained a priest, April 2, 1899, in the Basilica of Saint Mary Major, in Rome.

Eugenio Pacelli at the age of seven, Rome 1882.

Nunzio Pacelli visits Italian prisoners of war in Bavaria, 1918.

Pacelli distributes gift packages sent by the Vatican after WWI.

Pacelli visits the mines in Berlin, 1927.

Pope Pius XI and Cardinal Pacelli, accompanied by Guglielmo Marconi, visit the Vatican Radio facility.

Monsignor Pacelli is present for the signing of the Concordat
between the Holy See and Serbia, 1914.

Refugees, mostly women and children,
make a home in the papal apartments at Castelgandolfo,
outside Rome, during the fighting in Italy.

In 1936, Cardinal Pacelli visited Fordham University and received
an honorary degree. At his side are Cardinal Spellman
and Bishop Kearney.

(Left) An autographed message from Cardinal Pacelli
to the Apostolic Nunzio in Bucharest.
(Right) Pacelli's message to Cardinal Hinsley.

"The important political events which marked the two following years and then the war did not bring any attenuation to the hostility of National Socialism toward the Church, a hostility which was manifest up to these last months, when National Socialists still flattered themselves with the idea that once they had secured victory in arms they could do away with the Church forever.

"Authoritative and absolutely trustworthy witnesses kept us informed of these plans—they unfolded themselves actually in the reiterated and ever more intense activity against the Church in Austria, Alsace-Lorraine and, above all, in those parts of Poland which had already been incorporated in the old Reich during the war: there everything was attacked and destroyed; that is, everything that could be reached by external violence.

"Continuing the work of our predecessor, we ourselves have during the war and especially in our radio messages constantly set forth the demands and perennial laws of humanity and of the Christian faith in modern scientific methods to torture or eliminate people who were often innocent.

"This was for us the most opportune—and we might even say the only efficacious—way of proclaiming before the world the immutable principles of the moral law and of confirming, in the midst of so much error and violence, the minds and hearts of German Catholics, in the higher ideals of truth and justice. And our solicitude was not without its effect. Indeed, we know that our messages and especially that of Christmas, 1942, despite every prohibition and obstacle, were studied in the diocesan clergy conferences in Germany and then expounded and explained to the Catholic population.

"If the rulers of Germany had decided to destroy the Catholic Church even in the old Reich, Providence had decided otherwise. The tribulations inflicted on the Church by National Socialism have been brought to an end through the sudden and tragic end of the persecution! From the prisons, concentration camps and fortresses are now pouring out, together with the political prisoners, also the crowds of those, whether clergy or laymen, whose only crime was their fidelity to Christ and to the faith of their fathers or the dauntless fulfillment of their duties as priests. For them all of us have prayed and have seized every opportunity, whenever the occasion offered, to send them a word of comfort and blessing from our paternal heart....

"The present political and social situation suggests these words of warning to us. We have had, alas, to deplore in more than one region the murder of priests, deportations of civilians, the killing of citizens without trial or in personal vendetta. No less sad is the news that has reached us from Slovenia and Croatia.

"But we will not lose heart. The speeches made by competent and responsible men in the course of the last few weeks made it clear that they are aiming at the triumph of right, not merely as a political goal but even more as a moral duty....It is essential that the hate, the diffidence, the stimuli of an extreme nationalism should give way to the growth of wise counsels, the flowering of peaceful designs, to serenity in the interchange of views and to mutual brotherly comprehension.

"May the Holy Spirit, light of intellects, gentle ruler of hearts, deign to hear the prayers of His Church and guide in their arduous work those who in accordance with their mandate are striving sincerely despite obstacles and contradictions to reach the goal so universally, so ardently, desired: peace, a peace worthy of the name; a peace built and consolidated in sincerity and loyalty, in justice and reality; a peace of loyal and resolute force to overcome or preclude those economic and social conditions which might, as they did in the past, easily lead to new conflicts; a peace that can be approved by all right-minded men of every people and every nation; a peace which future generations may regard gratefully as the happy outcome of a sad period; a peace that may stand out in the centuries as a resolute advance in the affirmation of human dignity and of ordered liberty; a peace that may be like the *Magna Charta* which closed the dark age of violence; a peace that under the merciful guidance of God may let us so pass through temporal prosperity that we may not lose eternal happiness.[19]

"But before reaching this peace it still remains true that millions of men at their own fireside or in battle, in prison or in exile must still drink their bitter chalice. How we long to see the end of their sufferings and anguish, the realization of their hopes! For them, too, and for all mankind that suffers with them and in them may our humble and ardent prayer ascend to Almighty God. Meanwhile, venerable brethren, we are immensely comforted by the thought that you share our anxieties, our prayers, our hopes; and that throughout the world Bishops, priests and faithful are joining their supplications to ours in the great chorus of the universal church."[20]

10. Conclusion

Two weeks after his promise of peace, Hitler said: "One is either a German or a Christian. You cannot be both."[21] The National Socialists had a violent hatred of Jews, believed in Aryan German race superiority, and called for the unification of all German-speaking peoples. Already in 1920, Clemens August Graf von Galen (the future Bishop of Münster) declared that Nazism contained ideas which no Catholic could accept without denying his faith upon cardinal points of belief.

On October 1, 1921, the *Bayerischer Kurier* quoted Nuncio Pacelli: "The Bavarian people are peace-loving. But, just as they were seduced during the revolution by alien elements—above all, Russians—into the extremes of Bolshevism, so now other non-Bavarian elements of entirely opposite persuasion have likewise thought to make Bavaria their base of operation."

"This [the message in the above paragraph] was Pacelli's first published warning to people about Nazism, but it was not his last. Of the forty-four public speeches that Nuncio Pacelli made on German soil between 1917 and 1929, at least forty contained attacks on National Socialism or Hitler's doctrines," wrote Ronald J. Rychlak, in *Hitler, the War, and the Pope.*[22] Other Catholic leaders joined with him. German bishops warned against Nazism on five occasions between 1920 and 1927.[23] They stated that National Socialism was totalitarian, racist, pagan, and anti-Christian.

Pope Pius XI had already warned Catholics in 1925, not only against Communism, but against "every political conception which makes society or the State an end in itself, from which naturally, fatally indeed, it finishes in absorbing or destroying private rights."[24]

In a letter to Sir Robert Vansittart,[25] Ivone Kirkpatrick, British Chargé d'Affaires at the Holy See, recorded an encounter he had with the Secretary of State: "Cardinal Pacelli…deplored the action of the German Government at home, their persecution of the Jews, their proceedings against political opponents, the reign of terror to which the whole nation was subjected"[26]

Cardinal Pierre Gerlier, Archbishop of Lyons, became an outspoken critic of the Vichy Government. Shortly after the Germans split France into the occupied north and unoccupied Vichy, France, further south, Pius XII sent a secret letter to the Catholic bishops of Europe, to be read in all the churches, reminding the faithful that racism is "incompatible with the teachings of the Catholic Church." From the summer of 1941, the Church denounced the deportations and the treatment of Jews. On July 16, 1942, when the police rounded up thirteen thousand Jews in Paris, the French bishops issued a joint protest: "Our Christian conscience cries out in horror. In the name of humanity and Christian principles we demand the inalienable rights of all individuals...."

Part II
Remembering the Truth

Chapter III
Defense of the Pope

1. The Nazi Race-Myth

*P*ius XII had condemned the Nazi race-myth even before his election as Pope. The manner in which the debate about him is now conducted involves taking a contemporary conceptualization of Nazi-Jewish relations and illicitly foisting it upon an earlier era. This fact is well-analyzed in Peter Novick's seminal work, *The Holocaust in American Life.*"[1]

A respected historian at the University of Chicago, Novick points out that even when the concentration camps were opened in 1945 to eyewitness press reports, the killing was still seen as part of a world-wide campaign, not directed specifically against the Jews. There was nothing about the reporting of the liberation of the camps that treated Jews as more than among the victims of the Nazis; nothing that suggested the camps were emblematic of anything other than Nazi barbarism in general; nothing, that is, that associated them with what is now designated "the Holocaust."

Novick's thesis is that the conditions for praise or blame were not present during the war years, and so it is literally senseless to debate whether Pius XII ought to have publicly condemned the Holocaust. This explains why large numbers of Jews praised him immediately following the war. They did not have our contemporary concept of the Holocaust, but rather were simply grateful for what Pius XII had done for them during the war years.

How does one explain the present delusional obsession with Pope Pius XII? For the first twenty years after the war, very little was said about the destruction of European Jewry, especially by Jews themselves, who wanted to get on with life, to assimilate, and to forget the painful past. However, in the late 1960s, the State of Israel seemed to be under increasing threat as the Cold War moved into full swing. The Pan-Arab movement of the 1950s was now allied with the Soviet Union. Israel's enemies were emboldened to call for her destruction. The slogan "never again" was coined. All living Jews were to be understood as Holocaust survivors subject at any moment to destruction.

The world divided into those who accepted the new definition of the Jewish mission and those who did not. The destruction of European Jewry was understood at the time to be embedded in the much larger context of the deaths of fifty million people in World War II. Judging Pius XII in any other context is not only unjust but intellectually irresponsible.

This reinterpretation of history has become firmly entrenched in modern consciousness. Any criticism of these false perspectives automatically draws the charge of anti-Semitism. Some critics say that Pius XII ought to have suffered martyrdom and that the Church ought to have been destroyed, if necessary, for the sake of the Jews. Such a statement would have been unintelligible to most European and American Jews of the period.

Catholic apologists to the Jews as well as defenders of Pius XII are usually operating from the same premises. In the face of the revised history, their apologies and defenses will never be enough. Everything Pius XII or anyone else did will seem inadequate.

The murder of European Jewry, insofar as it was understood or acknowledged, was just one among the countless dimensions of a conflict that was consuming the lives of tens of millions around the globe. It was not "the Holocaust"; it was simply the (underestimated) Jewish fraction of the holocaust then engulfing the world. [2]

2. Opere et caritate

Pius XII was a good and holy man who responded to the challenges of his time with courage and intelligence. Mentioned in the literature of the period is a document, *Opere et caritate,* that the Pope sent to the bishops of Europe. After it was read, it was destroyed immediately to avoid any chance that the Gestapo would find it. Even in the Vatican, where there was danger of invasion by Hitler's troops, there was great fear of the document ending up in the hands of the Gestapo.

Joseph L. Lichten, a Jewish Rabbi, wrote: "It is known that in 1940 Pius XII sent out a secret instruction to the Catholic bishops of Europe entitled *Opere et caritate* (By work and Love). The letter began with a quotation from Pope Pius XI's encyclical, *Mit brennender Sorge,* and ordered that all people suffering from racial discrimination at the hands of the Nazis be given adequate help. The letter was to be read in churches with the comment that racism was incompatible with the teachings of the Catholic faith."[3] Research has been done in the Vatican, in France, and in Holland, and the background reference to this document is the same as reported by Rabbi Lichten.

Jews around the world concluded that Pius XII's public statements were directed against the Nazis. They knew that Catholics in the Nazi-occupied and Axis countries were trying to save Jewish lives. The allegations that Pius XII was a Nazi collaborator and that Catholics were indifferent toward the extermination of Jews are unjust. The general opinion of Jews in the years during and immediately following the war was one of praise and gratitude toward Pope Pius XII. Were these Jews insincere, or are the attacks today unfair?

How did Jews react when Eugenio Cardinal Pacelli was elected Pope on March 2, 1939? The Jerusalem *Palestine Post* editorial of March 6, 1939, stated: "Pius XII has clearly shown that he intends to carry on the late Pope's [Pius XI] work for freedom and peace....We remember that he must have had a large part to play in the recent Papal opposition to pernicious race theories and certain aspects of totalitarianism."

The *Jewish Chronicle* in London, March 10, 1939, stated that the Vatican received congratulatory messages from "the Anglo-Jewish Community, the Synagogue Council of America, the Canadian Jewish Congress, and the Polish Rabbinical Council."

The *Canadian Jewish Chronicle* editorial quipped on March 10, 1939: "The plot to pilfer the Ring of the Fisherman has gone up in white smoke." Why such a statement? Because the cardinals resisted Nazi attempts to influence the election and prevent Cardinal Pacelli from becoming Pope.

The London *Zionist Review,* March 16, 1939, reacted very favorably to the appointment of Luigi Cardinal Maglione as Secretary of State: "This confirms the view that the new Pope means to conduct an anti-Nazi and anti-Fascist policy."

Jews considered the Pope a friend of democracy and peace, and an enemy of racism and totalitarianism. With the issuance of Pius XII's first encyclical, the Jewish Telegraphic Agency in New York (October 27, 1939) reported that "the unqualified condemnation which Pope Pius XII heaped on totalitarian, racist and materialistic theories of government in his encyclical, *Summi Pontificatus,* caused a profound stir....few observers had expected so outspoken a document."

The editorial of the *American Israelite* in Cincinnati, November 9, 1939, speaking about the fundamental equality of men, observed: "This concept of democracy is reiterated in the Pope's Encyclical, stressing again the inviolability of the human person as a sacred being...."

On January 19, 1940, the *Jewish Ledger* in Hartford, Connecticut, described the gift of $125,000 to the Vatican, in order to assist its efforts on behalf of all victims of racial persecution, from the United Jewish Appeal for Refugees and Overseas Needs as an "eloquent gesture," which "should prove an important step in the direction of cementing the bonds of sympathy and understanding" between Catholics and Jews.

On January 26, 1940, the *Jewish Advocate* in Boston reported: "The Vatican Radio this week broadcast an outspoken denunciation of German atrocities in Nazi [occupied] Poland, declaring they affronted the moral conscience of mankind." This broadcast confirmed the media reports about Nazi atrocities, previously dismissed as Allied propaganda.

The *Canadian Jewish Chronicle* (January 26, 1940) published a story about Jacob Freedman, a Boston tailor who wrote to the State Department and the Red Cross for information about the fate of his sister and nephews in German-occupied Poland. They could not provide any information, so Mr. Freedman sought Pius XII's assistance. Several months later, Cardinal Maglione answered that the members of his family were alive and well in Warsaw. Jewish historian Pinchas Lapide stated that the Vatican Information Office helped tens of thousands of Jews locate missing relatives in Europe.[4]

The *Jewish Chronicle* in London (March 14, 1940) commented on Pius XII's conditions for a "just and honorable peace" especially the protection of racial minorities, and praised him for standing up for the "rights of the common man." The *Kansas City Jewish Chronicle* (March 29, 1940) reported that Pope Pius XII appointed several displaced Jewish scholars to posts in the Vatican Library, when Italy's anti-Semitic laws went into effect. The front page of the *California Jewish Voice* (January 2, 1942) quoted the Holy Father's 1941 Christmas address: "Religious persecution and oppression of minorities must have no place in the world of the future."

Rabbi Naftali Adler and Dr. Max Pereles, representing the thousands of Jewish refugees interned at the Ferramonti concentration camp in Southern Italy, on April 14, 1942, thanked the Pope for the abundant supply of clothing and linen to the children at the camp and for his care of the prisoners' other needs: "This noble and generous gift proves anew what the whole world knows and admires that Your Holiness is...also the paternal guardian and promoter of the ideal of humanity for all mankind."

On March 12, 1943, the Union of Orthodox Rabbis of the United States and Canada sent a telegram to the Vatican, signed by Rabbis Israel Rosenberg, Eliezer Silver, Bar Levinthal: "In our anguish we call the attention of His Holiness to the following cable from Warsaw which came to us via London: 'January Germans started liquidation of remnants Warsaw Ghetto. All over Poland liquidation proceeding. Liquidation of remnants planned for middle of February. Alarm the world. Apply to Pope for official intervention. We suffer terribly. Remaining few hundred thousand threatened with immediate annihilation. Only you can rescue us, responsibility towards history rests with you.' As religious leaders of American Jewry in solemn convocation we plead to His Holiness in the name of humanity for positive action in this zero hour."[5] On March 19th, through the Apostolic Delegate in Washington, D.C., Cardinal Maglione responded that "...the Holy See has worked and continues to work on behalf of the Jews."

The *Australian Jewish News* (April 16, 1943) quoted Cardinal Gerlier, who strongly opposed the deportations of French Jews and sheltered Jewish children, as saying that he was obeying Pius XII's instructions by continuing to oppose France's anti-Semitic measures. On October 29, 1943, the *Jewish Chronicle* in London reported the Vatican's response to the deportation of Italian Jews to Auschwitz: "The Vatican has made strong representations to the German Government and the German High Command in Italy against the persecution of Jews in Nazi-occupied Italy...." Vatican protests brought the roundups to an end. Thousands of Jews in Rome sought refuge in convents, monasteries, and the Vatican itself.

According to the 1943–1944 *American Jewish Yearbook,* Pius XII "took an unequivocal stand against the oppression of Jews throughout Europe." Representing the World Jewish Congress, Rabbi Maurice Perlzweig wrote that "the repeated interventions of the Holy Father on behalf of Jewish Communities in Europe has evoked the profoundest sentiments of appreciation and gratitude from Jews throughout the world."[6] Jewish leaders expressed similar sentiments. When the Allies liberated Rome in 1944, Jews left their hiding places and openly told the world they were saved by the Vatican.

The July 7, 1944, *Jewish News* in Detroit and the July 14th editorial in *Congress Weekly*—the official journal of the American Jewish Congress—revealed that Jews had been sheltered within the walls of the Vatican and that the Vatican provided Jewish refugees with kosher food. It also stated that during a meeting with Allied soldiers, Pius XII blessed a Jewish soldier from Palestine in Hebrew.

The *American Hebrew* in New York published an interview with Chief Rabbi Israel Zolli of Rome on July 14th. Zolli, who was hidden in the Vatican during the German occupation of Rome, stated: "The Vatican has always helped the Jews and the Jews are very grateful for the charitable work of the Vatican, all done without distinction of race." After the war he converted to Catholicism and wrote his memoirs, *Before the Dawn* (1954), claiming to have witnessed a vision of Christ, who called him to the faith.

Both the National Jewish Welfare Board and the World Jewish Congress sent telegrams on July 21st expressing their gratitude to the Pope: the former, for "the aid and protection given to Italian Jews"; the latter, for the "noble humanitarian work on behalf of Hungarian Jews."[7]

Protesting the deportations of Hungarian Jews, the president of the American Jewish Committee, Judge Joseph Proshauer, declared in his speech at a rally in Manhattan's Madison Square Park on July 31st: "We have heard…what a great part the Holy Father has played in the salvation of the refugees in Italy, and we know from sources that must be credited that this great Pope has reached forth his mighty and sheltering hand to help the oppressed of Hungary."

After the war in Europe ended, Moshe Sharrett, the future Foreign Minister and Prime Minister of Israel, wrote: "My first duty was to thank him, and through him, the Catholic Church, on behalf of the Jewish public, for all they had done in the various countries to rescue Jews, to save children, and Jews in general."[8]

According to the *New York Times* of October 12, 1945, the World Jewish Congress presented a $20,000 gift to Vatican charities "in recognition of the work of the Holy See in rescuing Jews from Fascist and Nazi persecution." During a St. Louis conference on March 17, 1946, William Rosenwald, chairman of the United Jewish Appeal for Refugees, Overseas Needs and Palestine, spoke on the plight of displaced Jewish refugees. In his speech, he said: "I wish to take this opportunity to pay tribute to Pope Pius for his appeal in behalf of the victims."

The Pope was honored publicly during and after the war. Were Jews on six continents ignorant of the facts? How could they be mistaken? How do Pius XII's detractors explain the praise and the gratitude of these survivors?

Oral and written testimonies of Catholic rescuers, acting under Pius XII's direct orders, are available. Pope John XXIII explained the motivation for his efforts in Istanbul during the war: "For all these painful matters I have referred to the Holy See and simply carried out the Pope's orders: first and foremost to save Jewish lives."[9]

The Chief Rabbi of Rome, Elio Toaff, upon learning of Pius XII's death, said: "More than any other people, the Italian Jews had experienced the great pity and supreme generosity of the Pontiff during the unhappy years of persecution and terror, when it seemed to them that they had no way of escape. His Jewish compatriots will everlastingly remember with gratitude the papal ruling to open the doors of convents and parish houses to them. The Jewish community is in mourning for the death of Pope Pius XII, and with sincere sentiments it raises its prayers to the Lord that He may grant His generous and chosen soul every beatitude."[10]

3. Books: Pro and Con

In an interview, British researcher Sir Martin Gilbert noted that Christians were among the first victims of the Nazis and that the Churches took a very powerful stand. On the question of Pope Pius XII's alleged silence, he added, "So the test for Pacelli was when the Gestapo came to Rome in 1943 to round up Jews. And the Catholic Church, on his direct authority, immediately dispersed as many Jews as they could." After years of research that began in 1959, Gilbert wrote *Never Again: The History of the Holocaust,*[11] which contains an extraordinary chapter on Pius XII's humanitarianism. Here Gilbert thanks the Vatican for what was done to save Jewish lives. We owe this historian a debt of gratitude.

Books by authors who defend Pope Pius XII are veritably dismissed by the media. This is an injustice. On the other hand, authors of several new books who condemn the Pope are called "scholars." It suffices to mention Michael Phayer and Susan Zuccotti, whose books are filled with falsehoods that clearly and directly attack Pope Pius XII's integrity.

One need only glance at the jacket of Michael Phayer's book *The Catholic Church and the Holocaust, 1930–1965*[12] to understand his thesis. It is the most anti-Catholic illustration ever published by a supposedly reputable American press—a sketch of a faceless Catholic prelate and an SS officer standing on the corpse of an emaciated victim wearing the Jewish Star of David. To the left of the figures is an inscription, in epitaph style: "AD 1933–1945 the Concordat." The jacket portrays a historical falsehood. The Concordat was not an alliance with Hitler; it was a treaty guaranteeing freedom and rights.

Phayer notes Pius XI's encyclical *Mit brennender Sorge* but does not state that Cardinal Pacelli drafted it. He states that when Hitler visited Rome on an official visit to Fascist Italy, Pope Pius XI "snubbed the dictators by leaving the city" and fails to mention that Cardinal Pacelli departed with the Pontiff. Phayer complains that "Pius XII chose a diplomatic rather than a moral approach," without citing what other approach would have been feasible or successful in the face of Nazi aggression. He accepts the allegation of "silence" on the part of Pius XII as a given but does not examine it.

Does Phayer take into consideration that the Nazis considered Pius XII an implacable foe, that he was hailed as the only voice speaking out in Europe against the Nazi terror, that his intent was to provide shelter to the persecuted Jews and other refugees? Pope Pius XII served the Catholic Church with remarkable consistency. He coordinated the Church's efforts and cared for suffering humanity. By combining diplomatic pressure, careful but sustained criticism while maintaining neutrality in war-torn Europe, as well as direct action through his nuncios and the local Church, Pius XII saved hundreds of thousands of Jewish lives. Following the Pope's directives, the Vatican Secretary of State encouraged all the superiors of religious orders to open their doors, according to a document published in 1975, by Andrea Ricciardi in *Vita e Pensiero.*[13]

In his review of Phayer's book, historian John Jay Hughes states that a major weakness in the book is its failure to consider other points of view. Phayer, according to Hughes, undermines his arguments by failing to take account of other positions, as, for example, in his treatment of Ernst Heinrich von Weizsäcker, Hitler's wartime ambassador to the Holy See. Hughes adds: "Like many anti-Nazi Germans who held government posts in Hitler's Germany, Weizsäcker used his position to sabotage Nazi policy when he could. Many of these heroic covert resisters paid with their lives. Weizsäcker survived the war, only to be sentenced to imprisonment by the Nuremberg War Crimes Tribunal."

Indeed, the ambassador to the Vatican did everything in his power to save Jews. Writing to his mother, Weizsäcker expresses the conviction that "Hitler's persecution of the Jews was a violation of all the rules and laws of Christianity." Hughes writes that Weizsäcker was "forced to play a double game: on the one hand assuring Berlin that the pope remained well disposed toward Germany and was not much concerned with the Jews; while at the same time urging Pius XII to work quietly behind the scenes, avoiding any public protest which would only enrage Hitler and thus hasten the Jews' destruction."[14]

Many have testified that they received clear directives from Pope Pius XII to do everything possible for the Jews. On October 29, 1943, the *Jewish Chronicle* of London recorded the well-publicized protests Pius XII had launched against the Nazi roundup of Roman Jews: "The Vatican has made strong representations to the German government and the German high command in Italy against the persecutions of Jews in Nazi-occupied Italy." In the diary of an American nun, published in 1945 under the pseudonym of Jane Scrivener, there is reference to the roundup of October 16, 1943: "It is understood that the Pope has asked the German Ambassador to make an effort to help the Jews. It is difficult for von Weizsäcker, of course, as the SS are independent of him. However, he did have some measure of success, for we hear that the women and children will be released."[15]

In the face of so much evidence, how can any historian claim that the Pope's antagonism was not understood. Foreign Minister Count

Ciano, Mussolini's son-in-law, wrote in his diary that the Duce was furious at the Pope's 1942 Christmas message. German ambassador to the Holy See, Diego von Bergen, protested that the Pontiff was "clearly speaking on behalf of the Jews." To reinforce this protest von Bergen absented himself from the Midnight Mass. In Berlin an official report called the speech "one long attack on everything we stand for." [This was a Nazi Internal Report from the Reich Central Security Office, January 22, 1943, in response to Pius XII's 1942 Christmas address. It is printed in *The Vatican in the Age of the Dictators, 1922–1945,* by Anthony Rhodes (New York: Holt, Rinehart and Winston, 1973), pp. 272–73.]

The *New York Times* spoke of "a lonely voice crying out of the silence of a continent.…No one would expect the Pope to speak as a political leader, or a war leader, or in any other role than that of a preacher ordained to stand above the battle, tied impartially, as he says, to all people and willing to collaborate in any new order which will bring a just peace.…Pope Pius expresses as passionately as any leader on our side the war aims of the struggle for freedom when he says that those who aim at building a new world must fight for free choice of government and religious order" (December 25, 1942).

Phayer contends that in 1943, Pius XII failed to assist Jews during the war and was obsessed with the threat of Communism. *The Black Book of Communism,* published in France in 1997, estimates its victims worldwide at one hundred million. The Pope did not support Nazi Germany against the Soviet Union. He was deeply concerned about Communism. Yet, he informed the bishops in the United States that the Church's continuing opposition to Communism should be no barrier to Catholic support for President Roosevelt's Lend-Lease program in aid of the Western Allies.

In fact, though critical of papal policy in many respects, the Catholic-Jewish Commission to study Vatican documents stated in October 2000: "The case has repeatedly been made that the Vatican's fear of Communism prompted it to limit its criticism of Nazi atrocities and occupation policies. We are struck by the paucity of evidence to this effect and to the subject of Communism in general. Indeed, our reading of the volumes presents a different picture.…" Phayer claims that Pius XII wanted a strong Germany to face down the threat of Communism. Yet, nowhere in the book does Phayer cite documented statements to support this assertion.

In *Under His Very Windows: The Vatican and the Holocaust in Italy,*[16] Susan Zuccotti repeats the discredited claim, made popular by John Morley's flawed study that the Vatican protested only on behalf of converted Jews *(Vatican Diplomacy and the Jews during the Holocaust: 1939–1943)*. Morley writes that in January 1942 the Vatican asked the Berlin Nuncio to try to get exit visas for three Czech Jews and that "the note does not indicate they were baptized although that must be suspected [*sic*]." Father Robert Graham, in *America* magazine, August 9, 1980, states that the three Czechs were not Catholics and theirs was "only one case of innumerable papal interventions."

Perhaps one can say that Zuccotti admits the truth about the role of the Catholic Church and then adds personal remarks that serve to dissuade the reader of the historical truth. She also claims that there are no witnesses who can testify that, at the direction of Pius XII, they made efforts to save Jews.

The following document destroys Zuccotti's thesis that there is no evidence of a papal directive to Church institutions to shelter Jews. It was written on September 26, 2000: "I, Sister Domenica Mitaritonna, declare under oath that during the period of the war 1942–1943, I was living at 16 Via Caboto, Rome, and assisted two or three Jewish families who sought refuge in our convent. They were welcomed with immense hospitality by the Superior who had been solicited by the Vatican to help them. With joy we received the Jews and tried to make their stay, living in the little theater of our school, less painful. Another Sister and I took turns near a window each evening for fear that the Germans would arrive. One night, German soldiers stopped their truck near our school. We were frightened and spread the word. The Jews were rushed to the trap door beneath the stage to hide. When a shoemaker who lived near us told them it was an elementary school, the soldiers departed. The Jews were saved. With fraternal affection, Sister Domenica Mitaritonna." This story and many others are told in *Yours Is a Precious Witness: Memoirs of Jews and Catholics in Wartime Italy* (p. 112).

It is incredible that Zuccotti failed to consult the nine hundred pages of sworn depositions for Pope Pius XII's cause for beatification. These testimonials make it perfectly clear that he was not anti-Semitic or indifferent to the fate of the Jews and that he did everything possible to help them.

Seemingly, Susan Zuccotti's contradictory statements and the contempt she expresses in *Under His Very Windows* surpass those of other contemporary writers. The author makes no mention of the evidence presented at the Nuremberg trials demonstrating the Vatican's repeated protests, nor does she describe the anger these protests provoked within Nazi ranks. Did Zuccotti read Hitler's notorious *Table Talks,* Joseph Goebbels' diaries, Martin Bormann's decrees, Alfred Rosenberg's diatribes, and Heinrich Himmler's orders to the SS and the Gestapo? Did she not read explicit statements in defense of Jews and against Hitler, Germany, and Nazism that were published in *L'Osservatore Romano* and used by the Vatican Radio? These statements were often written by Pope Pius XII himself.

By refusing to grant Pius XII credit for his leadership during World War II, by ignoring the testimony of contemporary witnesses and the innumerable statements in the media that acknowledge his words and actions on behalf of the Jews, by denigrating the many Catholic leaders who endangered their own lives to protect Jews, Zuccotti clearly exposes her prejudices.

How can Zuccotti or any writer ignore the many documents that contradict her statements? If, as Zuccotti contends, Pius XII did not speak out against the Nazis, why did newspapers in Germany condemn him for speaking out? Why did the *New York Times* and the media throughout the world praise him? If indeed the Pope had been "silent," why did past historians claim that he had condemned racism and totalitarianism? Has she correctly interpreted the twelve volumes of Vatican documents prepared by four Jesuit historians between 1965 and 1981? There are twenty volumes of *Discorsi e radiomessaggi* and twenty volumes of *Atti e discorsi di Pio XII* where one can fully and honestly interpret his religious and political point of view. Has she studied them?

Errors and inaccuracies abound in Susan Zuccotti's book. She claims that the Vatican's official condemnation of anti-Semitism in 1928 was "soon forgotten," when in fact it was frequently cited as a basis to resist the "Final Solution";[17] that Pope Pius XI's statement— Anti-Semitism is unacceptable. Spiritually, we are all Semites—was censored and also forgotten. Instead it was publicized throughout the world. Catholic philosopher Jacques Maritain, wrote: "No stronger word has been uttered by a Christian against anti-Semitism, and this Christian was the successor to the Apostle Peter."[18]

Zuccotti claims that the Vatican failed to resist Mussolini's anti-Semitic laws, but Haim Nahum, the Grand Rabbi of Egypt, thanked Pius XII for his resistance and the Nazi newspaper *Das Schwarze Korps* bitterly attacked the Pope. She also states that Pope Pius XII's first encyclical *Summi Pontificatus* "never mentioned Jews." But paragraph 48 not only explicitly uses the word "Jew," but does so in the context of condemning Nazi racism by quoting St. Paul: "The spirit, the teaching and the work of the Church can never be other than that which the Apostle of the Gentiles preached: 'putting on the new man...who is renewed unto knowledge, according to the image of Him that created him. Where there is neither Gentile nor Jew, circumcision nor uncircumcision, barbarian nor Scythian, bond nor free. But Christ is all and in all' (Col 3:10–11)."

In *Under His Very Windows,* Zuccotti presents the Church's theological differences with Judaism as antireligious bigotry: "The Catholic Church would protest against 'exaggerated nationalism' and against racism that made no allowance for religion, but it would not protect the rights of individuals of different faiths." She does not mention that, in 1916, the Secretariat of State directed by Eugenio Pacelli, the future Pope Pius XII, prepared the following document: "The Supreme Pontiff—as Head of the Catholic Church, which, faithful to its divine doctrine and to its most glorious traditions, considers all men as brothers and teaches them to love one another—never ceases to inculcate among individuals as well as among peoples, the observance of the principles of natural law and to condemn everything which violates them. This law must be observed and respected in the case of the children of Israel, as well as all others, because it would not be conformable to justice or to religion itself to derogate from it....[19]

Zuccotti's claim that Pope Pius XII never instructed religious to protect Jews during the war, is contradicted by the Chief Rabbi of Rome, Israel Anton Zolli, who devoted an entire chapter in his memoirs, *Before the Dawn,* to the German occupation of Rome and praised the Pope's leadership: "...The people of Rome loathed the Nazis and had intense pity for the Jews. They would willingly have assisted in the evacuation of the Jewish population into remote villages, where they would have been concealed and protected by Christian families. Christian families in the heart of Rome would have accepted Jews. There was money in the treasury for the support of destitute refugees thus hidden.

The Holy Father sent by hand a letter to the bishops instructing them to lift the enclosure from convents and monasteries, so that they could become refuges for the Jews. I know of one convent where the Sisters slept in the basement, giving up their beds to Jewish refugees. In face of this charity, the fate of so many of the persecuted is especially tragic" (New York: Sheed and Ward, 1954).

Why was Zolli's testimony ignored? Why did Susan Zuccotti ignore the testimony of Cardinal Paolo Dezza, whose article in the June 26, 1981, issue of the *Osservatore della Domenica* relates how he was ordered by Pius XII in a face-to-face meeting to assist the Nazi victims "willingly," especially the "poor, persecuted Jews."[20] Zuccotti mentions Cardinal Pietro Palazzini, but insinuates that he never claimed Pius XII directed him to assist Jews. This is not true. In 1985, when Palazzini was honored by Israel's Yad Vashem as a "Righteous Gentile," he explicitly stated that Pius XII ordered him to save Jews. His testimony is also clearly expressed in his memoirs: "Amidst the clash of arms, a voice could be heard—the voice of Pius XII. The assistance given to so many people could not have been possible without his moral support, which was much more than quiet consent."[21] Zuccotti misrepresents Palazzini's book, which is a tribute to Pope Pius XII's courage, heroism and charity during the German occupation of Rome.

Why did she ignore the testimony by an eyewitness, Monsignor John Patrick Carroll-Abbing, whose book *But for the Grace of God* provides information on his personal relationship with Pope Pius XII and his direct involvement with saving Rome's Jews? He points out that the loudest critics are those who never knew him, whereas those who actually worked with him, have nothing but the highest praise. As a participator in this effort, he clearly states: "Nothing easier than for Pius XII, at a distance, to have made a clamorous protest against the German—and, of course, the Russian—war crimes, if he had been willing to ignore the inevitable consequences for millions of already tortured people."[22]

In her acknowledgments, Susan Zuccotti writes about the survivors, rescuers, priests, historians, archivists, friends: "Some of them will be pleased with this book. Others may not welcome an association with it." Why would anyone whom Zuccotti interviewed "not welcome an association with it," if the book is an honest account of their words? Did she misinterpret their statements on behalf of Pius XII? How could she not mention the fact that thousands of Jews and other refugees were saved in Castelgandolfo?

The background of a photo (seven women and ten children among those living in the Pope's summer home) in *Pope Pius XII: Architect for Peace* shows a tapestry depicting the papal coat-of-arms. Here, too, on page 134, is the story of Timothy T. O'Donnell, who made a private tour of the gardens of Castelgandolfo and visited the ruins of the palace of the Emperor Tiberius under the papal residence (November 30, 1988). He learned that, during the Second World War in these hidden chambers, Pope Pius XII hid thousands of Jews, who were to be deported to German concentration camps. On the walls one can still see the darkened ash where these fugitives from the Nazis lit fires to cook food and keep warm. In the dark stillness of this subterranean vault stands an enormous wooden cross, beautifully decorated. This Christian symbol of love was given to Pius XII at the end of the war by the Jews who lived there during those terrifying days. It was their way of expressing deep gratitude and veneration for this Pope who had heroically defied the Gestapo and had saved their lives. Such heroism and such gratitude must not be dishonored by ignorance.

In *Inside the Vatican* (March 2001), William Doino, Jr., a free-lance writer, describes Susan Zuccotti as having used far-fetched, antipapal arguments undermining the credibility of those who speak favorably of Pius XII. For example, Cardinal Luigi Maglione and General Rainer Stahel agreed that signs would be posted on the extraterritorial buildings to warn German soldiers that they should not search them—unless they had reasonable cause to believe deserters or resistance fighters were there.

In his article Doino states: "Every building was so marked. But it is Zuccotti's jaundiced view that when the Vatican put these notices on all of its buildings instead of just those crowded with refugees, it did so because it wanted to protect its property. She writes that they wanted to 'protect the special prerogatives of the Church…regardless of whether it was harboring illegal fugitives.' She thinks the warning signs should have been put on only those churches, monasteries and schools hiding Jews or other refugees. How long does she imagine it would have taken the Germans to figure out why some buildings were marked and others were not?"

Witnesses contradict Zuccotti's contention that Pius XII did not instruct Catholics to help the Jews. She rests her case on the absence of documents, knowing full well that during the reign of Nazi terror all recipients of Vatican directives regarding Jews were told to destroy those messages. Hungarian rescuer Baransky, a member of the U.S. Holocaust Memorial Council who was honored at Yad Vashem, told reporters in 1983 that he saw personal letters from the Pope telling Papal Nuncios to help the Jews. Senator Adriano Ossicini reported that in 1943, the Catholic hospital where he worked received direct orders from Pius XII to admit immediately as many Jews as possible.

On February 4, 2001, Christopher Duggan, a historian at the University of Reading in England, reviewed Susan Zuccotti's book in the *New York Times Magazine.* Continuing the debate over Pope Pius XII and the Holocaust, Duggan writes: "This is a serious and well-researched book that certainly raises yet more questions about the conduct of the papacy in World War II. But is it good history? For all its scholarship, it feels driven by a remorseless desire to find wanting. Only in the conclusion does Zuccotti face what for the historian must be the most important question; not so much the fact of silence or relative silence, but how that silence is to be understood and interpreted. Credit is given in places; but for the most part the text is a litany of phrases like 'it was not enough,' 'that was all,' 'it was very little,' 'lamentable,' 'he was wrong,' 'should have'—phrases that repeatedly raise questions about the author's intellectual, as well as moral, vantage point. All historians make judgments, but their first duty is surely to try to understand. Zuccotti condemns, but offers little new insight into why the Vatican and Pius acted as they did."

4. A Righteous Gentile

No one deserves the title of "a righteous gentile" more than Pope Pius XII. In the February 26, 2001 issue of *The Weekly Standard,* Rabbi David G. Dalin writes about the vilification of the Pontiff and defends him against his detractors. The lengthy article is entitled "Pius XII and the Jews: A Defense."

Rabbi Dalin describes Susan Zuccotti's recent book, *Under His Very Windows,* in which she "dismisses—as wrong-headed, ill-informed or even devious—the praise Pius XII received from Jewish leaders and scholars as well as expressions of gratitude from Jewish chaplains and Holocaust survivors who bore personal witness to the assistance of the Pope.

"That she does so is disturbing. To deny the legitimacy of their gratitude to Pius XII is tantamount to denying the credibility of their personal testimony and judgment about the Holocaust itself."

Rabbi Dalin rightly states: "To make Pius XII a target of our moral outrage against the Nazis, and to count Catholicism among the institutions delegitimized by the horror of the Holocaust, reveals a failure of historical understanding. Almost none of the recent books about Pius XII and the Holocaust is actually about Pius XII and the Holocaust. Their real topic proves to be an intra-Catholic argument about the direction of the Church today, with the Holocaust simply the biggest club available for liberal Catholics to use against traditionalists.

"A theological debate about the future of the papacy is obviously something in which non-Catholics should not involve themselves too deeply. But Jews, whatever their feelings about the Catholic Church, have a duty to reject any attempt to usurp the Holocaust and use it for partisan purposes in such a debate—particularly when the attempt disparages the testimony of Holocaust survivors and spreads to inappropriate figures the condemnation that belongs to Hitler and the Nazis."

In conclusion, Dalin quotes the Bible: "The Talmud teaches that 'whosoever preserves one life, it is accounted to him by Scripture as if he had preserved a whole world.' More than any other twentieth-century leader, Pius XII fulfilled this Talmudic dictum, when the fate of European Jewry was at stake. No other Pope had been so widely praised by Jews—and they were not mistaken. Their gratitude, as well as that of the entire generation of Holocaust survivors, testifies that Pope Pius XII was, genuinely and profoundly, a righteous gentile."

Pius XII's role in rescuing hundreds of thousands of Jews from certain death at the hands of the Nazis cannot be denied. Chief Rabbi Elio Toaff clearly stated: "More than all others, we had the opportunity of experiencing the great compassionate goodness and magnanimity of the Pope during the unhappy years of the persecution and terror, when it seemed that for us there was no longer an escape."

Pope Pius XII was indeed "a righteous gentile," a true friend of the Jewish people, who saved more Jewish lives than any other agency or individual, including Raoul Wallenberg and Oskar Schindler.

5. German Eyewitness

On May 7, 1993, Father Robert Schlitt taped an interview with Sister Mary Matilda, a member of the Sisters of the Sorrowful Mother. She reflected on her time growing up in Nazi Germany and her experiences in wartime Rome. As she tells her fascinating story, she includes vivid recollections of Pope Pius XII, who arranged for a shipload of eleven sisters and eight hundred Jews to settle in the United States. When the sisters ran into difficulty with the Portuguese government, they were able to present a handwritten letter from the Pope recommending that they be respected and cared for.

Historians who documented the resistance of German Catholics point out that Catholics voted against Hitler by and large. Hitler provided jobs and fed the poor. These people, of necessity, became Nazi supporters. However, when Catholics learned that the Nazis were against the Church, they did not favor Hitler.

But it was too late. Germans were afraid of the Nazis. They were afraid to speak. Sister Mary Matilda's uncle, who was a Nazi mayor of his town, sent those who spoke out against Hitler to concentration camps. The local residents witnessed the cattle cars that passed by with Jewish friends who disappeared. People did not know what went on in these camps.

Children were taught to say, "Heil Hitler!" instead of "Guten Morgen." Catholic schools were closed. Churches were surrounded by Nazis who reported on bishops, priests, and laypeople. Although Mary Matilda defied the Nazis and went to church with her sister, other young people were forced to join Hitler's Youth Group and would be taken from church and forced to march and sing. She never joined them.

In 1936, Sister Mary Matilda entered the convent. A few years later, fleeing the Nazis, she was able to escape to Rome with a group of other nuns. They remained there for three years. They had the opportunity to visit Pope Pius XII frequently in St. Peter's Basilica and in Castelgandolfo. The sisters received bread from the Vatican. Food was scarce. With the Pope's permission she and other young sisters were invested and then, in June 1941, secretly boarded a small plane for Lisbon, Portugal, where they remained for four or five weeks. In August 1941, they finally departed on a dirty ship with no running water, inadequate toilet facilities, and little food. The trip lasted about two months because it had to avoid the mines and enemy ships. Only when its passengers stopped in Bermuda for one day did they have water and food. When they finally docked in the United States, the sisters had typhoid fever and had to spend several weeks in a hospital in Wisconsin. One of them died within a few days. Soon after, these sisters joined the Sisters of the Sorrowful Mother in Milwaukee. Sister Mary Matilda is now living in Broken Arrow, Oklahoma.

6. Zenit News Agency

On October 26, 2000, Zenit News Agency praised Pope Pius XII's wartime conduct and refuted those who accused him and the Holy See of not doing enough to save Jews persecuted by the Nazis. To shed light on the Pope's role, Zenit News Agency interviewed Jewish historian Michael Tagliacozzo, responsible for the Beth Lohame Haghettaot Center in Italy.[23]

- *Tagliacozzo:* I know that many criticize Pope Pacelli. I have a folder on my table in Israel entitled "Calumnies Against Pius XII," but my judgment cannot but be positive. Pope Pacelli was the only one who intervened to impede the deportation of Jews on October 16, 1943, and he did very much to hide and save thousands of us. It was no small matter that he ordered the opening of cloistered convents. Without him, many of our own would not be alive.
- *ZENIT:* Some maintain that the Holy See looked on in silence while Roman Jews were deported on October 16, 1943.
- *Tagliacozzo:* It's not true. The documents clearly prove that, in the early hours of the morning, Pius XII was informed of what was happening and he immediately had German Ambassador von Weizsäcker called and ordered State Secretary Luigi Maglione to energetically protest the Jews' arrest, asking that similar actions be stopped. If this did not happen, the Pope would denounce it publicly. In addition, by his initiative he had a letter of protest sent through Bishop Alois Hudal to the military commander in Rome, General Rainer Stahel, requesting that the persecution of Jews cease immediately. As a result of these protests, the operation providing for two days of arrests and deportations was interrupted at 2 P.M. the same day. Instead of the 8,000 Jews Hitler requested, 1,259 were arrested.

After meticulous examination of identity documents and other papers of identification, the following day an additional 259 people were released. Moreover, after the manhunt in Rome on October 16, the Germans did not capture a single Jew. During the trial, Herbert Kappler said: "The Jews were not handed over." Those who were arrested were betrayed by collaborators.

- *ZENIT:* You maintain that in the German army and diplomatic corps there were people who opposed persecution.

- *Tagliacozzo:* From the material in the archive it can be deduced that, no sooner had they learned about the extremely secret dispatch in which Himmler ordered the arrest of all Jews in Rome and their transportation to Germany for liquidation, General Stahel and Consul Eitel Frederick Moelhausen were vehemently opposed. Stahel said he would never take part in such nastiness. Moelhausen exerted pressure on Kappler to raise the matter with Albert Kesserling. Moelhausen was a practicing Catholic; he regarded the deportation of Jews as useless and inhuman and, in order to convince Kesserling, raised questions regarding the political and military inopportuneness of the deportation. Commander in chief Kesserling, fearing an imminent Allied disembarkation on the coasts of the Tyrrhenian Sea, denied his soldiers' availability to arrest Jews. Thus, on October 16, 1943, Kappler had to use 365 SS members to make the raid.

- *ZENIT:* Why was the Roman community so ill-prepared for the Nazi raid?

- *Tagliacozzo:* The representatives of Judaism and, with them, the leaders of the Roman Jewish community, showed the same defects as the Italian ruling class, and they failed at the moment of trial. In his book *Before the Dawn,* Chief Rabbi Israel Zolli recounts that in mid-September of 1943, in the course of a community meeting, he proposed to dissolve the community, pay employees' salaries six months in advance, and hide himself. However, President Ugo Foà said that Zolli was an alarmist and that nothing would happen. The minutes of that meeting cannot be found now. Zolli wasn't the only one worried. I have found the testimony of Amadio Fatucci, who had the courage to stop the president of the community and said: "Mr. President, need we fear?" Foà replied: "The authorities have no interest against the people, and the people must be tranquil. When people are tranquil, the authorities do not intervene." Foà's conduct was serious in the circumstance of the raid. On the morning of October 18, while the Nazis had the deported enter train wagons, the president took his children and escaped to Livorno. He returned on November 2, having done nothing to find out what happened to those deported. On that occasion, the community demonstrated superficiality and incomprehension of the dangers and surprises of the new situation.

- *ZENIT:* Some scholars deny that there were instructions from the Pope to help the Jews.

- *Tagliacozzo:* There was much confusion in those days, but all knew that the Pope and the Church would have helped us. Monsignor Giovanni Butinelli, the pastor of Transfiguration parish, told me that the Pontiff had recommended that priests be told to shelter Jews. After the Nazis' action, the Pontiff, who had already ordered the opening of convents, schools and churches to rescue the persecuted, even opened cloistered convents to allow the persecuted to hide. I personally know a Jewish family that, after the Nazis' request for 50 kilos of gold, decided to hide the women and children in a cloistered convent on Via Garibaldi. The nuns said they were happy to take the mother and girl but they could not care for a little boy. However, under the Pope's order, which dispensed the convent from cloister, they also hid the boy. I myself was saved from persecution thanks to the Church's help. I remember it was October 16, a rainy day. It was a Saturday, the third day of the Jewish feast of Sukkot. I had sought refuge in Bologna Square. When the Germans arrived, I was able to escape through a window and I found myself on the street in my pajamas. A family helped me and hid me. I then went to my former Italian teacher who let me stay in her home and asked several priests to find me a safe place. Finally, after almost a week, thanks to a recommendation of Father Fagiolo, I was hidden in the Lateran. I remember they treated me wonderfully. After not having eaten for two days, Father Palazzini gave me a meal with all God's goods: a bowl of vegetable soup, bread, cheese, fruit. I had never eaten so well.

- *ZENIT:* What do you think of John Cornwell's book, *Hitler's Pope?*

- *Tagliacozzo:* I haven't read it, but I know that much nonsense is written and, unable to contribute new arguments, they give exaggerated interpretations. I am a historian and I do not look for controversies. From the diaries on table conversations we learn that Hitler said: "I hate the Jews because they have given that man, Jesus, to the world."[24] By what right do some critics discount the testimonials of survivors and rescuers? Beyond doubt, Pius XII engaged in the greatest Christian rescue program in the history of Catholicism. He was a diplomat who steered a careful course through chaos. His many acts of mercy speak for themselves. Editorials of the time attest that Pius XII served as a beacon of hope.

7. The Record

German Ambassador von Weizsäcker played an ambiguous role. Afraid that a formal protest made by the Holy See would enrage Hitler, he gave a too bland impression of the attitude of the Holy See, and this became patently clear in the Nuremberg trials. On the order of Pius XII, the German military commander of Rome, Brigadier General Rainer Stahel, an Austrian officer of the old school, was approached. The General, who was a very compassionate man, sent a phonogram directly to Himmler. He gave the following reason: "This kind of violent action against the Italian Jews disturbs my military plans to reinforce the German divisions still fighting far to the south of Rome, and can also create serious problems here in Rome." This was true; but no less important was another one—his indignation about the criminal acts of the Gestapo and his compassion for the Jews. His intervention had success. Himmler immediately ordered a stop to further deportations. In this way thousands of Jews could be hidden, at the order of Pius XII, in the Vatican and in more than 150 ecclesiastical institutions in Rome.

A brief survey of the facts reveals that charges against Pope Pius XII have been repeated without critical evaluation. Unlike so much misrepresentation in the media today, Pius XII's past record presents a totally different picture.

Dr. Robert W. Kempner, Deputy Chief U.S. Prosecutor at the Nuremberg trials, rejected the charge that Pius XII never opposed Hitler's so-called "Final Solution." Kempner wrote: "The archives of the Vatican, of the diocesan authorities and of Ribbentrop's foreign ministry contain a whole series of protests—direct and indirect, diplomatic and public, secret and open." He also stated: "All the arguments and writings eventually used by the Catholic Church only provoked suicide; the execution of Jews was followed by that of Catholic priests."

On January 27, 1940, Vatican Radio and the *L'Osservatore Romano* revealed to the world the dreadful cruelties of uncivilized tyranny that the Nazis were inflicting on the Jewish and Catholic Poles. The German ambassador protested.

In May 1940, when Pius XII came into possession of vital military intelligence concerning when and where the German attacks against Belgium, Holland, and Luxemburg were going to take place, he did not hesitate to communicate with Paris and London, but he was not believed. He had been in contact with German generals who wanted to get rid of Hitler. They informed him that they would be able to prevent the attacks on the three aforementioned countries if, after they removed the Führer, a subsequent peace treaty guaranteed Germany honorable terms. Reports in the British Embassy confirm that the Pope passed on this information, but the British mistrusted his disclosure and did nothing.

Several years ago, I interviewed Princess Enza Pignatelli Aragona, who personally informed Pope Pius XII about the October 16, 1943, Nazi raid in the Jewish ghetto. One must not fail to remember that Rome was occupied by the Germans. In a rapidly executed Nazi raid, special SS squads acting on Hitler's orders seized over a thousand Roman Jews for dispatch to "Poland," from which few ever returned.

A Jewish friend notified the Princess when the Nazis arrived and begged her to go to the Vatican and intercede for the victims. But no public transportation was available at that hour. The Princess telephoned and awakened her German friend Gustav Wollenweber, who was an aide in the German Embassy, and asked him to bring his car and take her to the Vatican at once. Ironically, a German diplomat of an anti-Semite government was accompanying an Italian princess to the Vatican to protest the arrest of Jews! The Pope's intervention allowed the Jews to hide.

An undated report of the Research Committee of Deported Jews states that the raid had begun toward 11 P.M. on October 15th. The Jews were taken to the military college. When the Pope was informed the morning of October 16th, he immediately sent for Secretary of State Cardinal Maglione to protest to the German Ambassador, Ernst von Weizsäcker. The Ambassador promised to intervene, but without mentioning the Cardinal's request in order not to compromise the desired results.

The Cardinal recorded the following: "Upon learning that the Germans had made a raid on the Jews, I requested that the German Ambassador come to see me and I asked him to intervene on behalf of those poor people. I spoke as best I could in the name of humanity, in the name of Christian charity. The Ambassador, who already knew about the arrests, but doubted that specifically only Jews were arrested, told me with sincere emotion: 'I always expect someone to ask me: How come you remain in this office?'

"I exclaimed: No, Mr. Ambassador, I am not asking you nor will I ever ask you that question. I simply say: Your Excellency, you have a tender and good heart, try to save these innocent people. It is sad for the Holy Father, sad beyond imagination that just in Rome, under the very eyes of the Common Father, that so many people should suffer only because they belong to a specific race.…The Ambassador, after a few seconds of reflection, asked me: 'What would the Holy See do if this situation were to continue?' I answered: 'The Holy See would not want to be in a position to express words of disapproval.'

"The Ambassador observed: 'For more than four years I follow and admire the attitude of the Holy See. She has succeeded in guiding the boat [the Church] in the midst of rocks of all kinds and sizes without rocking it and, even though she has had greater faith in the Allies, she knew how to maintain a perfect equilibrium. I ask myself if, right now that the *boat* is arriving in the Port, is it worthwhile to endanger everything. I am thinking about the consequences that one wrong step of the Holy See would provoke.…The known directives come from the highest place. Your Eminence, will you give me the liberty of not *faire état* [to not make known] this official conversation?' [It should be noted that Weizsäcker speaks about this meeting in the same way.]

"I observed that I had begged him to intervene by appealing to his humanitarian sentiments. I left it up to him to use his judgment whether to mention or not to mention our conversation that had been so friendly. I wanted to remind him that the Holy See, as he himself had noted, was very prudent in order not to give the German people the impression of having done or wanting to do the least thing against Germany during this terrible war.

"However, I had to tell him that the Holy See should not be placed in a position to be forced to protest: if the Holy See were forced to do it, for the consequences, she would place herself in the hands of Divine Providence.

"Meanwhile, I repeated: 'Your Excellency told me that you will try to do something for the poor Jews. I thank you for this. Regarding the rest, I leave this to your judgment. If you believe it more opportune not to mention this conversation, so be it.'"

Why did Susan Zuccotti delete parts of the first and last paragraphs of Cardinal Maglione's report? No doubt because they both mention "Jews." The complete document is found in *Actes et Documents* (volume 9, no. 368, pp. 505–6). Zuccotti omitted phrases, such as, "a raid on the Jews"; Weizsäcker "doubted that specifically only Jews were arrested"; "I repeated: Your Excellency told me that you will try to do something for the poor Jews."

In this regard the British Minister reported on October 31st: "As soon as he heard of the arrests of Jews in Rome, the Cardinal Secretary of State sent for the German Ambassador and formulated some [sort] of protest. The Ambassador took immediate action with the result that large numbers were released....Vatican intervention thus seems to have been effective in saving a number of these unfortunate people. I inquired whether I might report this and was told that I might do so but strictly for your information and on no account for publicity, since any publication of information would probably lead to renewed persecution."[25]

In the aftermath, those Jews who had escaped the Nazi fury in Rome found secret shelter by the hundreds in the convents and religious houses of the Eternal City for the agonizing nine months of the German occupation. What would have happened to the eight thousand Jews in Rome if the Nazis had continued the raid?

Pope Pius XII did everything in his power to alleviate the sufferings of the Jews during the Holocaust. Yet, some critics do not want to accept the truth. It is time to dissect the "big lie" that the media continues to spread about Pius XII's "silence." It is time to expose the truth as to his role during the Holocaust and to address the unjust attacks upon his unequaled historic efforts to save the lives of Jews in Europe.

8. Eichmann's Trial

Even Adolf Eichmann, the Nazi leader condemned to death in Jerusalem in 1961 for crimes against the Jewish people, affirms the truth about the Holocaust and the undeniable evidence that exists and has been ignored regarding Pius XII's humanitarianism. Eichmann clearly states in his *Diary* that the Vatican "vigorously protested the arrest of Jews."

Why did the Israeli government wait so long to release this documentation? To prove that the Holocaust existed, the Israelis—relying on Eichmann's credibility—finally released the *Diary* they had in their possession for the past forty years. Apparently, Gideon Hausner, the prosecutor in the Eichmann trial, cautioned that publication of the memoirs could compete with the verdict. That is why Prime Minister Ben-Gurion ordered the manuscript locked away for fifteen years. Only recently was it decided to make the memoirs public. A copy of the manuscript was sent to London, after a request by defense lawyers. The book serves as evidence of the Nazi genocide. A photocopy and typed versions of the text in the original German are available at the Israel State Archives in Jerusalem.

The Holocaust took place during a complex and dark period of human history. The Church was the only institution that had the courage to denounce the Nazi action. Eichmann's words confirm the thesis of those historians who have collected documents on the action undertaken by the Vatican to defend Jews. In a chapter dedicated to Italy, Eichmann explains that on October 6, 1943, Ambassador Moelhausen sent a telegraphic message to Foreign Minister Ribbentrop in which he said that General Kappler, SS commander in Rome, had received a special order from Berlin; he had to arrest eight thousand Jews who were living in Rome, to deport them to northern Italy, where they would be exterminated. General Stahel, commander of the German forces in Rome, explained to Moelhausen that, from his point of view, it would be better to use the Jews for fortification works. On October 9th, however, Ribbentrop answered that the eight thousand Jews of Rome had to be deported to the Mathausen concentration camp. Under oath in the military prison of Gaeta on June 27, 1961, he emphasized that this was the first time he heard the term "Final Solution."

The truth is told in Kappler's own words: "At that time, my office received the copy of a letter, that I immediately gave to my direct superiors, sent by the Catholic Church in Rome, in the person of Bishop Hudal, to the commander of the German forces in Rome, General Stahel. The Church was vigorously protesting the arrest of Jews of Italian citizenship, requesting that such actions be interrupted immediately throughout Rome and its surroundings. To the contrary, the Pope would denounce it publicly. The Curia was especially angry because these incidents were taking place practically under Vatican windows. But, precisely at that time, without paying any attention to the Church's position, the Italian fascist government passed a law ordering the deportation of all Italian Jews to concentration camps."

Eichmann wrote in his diary: "The objections given and the excessive delay in the steps necessary to complete the implementation of the operation, resulted in a great part of Italian Jews being able to hide and escape capture." A good number of them hid in convents or were helped by men and women of the Church.

Adolf Eichmann organized the deportation of millions of Jews to death camps during World War II. He wrote his memoirs in an Israeli jail in the summer of 1961, after Israeli agents seized him in Argentina and brought him to trial in Jerusalem. Over a period of four months he laboriously penned his autobiography, which he apparently intended to publish as a book entitled *The False Gods*. Totaling 1,100 pages (including drafts, diagrams, and footnotes) the book recounts at length Eichmann's defense in his trial: that he was no more than a cog in the Nazi machine, that he was not anti-Semitic but misguidedly drawn to the nationalist ethos of Nazism. He also portrays himself as an official with limited authority who was simply following orders. In one diagram he places himself at the bottom of the Nazi hierarchy.

About his relationship with Jews: "I was never an anti-Semite," he declared. Other statements are: "My sensitive nature revolted at the sight of corpses and blood....I personally had nothing to do with this. My job was to observe and report on it."

Regarding his involvement in the Holocaust, Eichmann stated: "Because I have seen hell, death and the devil, because I had to watch the madness of destruction, because I was one of the many horses pulling the wagon and couldn't escape left or right because of the will of the driver, I now feel called upon, and have the desire, to tell what happened."

The release of Adolf Eichmann's memoirs raises questions about their veracity and value to current Holocaust debates. It certainly helped in Deborah Lipstadt's libel defense against David Irving in London, and helped bolster her arguments. The *Jerusalem Post*[26] stated that it would be difficult for Irving to twist the document in his favor. Furthermore, evidence Eichmann gave at his trial "is much more persuasive" than his memoirs, according to Professor Yehuda Bauer. He thinks that reading the memoirs alone will give a distorted view of the Shoah.

"It was a different time," says historian Yisrael Gutman, "a time when most talk about the Shoah centered on the perpetrators. We did not know then enough about the victims, about their destiny, their suffering, their end....There was no reason for our side, from our archives, to help in this exploitation and in the publication of such a thing....Keeping documents in state archives for 30 or 50 years is standard practice of democracies worldwide."

Some critics do not want to accept the truth and continue to reiterate the contention of several contemporary Jewish leaders that the Vatican is withholding evidence about its participation in World War II. Indeed, there are no such documents, and these allegations are unjust.

Ernst von Weizsäcker, Germany's Chief Secretary of Foreign Affairs until 1943 and then Ambassador to the Holy See, testified: "It was well known—everybody knew it—that the Jewish question was a sore point as far as Hitler was concerned. To speak of interventions and requests submitted from abroad, requests for moderation of the course taken, the results of these, almost in all cases, caused the measures to be made more aggravated, and more serious even, in effect."

Albrecht von Kessel, aide to Ernst von Weizsäcker in the Roman embassy, also testified: "I am convinced, therefore, that His Holiness the Pope did, day and night, think of a manner in which he could help the unfortunate Jews in Rome. If he did not lodge a protest, then it was not done because he thought, justifiably, that if he protested, Hitler would go crazy, and that would not help the Jews at all, that would give one the justified fear that they would be killed even more quickly. Apart from that, the SS would probably have been instructed to penetrate into the Vatican and lay hands on the Pope."

Jewish organizations took note of Pius XII's efforts, and they turned to him in times of need. Grand Rabbi Herzog wrote to Cardinal Maglione on behalf of Egyptian Jews, expressing thanks for the Holy See's charitable work in Europe and asking for assistance for Jews being held prisoner in Italy. The following month he wrote back thanking Pius for his efforts on behalf of the refugees that "had awakened a feeling of gratitude in the hearts of millions of people."

On August 2, 1943, the Jewish Congress sent the following message to Pope Pius XII: "World Jewish Congress respectfully expresses gratitude to Your Holiness for your gracious concern for innocent peoples afflicted by the calamities of war and appeals to Your Holiness to use your high authority by suggesting Italian authorities may remove as speedily as possible to Southern Italy or other safer areas twenty thousand Jewish refugees and Italian nationals now concentrated in internment camps…and so prevent their deportation and similar tragic fate which has befallen Jews in Eastern Europe. Our terror-stricken brethren look to Your Holiness as the only hope for saving them from persecution and death."

Later that same month, *Time* magazine reported: "No matter what critics might say, it is scarcely deniable that the Church Apostolic, through the encyclicals and other papal pronouncements, has been fighting totalitarianism more knowingly, devoutly, and authoritatively, and for a longer time, than any other organized power."

In September, a representative from the World Jewish Congress reported to the Pope that approximately four thousand Jews and Yugoslav nationals who had been in interment camps were removed to an area that was under the control of Yugoslav partisans. As such, they were out of immediate danger. The report went on to say: "I feel sure that the efforts of your Grace and the Holy See have brought about this fortunate result, and I should like to express to the Holy See and yourself the warmest thanks of the World Jewish Congress. The Jews concerned will probably not yet know by what agency their removal from danger has been secured, but when they do they will be indeed grateful."

Two months later, Rabbi Herzog again wrote to Pope Pius XII expressing his "sincere gratitude and deep appreciation for so kind an attitude toward Israel and for such valuable assistance given by the Catholic Church to the endangered Jewish people." Jewish communities in Chile, Uruguay, and Bolivia also sent similar offers of thanks to the Pope.

Those who continue to malign Pius XII and the Church also offend the Jews who have testified that they were hidden and "saved" by the Vatican during World War II. As a result of Pius XII's directives many Jews survived in Rome and have left us testimonials, interviews, and public acknowledgments toward the Pope, the Catholic Church, and its religious organizations.

Pope Pius XII's peace efforts are incontestable. Recent appeals for peace by Pope John Paul II were also not heeded. Will he be accused, as was Pius XII, of not doing enough for peace? This is an injustice.

When will the indictment against the Catholic Church and, in particular, against Pius XII end? Without justification, the following statement appeared in the Catholic News Service: "Pope John Paul II is pushing the canonization of Pope Pius XII." Except for those who are prejudiced, most people would consider those ill-chosen words to be both unworthy and provocative.

9. Jews Speak Out

Toward the end of the war, the *New York Times* published an article by Herbert L. Matthews, "Happier Days for Pope Pius: Shadows of war are lifting for a Pontiff whose greatest interest is world peace (October 15, 1944)." In it the well-known journalist summarized the Pope's peace plan based upon the five points he first put forth in his 1939 Christmas speech: "These proposals contained, among other things, the defense of small nations, the right to live, disarmament, some new kind of league of nations and a plea for the moral principles of justice and love." The same themes were reemphasized in the Pontiff's first important pronouncement after the United States was at war—his Christmas speech of 1941.

Some Jews feel the attacks on Pius XII are fueled by those opposed to the Church's strong moral position on some of the burning issues of modern society. Can it really be that the increasing slanderous attacks on Pope Pius XII in recent years are motivated by a desire to discredit the Church because of its leading role in the abortion and euthanasia issues, its opposition to pornography, and its defense of traditional family values?

Rabbi Marvin Hier[27] claimed that Pius XII "sat on the throne of Peter in stony silence, without ever lifting a finger" during World War II. He also argued that "the Vatican adamantly refuses to open its files on this period," because the evidence contained in the Vatican archives would prove the Pope's guilt. There is overwhelming evidence that he did speak out and that open defiance against the Nazis would have been unreasonable and detrimental since Hitler would have responded with unrestrained retaliation. One might ask, what did the Allied powers do to save Jewish lives? Did not the Immigration Offices of both the United States and Great Britain refuse to accept Jewish refugees?

In 1944, President Franklin D. Roosevelt decided to grant asylum to one thousand European Holocaust refugees. The incredible story of this group is told in *Haven on Earth,* a CBS miniseries based on the memoir of Ruth Gruber, a young Jewish-American employed by the Department of the Interior. Gruber accompanied these refugees on their hazardous transoceanic journey from Europe. She was dismayed when her charges, many of them survivors of concentration camps, were quarantined in a compound complete with barbed wire and armed guards in Oswego, New York. She was shocked to learn that the State Department had tried to prevent many Jewish refugees from seeking asylum here.

Despite Nazi attempts to keep the Einsatzgruppen extermination of Jews secret, news of the mass murders did find its way back into Germany and Allied countries. Reports of atrocities were met with disbelief and skepticism and were assumed to pertain only to military actions involving Russian defense forces.

But state papers now reveal that in 1941 the Allies knew about the Jewish genocide. The British government had detailed knowledge of the scope of the exterminations. In a radio address on August 24, 1941, Prime Minister Churchill disclosed that "whole districts" were being exterminated, and that "scores of thousands of executions in cold blood" were being perpetrated by "German police-troops upon the Russian patriots who defend their native soil." However, Churchill did not mention that Jews were being killed because he did not want the Germans to know that British intelligence forces had cracked their secret radio codes. The Allies did not bomb the railway line to Auschwitz, which would have saved thousands, and did little to save the Jews until the war was over. Martin Gilbert's book tells the sad story.[28]

Through diplomacy, personal contact with heads of state, and the underground railroad, Pius XII protected the Jews and other victims of the Nazis in a way that no other leader with mighty war weapons could provide. It was his charity and love that prevailed.

How long will honest scholars condone statements by those who defame Pope Pius XII? Numerous books have followed the route of *The Deputy,* that slandered Pius XII as a cold, "silent" pope who allegedly placed the Church's interests above those of the victims of

Nazi atrocities. This "black legend" repeats falsehoods that slander Pius XII's wartime record.

Following the footsteps of Rolf Hochhuth, Carlo Falconi, author of *The Silence of Pius XII,*[29] repeats the same calumnies. Robert A. Graham reviewed Falconi's book in an essay published in *The Pilot,*[30] and shows, contrary to Falconi's assertions, that there was no papal "silence" regarding Nazi atrocities. When the English translation appeared, six volumes of the Vatican's wartime documents had been published. Falconi made no reference to these documents.

Dr. Joseph Lichten, a Polish Jew who served with the Polish Government in exile during World War II and a former director of the Intercultural Affairs Department of the Anti-Defamation League of B'nai B'rith, suffered personal family tragedy from the Nazis. It is paradoxical that he has provided one of the best personal defenses of Pope Pius XII. Dr. Lichten wrote thirty-five pages of documentation in support of his belief that Pius XII did "everything humanly possible to save lives and alleviate suffering among the Jews" and that "the evidence moves against the hypothesis that a formal condemnation from Pius would have curtailed the mass murder of Jews." He also stated that "the Pope's opposition to Nazism and his efforts to help Jews in Europe were well-known to the suffering world."

In his introduction to Father Robert Graham's monograph *Pius XII's Defense of Jews and Others* (Catholic League, 1987), Lichten answered critics who maintain that the Vatican was primarily interested in helping only baptized Jews. Efforts to save converted Jews "did not detract from their action in defense of the hunted Jews.…Their pleas for the baptized were as natural as was the anxiety of the Jewish institutions over the fate of their own coreligionists. Finally, a countless number of baptized certificates were not genuine. When a Red Cross worker objected, saying that forged documents violated the Geneva Convention, the Apostolic Nuncio in Hungary replied: 'My son, you need have no qualms of conscience because rescuing innocent men and women is a virtue. Continue your work for the glory of God.'"

Shortly after Pius XII's death, an article in *The Jewish Newsletter* expressed the uniqueness of his extraordinary contribution: "It is to the credit of Pope Pius XII that…instead of preaching Christianity, as the Christian Churches had done for centuries, he and the churches practiced its principles and set an example by their acts and lives, as did the Founder of Christianity."[31]

Perhaps one can call the present media attacks an anti-Catholic "cultural war." In the late 1940s and 1950s, there were no "organized" efforts to undermine morality (legitimization of abortion and gay marriage were unthinkable; there was legal censorship against pornography). The attacks on Pius XII, starting with the play *The Deputy,* began in the early 1960s, at a time when Judeo-Christian moral and family values began to decline.

In fact, the increasing slanderous attacks on Pope Pius XII by both Jews and Gentiles (including some renegade "Catholics") have nothing really to do with Holocaust history, but have everything to do with the present cultural war. It is a determined effort to discredit the Church.

Richard Breitman, author of *Official Secrets: What the Nazis Planned, What the British and Americans Knew,*[32] explored the relationship among Nazi decisions, German behavior, and Western responses. The OSS documents of U.S. espionage during World War II and corresponding British secret service documents demonstrate the positive action of the Vatican in favor of the persecuted Jews and other Nazi victims. This was confirmed on July 7, 2000, by the Zenit News Agency.

Breitman, a professor at American University in Washington, D.C., is a consultant for the working group for the restitution of Jewish property, which group has obtained the declassification of the OSS dossier. In an interview with the Italian newspaper *Corriere della Sera,*[33] he explained that the documents "are only the tip of the iceberg. Over the next three years, additional millions of pages will be made public." But what impressed him most in regard to Italy was German hostility toward the Pope and the September 1943 plan to "Germanize" the country. He also found "the Allied silence on the Holocaust surprising. Their first testimonies are from the end of 1942...."

Asked about relations between Pius XII and the Germans, Breitman responded: "In general, the Germans considered the Pope as an enemy. In a telegram, someone suggested to play on his old anti-Communism, to induce him to 'understand' Nazism, and to take him from Rome to the North: the Vatican and Germany would have formed a common front against the USSR, and the Vatican would fall under

Berlin's control. But the proposal was rejected because the majority knew that Pius XII would never leave Rome, and that the Vatican was on the side of the Allies." The Nazis had spies in the Vatican and knew that Jews were being helped to safety. Aware of this activity, Berlin distrusted the Pope and considered him an enemy.

Unfortunately, several Catholic historians have been denied permission to see these documents. However, sooner or later, the truth will be revealed in the public domain. In fact, the Italian newspaper *Il Giornale*[34] published an article by Washington journalist Mariuccia Chiantaretto entitled "The Holocaust Wall of Silence Is Falling."

The article reports the words of Richard Breitman's colleague Timothy Naftali, professor of contemporary history at the University of Virginia, who also reviews books of espionage for the *New York Times*. Breitman and Naftali are consultants for the Nazi War Criminal Record Interagency Working Group, established by Congress to study secret documents of Nazi atrocities.

With regard to the deportation of over one thousand Roman Jews, Naftali states that the British could have prevented the tragedy. The British had broken the Nazi code several days before the orders were implemented. Prime Minister Winston Churchill knew about the Nazi plans. There is also proof that an American, Andrew H. Berding of the Office of Strategic Services, obtained this information during an agreement for the exchange of information by the secret services of both countries.

Naftali explains that the Allies remained silent for two reasons. Espionage was the priority for the military (e.g., the number of German agents in Rome). They considered atrocities against the Jews of secondary importance. The second reason is that the use of information about the Nazi roundup of Jews might have compromised the possibility of obtaining additional information in the future. At this time the Germans did not know that the Allies were able to decode their communications.

10. Warsaw Ghetto

On April 19, 1943, Jewish residents of Warsaw staged a desperate uprising in the ghetto. After twenty-eight days of resistance, the Germans blew up the synagogue and the Jewish quarter no longer existed.

Polish sources estimate that about twenty thousand Jews were killed in the streets of Warsaw and another thirty-six thousand in the gas chambers. Not only in Warsaw, but throughout Poland, Jewish people were in hiding. About two hundred convents hid more than fifteen hundred Jewish children, mainly in Warsaw and the surrounding area. It required courage for priests and nuns to provide shelter to Jewish people. Polish nuns in German-occupied areas were often persecuted and forced into hiding themselves. Nuns in Soviet-occupied areas were even sent to work in Siberia.

The Vatican Secretariat issued a memorandum on May 5, 1943, entitled: "The Jews: A Dreadful Situation." It reported that there were approximately four and a half million of them in Poland before the war; today the estimate is that not even a hundred thousand remain there, including those who have come from other countries under German occupation. In Warsaw a ghetto had been established that contained six hundred fifty thousand of them; today there would be twenty to twenty-five thousand. Some, naturally, have avoided being placed on the list of names, but there is no doubt that most were liquidated. "The only possible explanation here is that they have died....There are special death camps near Lublin (Treblinka) and Brest-Litovsk. It is said that by the hundreds they are shut up in chambers where they [are] gassed to death and then transported in tightly sealed cattle trucks with lime on their floors." [On August 30, the United States Secretary of State expressed doubt, sending a message that "there exists no sufficient proof to justify a statement regarding executions in gas chambers."]

On June 2, 1943 (the feast day of St. Eugenio), the Pope expressed in new and clear terms his compassion and affection for the Polish people and predicted the rebirth of Poland, in an address to the Cardinals that was broadcast on Vatican Radio and clandestinely distributed in printed form within Poland: "No one familiar with the history of Christian Europe can ignore or forget the saints and heroes of Poland, nor how the faithful people of that land have contributed throughout history to the development and conservation of Christian Europe. For this people so harshly tried, and others, who together have been forced to drink the bitter chalice of war today, may a new future dawn worthy of their legitimate aspirations in the depths of their sufferings, in a Europe based anew on Christian foundations."

Pius XII assured his listeners that he regarded all people with equal good will. He then, however, provided a bit more insight into his thoughts. "Do not be surprised, Venerable Brothers and beloved Sons, if our soul reacts with particular emotion and pressing concern to the prayers of those who turn to us with anxious pleading eyes, in travail because of their nationality or their race, before greater catastrophes and ever more acute and serious sorrows, and destined sometimes, even without fault of their own, to exterminating constraints."

The Pope warned the cardinals to be cautious about what they said. "Every word we address to the competent authority on this subject, and all our public utterances, have to be carefully weighed and measured by us in the interests of the victims themselves, lest, contrary to our intentions, we make their situation worse and harder to bear."

Leaders of the Catholic Church in Poland were very grateful for the address. On June 11, Cardinal Hlond sent his thanks for the "historic words" of the Pope, saying that "the Poles needed this, and they anxiously awaited this statement which put an end to the fables of Hitler's propaganda that the Holy See had simply given up in regard to the situation in Poland." Archbishop Sapieha wrote from Cracow that "the Polish people will never forget these noble and holy words, which will call forth a new and ever more loyal love for the Holy Father...and at the same time provide a most potent antidote to the poisonous influences of enemy propaganda." He also said that he would try to publicize the speech as much as possible by having copies printed, if the authorities would permit it.

In June 1943, Pius XII released his encyclical *Mystici Corporis Christi* (On the Mystical Body). This was an open attack on National Socialism: "The Church of God...is despised and hated maliciously by those who shut their eyes to the light of Christian wisdom and miserably return to the teachings, customs and practices of ancient paganism." He wrote of the "passing things of earth," and the "massive ruins" of war, including the persecution of priests and nuns. He offered prayers that world leaders be granted the love of wisdom and expressed no doubt that "a most severe judgment" would await those leaders who did not follow God's will.

The Vatican avoided taking a position that would violate its neutrality. By condemning Nazism, Pius XII would have endangered millions of Catholics and thousands of German priests. He would have jeopardized, as well, the safety of the Jews in Rome, which was the center of Fascist Italy occupied by the Germans.

Giovanni Miccoli's book *I dilemmi e i silenzi di Pio XII* reconstructs the facts and presents the mental attitudes and difficulties of the Vatican Curia during World War II. He states that for the Vatican to take a position against the Nazis would mean the transformation of the war into a crusade....

The Holy See could not identify itself with any of the contrasting ideologies. It would disappear as a "Catholic State." On the other hand, the Holy See could not avoid denouncing the errors and the horrors of the war without neglecting its mission. But to clearly denounce them and those responsible for them implied precise pronouncements. It meant going to battle with serious and dangerous consequences. Ultimately the results would block the action of persuasion, assistance, and peacemaking that was the role of the Pontiff. Miccoli concludes that the "compromising attitude" of the Church was inadequate with respect to the tragedy of the Church and the Shoah.

Was the attitude of any other leader or organization more adequate than that of Pius XII? In a letter to the Bishop of Berlin (April 30, 1943), the Pope stated: "For the Vicar of Christ to find a just balance between the contrasting needs of his pastoral office, the path he must follow becomes always more tortuous and paralyzed."

Pius XII appealed to "Catholics the world over" to "look to the Vicar of Jesus Christ as the loving Father of them all, who takes upon himself with all his strength the defense of truth, justice and charity." He explained, "Our paternal love embraces all peoples, whatever their nationality or race. Christ, by his blood, made the Jews and Gentiles one...." Pius XII noted that Jews were among the first people to adore Jesus. He then made an appeal for all to "follow our peaceful King who taught us to love not only those who are of a different nation or race, but even our enemies."

Chapter IV
Church Leaders versus Tyrant

---

1. Six Churchmen Defy Hilter

"Church leaders in Europe did not defy the Nazis" has been the media's mantra. This is particularly regrettable since the allegations that Catholic Church leaders were "silent" and other monstrous calumnies against the Church are totally baseless. Resolute in his refusal to bow to the Nazis, the Pope followed the courageous path of direct action and saved the lives of hundreds of thousands of Jews. His correspondence with the bishops shows that he guided them throughout the war. Indeed, under his direction the hierarchy played a pivotal role in combating Nazism.

In a letter to the archbishops and bishops of Germany, dated August 6, 1940, Pius XII explains the tasks of the Church in times of war and recalls his own activities and efforts to stop the battle against the Church. The Pope insists on the unity and constancy of action by the episcopacy. He reminds them that the accusations against the Church and its mission are without foundation; that the Pope must be impartial and maintain the principles of justice—an essential part of the Church's mission of truth. Pius XII repeats the conditions of a just peace and refers to his declaration at the moment of the invasion of Belgium. He mentions also that his task is laden with responsibilities as he multiplies his efforts to take care of the needs of so many people. He praises the German Catholics and their fidelity to the Church manifested during the persecution. Finally, he reminds the bishops of the dangers for the life of faith, the necessity of personal piety, and the need to encourage the clergy.

Unfortunately, there is an abundance of Holocaust literature that does not include the truth. Guenter Lewy in *The Catholic Church and*

Nazi Germany—published by Da Capo Press (New York, 1964) and republished with a new introduction (2000)—defames the Church by falsely accusing it of silence, collaboration, and indifference during the Nazi Holocaust. Why does the media ignore the significant syndicated series of six unforgettable articles that appeared in the *New York Times* from June 8 to June 13, 1942? The caption is self-explanatory: "Churchmen Who Defied Hitler," by Henry Smith Leiper, Foreign Secretary, Federal Council of Churches. These articles illustrate and confirm that the hierarchy of Germany, Norway, Holland, Yugoslavia, Belgium, and Switzerland did speak out in Europe.

2. Bishop von Galen of Germany

(Monday, June 8, 1942)

Religion versus tyranny could well be the title of the gigantic struggle going on in Germany today. Nazi attempts to stifle religion are meeting with the determined opposition of church leaders, who are virtually the only Germans still speaking up against the Nazi regime.

Most persistent opponent of the Nazi anti-Christian program is the rugged, fearless Bishop of Müenster, Count Clemens August von Galen, a man idolized by his native Westphalia and respected by all Germany.

Bishop von Galen received international acclaim a few months ago after the news leaked out of Germany that he had preached three "amazingly bold" sermons last Summer denouncing Nazi principles.

The first sermon was delivered a few days after a heavy Royal Air Force bombardment of Müenster. As an outcome of the Bishop's attack, all Roman Catholic orders in the Province of Westphalia were reported to have been dissolved and a number of prominent Roman Catholics imprisoned.

The Bishop's reaction was again to denounce the Nazis. The city, he said, had suffered first "from our opponents in war," and secondly, from an "inner enemy," that "spiritually was most dangerous."

"No German citizen," he added, "has any longer any security and justice has come to be a thing of the past."

A week later the Bishop mounted his pulpit to decry the injustices within the country that "cried aloud to heaven for redress." There was, he said, no longer any law in Germany. He believed, however, that the resistance of Christians was like a strong anvil and that, in the long run, all hammers would break if the anvil were sufficiently strong.

In outspoken terms, Bishop von Galen has condemned unauthorized killings of invalids and the insane, and Nazi racial doctrines.

"People speak of 'blood and soil.' If these words had any significance whatever, I more than anyone should have the right to invoke this doctrine, for my ancestors have been established in this country for over 500 years. Here in this Rhenish land we are on our own soil and have no need of prophets who come from abroad."

The Bishop was alluding to the standard-bearer of the anti-Christian forces, Dr. Alfred Rosenberg. Dr. Rosenberg, official Nazi philosopher, was born in Russia.

On November 8, 1938, Bishop von Galen came out of a church in Westphalia where he had been administering confirmation. He moved slowly through the crowds, blessing the people as he passed. A police inspector, accompanied by twenty of his men, ordered the Bishop to stop. The Bishop, six feet tall, an impressive figure in his episcopal robes, paused momentarily. Quietly he told the official that never before in his diocese had his right to do such things been denied, and he meant to continue.

"I forbid you!" shouted the inspector.

The Bishop looked at the crowd, and went calmly on his way, giving his blessing. The inspector and his twenty henchmen also looked at the crowd and decided that it was wiser to leave him alone.

Since 1934, when he and other Catholic Bishops denounced Nazi neo-paganism to Reichsfuehrer Hitler during a conference with the German leader, Bishop von Galen has been speaking his mind with forceful and uncompromising honesty.

He knows that a decree for his execution or imprisonment in a concentration camp depends solely upon the Nazi sense of expediency. He has said as much in his sermons, telling his flock that neither he nor any man is safe under a regime that is pitiless in its suppression of free speech and religion.

His fearlessness is a byword. He has not hesitated to tell Herr Hitler by telegram or letter whenever he violates the concordat he signed with Rome, which is often enough. He has gone straight to high-ranking ministers to denounce the persecution of religion. He has demonstrated his oneness with his people in defending what he holds dear to religion and personal freedom. In July of that year a great procession was held in Müenster, as it had been for 550 years, to commemorate the salvation of Müenster from fire and pestilence.

For the first time in all those years, the procession was marred by the hostility of the Nazi police, who roped off and placed under guard that part of the Cathedral Square through which the Bishop would pass after the ceremony. Mounting his pulpit, Bishop von Galen cried out in tones that moved his hearers to applause:

"If anybody thinks that physical force, ropes and police measures are going to separate me from you, or you from me, he is making a serious mistake."

Persuading his people to remain peaceful, he left the cathedral and deliberately passed across the square in such a way as to be seen by the crowds gathered beyond the ropes. His courage and the salvo of cheers that greeted him convinced the police it was safer to leave him alone.

His friends chuckle as they recall the quick-witted rebuke he once administered to a uniformed Nazi as he was preaching in his cathedral against State interference with the family, youth and education. By what right, the Nazi interrupted, did an unmarried cleric, a celibate, talk about the problems of youth and marriage?

Striking the pulpit a great blow, the Bishop retorted instantly:

"Never will I tolerate in this cathedral any reflection on our beloved Fuehrer!"

His courage flows from his faith and his kinship with his people.

"We Galens are neither particularly clever nor handsome," he once said. "But we have Catholicism in our bones."

Among his ancestors is Christopher von Galen, who was Bishop of Müenster in 1650 and helped to restore peace and prosperity to the countryside after the Thirty Years' War. Other ancestors also have been Bishops. In 1877 Ferdinand von Galen introduced the first piece of social legislation ever considered by the German Reichstag.

The Bishop's own father was a leader of the German Center party. The family's record of religious attachment and social reform has been carried on by the Bishop himself.

Born at Dinklage, Oldenburg, on March 16, 1878, and ordained in 1904, Monsignor von Galen worked in Berlin, and became president of the Workers Circle before being elevated to the episcopacy on October

8, 1933, by the late Cardinal Schulte, the first German Cardinal to recognize the dangers of Hitlerism.

Last November, according to a report from Müenster, the entire regiment of that city marched to the office of the Nazi Gauleiter upon hearing that Bishop von Galen had been banned from preaching and demanded that the ban be removed. A number of young men, who had appointed themselves as a voluntary bodyguard, attacked a Gestapo agent who had been assigned to spy on the Bishop's palace.

The Bishop has become a front rank leader in the Christian opposition to the program of National Socialism. His enemies in the Nazi stronghold are many, but so are the friends whose cause he upholds with such singleness of purpose.

3. Bishop Berggrav of Norway

(Tuesday, June 9, 1942)

At the Royal Palace at Oslo, Norway, late last Winter, two men faced each other across a conference table. Surrounded by his uniformed aides, the head of Norway's pro-Nazi government, Premier Vidkun Quisling, scrutinized the quiet, impassive features of Eivand Berggrav, Bishop of Oslo and Primate of the church of Norway, pondering the questions he would ask this man who had dared to defy the new Nazi order.

The Premier had many grievances against the Bishop. Had he not refused to give church support to attempts to recruit Norwegians to fight with the Germans against Russia? Had he not exasperated government circles by declaring that "for the Norwegians, only God—never Quisling—can be a leader?"

It was difficult for the Premier to pretend politeness toward this church leader, who, six days after the German invasion, had prevented him from becoming Premier at that time. That, indeed, was something to start on. He leaned forward.

Would the Bishop confess that the Administrative Council which succeeded the first Quisling regime and governed Norway throughout most of the Summer of 1940 had been instituted at the initiative of himself and Supreme Court Justice Paal Berg?

His fingers caressing the cross suspended from a gold chain around his neck, the Primate refused to answer.

"I can tell you, however," he said, "that two prominent members of the Nasjonal Samling [Quisling's party] participated."

Then, turning inquisitor himself, the quiet-spoken Bishop asked how Major Quisling could falsify his application for resignation by permitting newspapers to print that he had been dismissed after Major Quisling himself had used the word "resignation" in a telegram.

"We in the Nasjonal Samling see it thus," he was told.

"Then," responded the Bishop, "I have nothing to do here."

His patience exhausted, the Premier bellowed: "You triple traitor! You deserve to have your head chopped off."

"Well," came the Bishop's answer, "here I am."

Long considered the most dangerous opponent of the puppet government of Norway, Bishop Berggrav's subsequent deposition by the Nazi-sponsored Premier and his arrest on charges of having "incited the Norwegian clergy to rebellion" occasioned little surprises. There were some, in fact, who thought the Bishop lucky to have escaped the extreme penalty threatened by Major Quisling.

First interned in the Bretvedt concentration camp near Oslo, he was later released—on the personal orders of Reichsfuehrer Hitler, it was whispered—and is now said to be confined in a Summer cottage guarded by twenty men and surrounded by barbed wire. He has been forbidden to talk to any one except his nearest relatives and his servants.

His release from the concentration camp was believed to have been dictated by Norwegian political conditions—a euphemism for public unrest over his imprisonment. Meanwhile, the struggle between the Quisling government and the Lutheran Church, headed by Bishop Berggrav and comprising 97 percent of Norway's population, continues.

Valiant champion of Norwegian rights, Bishop Berggrav was born fifty-eight years ago in the much-bombed town of Stavanger. He became Bishop of Oslo in 1937, having previously been Bishop of Halogaland, scene of many Commando raids. His father also had been a Bishop, so he came to this work with a deep insight into its responsibilities.

His wife, Katherine Selp, whom he married in 1909, is a sister of Professor Didrik Akup Selp, the Rector of Oslo University, who has been reported cruelly treated by the Nazis, confined in a dark cell on a diet of bread and water. Both Bishop Berggrav and Professor Selp represent the independent spiritual life of Norway which the Nazis would like to crush.

In the early days of the war, it was said, Bishop Berggrav publicly urged the Norwegians to cooperate with the Nazis, but soon realized how fully the invaders threatened everything Norwegian and Christian.

It was not long before he was forced to gather round him the other six Bishops of Norway and to address to the Quisling authorities a spirited protest against the miscarriages of justice and the interferences with church work that was becoming increasingly apparent under the Nazi regime.

Timed with the sinister visit to Norway of Gestapo Chief Heinrich Himmler, the protest recalled broken Nazi promises to respect Norwegian church and civil laws, resoundingly detailed examples of brutal violence by Premier Quisling's "uniformed hooligans," and challenged Nazi banning of preachers' vows of secrecy—"the foundation of the church, the *Magna Charta* of the conscience."

Circulation of the Bishop's protest was expressly prohibited by the Nazis, but the message was printed in enormous quantities and read in churches throughout the country. Its effect was to consolidate opposition among the people to the threats inherent in the new Nazi creed. Despite the police, Norwegian congregations continued to pray for exiled King Haakon, and the Lutherans were backed in their struggle by the Congress of Dissenting Faiths, the Salvation Army of Norway, and numerous school and mission groups.

Out of Norway's 1,100 ministers, the pro-Nazis could persuade only twenty-seven Lutheran pastors to support the German invasion of Russia. The great majority joined with Bishop Berggrav in refusing to issue a call to their people "to put old quarrels behind" and unite with Germany in "the defense of European culture."

While the controversy was at its height, a cartoon appeared in a Swedish newspaper showing the Bishop preaching, a Gestapo official holding a club over his head.

The uncompromising Bishop brought the Church-State struggle to a climax by opposing measures to bring the schools under Quislingist domination, a move that would have extended a Nazi influence over Norwegian youth.

"The inner freedom of a good home," he wrote, "has always been a main pillar of our society, and no one can break into a home by force and upset the relationship between parents and children without God's Commandment being trampled underfoot."

Defiantly, he went on: "He who seeks to force the child out of the ties of parental responsibility and to break the divine right of the home, immediately forces the parents to the most extreme acts of conscience. Every father and mother knows that they will one day have to account to the Almighty for the way in which they brought up their children, or permitted them to be brought up. They must here obey God more than man."

Most of the 1,100 Norwegian pastors echoed these convictions and resigned from the State Church in protest.

Bishop Berggrav is no longer in a position to exert direct influence over his people, but he has laid the groundwork of an opposition the Nazis will find it hard to overcome.

4. Archbishop de Jong of Holland

(Wednesday, June 10, 1942)

In the Roman Catholic churches of the Netherlands, on the morning of Sunday, Aug. 3, 1940, parishioners settled back in their pews as the priest slowly mounted the pulpit to read a pastoral letter bearing the signatures of Dr. J. de Jong, Archbishop of Utrecht, and the Bishops of Breda, Bois le Duc, Roermund and Haarlem.

In the streets outside, men in German uniforms and agents of the Gestapo mingled with the early-morning crowds. Knowing this, worshipers in the dimly lit churches grew taut as words of defiance, spoken by their priest, and written by Bishops of the Netherlands, bade them beware of the enemy who had come to persecute and despoil their church.

What they did not know, as they listened intently to the pastoral letter, was the secrecy and spirit of determination that had made it possible for them to hear the outspoken message from their spirited leaders. Only a few hours before, a high official of the Gestapo had stalked arrogantly into the palace of Dr. de Jong. He demanded to see the Archbishop—at once.

The agent of the Gestapo was angry. The German secret police had only just learned that, in spite of all their cleverness, a pastoral letter, signed by the Netherland Catholic bishops, was to be read that morning from the pulpits of all Netherland churches.

A document that had been written, printed and distributed with such efficient secrecy could not but be dangerous to the occupying forces of Nazi Germany. It must be suppressed and the Archbishop must see to it immediately that none of his priests read it in church.

The demand was made in a bullying tone. But the Archbishop listened courteously. He assured the official that the matter could not be dealt with as expeditiously and easily as the Gestapo seemed to think.

There would have to be a delay while he consulted his cosignatories.

The Archbishop left his visitor alone and a considerable time elapsed before he returned. He apologized. At such an early hour, and the day being Sunday, the telephone service was not as one might wish. However, if the gentleman would be patient a little longer, he would try again to make a connection.

But an angry Nazi official, left cooling his heels for hours, could become too furious even for a dignified and courteous Archbishop to placate. When Dr. de Jong returned with yet another expression of regret, the Gestapo agent sprang to his feet shouting: "The letter must on no account be read in public. If it is, there will be heavy consequences."

The Archbishop sighed and looked at his watch. "That is regrettable," he said, "for now I fear it is too late. The letter has already been read at all our early Masses."

Too late, indeed, for even as the Gestapo official made his way back to headquarters all the Catholic Netherlands had been keyed to stiff resistance to Nazi tyranny by the explicit condemnations of its Bishops. It had been told that no Netherland Catholic could join Nazi organizations except under pain of being refused the sacraments.

The Bishops had struck an effective blow at attempts to popularize National Socialism in the Netherlands.

From the pulpits of the Netherlands on that August morning workers, miners, teachers and others had been told they must not enroll in the one big Nazi workers' association that was to do away with all other Netherland unions. There was to be no compromise with Nazi principles. The Bishops condemned the moral persecution waged against the Netherlands and the church. A year later the Netherland hierarchy reaffirmed its condemnation of the Nazi menace. In their pastoral letter, relayed here from Montevideo, the bishops, with reference to the National Socialist movement, asserted: "We again emphasize with greater insistency what we said previously, because since that time every one has been able to comprehend with increasing clarity that this movement not only threatens the Church in the free exercise of her essential mission, but also constitutes a grave danger for those belonging to this movement, in everything that pertains to the fulfillment of their duties as Christians."

Again Archbishop de Jong and his fellow-Bishops declared that they would continue refusing the sacraments in the case of death without repentance, and would also refuse ecclesiastical funeral, in the case of Catholics who in any way supported the Nazi ideology.

Linking forces with Protestant church leaders, the Netherland Catholic Bishops have protested attempts on the part of the Nazis to gain control of the Christian schools. Twelve hundred Christian schools throughout the Netherlands have joined in their protest by refusing to permit any interference with their affairs.

The Archbishop of the Netherlands has been fined by the Nazi authorities for his defiance of their regime, but, as is characteristic of the entire Netherland hierarchy, neither fine nor threat is likely to hold him to silence when the spiritual welfare of his people hangs in the balance.

5. *Patriarch Gavrilo of Yugoslavia*

(Thursday, June 11, 1942)

Yugoslavia is a subdued nation that refuses to be subdued. In its rugged hills an army under the leadership of General Draja Mikhailovitch is carrying on active warfare against the occupying legions of Hitler. The fearless General is continuing a tradition of courage and love of freedom which have, for centuries, been characteristics of the south Slavs—the Serbs, Croats and Slovenes—who make up the population of the Yugoslav kingdom.

Gavrilo Dozitch, 61-year-old Patriarch of the self-governing Orthodox Church of Yugoslavia, might have fled the country, as did King Peter II with members of his government, to carry on the struggle for Slav freedom from a foreign land. But he decided to stay with his people, a symbol of Yugoslav resistance to the Axis forces.

Elected Patriarch in 1938, Gavrilo Dozitch made himself a national hero by his conduct on March 27, 1941, when young King Peter ascended the throne on the heels of a bloodless coup d'état. Jubilant crowds cheered when he exhorted: "Rally round the King and be prepared for what comes. The church is always with you!"

Threats of Blitzkrieg already loomed over the Yugoslav State when the Patriarch was asked if he approved the demonstrations staged in the streets of Belgrade against Germany.

"Approve of them?" he replied. "I place myself at the head of them!"

January 27 is celebrated in Yugoslavia as the Festival of St. Sava, the Prince of the House of Nemanja, who, in the thirteenth century, left his father's court to become a monk and has since been revered throughout the Balkans as one of the founders of the south Slav culture.

On this feast in 1940 Patriarch Gavrilo warned the clergy against destructive propaganda being disseminated by Nazi agents. "There are various sinister organizations of foreign origin," he said, "which have aims alien and very dangerous to us. Our young people may fall a prey to these dark and alien forces, which bear in themselves a national danger to our State.

"Our clergy are called in the first place to exercise their serious and constant influence on the people and to destroy at the root all such agitations and efforts which belittle our traditions, weaken our national strength. Let us be wakeful, wise and watchful and let us 'take good care that no man deceive us.'"

When Regent Prince Paul's government signed its pact with the Axis in March, 1940, the Patriarch called a Bishops' meeting to protest it. At the White Palace he warned the Regent against giving the Germans power over the church.

The Patriarch was threatened with arrest and internment if he did not take a different attitude and restrain the Bishops from persisting in their hostility to the government's policy. To which the head of Serbia's Orthodox Church replied: "My own fate is a small matter compared with the fate of Yugoslavia. In no circumstance will the church support the betrayal of national honor now and endanger the future of the State."

Then came the fateful day of March 27, last year, when young King Peter, taking the law in his own hands, ascended the throne. From his palace balcony the stalwart Patriarch made his now famous promise of church support. The pro-Nazi government was swept from power. The nation rose exultantly to uphold and defend its royal ruler.

To the crowd which cheered wildly for the King, the Patriarch declared: "At dawn this morning the Yugoslav nation chose the road of truth and justice, of national unity and freedom. The eternal ideals which every Serb has always carried and cherished in his heart rose this morning clean and shining like the sun in the heavens.

"The bearer of these, our national ideals, the son of our noble Czar Alexander and the Almighty has preserved us today from decline. He heard our prayer and directed us back to the road of truth. Let us bend our knee before God and rise before man."

But even as he spoke the shadow of an irresistible terror was already lengthening over the Balkans. With the same paralyzing speed that marked the conquest of Poland, Norway and France, the Nazi armies smashed into Yugoslavia.

But Patriarch Gavrilo decided he could best carry on the struggle where he was. He refused to leave, and was taken prisoner by the Italians. In his place, fiery, black-bearded Bishop Nikolai Velimirovitch urges the guerrillas to continue their fight.

Whatever the future holds for the Patriarch Gavrilo and his country, he has lived up to the precepts of his predecessors. Courageously the nation suffers, awaiting patiently the day of deliverance.

6. Cardinal van Roey of Belgium

(Friday, June 12, 1942)

The Nazis have learned that the people of Belgium, a land "saturated with Catholicism," cannot easily be wooed into joining the "new order." They have found in Cardinal van Roey, Archbishop of Mechelen (Malines), a spiritual opponent deaf alike to blandishments and threats.

The Nazis were not unmindful of the trouble the German Army of Occupation had had in the last war when Cardinal Mercier, that brilliant, ascetic and courageous Primate, had defied their armies. They remembered the scorn of his words in 1914: "When we speak of German warfare, we try to attenuate the impression, for we feel that the naked truth exceeds the limits of what can be believed."

But Cardinal Mercier had been dead since 1926. In his place was slow-moving Cardinal Ernest van Roey, a man of few words, heavyset and phlegmatic. They had put him down as a negligible quantity. The task of winning Belgium was going to be a lot easier this time, the invaders told themselves.

Their mistake was in not knowing what type of man stood at the head of Belgium's Catholic people.

Only by degrees did the Nazis come to realize that Belgian resistance could show itself in other ways than through the lean courage of a Mercier. Now they stand irritated and baffled before the quiet, implacable resolve of 67-year-old Joseph Ernest van Roey, who refuses to have his people Germanized, who insists on heeding the voice of the Pope rather than the precepts of National Socialism.

Cardinal van Roey commands his people to obey the occupying power so far as international law demands. But that is not submission.

"The Belgian fatherland continues to exist," he insists, "and all its children owe it loyalty and service."

Fifth Columnists wage a fruitless campaign. The people refuse to look upon the Nazis as friends. They will not believe the stories told them about the wicked English. With quiet contempt they turn their back upon the Nazi organizations created to persuade them of the blessings of a world remade to Hitler's design. They cold-shoulder any Belgian who struts about in a Nazi uniform. Often, the Belgian Fifth Columnist gets rough handling. The Cardinal's priests refuse them the ministrations of the Church.

The Belgians can be a dour as well as a vivacious people. Their undemonstrative aloofness is thoroughly exemplified in the Archbishop of Mechelen. He has made no attempt to conceal his feelings toward the Nazi aggressors.

"The invasion of a country such as ours is clearly contrary to every law of justice," he has said. "The war is in itself a tremendous crime. It is a moral evil in all its horror."

In the days when Quislings were carrying on their traitorous activities, priests refused to countenance Masses for those "martyrs" who were shot, but with every show of reverence and respect they continued to bury dead British airmen. Cardinal van Roey forbade his priests to give communion to any pro-German in uniform or to sanction Masses for the dead. He would not even permit uniforms in church.

The Germans wanted to control education both in the schools and universities. But the Cardinal preferred to shut them down, as he did at Brussels, rather than hand them over to Nazi professors. He foiled attempts to divide the country by setting Flemings against French-speaking Walloons. He told his people that any sort of support to a government persecuting the church was unlawful.

Even the Flemings, regarded as "Germanic stock," scorned the call of "blood and soil." Emulating the Cardinal's example, priests mounted their pulpits to recount the stories of Nazi wrongs, to urge their congregations to resist adamantly any effort to Germanize them.

The Germans, baffled, were told by Degrelle and other pro-German leaders: "It's the church interfering in politics. Clericalism must go!"

They scribbled "away with the priests" on the walls of the Archbishop's palace. The Nazi-controlled press indulged in invective and abuse. Hints were made of a dire vengeance to come. The churches throughout the country were closed for three days to punish priests for having read the Cardinal's Pastoral Letter without permission. Again, the walls of the Cardinal's palace were smeared with tar and lurid threats chalked over them.

The Primate of Belgium seemed to take no notice of these acts except to declare bluntly that the first nine months of the Nazi occupation had proved worse than the three years' occupation during the last war.

In vain have the Germans urged collaboration in their campaign of Nazifying the Catholic people of this small but resolute nation. Even as a theory, the Cardinal reminds them, collaboration is unthinkable. It is true, he says, that "the Catholic Church adapts itself to all governments that safeguard her liberty of conscience, but as for adapting herself to governments that oppress the rights of conscience and persecute the Catholic Church, the answer must be—no! Never!"

The Nazis know now how utterly unshakable that "no" can be. "Intelligence and good sense," the Cardinal assures his people, "help us to find our way to confidence and resistance because we are certain our country will be restored and will arise again."

7. *Karl Barth of Switzerland*

(Saturday, June 13, 1942)

During the spring of 1940, when frontier skirmishes were taking place between France and Germany north of the Black Forest, students at the cosmopolitan University of Basle, in neutral Switzerland, listened to the sound of distant cannon and asked themselves. "Where is Professor Barth?"

The professor was not to be found in his classroom. Not until his return some time later did the students learn that Karl Barth, former head of the theological faculty of the University of Bonn, in Germany, had temporarily forsaken the role of lecturer to shoulder a rifle and perform sentry duty on Switzerland's frontier.

Remembering that the internationally distinguished Protestant theologian had been a pacifist in the first World War, some expressed surprise at his action.

Others recalled, however, his frequent and now-famous condemnations of National Socialism, which have echoed around the world and earned for him the reputation of being one of the most convinced and outspoken opponents of Hitlerism and all it stands for. They remembered also that in between lectures Dr. Barth performed voluntary service with the Auxiliary Corps of the Swiss Army.

Karl Barth is in Switzerland today because he was expelled from Germany. First he aroused the ire of the Nazis when, while still teaching in a German university, he published his much-discussed pamphlet, "I say No!"

In it he ridiculed the blood and race theories of the Nazis. "Membership of the church," he said, "is determined, not by blood and race, but by the Holy Spirit and by baptism. If the German Church were to exclude Jews who have adopted the Christian faith or were to treat them as Christians of an inferior kind, it would have ceased to be a Christian church."

Dr. Barth infuriated the Nazis still more when he refused to take the oath of loyalty to Hitler—compulsory for German officials—without supplementing it with the words, "in so far as, being a Christian, my conscience permits me to do so." Furthermore, he refused to open his lectures on God by giving the customary "Heil, Hitler" salute.

For these reasons he was dismissed from office and later expelled. He returned to his native Switzerland and was welcomed by the University of Basle, where he now remains as Professor of Systematic Theology. The Nazis retaliated by forbidding German students to attend the University of Basle and withholding recognition of studies carried on under its roof.

Born in Basle in 1886, the son of a Reformed church professor, Karl Barth received his early training in the democratic, progressive schools of German Switzerland. He studied at the University of Berne, and then, in the Central European custom, at Berlin, Tubingen and Marburg. After ten years in the Swiss pastorate and a brief period of religious journalism, he embarked on his illustrious career as professor of theology. He taught, successively, in three German universities, at Gottingen, Müenster and Bonn, on the Rhine, just above Cologne.

During his years at Bonn (1930–1935), he witnessed with growing concern the inception and growth of the Nazi power and the attacks on the spiritual freedom of the German Church. Because he would neither take the oath of support to Hitler nor cease to defend the old faith, his expulsion from the new Germany was inevitable.

His Swiss nationality and the fact that the Nazi revolution was as yet in its early stages spared him from the harsh personal treatment suffered by subsequent Protestants against the new regime. He was simply requested to absent himself and was given some months' pay in advance. His post was given to another professor, his writings were burned and his future publication or circulation in Germany was forbidden.

Protestant Christians of Britain, France, Czechoslovakia, Germany, and Switzerland have come to regard Karl Barth's anti-Nazi pronouncements as something to look forward to. Catholics read his words and admire the spirit that dictates them. All creeds respect the courage that prompts his comments on current affairs. So outspoken are his views, that the Swiss censorship has felt obliged at times to put a ban on his pronouncements and speeches.

Writing in the Fall of 1938 to a fellow-theologian in Prague, Dr. Barth warned that the freedom of Europe might fall if freedom was lost in Czechoslovakia.

"Is the whole world really under the ban of the evil look of the boa-constrictor?" he asked. "I dare to hope that the sons of the old Hussites will show in the face of effeminate Europe that yet there are men even now. Each Czech soldier who will then fight and suffer, will suffer also for us, and—I say it without reservation—also for the Church of Christ."

In December, 1939, he told French Protestants: "After having made Germany from end to end a land of fear and terror, Hitler's National Socialism has become to an increasing extent a menace to the whole of Europe. When this last fact became sufficiently clear even for the blind to see, war came. Our generation would be answerable before God and before men if the attempt were not made to put an end to the menace of Hitler. The church cannot remain neutral in things great or small where justice is at stake."

When France fell, his message to the French people was to keep on resisting the enemies of Christianity.

He warned his own Swiss people of the perils of totalitarianism, saying: "We should be fools if we were to allow our present correct and friendly relations to make us forget that we have certainly not been forgotten and that the steamroller of the so-called 'new order' will sooner or later reach us."

To the people of Germany, among whom he had lived, studied and taught, he broadcast a Christmas message of consolation. "We know," he said, "how hard it is for you to celebrate Christmas joyfully this year; we know of the grief and sorrow in many of your families, of the oppression which is the price you must pay if you make confession of the Gospel, of the terrible things which our Jewish brothers and sisters have had to undergo. We pray for you. Pray also for us."

Karl Barth's latest message is addressed to Norway's heroic pastors who have defied both the Quislings and the Nazis. "You will give us Christians in all countries," he assures them, "a moving, inspiring example, and you will come into particularly close fellowship with Him who governs all lands and powers in heaven and on earth. We are confident that nothing you have been called upon to suffer will be in vain."[1]

Chapter V
Survivors' Testimonials

---

1. Stefanie Hoffman

*N*o one will ever forget the tragedy of the Holocaust of World War II. How can the testimony describing the actions taken by Pope Pius XII be ignored? How can one dismiss the heroism of so many individuals? Recently, members of two families were reunited at a bat mitzvah for thirteen-year-old Stefanie Hoffman, the eldest granddaughter of a little Jewish girl who had been smuggled out of the labor camp a half-century ago. Throughout the ceremony, there was a palpable sense that such a celebration might never have taken place had it not been for the courage of a Catholic family in Czestochowa, Poland. The story illustrates what some members of the Catholic Church did during the Holocaust.

In the predawn hours of a spring day in 1943, a Jewish woman approached the fence inside a Nazi labor camp in Poland and delivered a blanket-wrapped six-year-old girl, her only child, into the arms of virtual strangers. She risked being shot. She had no other choice. Her husband had died in a concentration camp. She did not think she and her daughter could survive for long. For more than two years through the end of the war, the little girl was hidden from German authorities.

Rabbi Jehiel Orenstein, head of the Congregation Beth El in South Orange, New Jersey, stated: "In the Jewish tradition, there is a saying that one righteous deed leads to another....This is an attempt to make sure the people who did us this great kindness are recognized and publicly thanked. The world is still slightly insane and we have to remind ourselves that we have to band together for justice. This is a wonderful reminder of the decency of humanity."

During the service, Stefanie Hoffman read the closing chapters of the Old Testament book of Leviticus, which describe the laws by which Jews are to conduct themselves. At the end of the reading, the congregation stood. "Let us be strong and let us drink from one another," they answered in Hebrew. The little girl who had been hidden from the German soldiers during World War II, Ilona Mudweid, now sixty-three and living in San Diego, stood before the congregation and embraced Zofia Berczynski, the seventy-eight-year-old woman who was her surrogate mother for more than two years during the war and still lives in Czestochowa.

The event was overwhelmingly emotional. Zofia Berczynski explained that she, her husband, and her mother-in-law took the girl in even though they would be executed if anyone discovered what they were doing. They obtained fake birth and baptismal certificates that said the girl's name was Irena Gawronska. They told friends and German soldiers she was a distant cousin whose parents had been killed during bombing raids. They taught her Polish prayers and made her wear a cross. "It was dangerous to stay in one place" recalled Berczynski. "For more than two years, we moved constantly from farm to farm or other outpost, hiding from the soldiers. Together we stood in line for a piece of potato or bread or a drink of soup."

At the end of the war Ilona Mudweid was reunited with her mother in Opoczno. The little girl was wearing the same pair of shoes—the toes, cut out to make way for her growing feet. A short time later, they immigrated to the United States and settled in Brooklyn.

"The keeping of the Jewish child was very difficult and dangerous....As long as I live I will remember their sacrifice and their good heart," Mudweid's late mother, Roma Frydman, wrote in 1984 as part of her testimony given to Yad Vashem, Israel's Holocaust authority. In 1985, Zofia Berczynski was honored as "Righteous among Nations," the name for those who rescued Jews during the Nazi occupation. Ever since she was honored in 1985, she has been receiving financial assistance through the Jewish Foundation for the Righteous. Stanlee Stahl, a Foundation official and a friend of Stefanie Hoffman's family, stated: "To Zofia, I would like to say that the people you see standing before you are alive today and are here because of your bravery and that of your beloved husband and mother-in-law of blessed memory. This is your legacy. And to you, Stefanie, may you always remember what Zofia did for your family and that one person can make a difference."

Stefanie said she would donate some of her bat mitzvah money to the Jewish Foundation for the Righteous.

2. Dr. Zofia Szymanska

Few people are acquainted with the work of another Zofia, a Jewish survivor of the Holocaust. Dr. Zofia Szymanska was saved by nuns in Poland. In *I Was Just a Doctor*,[1] she writes: "I am trying to portray the development of the distinction between a child's psyche and a mature person—extrinsic as well as intrinsic elements which have had an influence on me."

A renowned Jewish neuropsychiatrist, Dr. Szymanska was born in 1888 in Lodz, a large industrial city in Central Poland. Her father, an engineer educated in Vienna, was a cloth manufacturer and factory owner; her socialite mother graduated from the Dresden School of Music.

Zofia had two younger sisters, Elisa and Stella. The three girls had French and, later, German governesses, who helped with their education. When Zofia was sixteen, she entered the Lyceum, completed a four-year program within two years, and wrote her thesis in four languages: French, German, Russian, and Polish. After graduation and a short stay in Warsaw and in Berne, Switzerland, in 1908 she moved to France and was accepted at the Sorbonne School of Medicine. There she divided her time between studying and working with children at different hospitals.

At the beginning of World War I, Zofia's parents moved to Russia, where she later joined them after defending her doctoral dissertation. The professors commended her on the concept of using a variety of reproductions representing the Madonna with Child to document her scientific thesis in the field of child psychiatry. She completed her education at the Sorbonne with great success.

In Moscow, after passing the examinations for foreign doctors, she started to work simultaneously at the Children's Clinic and at the Institute of Neurology and Psychiatry with Dr. Rossolimo, a well-known child psychiatrist. At first, she was assigned to organize the search for the homeless and for orphans who were wandering all over Russia as a result of the Revolution. Later she was sent to a military hospital as a surgeon.

At the end of World War I, Dr. Szymanska and her family returned to Warsaw. The newly independent Poland was devastated and flooded by waves of refugees from Russia who brought threats of cholera and typhoid fever. To protect Poland from the outbreak of this epidemic, the physicians were mobilized by the Army and sent to the areas where instances of disease were most common. Zofia, now an epidemiologist, was ordered to organize outpatient programs and temporary hospitals near the city of Vilnus.

The epidemic outbreak was averted after three years of struggle, and Zofia was discharged with the rank of Lieutenant Colonel. She returned to Warsaw in 1923 and founded a mental health clinic for children. She implemented an innovative treatment based on collaboration among physicians, psychologists, and social workers. Socially unfit children were referred to her by doctors, teachers, police, and juvenile courts. She made house calls for the very poor through the State Insurance Health Center. In 1927, the director of Centos (the Union of Welfare Societies for Jewish Orphans) asked her to establish a needed program for children with mental disabilities who were unable to adjust or comply with the routine at orphanages. Her clinics ceased to exist in 1939, by order of the Germans.

With the German occupation of Poland in 1939, the people of Warsaw faced a hopeless situation. Dr. Szymanska became involved in the work of helping thousands of Jewish children. While still working for Centos during the first winter of the war, she understood the future fate of Warsaw Jews and the lack of help from the Jewish organizations outside Poland, especially American Jews. She knew that this was the beginning of the end. With her two sisters, brother-in-law and nine-year-old niece, Jasia, she lived in the Warsaw Ghetto from October 1940. The Centos Building was bombed on the first day of the War. In 1942, the Germans closed the Centos and her permit was terminated. The program was liquidated. All two hundred residents were exterminated.

When the reality of the liquidation of the Warsaw Ghetto became imminent, Sister Golembiowska, who was working with the Polish underground network, persuaded Dr. Szymanska to leave the ghetto with Jasia. They were moved by the network to the Institute for Boys at 97 Pulawska Street. Another Catholic friend, Irene Solska, took Dr. Szymanska to Sister Wanda Garczynska of the Immaculate Conception Sisters on Kazimierzowska Street. This convent was a link in the underground network to "help those who were hiding and living in danger and misery." Within seventeen days she was relocated with the Ursuline Sisters. Jasia, entrusted to a family friend and colleague, spoke about the bombings of the Warsaw Ghetto, accidentally disclosing her Jewish background. Immediately she was transferred to Kazimierzowska Street and instructed to approach the gate alone. She knocked and said: "I'm Jasia and I don't have anyone." Sister Wanda responded, "No, my child, you are not alone, you have me." During these years of hiding, Jasia was moved many times among the villages of Wrzosowo and Szymanowo and Kazimierzowska Street. The Gestapo suspected that the nuns, under the pretext of foster care for Polish orphans, were saving the lives of many Jewish children. In spite of constant danger the girls attended classes regularly in a serene atmosphere. Indeed, the heroic role of the Immaculate Conception Sisters in saving Jewish lives needs to be told.

In her book, Dr. Szymanska writes: "The example of the Sisters allowed me and others not to lose faith in human beings during those years of atrocities and cruelty." At the end of August 1942, with the approval of the Mother General Pia Lesniewska, she was moved to the Ursuline Gray Nuns' convent in the village of Ozarow. There she remained for two years and eight months in a small room and was visited by Sister Urszula Gorska, a student of classical philology at Warsaw University. From her small convent cell, she looked closely at the lives of the nuns but could not understand their obedience to suspend their obvious enjoyable work routine and their readiness to pray and contemplate. Only later was she able to understand the power of contemplative devotion to God—the sole source of their strength—which gave a sense of meaning and purpose to their lives.

She frequently asked herself: Why did God allow this to happen? Why wasn't Hitler excommunicated? Why didn't the American Jews organize assistance and intervene with the American Government to help the European Jews perishing in the concentration camps? The Germans began the liquidation of the ghetto in 1942. They transported whole orphanages of children to the concentration camps. After the Warsaw Ghetto uprising, only her younger sister Eliza was still alive and trapped in the Ghetto. Stella and her brother-in-law had been transported to the concentration camp. When she learned the fate of her family, she shared her thoughts of depression and suicide with Sister

Gorska. Responding to her needs, one of the sisters moved to her cell to help her. Many were the conversations they had about the need for people to assume responsibility and help save lives. In this crisis, the sisters were influential and encouraged her, but never did they try to persuade her to convert to the Catholic faith.

After the Russian offensive in the Spring of 1945, Dr. Szymanska spent the last Easter with the Ursuline Sisters. From documents and statements of eyewitnesses, she found out that the entire village of Ozarow knew that she and others were hiding in the convent. The sisters were aware of the consequences of hiding Jews; yet, without hesitation, they continued the dangerous task and saved many lives. She states: "No other country but Poland paid such a tremendous bloody tribute to the cause of saving Jewish lives. It is an undisputed fact that it is much easier to demonstrate and march for the cause of Jews, as happened in some Western countries, than to hide one of them for years during the German occupation of Poland." After the war, she returned to completely devastated Warsaw and worked for the Ministry of Education, Department of Child Welfare. She inspected the care given in orphanages. She learned that under the direction of Mother Getter, who saved the lives of several hundred Jewish children, the Sisters of the Family of Mary was one of the most active congregations protecting Jews during and after the war.

From 1949 to 1971, Dr. Szymanska worked for the Institute of Mental Hygiene and was given the opportunity by the government to create counseling programs devoted to the rehabilitation of children and adolescents. There again, as before the war in the Centos, she organized psychiatric care for children and training programs for future medical doctors and psychologists. The Center at Josefow was established as a mental health facility for boys. It was one of the first modern psychiatric institutions in Poland. Because of health problems and the inability to walk, in 1971, Dr. Szymanska retired at the age of eighty-nine. Dedicated to helping others and grateful to God for giving her the opportunity, she promoted issues of mental health hygiene throughout her life as a physician, teacher, and organizer. Even in the darkest hours of Fascism and Nazism, she never stopped believing in humanity. Dr. Zofia Szymanska expressed gratitude to the Catholic Church in her book, *I Was Just a Doctor.* She died in 1978, after many fruitful years of humanitarian services during and after World War II.

3. Leone Pontecorvo

Among the living Jewish survivors of the Nazi occupation in Italy during the Holocaust is Leone Pontecorvo, a well-known attorney in Rome.

Pontecorvo sent a letter, dated July 23, 1999, to Margherita Marchione with the following testimonial: "I was one of those saved by the Vatican. In October 1943, my father sent me (I was eight years old) and my brother Bruno (four and a half) to the boarding school of the Sisters Oblates of Mary in Rome, Via delle Mura Aureliane, where we remained until June 4, 1944.

"Only the principal and her assistant knew we were Jewish. We were well received and lived a normal life. We missed our parents who were with Catholic friends, hidden in a sealed room. There was no way we could communicate with them throughout this period. We were happy and followed the routine of the other children with morning and evening prayers, Mass, and participation in processions dressed as altar boys! Our stay was rich with episodes that were both moving and entertaining...."

4. The Nightmare of the Swastika

Michael Tagliacozzo's study, *La comunità di Roma sotto l'incubo della svastica* (The Roman Community during the Nightmare of the Swastika)—published by the Centro di Documentazione Ebraica Contemporanea (Quaderno No. 3, November 1963)—was later translated into Hebrew and published in 1970.

Professor Tagliacozzo sent a copy of this publication with a letter addressed to Margherita Marchione (June 18, 1997), in which he stated: "In my study of the conditions of the Jews of Rome during the German occupation, I pointed out the generous and vast activity of the Church in favor of the victims. During my research, conducted *sine ira et studio,* I learned how great was Pope Pacelli's paternal solicitude. No honest person can discount the merits attributed to him."

5. Vox populi, Vox Dei!

In a letter to Margherita Marchione (December 26, 1998), Michael Bobrow, an American Jew and foreign correspondent in the Holy Land in the late 1960s, stated that his cousin was hidden by Catholic nuns and saved, thanks to the directives of Pope Pius XII, whose "canonization would be an act of supreme justice, charity, and truth...."

Referring to Pius XII's sanctity in his letter to Margherita Marchione (February 22, 2001), Bernard Tiffany quoted the following letter from Padre Pio's secretary, Reverend Dominic Meyer, O.F.M., Cap.: "Padre Pio told me he saw the Pope in Heaven during his Mass. And many miracles have been attributed to His intercession in various parts of the world. Pictures of the Pope have been printed with a prayer for His beatification. But so far I have not seen any with the prayer in English (June 30, 1959)."

In *Diario* (p. 225), one finds a confirmation of the above statement. When Pius XII died on October 9, 1958, Padre Pio was consoled "by a vision of the former pontiff in his heavenly home," according to Padre Agostino.

Vox populi, Vox Dei! One cannot fail to note that immediately after his death the world at large proclaimed Pope Pius XII worthy of the title, Saint. One of the most charismatic figures of the twentieth century, Padre Pio, a mystic from Pietrelcina, in the province of Benevento, Italy, was beatified on May 2, 1999.

Chapter VI
Meeting the Challenge

1. "Be not afraid...."

*C*atholicism defends certain propositions about God, man, and the world as absolutely true and binding on all men. It is necessary to know the truth that "will make us free" (John 8:31–32). The Catholic Church has never compromised on matters of truth. With Pope John Paul II, we must give witness to the truth. We must repeat: "Be not afraid....Only in honest dialogue and acceptance of truth, can Catholics enter a new era of love and understanding with our elder brothers" (Catholic News Service).

Today, there are many dimensions to the present culture war, including both the rise of atheism and the decline of Christianity. Individualism, secularism, materialism, socialism, and relativism in truth and morals are the dominant philosophies. God and religion are subtly attacked through innuendoes and ridicule propagated in films, television, and the print media. The reality of religion or of the soul is rejected. Though we are living in an atheistic and secularistic world, we must not be intimidated; we must forge ahead in faith and hope.

To present the true role of Pius XII, one cannot assume as factual the many allegations that are contrary to evidence that has been available for many years but is studiously ignored by postwar critics. During the war and after the cessation of hostilities, the historic truth that he did his utmost in the saving of Jewish lives from Nazi terror was universally accepted until 1962.

In the 1960s, based on the purely fictional play *The Deputy*, the "big lie" intended to debase the memory of Pius XII and to demean his efforts was concocted by Rolf Hochhuth. Critics of Pius XII, through

107

repetition of baseless allegations and insinuating questions, continue to perpetuate the "big lie" as factual.

The body of probative evidence of Pius XII's efforts on behalf of the Jewish victims consists of the twelve volumes of the *Actes,* containing more than five thousand documents, describing the activities of the Vatican during World War II. This proof is supported by the many news reports of that era; documents in the archives of governments that had diplomatic relations with the Vatican at that time; and testimony at the Nuremberg trials. One must not discount the research of reputable Jewish, Catholic, and other historians who witnessed the events of World War II. Messages of highest praise for the rescue efforts of Pius XII by Jewish and government leaders are also recorded.

2. Rabbi Israel Zolli

The most important non-Catholic witness to the role of Pius XII in wartime Italy is Rabbi Israel Zolli, Chief Rabbi of Rome during the Nazi occupation and persecution of Jews.

A biblical scholar whose courage and integrity cannot be challenged, Rabbi Zolli was hidden in the Vatican. He and his twenty-year-old daughter Miriam were eyewitnesses of the deportation of Rome's Jews by the Gestapo in 1943. Yet, their testimony is generally ignored.

In his book *Antisemitismo* Rabbi Zolli states: "World Jewry owes a great debt of gratitude to Pius XII for his repeated and pressing appeals for justice on behalf of the Jews and, when these did not prevail, for his strong protests against evil laws and procedures."

Miriam recalls the prophetic words of her father about Pope Pius XII: "You will see, they will blame Pope Pius XII for the world's silence in the face of the Nazis' crimes!" She insists that her father, who was baptized in 1945, never abandoned his Judaism: "He felt he was a Jew who had come to believe in the Jewish Messiah."

Zolli, who found shelter in the Vatican during the war, stated: "No hero in all of history was more militant, more fought against, none more heroic than Pius XII in pursuing the work of true charity!...and this on behalf of all the suffering children of God."

In 1964, a special enlarged edition of the Vatican's weekly publication, *L'Osservatore della Domenica*[1] defended Pius XII. The issue, entitled *The Pope, Yesterday and Today,* included testimonials of contemporary historians, poets, literary and religious writers, and others of international stature who wrote in defense of Pius XII.

These writers were: Monsignor Cesare Angelini, Cardinal Domenico Tardini, Pope Paul VI, Pope John XXIII, Angelo Martini, S.J., Georges Jarlot, S.J., Cardinal Carlo Confalonieri, P. Robert Leiber, S.J., Luigi Salvatorelli, A. C. Jemolo, Vincenzo Fagiolo, Giuseppe DeMarchi, Gianluca André, Federico Alessandrini, Jean Toulat, Bishop Carlo Marziana, Minister Paul von Zeeland, Lutheran Bishop Fuglsang-Damgaard, Michel Riquet, S.J., President Luebke of Germany, Paolo Vincentin, Monsignor Walerian Meystowicz, Ambassador Gunnar Hagglof, Antonio Cederle, Dino and Pia Secco Suardo, Primo Mazzolari, Giuseppe Dalla Torre, Pinchas Lapide, Ambassador G. A. Gripenberg, Ennio Francia, Benvenuto Matteucci, Carlo Adami, Mario Toscano, Raffaele Cantoni, Cardinale Paolo Dezza, S.J., Cesidio Lolli, Herman Herskovic, Ettore Della Riccia, Rabbi Elio Toaff, Father Pancrazio Pfeiffer, and Enrico Zuppi.

3. Sir Martin Gilbert

An outstanding Jewish historian, Sir Martin Gilbert paints a deeply personal and cultural portrait of the Holocaust in *Never Again: The History of the Holocaust.*[2] Gilbert's new book demolishes John Cornwell's book *Hitler's Pope: The Secret History of Pius XII,* which charges the Catholic Church with having been responsible for the Holocaust.

Sir Martin Gilbert is also the author of *Auschwitz and the Allies*[3] and *The Holocaust: A History of the Jews of Europe during the Second World War.*[4] In the latter he writes: "In addition to the six-million Jewish men, women and children who were murdered, at least an equal number of non-Jews were also killed, not in the heat of battle, not by military siege, aerial bombardment or the harsh conditions of war, but by deliberate planned murder." Why the silence about these dead? Is it because they were mostly Christian? Is it because mentioning them might possibly point up Hitler's hatred of Christianity—which might tend to undercut the theory that Christianity was the source of Nazism? Would mention of Christian victims somehow make it more difficult for anti-Christians to see Nazism as perverted Christianity?

It is time for a resurrection of the truth. The infamous *Kristallnacht* pogrom took place on the night of November 9, 1938, and was accompanied by hysterical anti-Semitic diatribes from the Goebbels propaganda machine coupled with severe measures that terrorized German Jews to new levels of intensity. Reaction abroad was limited: President Roosevelt called his ambassador back to Washington to report. France received the German foreign minister, Ribbentrop, with full military honors four weeks later.

On a positive note, Cardinal Pacelli sent a recommendation dated November 30, 1938, on behalf of converted Jews obliged to leave Germany and Italy, to the Representatives of the Holy See.

This circular telegram was transmitted to nuncios in Dublin, Buenos Aires, Santiago in Chile, Lima, La Paz, Bogotà, Habana, San José de Costarica, and to the apostolic delegates in Washington, North Sydney, Scutari, Leopoldville, Hué, Beirut, Le Claire, Bloernfontein: "A good number of converted Italians and Germans are forced by law to abandon their country and to live elsewhere in order to exercise their professions, especially in teaching and medicine. His Eminence Cardinal Mercati is also prepared to suggest for university teaching illustrious professors in various fields of science. I ask Your Excellency to communicate this information to all concerned if there are Universities, Catholic Institutions, Hospitals, or other entities disposed to assume these persons and inform us of the requirements they may have."[5]

By word and deed, Pius XII rescued Jews during the Holocaust. How can a single person, among the millions that were a part of that dark period, be the object of so much blame and bitterness on the one hand, and so much praise and gratitude on the other?

With John Cornwell's book *Hitler's Pope,* the myths of Pius XII's so-called silence and criticism of Pope John Paul II have been revived. But the present-day Pope has not apologized for Pius XII's failings. The truth of the matter is: Pope Pius XII did not fail. He set up a Catholic refugee committee in Rome, which provided thousands of Jews with baptismal certificates, financial aid, and other arrangements so they could enter the United States as "Catholics." He initiated and sustained rescue programs all over Europe, primarily through his nuncios.

4. Information Office

Pius XII instituted the Vatican Information Office to take care of prisoners of war throughout the world. He lifted restrictions on cloisters of convents and monasteries so they could provide refuge for Jews, who were also housed in churches, administration buildings, parish houses, the Pope's own summer home in Castelgandolfo, and in the Vatican. He provided millions of dollars of aid to Jews and spent all his family inheritance on behalf of the Jews. Throughout the war, funds were at the disposal of the Quakers, the Swedish mission, and the Jewish Community, but none were available for baptized Jews. It was a tragic situation for, in the eyes of their coreligionists, Catholics of Jewish origin were apostates and, therefore, were to be neglected. The relief Pius XII sent was insufficient. Promises to assist refugees and issue visas allowing immigration to North and South America were not kept by some countries. However, the Pope continued his efforts to mitigate racial laws, to obtain the release of Jewish internees, to improve the conditions of prisoners, and to provide economic aid to families.

As early as 1939, Pius XII created a special department for Jews in the German section of the Vatican Information Office. According to the *Canadian Jewish Chronicle* and other Jewish publications, some 36,877 papers were processed in favor of Jewish refugees. The Jewish community has attested that the Church saved 4,447 Jews from Nazi persecution in the city of Rome alone. In fact, in the Museum of the History of the Liberation of Rome there is an inscription: "The Congress of delegates of the Italian Jewish community, held in Rome for the first time since the liberation, feels the urgent duty to render reverent homage to Your Holiness, and expresses the most profound feeling of gratitude that inspires all Jews, for the evidence of human fraternity shown to them by the Church during the years of persecution, when their life was endangered by Nazi barbarism."

After the war, the World Jewish Congress presented a large monetary gift to the Vatican "in recognition of the work of the Holy See in rescuing Jews from Fascist and Nazi persecution."[6] While Jews were the immediate target for persecution and extermination, it is clear from reading Hitler's writings or listening to his speeches that he pursued a systematic and tireless war against the Roman Catholic Church.

There has been some confusion, as to Pius XII's efforts in behalf of the Jewish victims of the Nazi atrocities. The documents indicate that initially, the baptized of Jewish origin appeared to be the only group who had been without help. However, the records show that the

Catholic Church consistently assisted many Jewish victims of Nazi anti-Semitism, even before the outbreak of World War II.

Father Blet's book *Pius XII and the Second World War* contains a summary of Vatican activities. It reveals Pope Pius XII's appeals on behalf of peace before the outbreak and during the war. His accomplishments were extraordinary when one considers his persistence in the face of so many efforts that failed. There were, however, many that succeeded.

One of the purposes of the Pope Pius XII Society, founded in 2000, is "to organize rapid response teams to defend the Church and comment in the media." In particular, it will promote the truth about Pius XII and the Holocaust—an important contemporary issue. The vilification of the person of Pope Pius XII and the denigration of our present Pope John Paul II are matters that affect the Magisterium of the Catholic Church.

Both are accused of silence. The Vatican chastised the Anti-Defamation League for its ads in the *New York Times* and the *International Herald Tribune.* According to correspondence obtained by *The Jewish Week,* Walter Cardinal Kasper, head of the Commission for Religious Relations with the Jews, defended John Paul II on May 18, 2001, in a letter to Abraham Foxman: "To defame the Holy Father by attributing 'silence' to him is quite unjust and cannot go uncontested....It wounds our relationship."

Throughout World War II, Pius XII continually attacked Nazi policies. Who can deny that Pius XII's voice was heard? Vatican Radio[7] explicitly condemned "the immoral principles of Nazism" and "the wickedness of Hitler," citing Hitler by name.[8] The London *Times* praised Pius XII: "There is no room for doubt. He condemns the worship of force...and the persecution of the Jewish race."[9] Later *The Tablet* of London reported that Nazi leader Goebbels issued pamphlets in many languages condemning Pius XII as a "pro-Jewish Pope."[10]

But nothing that has been said or written can compare with the terrible accusations in *Hitler's Pope.* Contrary to what Mr. Cornwell states, Pius XII was not responsible for the outbreak of both World War I and World War II, and the "final solution" of the Jews. He was not a "silent" Pope. The wisdom of his words and actions is supported by the evidence, including the Nuremberg trials.

The *New York Times Magazine* article "Papal Sin: Structures of Deceit" by Garry Wills[11] is part of "the real structure of deceit," together with *Hitler's Pope.* In his review of Wills' book, Richard

Rorty's condemnation of the Catholic Church is a travesty of justice. By stating that the hierarchy "lied and weaseled about what the Church did and did not do during the Holocaust," these writers are ignoring the 1939–1945 statements in the *New York Times,* where one can undoubtedly find documentation that describes what "the Church did and did not do during the Holocaust."

In this current cultural war, apparently some writers are not aware of the many 1939–1945 statements in the *New York Times* or elsewhere in the media. Are they repudiating this documentation? Are they suggesting that Herbert L. Matthews, Anne O'Hare McCormick, and other reputable *New York Times* correspondents during this period are liars? What about statements recorded in other newspapers, such as the London *Times* and *L'Osservatore Romano?* Indeed, the Vatican Radio was the voice of Pope Pius XII. Can his voice be ignored?

Historians continue to probe the character of Pope Pius XII. What did he know about the Holocaust and when did he know it? Was his caution warranted? How many lives—Jewish and Christian—did he save by relying on diplomacy rather than moral rhetoric? According to Kenneth L. Woodward, "Such questions require care in using archives, intellectual skill in interpreting documents and dispassionate judgment in assessing the peculiar circumstances of European politics in the dark age of Adolph Hitler."[12]

There is a current campaign underway to vilify Pope Pius XII, to divide Catholics, and to undermine papal authority. Catholics must confront the unjust and vindictive attacks on Pius XII, aimed at eventually silencing the strong moral voice of the Church in the person of the Vicar of Christ, John Paul II.

Monsignor Stephen M. DiGiovanni generously shared his well-researched monograph, *Pius XII and the Jews: the War Years,* as reported by the *New York Times.* His specific quotes in support of the rational conclusion that Pius XII was not "silent" provide additional incontrovertible proof of the historic truth.

DiGiovanni justly states: "Pius XII's work to save the Jews against Hitler and Stalin and their systematic debasement of the human person as slave of the totalitarian state is one of the greatest and most heroic works in the history of the Church. It is an understandable tragedy that he is attacked by the media as a means of undermining the

Church's credibility in the modern 'global' society. The Church is *in the way,* just as it was *in the way* of Hitler and Stalin."[13]

Indeed, no longer can one ignore the documentary evidence found not only in the *New York Times,* but also in *L'Osservatore Romano* and through the recordings of Vatican Radio.

5. The Catholic League

Vatican documents reveal that the Jewish community received tremendous help from Pope Pius XII. He used his personal funds to ransom Jews from the Nazis; his nuncios in Croatia, Romania, and Hungary intervened—at their own peril—to stop deportation; he was in constant communication with German generals who sought to overthrow the Hitlerian regime. To set the record straight, the Catholic League for Religious and Civil Rights recently sponsored a full-page ad in the *New York Times* entitled "Was the Church Silent During the Holocaust?" The ad provides the answer to that question by quoting from the editorial comments in the *New York Times* which prove conclusively that Pius XII was not silent during the Holocaust.

William A. Donohue, President of the Catholic League for Religious and Civil Rights, wrote: "The March 19, 2000, edition of *Sixty Minutes* did a segment on the Vatican's response to the Holocaust that drew on the work of John Cornwell. Ed Bradley interviewed Cornwell who claimed to be 'a practicing Catholic' and also claimed he was given 'unprecedented access to the Vatican archives'; Cornwell's thesis is that Pope Pius XII was *Hitler's Pope.*" The Catholic League for Religious and Civil Rights in the *New York Times* had a full-page ad on March 31, 2000: "The Revisionist History of *Sixty Minutes*—CBS Television Program." The Catholic League continues to respond to this "revisionism."

The media misrepresented the truth. Many people were appalled by the unbalanced and unfair CBS presentation of Pius XII and the Catholic Church on *Sixty Minutes.*[14] It was not an impartial presentation of historical facts. False statements were made. Vatican records show that except in Denmark, nowhere in all of Europe did more Jews survive than in Italy (85 percent), thanks in large part to the efforts of Pius XII. During and after the war, and at the time of the Pope's death in 1958, Jews all over the world commended Pius XII for his heroism in saving the lives of as many as 860,000 Jews. No mention was made of this historical fact.

Nor did Ed Bradley acknowledge letters in defense of Pius XII. I have copies of several letters from Jews and Catholics. Renée Keane also wrote to Mel Karmazin, President of CBS: "As a Jew I watched with anticipation your show and I was terribly disappointed by your one-sided presentation.... You have really slighted the Catholics of America and not helped the Jews either, just fanned the flames of discord." Yet, despite all the objections, this CBS Program[15] was reaired on July 16, 2000, with no corrections or additions.

The following is a transcription of Ed Bradley's introduction to the program: "Last week Pope John Paul II marked the Holy Year with an apology—at Mass in St. Peter's Basilica, Rome, he asked forgiveness for the sins committed by the Catholic Church over the last two thousand years. But one person John Paul II did not apologize for is Pope Pius XII whose silence in the face of the extermination of the Jews during World War II has often been criticized. John Paul II recently called Pius XII a 'great pope' and is planning to make him a saint. But now a new book by British author John Cornwell has renewed the controversy and claims that—far from being a saint—Pius XII was *Hitler's Pope*."

Most reputable scholars believe that Cornwell has produced a shoddy, superficial, and totally untrustworthy book that attempts a moral lynching and character assassination. His Pius XII is not Eugenio Pacelli; it is a fictitious Pius XII, a nasty caricature of a noble and saintly man.

Obviously, Cornwell—totally unaware of the psychological warfare especially waged by the English press in its divulging of false reports about the Vatican Radio and others—never heard about the Scattolini forgeries, which were widely believed. After the war, Scattolini was arrested by the Italian police and admitted that these reports (about one thousand) were purely and simply invented by him in order to make money. Cornwell has never checked whether and to what extent he has fallen a victim of this man who was condemned by the Italian Tribunal and sent to prison.

There is no mention of Pius XII's support for American Lend-Lease to Communist Russia or his threat of "dire consequences" for any U.S. bishop who opposed Roosevelt's declaration of war against the Axis powers, though this meant an alliance with the Soviet Union. The Nazis considered Pius XII to be their enemy. However, Cornwell does acknowledge that the Vatican put itself at great risk in 1940, by secretly agreeing to aid anti-German generals in their plot to overthrow Hitler.

The *Washington Post* reported that John Cornwell "was once a seminarian at the English College in Rome and knows the Vatican terrain, [but] he has long since left the seminary and the Catholic faith, and thus writes with that astringent, cool, jaundiced view of the Vatican that only ex-Catholics familiar with Rome seem to have mastered."

A Catholic writer would not have written, as Cornwell did in previous books, that human beings are "morally, psychologically and materially better off without a belief in God." A look at his books[16] makes it very difficult for a reader to accept his avowals that he is a "practicing" Catholic.

Sixty Minutes also interviewed Gerhard Riegner, who complained about Pope Pius XII's alleged "silence." Describing Riegner's March 18, 1942, memo, Cornwell gives the impression in *Hitler's Pope* that the Vatican failed to take any action in response to it. He ignores the letter of thanks that Riegner himself sent to the Apostolic Nuncio Philippe Bernadini in Berne, Switzerland, on April 8, 1942, on behalf of the World Jewish Congress: "We have received your communication of April 2nd, and we hasten to thank you very sincerely for so graciously calling the attention of the Secretariat of State of the Holy See to the situation of Jews in Central Europe and specifically in Slovakia.…In renewing the expressions of our profound gratitude, for whatever the Holy See, thanks to your gracious intermediation, was good enough to undertake on behalf of our persecuted brothers, we ask Your Excellency to accept the assurance of our deepest respect."

When Ed Bradley asked about the numerous letters sent by Jewish groups, no mention was made of Riegner's own letter of thanks. According to Riegner, the expressions of thanks and praise for Pius XII's efforts to save Jews from the Nazis were merely "political maneuvers."

Father Gumpel responded to those who complained that a report sent by Riegner from Switzerland to Rome was not published in the *Acts and Documents of the Holy See Related to the Second World War.* Riegner handed this report to the Nuncio in Switzerland in March 1942, a few months after the Wannsee Conference of January 20th, in which the systematic murder of the Jews was finalized. This report reached the Vatican, as is clear from the dispatch of the Nuncio published in the *Acts and Documents* (vol. 8, p. 466), where Riegner's report is mentioned as well as his subsequent thanks expressed to the Nuncio in Switzerland for having transmitted it. However, at that time it was not possible to check whether the facts mentioned in this report were objectively true. The U.S. State Department had expressed doubts about this report and asked the Vatican whether they would confirm them.

During the Second World War and until five years after his death (October 9, 1958), Pius XII was greatly praised by all Jewish organizations, chief rabbis of diverse countries and especially from the USA. Why would Jewish organizations express thanks for Pope Pius XII's good works and, later, sorrow when he died in 1958? How does one explain the gratitude of survivors? It suffices to mention some groups of grateful Jews: the Anti-Defamation League, the Synagogue Council of America, the Rabbinical Council of America, the American Jewish Congress, the New York Board of Rabbis, the American Jewish Committee, the Central Conference of American Rabbis, the National Conference of Christians and Jews, the National Council of Jewish Women.

The statement of *The Jewish Post* in 1958 is representative of newspapers throughout the world: "It is understandable why the death of Pius XII should have called forth expressions of sincere grief from practically all sections of American Jewry. For there probably was not a single ruler of our generation who did more to help the Jews in their hour of greatest tragedy, during the Nazi occupation of Europe, than the late Pope."[17]

Neither Cornwell's books nor *Sixty Minutes* cited the gratitude of the then Israeli representative to the United Nations and future Prime Minister of Israel, Golda Meir: "When fearful martyrdom came to our people in the decade of Nazi terror, the voice of the Pope was raised for the victims. The life of our times was enriched by a voice speaking out on the great moral truths above the tumult of daily conflict. We mourn a great servant of peace."

With regard to the inaccuracies about Pope Pius XII on *Sixty Minutes,* after each of the programs I wrote to CBS and requested an appointment. These were serious errors, and I wanted to clarify the misrepresentations. It seemed to be deliberate anti-Catholicism. My letters were ignored.

I challenged John Cornwell's distorted and false statements and wanted to correct Bradley, who claimed that Pius XII requested the Allies not to send any black troops into the Vatican. The facts he quoted were totally out of context and misrepresented the truth. I explained that historical evidence is available in the Office of Strategic Services, Washington, D.C.[18] This important information is incontrovertible proof of the historic truth.

I informed Ed Bradley that my own books contain evidence that supports the rational conclusion that Pius XII was not "silent."[19] This evidence effectively refutes "the big lie" which, unfortunately, has been disseminated and enhanced by certain elements of the media. I concluded my letter with a "prayer that enmities will cease, and that genuine reconciliation and regard for the sanctity of life, to which Pope Pius XII and Pope John Paul II each have dedicated a lifetime of saintly efforts, will motivate Jew and Christian, and all members of the human family."

The June 1999 Catholic League issue of *Catalyst* published some responses to another Op-Ed ad on the *Five Million "Others."* While some negative responses merely repeated anti-Catholic statements, others congratulated William Donahue for promoting the truth in the *New York Times* (April 23, 1999).

Positive responses include: "Since I have spent five-and-a-half years in German concentration camps, I feel obligated to debunk the vicious propaganda that the Church was idle when millions of Jews and others were being murdered."

"You have performed a great service in reminding Americans of the other victims of the Holocaust in addition to pointing out to Americans that German National Socialism (Nazism) has no roots in Christianity."

"It is about time, especially bringing to the attention of the public the suffering of the Polish Catholics during the Holocaust."

"Many non-Jews perished in the Holocaust and, in fairness to all the victims, this fact should not be ignored."

"The attention that has been focused on the Jewish experience under the Nazis has all but obscured the sufferings of others who were also tortured and put to death."

"My father won the Virtuti Militari (Poland's medal of honor) after fighting the Germans for five years. He lost his friends, family and land. The greatest tribute we can give to those who laid down their lives for freedom is *remembering*."

The Catholic League for Religious and Civil Rights is to be commended for *remembering* all the victims of the Holocaust, for rendering this information accessible to the public, and for promoting the "Truth" about the efforts of the Catholic Church during World War II.

Part III
The Media

Chapter VII
The New York Times

---

1. Encyclicals

*T*he *New York Times,* while not offering the complete story, gives valuable historical information about the Church, the Jews, and the Nazis during World War II. It provides a portrait of the contemporary scene and is conveniently found on microfilm in major libraries and universities.

The *New York Times* reported that both Pius XI and Pius XII spoke out repeatedly against the racist policies of the totalitarian governments and worked to save hundreds of thousands of Jews from extermination. It also gives evidence that the entire world applauded Pius XII and the Church in Europe, publicly thanking the Pope for his efforts in the condemnation of the horrible reality of Hitler's ultimate goal.

In their encyclicals both Popes expressed the fundamental errors of modern society: the denial of natural law; the deification of the state; racism. Indifferent to the dignity of man and the rights of the human person, totalitarian governments sought to implement a "final solution" for undesirable races, groups, and individuals.

For many years, Eugenio Cardinal Pacelli, as Secretary of State, had collaborated with Pius XI. The *New York Times* published what Pius XI said, despite protests from the Fascists and Nazis claiming that he was interfering in political matters.[1] Pius XI condemned Nazi and Fascist notions of race, blood, soil, and nation. He spoke of "excessive nationalism—which we have already had painful occasion to denounce as erroneous and dangerous."[2] When Pope Pius XI died, the Union of American Hebrew Congregations, through its president, Robert P. Goldman, issued a statement offering its sympathy to its friends in the

Catholic Church: "He was a lover of peace and humanity, and upheld the ideals of spirituality with courage and wisdom. He has clarified the thinking of the world by his firm declaration that the law of God must mold the standards of society.…His life was an inspiration and his passing is a loss to the people of all religious faiths"[3]

Smuggled into Germany and secretly printed, Pius XI's encyclical *Mit brennender Sorge* was read from all Catholic pulpits in March 1937: "Whoever exalts race, or the people, or the State, or a particular form of State, or the depositories of Power, or any other fundamental value of the human community—however necessary and honorable be their function in worldly things—whoever raises these notions above their standard value and divinizes them to an idolatrous level, distorts and perverts an order of the world planned and created by God; he is far from the true faith in God and from the concept of life which that faith upholds.…None but superficial minds could stumble into concepts of a national God, of a national religion; or attempt to lock within the frontiers of a single people, within the narrow limits of a single race, God, the Creator of the universe, King and Legislator of all nations before whose immensity they are 'as a drop in a bucket' (Isaiah, 40, 15)."

Appeals from both Europe and the United States reached Pope Pius XII soon after his election to a symbolic post of leadership of the religious forces of the Western World, including the harassed ranks of Judaism. According to the Catholic editor and writer Michael Williams, one message petitioned the Pope to "give consideration to the cooperative work being done in the United States by organizations made up of leaders of both Protestant and Catholic Christianity and of Judaism to foster religious and civil liberties and to stem efforts to introduce into the Western World the disruptive and degrading hatreds and persecutions now rife in so large a part of the Old World."[4]

Pius XII endeavored to end the bitter struggle between Catholics and Nazis. The atmosphere improved when *L'Osservatore Romano,* which had been denouncing the anti-Catholic policy of Germany, no longer printed articles against Nazism. Pope Pius XII called the four German cardinals who were in Rome for a conclave to obtain reports on the condition of Catholics in Germany. They were: Adolf Cardinal Bertram, Michael Cardinal von Faulhaber, Karl Josef Cardinal Schulte, and Theodor Cardinal Innitzer. The Pontiff also granted an audience to

Ambassador Diego von Bergen, with whom he reviewed Vatican-German relations.

From Vatican City, Camille M. Cianfarra wired the *New York Times:* "Nobody thinks that the conflict in principle between Catholicism and Nazism may be overcome since compromise is obviously out of the question between ideologies starting from such diametrically opposite premises."[5]

2. Pius XII Speaks Out

In his Easter sermon Pius XII deplored the breaking of pledged word: "How is peace possible," he asked, "if pacts solemnly sanctioned and the plighted word have lost that security and value which are the indispensable bases of reciprocal confidence and without which ardently desired disarmament, both material and moral, becomes with each passing day less possible of realization?" His homily showed great balance and calm judicial judgment. His reproach may be presumed to have been directed against the totalitarian States, but he made it clear that he did not consider the other side free from blame for the unrest that at present was agitating the world. Peace is impossible without justice and justice requires, among other things, "that those goods and riches which God has showered upon the world for the benefit of his children be conveniently distributed."[6]

Pius XII spoke about the dignity of work: "How may peace be had while so many thousands of men lack work—honest work, which not only maintains life for individuals and their families but represents, furthermore, a necessary and decorous explanation of the complex energies nature has exercised, study of which has endowed and honored the dignity of the human person? Who can fail to see that enormous masses are being formed whom impoverishment and misery—so much more exasperating because in strident contrast with the luxury and excessive comforts of those privileged ones who do not feel the duty of helping those suffering—render easy prey to deceptive mirages insidiously proposed by shrewd propagandists of fatal theories?...Here then, venerable brothers and beloved sons, is a basis unique and unshakable upon which true peace rests: God; God known, respected, obeyed....When the arms of violence are substituted for the scepter of justice, no one need marvel at the appearance on the horizon of the gloomy forebodings of war instead of the longed-for dawn of peace."[7]

Pope Pius XII invited the prime ministers and foreign ministers of five European countries (Germany, Great Britain, France, Italy, and Poland) to confer in Vatican City according to the *New York Times*.[8] He suggested that the meeting be held as soon as possible. He would open the first session in person and would put his palace and staff at the disposal of the plenipotentiaries. He would take no part personally but would be at the disposal of the conference through his Secretary of State as counselor and conciliator if needed. He further suggested that the aim of the conference would be to settle amicably the German-Polish dispute and eventually to begin the settlement of other problems. The article, by Jules Sauerwein, concluded: "Until now the Pope's proposal has been kept closely secret. That he has made it, is a mark of his high intelligence and exceptional courage. He believes it his duty to make this proposal so as to save Europe from war, even though he is not sure he will succeed."[9]

The *New York Times* editorial evaluated the political situation: "As Cardinal Pacelli, Pope Pius XII showed himself to be so devoted a friend of peace and so tireless an emissary of better understanding that it is wholly natural that he should now seek to use the authority of his great office to avert the threat of war in Europe. Tension is greatest at two points; between Germany and Poland, and between Italy and France. It is primarily for the purpose of effecting a settlement of these two controversies that Pius XII is reported to have acted. In both cases the primary question is whether the nations which have created the controversies really desire a settlement by peaceful methods and on practicable terms. Italy's statesmen have talked interminably of their alleged mistreatment by France, but they have never to this day accepted the invitation of the French Government to state their grievances in specific terms. Germany has presented to Poland a demand which Hitler described as his 'one and only offer,' and accompanied this virtual ultimatum by the abrogation of a pact of non-aggression which still had five years to run. The essential problem which any intermediary in Europe must face today is the problem of creating a will to peace on the part of nations which have been ready to resort to violence in order to achieve their ambitions."[10]

In the following Sunday issue of the *New York Times* Herbert L. Matthews stated that "in relation to the present situation, for the Catholic Church, in throwing its spiritual force on the side of peace, is merely exercising its traditional role....The fact that Pope Pius stepped in so soon after his election and in such relatively open fashion would seem to demonstrate that he regards the situation most seriously....Pius XII can work only through normal diplomatic channels, which is to say through his nuncios and apostolic delegates or trusted envoys in various countries....If armed conflict does come to Europe, none will be able to say the Vatican has not done everything possible to prevent it."[11]

Camille M. Cianfarra describes the Vatican peace efforts and quotes from an editorial in *Avvenire d'Italia,* an independent Catholic newspaper: "Pope Pius's peace efforts have passed from the first to the second stage, from the motherly advice of the church to motherly services, to new eagerness and earnestness. There were two factors: the limitations on the Holy See's international moves and that although Pope Pius began his soundings early in May, nothing authoritative was mentioned about them until a month later. Throughout these recent negotiations it has been insisted at the Vatican that the Holy See does not mix in international conflicts nor material interests and it keeps itself apart from specific questions, limiting itself to recommending universal peace."[12]

The Pope's normal diplomatic channels are through his nuncios or apostolic delegates in every important country, who report back, convey missions assigned to them, and receive messages just as ambassadors and ministers of other governments do. It is also possible for the governments to communicate directly with the Pope through the Secretary of State, Cardinal Maglione, instead of through the nuncios, but only when the Pope makes the first move. On August 13, 1939, the *New York Times* reported that the Nuncio to Berlin conferred with the Pope when the Austrian concordat of 1934 was violated by the Nazis.[13]

The *New York Times* reported on September 16, 1939, that "Vatican circles took the unusual step today of calling attention to the Catholic persecution in Germany by permitting *L'Osservatore Romano,* its official organ, to comment critically on a Stefani News Agency dispatch from Berlin excusing German measures."[14]

The front-page caption of the *New York Times* was in very large print: "Pope Condemns Dictators, Treaty Violators, Racism; Urges

Restoring of Poland." The Pope's entire encyclical was printed on pages 8 and 9. Journalist Herbert L. Matthews wrote: "A powerful attack on totalitarianism and the evils which he considers it has brought on the world was made by Pope Pius XII in his first encyclical, issued today from his Summer villa at Castelgandolfo. In this document he raises the banner of Christianity against totalitarian paganism, which idolizes purely human values, and against atheism which denies the existence of God.

"Presenting a picture of contemporary life as devastating as any of the Old Testament prophets could have drawn, the Pontiff proclaimed his determination to step forward boldly into 'the immense vortex of errors and anti-Christian movements' and to fight the enemies of the Church, defending the rights of the individual and the family against State autarchy. In his own words, he spoke today as 'one of those who make up the church militant.'"[15]

The encyclical is a clear continuation of Pius XI's policy. It denounces Fascist tenets and hopes for Poland's rebirth. Pope Pius XII stresses that this is not "a full statement of the doctrinal stand to be taken in the face of the errors of today," but simply "some fundamental observations. It is Germany that stands condemned above any country or any movement in this encyclical—the Germany of Hitler and National Socialism."

Pius XII forcefully states: "Before all else, it is certain that the radical and ultimate cause of the evils which we deplore in modern society is the denial and rejection of a universal norm of morality as well for individual and social life as for international relations; we mean the disregard, so common nowadays, and the forgetfulness of natural law itself, which has its foundation in God."

The Pontiff cites two "pernicious errors" that render almost impossible, or at least precarious and uncertain, the peaceful intercourses of peoples: (1) forgetfulness of that law of human solidarity and charity, which is dictated and imposed by our common origin and by the equality of rational nature in all men, to whatever people they belong; (2) the error contained in those ideas, which do not hesitate to divorce civil authority from every kind of dependence upon the Supreme Being.

The editorial of the *New York Times* summarizes the aim of Pope Pius XII in this first encyclical: "No reader can miss the passionate earnestness of the Pope's words or their vital application to immediate issues. In denouncing the unilateral breaking of treaties as a death-blow to mutual trust among States, he emphasizes the obligation of all nations, for their own order and prosperity, to keep intact what he describes as the unity of supranational society."

The editor stressed the Pontiff's experience in the diplomatic field and stated that he speaks not only with the high authority of his office but with wide knowledge of the problems with which he deals. His efforts to avert the war failed. His advice was listened to with respect, but not followed. He will continue to work for a negotiated peace, embodied in treaties "animated by justice and equity toward all."[16]

Pius XII attacks the racial theories of the Nazi regimes. The dignity of the individual made to the image of God cannot be diminished. It does not derive from blood, race, nationality, or utility. In *Summi Pontificatus,* Pius XII not only publicly defended his Jewish brethren—explicitly using the word "Jew"—but did so in the context of condemning racism by quoting St. Paul (Col 3:10–11).

In paragraph 53, he states: "Once the authority of God and the sway of His law are denied in this way, the civil authority as an inevitable result tends to attribute to itself that absolute autonomy which belongs exclusively to the Supreme Maker. It puts itself in the place of the Almighty and elevates the State or group into the last end of life, the supreme criterion of the moral and juridical order, and therefore forbids every appeal to the principles of natural reason and of the Christian conscience." The encyclical continues with a plea for the family as the essential cell of human society, whose existence is antecedent to the state, and whose rights are sacrosanct, which the Church will defend against the encroachments of the state (pars. 61–63).

Addressing the Belgian ambassador on September 14, 1939, Pius XII condemned the Nazi invasion of Poland as "an immeasurable catastrophe!" and declared "of this new war, which already shakes the soil of Europe, and particularly that of a Catholic nation, no human prevision can calculate the frightful potential of carnage which it bears within itself, nor what its extension and its successive complications will be." In the same speech he pleaded "that civilian populations will be preserved from all direct military operations; that, in the occupied territories, the life, property, honor, and religious sentiments of the inhabitants will be respected; that the prisoners of war will be treated humanely and that they will be able, without any hindrance, to receive the comforts of religion." The speech ended with a demand that "the use of asphyxiating and poison gases will be excluded."

On September 26, he counseled a group of German pilgrims against political fanaticism. He declared that the war was in fact "a terrible scourge of God" and urged the German clergy not only to resist it but to repent. "The priest must now, more than ever before, be above all political and national feelings. He must console, comfort, help, exhort to prayer and penance, and must himself do penance. Pray that God may shorten the misery of war and restore peace, peace in honor, in justice, in reconciliation and agreement for all participants, a peace that will again grant the Catholic Church in your beloved fatherland happier days and greater freedom."

Pius XII addressed a group of Polish pilgrims, September 30, branding the Nazis as "the enemies of God." He declared: "Before our eyes pass as a vision frightened crowds and, in black desperation, a multitude of refugees and wanderers—all those who no longer have a country or a home. There rise toward us the agonized sobs of mothers and wives, who weep for dear ones fallen on the field of battle. We hear the desolate lament of so many of the old and infirm, who too often are left deprived of every assistance; the cries of children who have lost their parents; the cries of the wounded in battle who are dying—not all of whom were soldiers. All of their sufferings, miseries, and mourning we make ours."

On October 29, 1939, after the publication of his first encyclical, Pius XII ordained twelve native priests as bishops of missionary dioceses and thus underscored his teaching of racial equality before God. The elevation of two blacks made history: Bishop Joseph Kiwanuka and Bishop Ignatius Ramaronandratana, the former, a native of Uganda, Africa, as Vicar Apostolic of Masaka, Africa; the latter, a Malgash from Madagascar, as Bishop of the Diocese of Marinarivo in Madagascar. In his homily the Pope issued a call to all Christians to defend religion: "It is absolutely necessary that all those who are proud of the name of Christian strive to give, in the measure of their possibilities, their contribution toward the attainment of this most important aim and this must be done especially in our times, when men too often are absorbed in a greedy search for things material and are distracted from the attainment of celestial gifts, so that the Kingdom of truth and life, of holiness and grace, of justice, love and peace is neglected or for-gotten or unhappily rejected altogether."[17]

Another article by Anne O'Hare McCormick clearly demon-strates what was at stake: "The present war is fought for many ends. It is fought on various fronts with new methods. In a way, it is a war too big to fight, at least with military weapons, for the reason that its funda-mental issue cannot be resolved on a battlefield, and everybody knows it. In the broadest sense it is a religious issue, and perhaps that is why the Pope has put his finger on it more surely than any secular states-man. The central theme of his long encyclical is the function of the State in the modern world, and that is the crux of the struggle of our time. The dictatorship of today is not simply a form of government; it is a form of life, a usurpation of every human and divine right, a growth of power so abnormal that it is like a tumor pressing on the whole social body and preventing other nations from functioning naturally."[18]

On November 8, 1939, it was learned that the Germans closed 687 monasteries and convents in Reich territory alone. Churches were forbidden by the Minister of the Interior to request alms since all offer-ings must be reserved for Germany's Winter Help campaign.

3. Editorials (1940)

Soon after, against protests by Mussolini's government, the Vati-can appointed two Jews to the Vatican Academy of Science.[19] Twelve hours before the new Italian laws went into effect prohibiting Jews from all professional life, Pius XII also appointed a Jewish professor to the Vatican Library to restore ancient maps.[20]

The *New York Times* reported that on March 14, 1940, the Pope defended the Jews in Germany and Poland, and that German Foreign Secretary von Ribbentrop left the audience "downcast." The *Times* called the visit "Hitler's Canossa," a reference to Emperor Henry IV humbling himself before Pope Gregory VII.

Louis Finkelstein—Provost of the Jewish Theological Seminary of America—referring to the Christian churches that offered resistance to the Third Reich, stated: "No keener rebuke has come to Nazism than from Pope Pius XI and his successor, Pope Pius XII." In a letter to the editor, Finkelstein wrote: "Jewish tradition, like Christian religious tradition, demands that in the face of evil we should renounce before we denounce, that before we demand the purification of others we should cleanse ourselves. In the midst of unprecedented horrors the Jews of Poland followed this tradition in proclaiming a special fast and singing the penitential hymns prescribed for such days, asking forgiveness for their own sins. This is not simple submission to evil. On the contrary, it is resistance to evil with the greatest possible hope of ultimate effectiveness.

"It is our constant prayer that the efforts of the enemies of religion to create dissension between the various denominations will fail and that following the teachings of our respective faiths we will be able to make a real contribution to the preservation of our liberty and of civilization. In expressing this hope we do not conceive of the possibility of reducing all religions to simple universalism. On the contrary, we should each strengthen his own tradition. This involves not opposition but cooperation, not the spread of hostility and recrimination but the increase of abiding affection. This attitude toward the current emergency in American life is the fruit of the religious experience of the ages."[21]

Finkelstein's parents survived the Holocaust, but other family members were exterminated. He strongly maintains that aspects of the "Holocaust industry" defame the dead of the death camps by insisting on "compensation" for survivors.

Also in 1940, the *New York Times* editorialized: "If the Pope in his Christmas message had intended to condemn Hitler's system, he could not have done it more effectively than by describing the 'moral order' which must govern human society. The Pontiff pointed out that the foundation of the moral order is trust, 'Fidelity in the observance of pacts.' Without trust—and this war has demonstrated the truth of his words—the coexistence of powerful and weak peoples is impossible. The moral order cannot be based on hatred, on the principle that 'might makes right,' on 'economic maladjustment,' on 'the spirit of cold egoism' which leads to the violation of the sovereignty of states and the liberty of their citizens. The moral order, in a word, is in complete contradiction to Hitler's order."[22]

The words of the Catholic hierarchies throughout Europe were based on the encyclicals of Popes Pius XI and Pius XII. The German bishops, too, spoke out against the racist, and in particular anti-Semitic policies of the Nazi government. The bishops met at their annual conference in Fulda in 1939 and published a pastoral letter "which was one of the sharpest attacks ever made by Catholics against Nazis."[23] The

Nazis seized Catholic presses and closed printing facilities used in the production and distribution of the pastoral letter. On January 21, 1939, a report stated that among recent Nazi measures "against the Roman Catholic Church" in German-held territories was the billeting of soldiers in convents, one of which, the convent and girls' school of St. Francis de Sales in Vienna, was to house 150 soldiers for two years.[24]

This was part of the organized "war on Christianity" waged by the Nazis, according to a letter written in June, 1941, to Pius XII by the bishops during their meeting in Fulda. The Pope lamented the attempt to destroy the Church in Germany and quoted the words of St. Cyprian: "Your present confession of faith is more illustrious and honored because of your greater strength in suffering....If the battle calls you, if the day of your struggle has come, fight bravely, fight constantly, knowing that you are battling beneath the gaze of our Lord who is ever present, that you are by your confession of His name attaining to His glory who not merely watches His warring servants but Himself joins battle, Himself crowns and is crowned by the decisive contest of our trial."

The bishops informed Pius XII that Catholic organizations were being disbanded, influential men in German society pressed to deny their faith, schools and Catholic institutions closed, printing houses destroyed, monasteries and religious houses confiscated, holy days canceled in favor of work days, priests and religious sisters arrested and sent to concentration camps. Responding to this systematic war against the Church, the *New York Times* stated: "In this and in other ways freedom of conscience is repressed to a degree that is simply intolerable for man made to the image of God and for Christians."[25]

The bishops' words were printed in the *New York Times*. Bishop Fidel Garcia y Martinez, Bishop of Calahorra in Spain, condemned Nazi propaganda and racism in his pastoral letter, published in February 1942. It included texts from the 1941 German Catholic bishops' pastoral letter from Fulda condemning Nazi doctrines, as well as sections from the pastoral letter by the Catholic bishops of the Netherlands.

The pastoral letter of the German bishops of the Roman Catholic Church—the first since the Fulda Conference—was dated March 22 and read in the German churches on that day, Passion Sunday. The document reveals that the bishops had recently submitted formal protests to the Nazi Government against the oppression of Christianity and the Church, and that they had demanded the cessation of the intolerable acts.

The letter protests specifically against all violations of personal freedom, against the killing of insane persons and the proposal to kill incurables, against the forcible confiscation of property, including churches and church property, from the lawful owners, and against the Gestapo's spying on and charges of treason against priests and laymen who stand up for religious freedom.

The bishops declared that they intended to defend "our sacred creed" against all attacks and that they "decisively and finally" refused the Nazi implication that they prove their patriotic faith through faithlessness toward Christ and the Church. The letter urges the German laity to support the Church and to "repulse all attempts to make you waver."

4. Pastoral Letter (1942)

A translation of the text of the pastoral letter of the German bishops follows:

Dear Diocesans: For years a war has raged in our fatherland against Christianity and Church, and has never been conducted with such bitterness. Repeatedly the German bishops have asked the Reich Government to discontinue this fatal struggle; but, unfortunately, our appeals and endeavors were without success.

Even in wartime, when solidarity has always been a matter of course, the fight continues; nay, increases in sharpness and bitterness and lies like a tremendous incubus on the German people, of whom at the last census 95 percent—in Bavaria even 98 percent—have professed to be Christians.

Therefore, the German bishops have considered it their duty toward Church and people to put an end to this internal war by a public declaration and an effective order. As we know that the faithful expect their bishops to do everything to protect belief and conscience, to reestablish the peace of religion and Church and to ease their souls from severe pressure, we feel obliged to make public the most important point of our memoir (to the Reich Government).

In the Concordat of July 20, 1933, the Reich Government granted the Catholic Church State protection for the free development of its functions. Actually, these grants have not been kept. Christianity and the Catholic Church have been denied State protection and are being fought and fettered through measures and organs of party and State.

1. Promised and pledged was "the liberty of creed and worship of the Catholic religion." In truth, pressure is frequently used on those who depend on State or party positions to force them to conceal or deny their Catholic religion or to compel them to abandon the Church. Through numerous ordinances and laws open worship of the Catholic religion has been restricted to such a degree that it has disappeared almost entirely from public life. It appears as if the sign of Christ, which in the year 312 was gloriously carried from the catacombs, is to be driven back to the catacombs.

Even worship within the houses of God is frequently restricted and oppressed. Quite a number of places of worship, especially in the Ostmark, in the newly conquered territories, but also in the old Reich, have been closed by force and even used for profane purposes. Services in rented rooms have been prohibited despite urgent necessities. Purchases of lots for the construction of new churches is being rendered impossible.

From time to time religious instruction for children and juveniles has been prohibited even in Church-owned premises and has been punished. Religious care in hospitals has been most severely restricted through new laws.

2. Catholic parents and the Catholic Church have the natural and divine right to educate their children religiously according to the principles of the Christian faith and ethical law and in conformity with their own consciences. Through concordats, the influence of the Christian churches on school and education has been expressly granted.

Actually, however, the rights of parents and Church are being more and more restricted and have become ineffective. Juveniles in State youth organizations, in hostels and labor camps, often even in schools and country homes for evacuated children are being influenced in an anti-Christian manner and kept away from religious services and celebrations. In the new State institutions (such as teachers' training schools, all-political educational homes, etc.) any Christian and religious influence is absolutely impossible.

3. The Catholic Church and its priests have the right and the duty to pronounce and defend, freely and unrestricted, orally and in writing,

the creeds and doctrines of the Christian religion. The clergy, by agreement, has been granted State protection for the execution of its duties.

In reality, Catholic priests are watched constantly and suspiciously in their teaching and pastoral duties; priests, without proof of any guilt, are banned from their dioceses and homes, even deprived of their freedom and punished for having fulfilled their priestly duties truthfully and scrupulously.

It is unbearable that clergymen are being punished with expulsion from the country or internment in a concentration camp without court procedure and any contact with the clergy, when approach to the bishopric could have resulted in the explanation of misunderstandings or the prevention of mistakes.

The holding of religious services and exercises is made almost impossible; the religious press has been destroyed almost entirely; the reprinting of religious books, even catechisms, school Bibles and diocesan prayer books is not permitted, while anti-Christian writings may be printed and distributed in mass circulation.

4. It is consented upon and granted by agreement: "Orders and religious societies are not subjected by the State to any specific restriction regarding their pastoral, educational, medical and relief work, conduct of their affairs and administration of their estates."

In fact, the Catholic orders have been expelled from schools almost entirely and are being curtailed in their other activities on an ever-increasing scale. A large part of their property and their institutions have been taken away from them and many are destined to perish because of the law prohibiting able-bodied men to work for them. Consequently, the German people will be in future without the pastoral services of the priests of the orders and without the sacrificing services of their nuns.

5. It has been promised and granted: "Within the limitations of the law, the clergy has the sole right to erect, conduct and administer the seminaries for priests as well as church refectories."

In truth, not only the Church refectories for students have been largely destroyed or taken from the administration of the Church authorities but even seminaries for priests have been confiscated and deprived of their clerical status. This is in conformity with the purpose of those who wish to deprive the Catholic priesthood of success.

We emphasize that before the authorities we not only stand up for religious and clerical rights but likewise for the human rights bestowed by God on mankind. Every honest human being is interested in the respect and preservation of these rights; without them the entire Western culture must break down.

1. Every man has the natural right for personal freedom within the boundaries designated by obedience to God, consideration of his fellow man and the common good and the just laws of the civil authorities.

We, German Bishops, protest against every disregard of personal freedom. We demand juridical proof of all sentences and release of all fellow citizens who have been deprived of their liberty without proof of an act punishable with imprisonment.

2. Every man has the natural right to life and the goods essential for living. The living God, the Creator of all life, is sole master over life and death.

With deep horror Christian Germans have learned that, by order of the State authorities, numerous insane persons, entrusted to asylums and institutions, were destroyed as so-called "unproductive citizens." At present a large-scale campaign is being made for the killing of incurables through a film recommended by the authorities and designed to calm the conscience through appeals to pity.

We, German Bishops, shall not cease to protest against the killing of innocent persons. Nobody's life is safe unless the Commandment "Thou shalt not kill" is observed.

3. Every man has the natural rights to the protection of his honor against lie and slander. On the front and in the homeland faithful Christians fulfill their patriotic duties like all their fellow citizens. Yet Catholic priests and laymen are suspiciously watched, secretly suspected, nay, publicly branded as traitors and national enemies, just because they stand up for the freedom of the Church and the truth of the Catholic faith.

Catholics of the religious orders have fulfilled their duty heroically in the field, at home and in war, a fact which has been frequently acknowledged through the bestowing of war decorations. In spite of this, many have been deprived of their monastic homes.

We Bishops protest against such violations of truth and justice and demand effective, honorable protection for all citizens, including faithful Catholics and members of Catholic orders.

For months, regardless of war misery, an anti-Christian wave of meetings and party pamphlets has been carried through the country with the clearly noticeable, even outspoken aim, to suffocate the vigor of the Catholic Church in German lands.

If possible, they wish to destroy Christianity in Germany during the war, before the soldiers, whose Christian faith gives them the strength for heroic battles and sacrifices, return home. The vast majority of the German people, whose deepest feelings are hurt by such attacks on Christianity, justly expect the immediate and frank rectification of the Reich Government of the unjust oppression and hated struggle against Christianity and the Church.

Dear Diocesans: We Bishops have informed you of our grave worries and ardent endeavor for inner peace in our German nation. We call upon you, with the devotion we have always shown you, to support our efforts through your prayer and your unshakable faith, and to repulse decisively and vigorously all attempts to make you waver.

We wish to prove through our attitude that we long for nothing but internal peace, and esteem nothing as highly and faithfully as our sacred creed, which we shall defend against all attacks. Decisively and firmly we refuse the suggestion that we should prove our patriotic faith through faithlessness toward Christ and our Church.

We remain eternally true to our Fatherland just because, and at any price, we remain faithful to our Saviour and our Church. God bless our country and our holy Church. God give an honest, happy, lasting peace to the Church and the Fatherland.

> **The German Bishops** *for the Diocese of Wuerzburg:*
> Matthias Ehrenfried.

The document reveals that the bishops had submitted formal protests to the Nazi government. It traces the broken promises of the state to protect the church, the restriction of worship and religious education, the expropriation of church property, the expulsion and internment of priests for no other crime than the practice of their faith. It shows with irrefutable logic that this assault is only part of a broader attack on all human rights, human freedom, and the human spirit. This was a call to "courage no less exalted than that of the Christian martyrs in pagan Rome." It was read in all churches during services on Passion Sunday, March 22, 1942. While reports indicated that the Nazi authorities restricted the circulation of this pastoral letter, a United Press dispatch from London stated that the British radio did broadcast it within the Reich in the German language. The *New York Times* printed it on June 7, 1942 (p. 12, cols. 1–5).

Vatican sources indicated how seriously the Secretariat of State viewed the situation. In spite of Italian censorship, Cardinal von Faulhaber's indictment reached and was reported in the media. The *New York Times* heading for the article was in large print: "German Cardinal Indicts Nazi 'War on Christianity'; Faulhaber Reports to Vatican That Regime 'Blackmails' Believers and Uses Spies to Put Pressure on the Clergy." [26]

From Berne, Switzerland, news reporter Daniel T. Brigham outlined the eleven-point indictment of the Church situation in Germany to the Holy See by Michael Cardinal von Faulhaber, militant leader of the religious opposition in the Reich:

1. A "veritable war against Christianity" waged in Germany has contributed largely to present "spiritual unrest" in the Reich, which is translated into "manifestations against the regime" that are catalogued by the authorities as "machinations of foreign Judeo-Communistic elements." There is a noticeable "armistice" between the Catholic and Protestant Churches in the Reich, to their mutual benefit.

2. The Church continues to be treated with mistrust by the regime, which maintains an elaborate system of "anti-Christian espionage" in the principal religious centers. This system attempts to prevent the reading of "certain episcopal documents" from the pulpits by the simple process of ordering the arrest of bishops or priests prior to their issuance; if the document is not read the ecclesiastic is released; if it is read, sometimes he is not.

3. Moral "blackmail" is being applied to faithful Catholics with reminders that "less faithful attendance at church means keeping your job." This "blackmail," says Cardinal von Faulhaber, also is applied to the Church itself, which is called on for proportionately greater sacrifices in money and property than the "unbelieving individual citizen of greater Germany." Larger contributions to the party and war funds also are required from well-known Catholics than from non-Catholics, the Cardinal asserts.

4. Intensified propaganda efforts are being developed among lower-paid workers to get them to disavow the Church. They also are

tempted against the Church by "cynical inferences as to how to avoid paying the 'blood tribute' of the Church."

5. Accusing the Church of being a "super-national organization," party functionaries ask "loyal Germans" how they can reconcile their duties to the State with those to the Church. The inference is stressed that they must quit the Church or quit the "future of Greater Germany," meaning oblivion in the "cultural life of the new order."

6. Violence is often employed in the "catechism" of a "doubtful" German, who must "develop a conscience of his nationality" or "suffer the consequences."

7. "Grave measures" have been taken in primary and secondary schools to prevent religious instruction. Pupils' "school cards"—a sort of "progressive diploma" that follows the pupil through his school life in Germany—are no longer permitted to bear the subject "religious instruction." Cards still bearing that inscription are withdrawn or amended.

8. Under the pretext of lack of paper, publication of religious textbooks and other church publications has been forbidden. On the other hand, the number and size of publications and pamphlets attacking the Church has "increased beyond measure."

9. Young persons of both sexes have been forbidden to attend church festivals in the evenings on the ground that "they last too long and prevent their getting sufficient sleep." Yet "attendance at party functions which often last well past midnight, is obligatory."

10. Church organizations have been prevented from acquiring land on which to build religious structures, even in places where no religious facilities exist. In many cases, where church organizations had acquired such land, it has been sequestered without indemnification.

11. Church property, such as bronze bells and even ritual vessels of immense real or intrinsic value, has been sequestered without warning and without indemnification "for the good of the country and the prosecution of the war." The Cardinal closes with a prayer that "the church stand together for the fight of its existence. Today it is a question of life or death for Christianity, for in its blind rage against religion the Nazi 'faith' does not or cannot distinguish between Protestantism and Catholicism."

The *New York Times* also printed Cardinal von Faulhaber's list of ten commandments distributed in churches throughout the Reich:

1. Resist evil with all your strength, courageously, wisely and perseveringly.

2. Neither spread false rumors nor be misled by empty claims of authority; instead, speak the truth and promote its realization.

3. Do not unleash anger, but conquer your vexations so that your conscience shall not become deadened by quiescence before injustice or your spiritual powers consume themselves in discontent and discord.

4. Rejuvenate your soul in keeping with the best examples of our culture so that peace may possess you more thoroughly than war has done.

5. Collaborate in the creation of a society that will afford to all men of good-will an honest opportunity to live in justice, freedom and truth.

6. Do not dissociate yourself from the sufferings of mankind, but instead love men with a warm heart and adjudge your enemy in justice.

7. Where you cannot act or intervene in the course of events, do not merely anticipate or plan, but enter into the reason of the Eternal Being.

8. Fulfill your destiny in the larger relations of the world, but not without humbly recognizing your share in the guilt....

9. Praise light, even in darkness, for light ever remains light.

10. Let us be men in order that we may become Christian.[27]

5. War on Christianity

By telephone to the *New York Times,* Daniel T. Brigham, from Berne, Switzerland, confirmed the circulation of the "list of ten commandments distributed to the faithful in churches throughout the Reich....[This is] one weapon the Church in Germany is reported to be using liberally to resist the 'veritable war against Christianity' cited in Michael Cardinal von Faulhaber's report to the Holy See, outlined in these dispatches yesterday...."

Despite Cardinal von Faulhaber's protest against the Nazis, the campaign against Christianity continued. The régime attempted to obtain acceptance of a hymn book throughout the Reich in which mention of "Jerusalem," "Zion" and other biblical allusions were deleted, "hallelujah" amended to "God be praised," and "Jehovah," "psalter," and "psalm" also eliminated.

Published by the "German Christian publishing house of Schneider & Co., Weimar," the new hymn book was issued under the auspices of the "Institute for the Examination of Jewish Influence on the Church Life of Germany." Entitled *National Socialist Hymn Book,* it had appeared in an experimental edition in Thuringia on June 13, 1941.

The new collection did away with a large part of the standard German hymnals' selections dating from the time of Martin Luther. The Orthodox hymnal contained 500 selections; the new book contained only 284, not all of which may even be considered religious hymns in the true sense of the word. Of the 284, only 143 of the old favorites were retained. The rest are songs and poems of the nineteenth and twentieth centuries in which former texts have been curtailed and sometimes altered to suppress "Judaistic" words. The obvious desire of the editors of the hymnal was to eliminate all reference to the Old Testament. Any reference to the New Testament also is deleted. They included ninety-three compositions from the "National Church Hymnal" glorifying the aims of the National Church. Concessions made to "the old school" included favorites under new classifications. The chapter headings betray a desire to give mundane matters precedence over religious and missionary themes. One finds, for example, the themes of the new political faith, labor, blessings of the soil, national unity and kindred subjects extolled without reference to God or Christ. Baptismal hymns also are "adjusted" to the "new order of things."

Reporter Anne O'Hare McCormick wrote: "The Bishops have taken the unusual step of circulating among the people the official protest they have addressed to the Government....This confirms that the Catholic Church has followed the Jews as the scapegoat of the Nazis."[28]

Justinian Cardinal Seredi, the Roman Catholic Prince Primate of Hungary, prohibited the participation of his priests in the Nazi movement as far back as in 1934. He declared in a speech in the presence of the Papal Nuncio that "Christ's teachings do not acknowledge difference between men and men and do not know prerogatives which would entitle a man or a nation to oppress another man or nation on racial or national basis....Human freedom is the greatest among all human rights and for it humanity has fought out innumerable battles; such a battle is going on also today and it will continue until freedom will have become such a natural need for people as air....Slavery and oppression are the antithesis of freedom. The Christian Church declared war on slavery and oppression because they are in contradiction to Christ's teachings. The Church is fighting not only against the physical but also against the spiritual oppression of humanity."[29] His speech was reprinted.

There is no doubt that cardinals, bishops, and clergy in Europe spoke out against the Nazis and the Fascists. Today, it is difficult to understand why an American bishop, in an effort to cultivate harmony and understanding between the Christian and Jewish people, would circulate the following letter to the people of his diocese on March 5, 2000: "The history of the Catholic community of faith has included many instances of injuries to others. An example is, of course, the fact that the Jews of Europe have over the centuries been herded into ghettos, forbidden property ownership, forced to convert, exiled and decimated in pogroms. This history of persecution was ultimately consummated in the unparalleled horror of the Holocaust....To complicate this we know that history also shows us that few church leaders distinguished themselves in speaking out against the Nazi terror. This passivity and complicity of Catholics and other Christians played a significant role in the death of 6 million Jews and millions of other innocent people." One need only to review the *New York Times* during World War II to learn that church leaders did speak out against the Nazi terror.

The *New York Times* reported that Michael Cardinal von Faulhaber issued a document that was sent to the Holy See about the confiscation of church property, arrest of bishops, priests, and religious, the closing of Catholic printing houses, labor organizations, and other Catholic institutions, the pressure upon Catholic workers and students, the characterizing of the Church as a "super-national organization."[30] On May 24, 1942, the newspaper pointed out that circulation of pastoral letters was forbidden in Germany.[31] The bishops vehemently protested Hitler's interference in Church affairs and education, and "all violations of personal freedom," against the killing of insane persons and the proposal to kill incurables, against unjust seizure of individuals and of property. The bishops condemned Hitler's policies of official murder of the innocent and of those judged "unproductive citizens."[32]

In 1942, Religion News Service provided a series of articles that appeared in the *New York Times* entitled, "Six Churchmen Who Defied Hitler." The newspaper observed that, since Germany's population was 95 percent Christian, "this, then, means that the Nazi dictatorship is waging war on its own people. Indeed, the bishops specifically call it a war and publicly protest its continuance. Step by step they traced the Reich's broken promises to protect the church, the restriction of both worship and religious education, the expropriation of church property, the expulsion and internment of priests for no other crime than the practice of their faith." The Catholic bishops go on to show with irrefutable logic that this assault on the Church is only part of a broader attack on all human rights, human freedom and the human spirit. Nobody's life is safe, they [the bishops] assert, "if the state assumes the power to kill at will. Above all, they repel the sickening charge that refusal to submit to this brutal creed is lack of patriotism." The editorial ends: "The measure of Nazi madness is to have precipitated a civil war in the midst of an effort to conquer the world."[33]

On June 8, 1942, the *New York Times* stated that the Church leaders "are virtually the only Germans still speaking up against the Nazi regime." Bishop von Galen condemned Himmler and the Gestapo as "tyrants and murderers." The outcome of the first of three sermons denouncing Nazi racial and antireligious principles was that the Nazi government dissolved all Roman Catholic religious orders in the province of Westphalia, and a number of prominent Roman Catholics were imprisoned. The next week, the Bishop mounted his pulpit to decry the injustices within the country that "cried aloud to heaven for redress." The *Times* stated that the bishop "in outspoken terms has condemned unauthorized killings of invalids and the insane, and Nazi racial doctrines."[34]

Also on June 10, 1942 Anne O'Hare McCormick summarized the protest against the Nazis by the Churches of Europe in her weekly column, "Abroad": "When the history of this new Reign of Terror is written, it will appear that the strongest centers of opposition to the claims of the God-State were not universities, trades unions, political parties, courts or organized business. In Germany and the occupied countries the institution that stands up most stoutly against the pretensions of the Nazi New Order is the church. The Protestant pastors of Norway dared to go on strike rather than accept orders from Quisling [Nazi head of the government]. The [Catholic] Primates of Holland and Belgium have defied the Nazi authorities as boldly as Cardinal Mercier did in the last war. Resistance to the collaborationists in France has been nourished by the parish priests, whose influence among their people has never been so strong, according to all reports, as it is today. Judging from the open resistance offered by the churches in Hitler's Europe, one might infer that of all human freedoms, freedom of conscience is the most cherished.

"The Fulda Conference document is not an underground report or a picture drawn from isolated incidents but a detailed disclosure of the actual situation of the church in Germany. The indictment confirms reports that the Catholic Church has succeeded the Jews as the scapegoat of the Nazis. This is a logical consequence. A regime that starts by oppressing one group must find another when the first is exhausted. A nation acquiescing in the persecution of one minority cannot expect any minority to escape the same fate, and since the majority is only the sum of minorities, eventually the policy of proscription will extend to the whole population. The bishops say, 'The Nazis wish to destroy Christianity in Germany during the war before the soldiers return home.' All we know for certain is that religion plays a vital part in this war."[35]

The record shows that, on June 10, 1942, the *New York Times* again noted that the August 3, 1940, pastoral letter by the Catholic bishops of the Netherlands, secretly prepared and sent to all parishes, was read from every Catholic pulpit. Archbishop de Jong was the force behind the condemnation of Nazi policies and forbade Catholics from joining any Nazi organization, without the explicit denial of Nazi ideology, under pain of being refused the sacraments. In 1941, the bishops issued another protest: "We raise our voices in protest against the injustice inflicted upon tens of thousands—to force them to accept a conception of life which is contrary to their religious convictions."[36]

Among other church leaders, Joseph Ernst Cardinal van Roey, Archbishop of Malines in Belgium, heeded the voice of the Pope rather than the precepts of National Socialism. Members of the Belgian Fifth Column, a Nazi military group, were refused the sacraments. He instructed his priests to refuse communion to any pro-German or German in uniform and to denounce the Nazi theories of blood and soil from their pulpits, recounting Nazi wrongs. The government then closed all Catholic churches in Belgium for three days, newspapers attacked the Church, and the Cardinal's residence was smeared with abusive graffiti. In his pastoral letter Cardinal van Roey wrote: "It is true that the Catholic Church adapts itself to all governments that safeguard her liberty of conscience, but as for adapting herself to governments that oppress the rights of conscience and persecute the Catholic Church, Never!"[37]

In the summer of 1942, Pope Pius XII intervened to save the Jews in France when the Vichy government began its deportation of Jews. Joining the Pope's protest was the "spirited written protest against racial and religious persecution" issued by Emmanuel Celestine Cardinal Suhard, Archbishop of Paris, and by Pierre Cardinal Gerlier, Archbishop of Lyons. The local bishops protested the government's action after the Vatican learned that the Germans had asked for Jewish deportations to supplement farm and mine labor in Silesia and Poland, and was to extend this policy throughout Germany, Austria, Poland, Czechoslovakia, and the Baltic states to include all Jews who had sought refuge since 1936.[38] A few days later, the editor called the Church's work "a noble insistence" to the Vichy government to save the Jews. The Vatican, through the Papal Nuncio, "repeated its past appeals to the Vichy government for tolerance for the Jews...but the Vichy government said they could do nothing in the face of German demands."[39]

In a pastoral letter read from all pulpits of the Diocese of Toulouse in late August, Archbishop Jules Gérard Saliège denounced the Jewish persecution openly: "In the concentration camps in our diocese horrible things are happening against the Jews, who are human beings like we are. Every imaginable cruelty is permitted against them. There are rights of man given by God to the human race which should not be violated. Jewish children, women and men are treated like cattle."[40]

According to the *New York Times,* Catholic and Protestant leaders protested against the maltreatment of Jews: "Some of their remarks have scarcely been veiled."[41] Noted, too, were the efforts by the Church to save the Jews in France: "Many Catholic leaders in unoccupied France are sheltering children of Jews, and their defiance of orders to surrender them has brought about an open rift between the Vichy government and priests."[42] In Belgium, a priest was shot for having hidden a hundred Jewish children.[43] Letters and protests by the Catholic bishops in occupied France were read from Church pulpits urging Catholics to help persecuted Jews. These protests created a "difficult situation" for the Vichy government: "It is semi-officially reported from Vatican sources that Pope Pius, through the Nuncio in Vichy, has sent to Marshal Pétain a personal message in which he intimated his approval of the initiative of the French Cardinals and Bishops on behalf of the Jews and foreigners being handed over to the Germans. It is understood the Pope asked the French Chief of State to intervene."[44]

When thirteen thousand Jews were rounded up on July 16, 1942, the French bishops issued a joint protest. At the direction of Pope Pius XII, the protests from French bishops were broadcast and discussed for several days on Vatican Radio. This angered Pierre Laval, who reaffirmed his decision to cooperate in the deportation of all non-French Jews to Germany. Archbishop Saliège instructed priests "to protest most vehemently from the pulpit against the deportation of the Jews." His pastoral letter stated: "There is a Christian morality that confers rights and imposes duties....The Jews are our brothers. They belong to mankind. No Christian can dare forget that!" *L'Osservatore Romano* praised Saliège as a hero of Christian courage.

Conversion was not the primary interest of Church leaders during the Holocaust. The Catholic Church helped produce thousands of false documents that were used to deceive the Germans. These documents were provided so that Jewish people could avoid persecution, even though they had not actually converted. Evidence suggests that most clergy did not undertake conversions lightly. At times, classes were established to let children study their own religion. However, the surest way to protect very young children from the Nazis was by actually baptizing them and indoctrinating them, in case they were ever challenged.

In a Papal Allocution of October 6, 1946, Pius XII addressed the charge that the Church had engaged in "forced conversions." He found the best evidence to be a memorandum, dated January 25, 1942, from the Vatican Secretariat of State to the Legation of Yugoslavia to the Holy See: "According to the principles of Catholic doctrine, conversion must be the result, not of external constraint, but of an interior adherence of the soul to the truths taught by the Catholic Church. It's for this reason that the Catholic Church does not admit to her communion adults who request either to be received or to be readmitted, except on condition that they be fully aware of the meaning and consequences of the step that they wish to take." After the war, the Secretary General of the World Jewish Congress reported on a meeting with Pius XII to thank him for helping hide Jewish children. The Pope promised to cooperate with returning the children to their communities.

In France, special efforts were made to protect an estimated seven thousand Jewish children. A force of Protestant and Catholic social workers broke into a prison in Lyons and "kidnapped" ninety children who were being held with their parents for deportation. The parents were deported the next day; the children were sheltered in religious institutions under the protection of Cardinal Pierre Gerlier with the assistance of Father Pierre Chaillet, a member of the Cardinal's staff. When the Cardinal refused to surrender the children, Chaillet was arrested and sent to a "mental hospital" for three months.

In an editorial dated August 28, 1942, the *California Jewish Voice* called Pius XII "a spiritual ally" because he "linked his name with the multitude who are horrified by the Axis inhumanity." The *Jewish Chronicle* (London) reported that "Catholic priests have taken a leading part in hiding hunted Jews, and sheltering the children of those who are under arrest or have been deported to Germany."

On September 4, 1942, the *Canadian Jewish Chronicle,* referring to Vichy leader Pierre Laval, ran this headline: "Laval Spurns Pope: 25,000 Jews in France Arrested for Deportation." Four days later, according to the *Geneva Tribune,* Vichy ordered the French press to ignore the Pope's protest concerning the deportation of Jews, but word spread rapidly about the courageous attitude of members of the French resistance, who knew that they had the blessing of Rome.

On April 16, 1943, the *Australian Jewish News* ran an article quoting Cardinal Gerlier, who stated that he was simply obeying Pius XII's instruction to oppose anti-Semitism.

During this period, Pope Pius XII met for more than ninety minutes with Myron Taylor, President Franklin D. Roosevelt's personal representative to the Vatican, and the general opinion was that the Vatican was on the verge of doing something more directly to help the Jews in the various occupied countries.[45]

From London, December 23, 1942, Chief Rabbi Hertz sent a telegram to Pope Pius XII, requesting that he intervene for the Jews in eastern Europe who were threatened with annihilation: "In the name of worldwide religious Jewry respectfully beseech intervention our Holiness to save annihilation of Israel Eastern Europe. We invoke the fatherhood of God and the brotherhood of Man to save one suffering people. At this momentous hour—Agudas Israel World Organization of Orthodox Jews."

Similar telegrams from Jews residing in Colombia were sent on December 2, 1942, by the Archbishop of Bogota, Monsignor Ismael Perdomo, and the Jewish Community of Costa Rica; the Jewish Community of Bolivia, on December 3; the Jews residing in the Diocese of Manizales (Colombia), sent by Bishop Luis Concha, on December 4; the Rotary Club of Managua (Nicaragua), on December 9; the Women's International Organization of Zionists in Egypt, sent by the Chargé d'Affaires in Cairo, Father Hughes, on December 12; the Jewish Community in Mexico, sent by the Archbishop of Mexico, Monsignor Luis Martinez, on December 15; the Jewish Community in Potosi (Bolivia), on December 22; the Union of Orthodox Rabbis of the United States and of Canada, on December 23.

In his Christmas address in 1942, Pope Pius XII clearly reaffirmed the Church's teaching on the dignity of the human person, and its denunciation of Marxist socialism, while calling on the world to reestablish the international rule of law.

The *New York Times* reported that the Pope "also castigated the authoritarian form of government for its denigration of the human person, and he called upon all those who recognized Christ to join the crusade for a new social order based on the Christian precept that to serve is better than to dominate."[46]

The Pope said: "He who would have the star of peace shine out and stand guard over society should cooperate for his part in giving back to the human person the dignity given to it by God from the beginning; he should oppose the excessive herding of men; as if they were a mass without a soul; their economic, social, political, intellecual and moral inconsistency; their dearth of solid principles and strong convictions, their surfeit of instinctive sensible excitement and their fickleness. He should favor, by every lawful means, in every sphere of life, social institutions in which a full personal responsibility is assured and guaranteed both in the earthly and the eternal order of things."

The error of today's life, "was to believe that civil life was based on the principle of gain." The Pope "reiterated the Church's stand against Marxist socialism." He ended by castigating a large part of humanity, including Christians, who "collectively bore the responsibility for the present universality of war....Did the peoples of the world wish to remain inert before the development of these disastrous events or should not the best of them unite against this ruin of the social order? A new and higher order must soon be born. It was demanded by the sacrifices of those who had lost their lives in this war, by the mothers, the widows, and the orphans, by the countless refugees in flight, by the thousands of men who through no fault of their own but for reasons of nationality or race had been doomed to death or decay."[47]

The *New York Times* was quick to applaud the Pope. "This Christmas," the *Times* wrote, "more than ever he is a lonely voice crying out of the silence of a continent....No Christmas sermon reaches a larger congregation than the message Pope Pius XII addresses to a war-torn world at this season." The *Times* understood what the Pope said, whom and what he condemned, even if the proper names were not pronounced: "But just because the Pope speaks to and in some sense for all the peoples at war, the clear stand he takes on the fundamental issues of the conflict has greater weight and authority. When a leader bound impartially to nations on both sides condemns as heresy the new form of national state which subordinates everything to itself; when he declares that whoever wants peace must protect against 'arbitrary attacks' the 'juridical safety of individuals'; when he assails violent occupation of territory, the exile and persecution of human beings for no reasons other than race or political opinion; when he says that people must fight for a just and decent peace, a 'total peace'—the 'impartial' judgment is like a verdict in a high court of justice." The editor ends, echoing the Pope's words that these new states "must refuse that the state should make of individuals a herd of whom the state disposes as if they were lifeless things."[48]

6. Persecutions (1943)

The *New York Times* reported that Cardinal Suhard of Paris visited Rome "with a detailed report on the results of French collaboration with the Axis, particularly the trend toward complete elimination of Jews from France."[49]

Already in 1940, Justinian Cardinal Seredi, Catholic Primate of Hungary, had attacked Nazi-inspired racial discrimination. Protesting in 1942, he stated: "Even if we see today that international law has received a new interpretation and innocent people have to suffer under physical and spiritual oppression, the church is fighting with all its might against the fashionable currents and for the protection of human rights....The endeavors which we witness today and which caused so much suffering also to the Christian church, will provoke such reaction, such vengeance, that also innocent people will fall its victims."[50]

On January 30, 1943, Hitler broadcast a speech in which he tried to revive the myth that Nazi Germany was the last barrier against the conquest of Europe by Bolshevism.[51] Among the petitions that followed asking for help was one from Rabbi Herzog, the Chief Rabbi of Jerusalem, to which the Pope replied, promising "to do all in his personal power to aid persecuted Jews in Europe."[52]

In its March 14, 1943, issue, the *New York Times* quoted: "In all the injustices that are now being committed, our sympathy goes out particularly to the youths who are being violently taken away from their parental homes. It goes out to the Catholic believers of Jewish origin and to those persecuted for their belief in religious freedom. Moreover, we are deeply moved [with shame] that in the execution of this persecution...the collaboration of our own fellow-countrymen has been demanded. Conscience cannot allow collaboration in such things. If the refusal to collaborate implies sacrifices for the individual, then he must be strong and steadfast in the knowledge that he is doing his duty before God and man. The Catholic Church does not wish to take sides in the conflict between States and people attempting to solve immense problems of national collaboration, but only as long as they respect divine law. With the mandate of Christ as guardian of Christian principles, it must not fail to proclaim inviolate the word of God, which is to obey Him rather than man."

Condemning the arbitrary arrest of Danes, as well as the German anti-Semitic propaganda in Denmark, eight Catholic bishops sent similar protests to Thune Jacobsen, the Minister of Justice.[53] Later, Protestant and Catholic bishops issued a joint pastoral letter condemning the German treatment of Jews and the deportation of four hundred Jewish children from Eastern Europe[54]

In the April issue of the Fascist periodical *Regime Facista,* Roberto Farinacci accused Vatican Radio of "inciting the people of Poland to make common cause with the Russian Army."[55] In May, the Nazi-controlled radio reported that the Catholic Church had "a crushing responsibility in unleashing the present war." The Nazis charged that the Catholic Church had invited oppression in the Reich by opposing Hitler's racialist theories.[56] Clearly, Pius XII had not been silent.

When the Nazi-controlled Paris radio blamed the Catholic Church for having unleashed the war[57] the Vatican responded by "recalling the Nazi charges that the Catholic Church in Germany had invited oppression by opposing Adolf Hitler's theories of 'racialism'...."[58] In September the Paris newspaper *Aujourd'hui* said that "Pope Pius XII was responsible for the hostile attitude of the French clergy toward German authorities and that his last speech had a particularly disquieting effect."[59]

The persecution of the Church by the Nazis resulted also in the incarceration of thousands of Catholic priests, religious sisters, and brothers. A report circulated by the Catholic International Press Agency of Freiberge, Switzerland, in 1943, claimed that Protestant and Catholic clergy were systematically being starved to death in the death camp at Dachau. It claimed that at least fifteen hundred Polish priests interned in Dachau had died of starvation. German clergy met the same fate. The report claimed that three thousand Catholic priests were still confined in Dachau, twelve hundred of whom were German.[60] The report continued on August 13, 1943: "The arrests are linked with strong anti-Nazi and anti-war movements in the preponderantly Roman Catholic section of Germany, in which Catholic students as well as priests are said to be active."[61]

Catholic protests continued through the following months in the Netherlands. There were mass deportations of youths and a policy of forced sterilization of those entering mixed marriages between Jewish and non-Jewish parties was implemented. The bishops wrote: "After all that has befallen the Jewish citizens of our country there is now taking place something so monstrous that it is impossible for us to refrain from addressing you in the name of Our Lord."[62] In that same issue a report stated that the Catholic and Protestant churches had been hard at work against the Nazi regime. It refuted charges made by some religious leaders in other countries that German churches followed a policy of resignation and inactivity in the face of Nazi tyranny. The churches had, in fact, protested frequently against the persecution of Jews. Catholic bishops had protested the persecution "of both Poles and Jews by affirming the fundamental rights of all men...."[63]

The Vatican and the religious institutions under its authority were sanctuaries not only for Italian but for refugee Jews in Italy, of whom there were many. Pius XII also sent an urgent appeal to Admiral Horthy and instructed Cardinal Seredi of Budapest to intervene in behalf of the Jews of Hungary.

Later a marked rise in the Nazi opposition to Roman Catholicism in particular and to Christianity in general was noted in occupied countries. In the Netherlands, *Storm,* the official organ of the Nazi party, attacked the Catholic clergy as "the prime instigator" of the general strike in May, stating that the strikers were "mostly sheep of the Roman Catholic Church, who incited our people until they stood opposite German firing squads."

Ragnaroek, the Nazi Norwegian publication—an ironic reference to the Norse equivalent of "Gotterdammerung" in German mythology, that is, "The Twilight of the Gods"—clearly stated: "We Nazis reject Christianity because we reject Judaism, and have acknowledged that both are inextricable allies. As a consequence both are capable of doing anything against us. We reject Christianity because we consider the Bible in its entirety a Jewish delusion, created in order to break the earthly will for life and the immortal belief of all Nordic peoples in their own part in things divine."[64]

The *New York Times* also reported a fresh wave of opposition against the French Catholic clergy because of its protests against the Vichy Government.[65] Broadcasting to occupied France, the Vatican Radio reiterated its denunciation of the Nazi racial laws, stating: "He who makes a distinction between Jews and other men is unfaithful to God and is in conflict with God's commands."[66] The following day the Vatican continued: "The peace of the world order and justice will always be compromised so long as men discriminate between members of the human family." Paraphrasing Scripture: "There are neither Greeks nor Jews. There are only men facing their God and their Father, and those who make distinctions between them abandon God and enter into disorder."[67]

By July, the Catholic hierarchy in Germany incurred the wrath of the Nazi regime when all the bishops signed a protest against the Nazi party plan to extend the wearing of the Star of David to the offspring of mixed marriages. As a result of the protest, three outspoken bishops were subject to house arrest: Michael Cardinal von Faulhaber, Archbishop of

Munich; Clemens Count von Galen, Bishop of Müenster; and Konrad Count von Preysing, Archbishop of Berlin. The Nazi response was to seize convents, Catholic hospitals, and other church property throughout Germany; Catholic labor organizations were disbanded, and religious images removed from schools.[68]

In August, during the Fulda Conference, the German bishops reiterated their protests against the Nazi practices and teachings. A report on the bishops' pastoral letter stated that "the letter abounds in sly but fearless thrusts at the false god and Nazi tenets. The Bishops addressed themselves also to 'those who saw fit to create a god after their own hearts, or one designed only for national or racial consumption.'" The article ended by thanking Pope Pius XII for leading the way in seeking peace and preserving human dignity.[69]

7. Nazi Attacks

On October 6, 1943, the *New York Times* reported that the Nazis had tortured to death a Catholic bishop and an archdeacon of the Diocese of Plock, both over eighty years old: "The German slaughter of Catholic priests is raging through all Poland. The Nazi concentration camp at Inowroclaw is filled with priests awaiting execution....In West Poland alone more than 1,600 priests have already lost their lives. Threats and violence against the clergy were common: Cardinal Faulhaber of Munich was shot, Cardinal Innitzer's residence in Vienna was ransacked, and Bishop Sproll of Rottenburg was manhandled."[70]

By early December, the Vatican protested the decision of the Italian government to intern all Jews in Italy, even Catholics of Jewish descent, and to confiscate their property.[71] As the Church continued its work to save Jews, churches began to be searched. Early in 1944 in Rome, the Roman police forced entry into the Basilica of St. Paul Outside the Walls and arrested eighty-four persons, including twenty-eight Jews who had been given sanctuary there. Any priests assisting "traitors" were to be arrested. After the protests by the Pope, Castelgandolfo was bombed three times, along with other Vatican property.[72]

By spring, 1944, Nazi attacks began against the Jewish communities in Hungary. There were many protests by Justinian Cardinal Seredi, Catholic Primate of Hungary. The newspaper reported his protest against the forced movement of over three hundred thousand Jews to "collection camps" in Hungary.[73] He had already, in 1934, attacked totalitarian principles and ideologies. In a pastoral letter that year, Cardinal Seredi wrote, "It is not possible for a Catholic priest to approve Nazi principles, and I decidedly prohibit participation in this movement or even a benevolent attitude of any of my priests toward it."[74]

On February 29, 1944, it was reported that by May 1, 1943, more than 3,400 Catholic monasteries and clerical institutions in Germany had been confiscated by the Nazis. 16,495 Catholic priests and seminarians were inducted forcibly into the German Army. Of these 1,597 were killed at the front, 593 were missing, and about 100 were so seriously wounded that they could not resume their priestly tasks. The arrests of priests continued through the year, especially in Bavaria and in the more industrialized areas of Germany. By November another 400 priests had been seized by the Reich since the beginning of October.[75]

In her weekly column "Abroad," Anne O'Hare McCormick observed that, despite the horrors of the war and even in the face of the tragic persecution of the Jews in Hungary, there was hope that it would end. She wrote: "But as long as they exercised any authority in their own house, the Hungarians tried to protect the Jews. The Italians, according to the testimony of the chief rabbi and every hunted Jew in Rome, did not carry out the Fascist racial laws, and endangered their own lives to hide Jews when the Germans took over. The Pope does not think it is hopeless....It is not hopeless because we can still count on forces of Christianity and humanity inside Europe to resist Nazi fury." This, plus the Russian advance into Germany, gave hope that the atrocities of the Nazi regime would soon come to an end.[76]

A week later Rome was liberated. The Pope, who gave no audiences to German forces during the war, received more than 150,000 Allied soldiers, according to the paper. The Chief Rabbi of Rome, Israel Anton Zolli, formally expressed the gratitude of Roman Jews "for all the moral and material aid the Vatican gave them during the Nazi occupation."[77]

McCormick added her observations: "Presiding over a worldwide church in a world-wide war that is also a civil and religious war, Pius XII comes out of the ordeal a stronger figure, as far as liberated Italy is concerned, than he was before." She interviewed "an old liberal" about the Italian Christian Democratic party in the coalition, who said, "The last thing that I expected in the crisis was the resurgence of the Catholic party in greater force than the Communists and Socialists. An equally surprising phenomenon is the rising prestige of the Pope. Mussolini has gone, the King has gone, and nobody mourns. The Pope remains the winner of Italy's one victory—the saving of Rome."

McCormick stated that the Pope was credited with having saved Rome: "But this is not the only cause for the popularity of Pius XII. During the nine months between the armistice and the entry into Rome, the Vatican was a refuge for thousands of fugitives from the Nazi-Fascist reign of terror. Jews received first priority—Italian Jews and Jews who escaped here from Germany and other occupied countries—but all the hunted found sanctuary in the Vatican and its hundreds of convents and monasteries in the Rome region. What the Pope did was to create an attitude in favor of the persecuted and hunted that the city was quick to adopt, so that hiding someone 'on the run' became the thing to do. This secret sharing of danger cleared away Fascism more effectively than an official purge. The Vatican is still sheltering refugees. Almost 100,000 homeless persons from the war zone and devastated areas are fed there every day."[78]

While Jews—charged with being the cause of every evil in the Reich—were Hitler's immediate target for persecution and extermination, it is clear from reading the German dictator's writings or listening to his speeches that he pursued a systematic and tireless war against the Roman Catholic Church throughout the war years.

8. Soviet Accusations

Both Hitler and Stalin blamed the Pope and the Catholic Church as responsible for the war and for the sufferings of millions, including Jews and Catholics. These accusations were repeated by both Nazis and Communists during the remaining years of the war in an attempt to weaken the loyalty of the peoples of Europe to Pius XII and the Roman Catholic Church. This is the origin of the numerous unfounded accusations about the "silence" of Pius XII, as reported by the *Times,* which are repeated even today.

The Soviet government newspaper, *Izvestia,* on February 1, 1944, asserted that Vatican foreign policy had disillusioned Catholics throughout the world and earned the contempt of the Italian masses because the Vatican had supported Fascism. The paper charged that the

Vatican had pledged its support to Italian Fascism following the conclusion of the Lateran Treaty in February 1929. However, "the Vatican's support for fascism wasn't limited solely to Italy, *Izvestia* continued. It approved many acts of aggression by Fascism although the true meaning of these aggressions was no secret."[79] The Vatican, according to the *Izvestia* article, supported Italy's aggression into Abyssinia and had played a "disgraceful role" in Hitler's and Mussolini's intervention in the Spanish Civil War. The Church had supported Franco's Spain, which was "the image of the clerical States of post-war Europe." The Vatican's "silence" when France was attacked in 1940, and its swift support of the Vichy government were typical of its policy, *Izvestia* charged. Despite the Pope's claims to neutrality, *Izvestia* wrote that the Vatican had worked to support the Nazi regime.[80]

This is, perhaps, the first report in the *New York Times* in which the Pope and the Church are attacked as cooperators of Hitler and falsely condemned for the supposed "silence" of the Pope. It is significant that the *Times* reported the *Izvestia* charges but gave them no credence and, in later pieces, expressed consternation that anyone could believe the charges as anything other than Communist propaganda against the Church.

An earlier U.S. Foreign Policy Report had stated that the Pope supported neither the modern dictatorships nor modern democracy, "...but is just what he claims to be—indifferent to political forms, accepting any government which will meet the minimum demands of the church."[81]

9. Fulton J. Sheen Responds

An American rebuttal of these charges was swiftly made by Monsignor Fulton J. Sheen on the same day the *Izvestia* article appeared. He stated that the report was an attempt to confuse the political atmosphere in Europe in preparation for a separate peace by Moscow with the German Army after the expected overthrow of Hitler. Sheen predicted an alliance between Communist Russia and the Nazis, minus Hitler, for the "bolshevization" of Europe, and declared that the *Izvestia* article was designed to help destroy religion as the one great obstacle to the achievement of this objective. "The Vatican within the last six months has been called Communist by the Nazis, Nazist by the Communists, and anti-Fascists by the Fascists. And they all mean the same thing, namely, the Vatican is opposed to every anti-religious ideology."[82]

Sheen observed that Russia's plans were to control Europe after the war. The only outspoken obstacle to Russia's plan in Europe was the Catholic Church. He continued: "As Soviet Russia has already served notice that America and Great Britain may not interfere in the question of Poland, so now it serves notice on religion that it may not interfere in the question of Europe."[83]

The first attacks claiming that the Church had endorsed silently the atrocities of the Nazis came from Communist Russia. Soon to control Poland and other vast areas in eastern Europe, Russia saw the need to break the loyalty to the Pope of Catholic majorities in those countries. The plan was a simple one: Convince all that the Pope supported the hated Nazis during the war and, therefore, neither he nor the Church could be trusted after the war. The destruction of the Church would leave the field wide open for Russian influence and control.

The *New York Times* published an angry editorial: "Of all the incendiary literary bombs manufactured in Moscow...and thrown with such light-hearted recklessness into the unity of the Allied nations, none is likely to do greater damage than *Izvestia*'s unjust and intemperate attack upon the Vatican as 'pro-Fascist.'

"The Vatican is a neutral state," the editor continued, "with which Russia's two allies, the United States and Great Britain have 'confident relations.' They have no doubt where the real sympathy of the Vatican lies in this struggle. They recognized the inescapable neutrality of the Pope's position; but they have had no difficulty in finding in his eloquent declarations clear evidence of his detestation for those who have violated the rights of the little nations, who have committed bestial acts from one end of Europe to the other, and who have attempted to elevate the dogma of totalitarianism to the dignity of a new religion. *Izvestia*'s attack is damaging to unity on which victory depends."[84]

American protests were not limited to those by churchmen or by the *Times*. Politicians made protests in local and state assemblies throughout the country, denouncing as false the accusations that the Pope was pro-Fascist or Nazi.[85] The New York State Legislature voted on March 18, 1944, unanimously to deplore the action of *Izvestia,* recognizing it as an official act of the Soviet government against the Vatican. The Legislature pointed out in its resolution that both Pius XI and

Pius XII had condemned Fascism and Nazism and "all other forms of totalitarian government in both public and private pronouncements dating back to 1931."[86]

The Russians continued their accusations. On February 8, the *Times* related that the Russian Army newspaper, *Red Star,* printed extracts from a pamphlet on Vatican policy in Europe. Written by a Leopold Mannaberg, a German businessman, the pamphlet was a criticism on "the constant interference of the Vatican in other lands' policies and the Vatican's intrigues on the international arena." According to Mannaberg, the Vatican played a leading role in the rise of the Nazi and Fascist regimes in Europe. A strong peace in Europe was impossible unless the Vatican was completely deprived of its political power, the pamphlet argued.[87]

Monsignor Sheen was quick to reply. He said it was only natural that the Catholic Church be opposed by a government "that has between eight and ten million political prisoners doing slave labor in Russia. No democratic nation has charged the Vatican with *lack of sympathy*."[88]

Hanson W. Baldwin penned an interesting article in the March 8, 1944, number of the *Times,* "Dual Policy of Russia Traced: Soviet Union Demands Voice in Western Europe's Problems While Pursuing Unilateral Course in East."[89] He wrote: "Since Teheran there have been many disturbing trends. Some of these stemmed from Moscow. The *Pravda* article rumoring that Britain was feeling out the Germans on a separate peace, the *Izvestia* denunciation of the Vatican as pro-Fascist, the virtual insistence of Russia upon settling her boundary dispute with Poland on her own terms and without Anglo-American mediation and the companion piece to this—establishment by Moscow of a Polish National Council, which obviously might be groomed to replace the Polish Government in Exile, are all straws in the wind."

Baldwin continued, "Russia plainly holds many of the cards in Europe and is playing them aggressively. She has demanded, on the one hand, a voice in the affairs of Western Europe, but she refuses similar representation to Britain and the United States in Eastern Europe. And her cards are military power, international Communism used to forward Russia's national ends and pan-Slavism. One part of the Russian pattern is plain. Russia's insistence on taking Eastern Poland up to the Curzon Line and the Baltic States, parts of Finland and Bessarabia may represent the limits of her territorial ambitions."

In addition to the acquisition of territory, Russia established governments friendly to her in contiguous territories or was laying the groundwork to do so, according to the article: support for Tito in Yugoslavia, the establishment of the Polish National Council in opposition to the Polish Government in Exile, the continued support of the Free German National Committee and some Communist support for Greek factions. She also made a treaty of mutual assistance with Czechoslovakia. Russia was interested in most of the European area east of a line drawn from Koenigsberg in East Prussia to Fiume on the Adriatic.[90]

The Church and the Vatican were in the way of Russia's plans for an easy territorial conquest. Not simply because the Catholic Church was so strong in those countries, but because the Pope publicly opposed Soviet aggression and unconditional surrender for Germany. The reasons are not because of any alleged pro-German sentiments on the part of Pope Pius XII or of the Church. He opposed unconditional surrender on principles of Christian mercy. An eye for an eye had been replaced by Christian forgiveness, and the Pontiff applied this, not only to personal relationships, but also to the relationship of one state to another, one government to another: Christian morality was to form the basis for international law and relationships—a truly new world order after the war. He was opposed because of this, especially by Russia.

On June 2, 1944, two days before the Allies entered Rome, the Pope addressed the Sacred College of Cardinals in which he deplored "reports of ill-dissimulated violence or openly declared vengeance." Opposed to the Allied demands for unconditional surrender, he wanted a "negotiated peace with as many elements of compromise in it as possible." Herbert L. Matthews closed his article: "...the Pope's feelings are unquestionably anti-Nazi and anti-Fascist. There can be no doubt about his personal feelings so far as Hitlerites are concerned"[91]

Archbishop Griffin of Westminster (London) sent a telegram July 3, 1944, to Cardinal Maglione, Vatican Secretary of State, requesting intervention on behalf of Hungarian Jews: "Have been requested by World Jewish Congress to support their appeal to Holy Father to intervene on behalf of Hungarian Jews." A response was sent assuring that the "Holy See even through Papal Nunciature Budapest has left nothing undone and is still doing everything possible to alleviate sorrowful plight of all those who are suffering on account of nationality or race."

The National Jewish Welfare Board of New York wrote to Pope Pius XII acknowledging his efforts on behalf of Italian Jews: "As freedom is being won back for the oppressed peoples of Europe, word comes to us from our army chaplains in Italy telling of the aid and protection given to so many Italian Jews by the Vatican and by priests and institutions of the Church during the Nazi occupation of the land. We are deeply moved by these stirring stories of Christian love, the more so as we know full well to what dangers many of those exposed themselves who gave shelter and aid to the Jews hunted by the Gestapo. From the bottom of our heart we send to you, Holy Father of the church, the assurance of our unforgetting gratitude for this noble expression of religious brotherhood and love. We glory in this bloodless victory over the forces of evil that are bent on uprooting religion's eternal teachings of the sacredness of life and the oneness of humanity under God. It is our fervent prayer that your example, your influence and your intervention may yet save some of the remnant of the Jews in other lands who are marked down by the Germans for murder and extinction, and we pray that just as liberty has been restored to the Eternal City, so may freedom very soon be restored to all mankind. Then, with all men rescued from human tyranny, they may once more serve their fellow men and the God of all mankind in love, in freedom and in enduring peace."[92]

The World Jewish Congress, London, sent the following telegram to Cardinal Maglione, thanking the Holy See for its intervention in Hungary and requesting a final appeal to Regent Horthy: "World Jewish Congress gratefully conscious His Holiness' aid behalf sorely afflicted and menaced Jews Hungary which has been followed by offer of Regent of Hungary secure release certain categories of Jews particularly children. His Holiness' efforts bring us new hope at eleventh hour of saving from death surviving remnants of decimated European Jewry and gives solace to our persecuted brethren at moment of their present extinction. In expressing gratitude for Holy Father's noble humanitarian work we would respectfully and earnestly request his continued aid in urging Regent of Hungary speedily and practically carry out his offer by arranging quickest release greatest number of Jewish children and adults for whom sanctuary will be prepared and found."[93]

The Vatican Secretariat of State requested British Minister Osborne's intervention on behalf of civilian internees in Egypt: "The

Secretariat of State of His Holiness presents its compliments to His Excellency the British Minister to the Holy See and begs to call to his attention the situation of the civilian internees in Egypt. There are still about three thousand men interned in Egypt the vast majority of whom are of Italian nationality. Internment has lasted many years and has resulted in very grave financial, social and moral difficulties amongst the families resident in Egypt. Active hostilities between Great Britain and Italy have long ago ceased. At the present stage of the war it is therefore suggested that the changed conditions are such as to make possible a general act of clemency which might not some months ago have recommended itself to the authorities responsible for military security. His Excellency will understand that the Holy See is actuated in making such a request by motives of a humanitarian and religious order. Wherever it is possible, no matter what the race or the religion of those suffering from the consequences of the war, it has been and is the Christian policy of the Holy See to intervene in the sense of mercy and clemency."[94]

On August 21, 1944, Anne O'Hare McCormick commented: "The idea that the Pope does not want a complete and decisive victory is erroneous. What concerns him is the policy to be pursued by the victors after the decision has been won. As a spiritual ruler he can hardly be expected to take the same view as the military and political leaders."[95]

10. Marxist Attacks

In January 1945, Harry Hopkins met with the Pope and Myron Taylor. According to the report, the Pope expressed his ideas concerning Poland, Germany, and war rehabilitation: a joint Allied government in Poland until a plebiscite was possible; armistice terms for the Germans "possibly severe but consistent with his previous declarations on the distinction between the more and less guilty Germans and his known critical attitude toward the formula of unconditional surrender"; a broad and comprehensive rehabilitation and relief program throughout the distressed areas of Europe. The report said the Pope had "intense interest in the Polish question," especially concerning totalitarian government control of postwar Poland.[96]

The Vatican continued to swipe at Communism. In January 1945, *L'Osservatore Romano* issued a strongly worded condemnation of Communism to clarify that Communism and Catholicism were incompatible.

The reason for the repeated condemnation was that the Catholic Communist party in Italy, then renamed the Left party, while its platform and ideology were Marxist, claimed to represent Christian principles and sought Catholic membership. The Vatican was justifiably anxious about the growth of Communism in postwar Italy and Europe.[97]

On February 9, 1945, and for some time thereafter, Moscow launched a series of attacks on the Pope. The bishops of the Russian Orthodox Church, gathered with their newly elected patriarch, Alexis, to broadcast a statement by Moscow Radio accusing Pope Pius XII of condoning Fascism by attempting to excuse Germany for its crimes. The Vatican, so the argument ran, was attempting to absolve Hitler and Germany, "who drenched all Europe in the blood of innocent victims," and to continue Fascism in Europe. The statement said that the Russian Orthodox Church was conferring its blessings "both on the arms that are now winning liberty from the Hitler tyranny for all peoples and on the great leaders of progressive humanity in the postwar organization of the world which will be theirs to undertake."[98]

In an article by Herbert L. Matthews, "Stalin's Hand Seen in Vatican Attack," appearing on February 12, it was reported that the Vatican had reacted to the attacks by Moscow. The Italian newspaper *Quotidiano,* an organ of Catholic Action, reported that Moscow attacked the Vatican because the Roman Catholic Church stood for liberty against dictatorship. The *Times* commented that "the fact that this attack came from the Patriarch and was addressed to the peoples of the world gives it a more serious aspect than the recent accusations in the Russian newspaper *Pravda....*" The *Quotidiano* continued: "The Church of Rome in Poland, Czechoslovakia, and the Balkans represents freedom of spirit. It represents an obstacle to dictatorship. Hence it must be fought. Moscow intends to make use of 'her' [Orthodox] church for gigantic imperialistic aims."[99]

In the midst of these European attacks against the Church by the Soviet Union, *The Protestant,* a New York periodical, published a declaration issued by sixteen hundred Protestant ministers and religious leaders in America, stating that the Vatican should not have any influence in the postwar deliberations, "since the papacy has thrown its weight into the present human struggle on the side of the enemies of democracy."[100] Addressed to Franklin Delano Roosevelt, Winston Churchill, and Joseph Stalin, the petition repeated what would become standard misrepresentations of the Pope's actions during the war, demanding that no religious body, especially not the Vatican, have any part in the postwar deliberations.[101]

Other than the *Izvestia* articles, this is the first time such accusations appeared. A similar action against the Church had been taken following World War I. The usual anti-Catholic rhetoric of nineteenth-century America was repeated then and now, as the Second World War came to a close.

The Soviet attacks, employing the Russian Orthodox Church to keep the Vatican out of the peace talks, could only have enhanced Russia's position at the table, since, without the Vatican's voice, Stalin could press his demands without much opposition. The traditional anti-Catholic bias of Protestant America unwittingly cooperated with Russia, lending its weight to the same goal, resurrecting all the old Anglo-American antipopery rhetoric in their petition to the Big Three. The American Protestant intervention raised another element, the Jewish claims to Palestine and the Vatican's lack of support for such a proposal. One of the signatories of the Protestant document wrote: "These are national, not ecclesiastical claims," and the Vatican should be kept out of the discussions.[102]

Another Russian attack on the Pope was issued February 10, 1945, by the former Russian ambassador to Rome, Boris Stein, who claimed that the Vatican was a "tremendous danger to world peace and post-war security." The Vatican had never been a purely religious institution, he charged, and favored only the winning side in war.[103]

In an address to the Central United Russian War Relief, Inc., in New York City, Metropolitan Benjamin, head of the Russian Orthodox Archdiocese of the Aleutian Islands and North America, attacked the Catholic Church for its "attitude of harmful leniency" toward defeated Fascist nations. Enthusiastically, the Russian Archbishop endorsed Stalin and other Soviet leaders since "they were doing everything possible to nourish the resurgence of religion now sweeping the Soviet Union." The Russian prelate continued, "And speaking of politics, what must the world think of those Roman Catholics who suddenly have become lovers of peace. These are the same priests who were so silent when their Fascist friends were killing women and children in Spain, when Hitler was ravaging all of Europe, murdering millions of human beings by the foulest of means. But now that the Red Army has snatched victory from defeat, when the Soviet Union and her allies have brought Fascism to its knees, these once so silent Roman Catholics suddenly clamor for what they call a just peace."[104]

C. L. Salzberger, the former publisher of the *Times* rightly observed, "The Soviet attitude toward the Vatican and the Roman Catholic Church in general strikes most Americans as rather amazingly caustic and perhaps somewhat ludicrous when one considers that this is the largest state in the world and Vatican City is the smallest." He reported the contents of an article published in the Communist party magazine, *Bolshevik,* which made fantastic claims about the Vatican having marshaled the world's Catholics into an immense international army financed by unlimited funds, guided by the bishops and clergy who served as Vatican spies around the globe. The Pope was not neutral, the false argument ran, but had intervened in purely political affairs, especially by his support for the Fascist and Nazi governments. The *Bolshevik* claimed that the present Pope, a friend of Germany, approved of Hitler and his policies.[105]

The *Times,* here and whenever these false charges were made against the Pope throughout the war, decried these Russian accusations as pure fantasy. On May 7, 1945, a photograph of the beer cellars of the Burger Brau Haus in Munich showed Nazi paraphernalia used by the Brown Shirts. Hanging from the gallows were statues of Jews saluting Nazis and desecrated Catholic crosses with swastikas.[106] The arrest, deportation, and murder of thousands of priests and religious that took place in the camps were documented June 3, 1945, on pages 1 and 22 (full pages). More priests were reported imprisoned in Dachau by the summer.[107]

On July 2, 1945, the *New York Times* disclosed that the Nazis had been responsible for the November 5, 1943, bombing of the Vatican.[108] On September 26, 1945, it was revealed that documents were uncovered in Berlin.[109] This was called "a secret struggle between the German Gestapo and the Catholic hierarchy which lasted from the rise of Nazism to its fall." The Gestapo agents had stolen, bribed, and worked to get access to messages from the Holy See to Catholic bishops in Germany and western Europe during the war years. The churchmen were seen as enemies of Hitler's new order. As the European war neared its conclusion, important international meetings were being held in San Francisco to consider plans for postwar Europe. The major question was Poland. Compromise between Russia, the United States, and Great Britain was thought to be at hand when sixteen leaders of the Polish underground, gathered in Moscow to confer with Red Army chiefs and others, were arrested. What was becoming clearer was that "the liaison between the Soviet official mind and ours [the USA and Britain] is still pretty tenuous," as Anne McCormick wrote. It all boiled down to the relationship between the United States and the Soviet Union.

Keeping up its own pressure, Russia sent out other attacks against the Vatican. In mid-May, 1945, *Izvestia* spoke of German war criminals it claimed the Vatican was hiding or was treating leniently. "At the head of these advocates stands the Vatican, which in the darkest years of the war never raised its voice against Hitler's barbarism."[110]

In a radio broadcast inside Germany later in the month, Moscow repeated its charge that "high standing officials connected with the church are pro-Nazi." Moscow continued: "Pope Pius, in calling for mercy and a more forgiving attitude, had not a word to say about the responsibility of those who had inundated the world with blood and carried out the most monstrous of crimes."[111]

11. Conclusion

On June 2, 1945, Pius XII addressed the Sacred College of Cardinals. It was time to set the public record straight, the Pope told them. While the war had ended in one part of the world, grave perils still existed in Europe, not the least of them, a new Communist tyranny. Among those perils were "...those mobs of dispossessed, disillusioned, disappointed, hopeless men who are going to swell the ranks of revolution and disorder in the pay of a tyranny no less despotic than those for whose overthrow men planned."

In a clear reference to the control of the Soviet Union in eastern Europe, Pius XII said that the people of smaller- and medium-sized nations "are entitled to refuse to accept a new political or cultural system which is decisively rejected by the great majority of their people."[112] The Pope reviewed the "sorrowful passion" of the Church under Germany's National Socialist regime, and hoped that Germany "can rise to a new dignity and a new life after it has laid to rest the satanic specter raised by National Socialism and the guilty have expiated the crimes they have committed."[113]

Speaking of the Church and the Nazi regime during the war, Pius XII stated that, while the Church entered into a concordat with Germany, unable to avoid the invitation by Hitler, the Church did so in order to provide for itself some juridic protection from possible encroachment by the government. Despite this, the Church suffered great hardship as the Nazis pursued its plan systematically.

He explained that, after the concordat had been broken repeatedly by Germany, Pius XI protested, and constantly called for fidelity to one's pledged word. Finally, in 1937, in his encyclical *Mit brennender Sorge,* the Pope condemned Hitler's regime as "the arrogant apostasy from Jesus Christ, the denial of His doctrine and of His work of redemption, the cult of violence, the idolatry of race and blood, the overthrow of human liberty and dignity."

Pope Pius XII expressed his confidence that with "the satanic apparition of National Socialism" out of the way, Germany would "rise to a new dignity and a new life." He pointed out that Nazi persecution of the Catholic Church both in Germany and occupied nations had been continuous, and that he had been aware of Nazism's ultimate goal: "...its adherents boasted that once they had gained the military victory, they would put an end to the Church forever. Authorities and incontrovertible witnesses kept Us informed of this intention."[114]

The world did not listen to the Church's warning. "But in any case nobody could accuse the Church of not having denounced and exposed in time the true nature of the National Socialist movement and the danger to which it exposed Christian civilization."[115]

The encyclical was clear: "Whoever sets up race or people or the state or a particular form of state or the depositaries' power or any other fundamental value of the human community to be the supreme norm of all, even of religious values, and divinizes them to an idolatrous level distorts and perverts an order of the world planned and created by God....The radical opposition of the National Socialist State to the Catholic Church is summed up in this declaration of the encyclical. When things had reached this point the Church could not, without foregoing her mission, any longer refuse to take her stand before the whole world....But by doing so she became once again 'a sign that shall be contradicted' (Luke 2, 34), in the presence of which contrasting opinions divided off into two opposed camps."[116]

The government reaction to the encyclical was immediate. A formal protest was sent from Berlin to Rome and equally swiftly rejected by Cardinal Pacelli. Hitler and Goebbels mobilized the propaganda machine; clerics found themselves arraigned on the old charges of "immorality" and "slandering" the Nazi state. Gestapo units were able to find the presses that had produced the encyclical; twelve were confiscated and the editors arrested. In one parish, Essen, in the diocese of Oldenburg, seven girls were arrested inside the church as they handed out copies of *Mit brennender Sorge* after the Palm Sunday service.

Violence against the Church in Nazi Germany began in 1937. The next two years, and throughout the war, National Socialists flattered themselves with the idea that once they had secured victory in arms they could do away with the Church forever.

The Pope wrote, "We ourselves have during the war and especially in our radio messages constantly set forth the demands and perennial laws of humanity and of the Christian faith in contrast with the ruinous and inexorable application of national socialist teachings, which even went so far as to use the most exquisite scientific methods to torture or eliminate people who were often innocent."[117] Such suffering alone convinced people to listen to the Church.

The Christmas message of 1942, in particular, was studied widely in Germany, "despite every prohibition and obstacle. The witness of thousands of Roman Catholics interned in prisons and camps is before us, whose only crime was fidelity to Christ. Those who suffered most were the Polish priests. From 1940–1945 approximately 2,800 Polish ecclesiastics and religious were imprisoned in Dachau. By April, 1945, only 816 survived. Priests from dioceses in Bavaria, the Rhineland, and Westphalia, as well as from the occupied territories of Holland, Belgium, France, Slovenia and Italy had died in the death camps."

The Pope concluded by referring to the "world to which might be applied the words of Christ: 'And the last state of that man becomes worse than the first' (Luke, 11, 24–26). The present political and social situation suggests these words of warning to us. We have had, alas, to deplore in more than one region the murder of priests, deportations of civilians, the killing of citizens without trial or in personal vendetta. No less sad is the news that has reached us from Slovenia and Croatia."

Pius XII and the Roman Catholic Church did much throughout the war to bring the world's attention to the plight of the Jews of

Europe, to reverse the genocidal policies and practices of Nazi Germany, Fascist Italy, and the regimes operating in the conquered countries of Europe, and to assist tens of thousands of Jews to survive and escape these regimes and their death camps. The *New York Times* reported that the Pope was not silent concerning the Jews, and often applauded him for what he did do and say. Whatever the editorial policy of the *Times* or the background of the reporters and their work, the newspaper itself proved that the Pope was not silent and that the Church was very active during the war.

The issue of May 7, 1939, states: "Pope Pius XII was reported on good authority to have put the moral force of the Catholic Church and the diplomatic resources of the Vatican into a campaign to preserve the peace of Europe. Sources familiar with Vatican policy said that the Papal nuncios to Germany, France, Italy, Poland, and other countries had been instructed by the Pontiff to confer with high officials—in some cases the heads of governments—in an effort to safeguard peace."[118] In particular, interviews mentioned were between Adolf Hitler and Monsignor Cesare Orsenigo, Nuncio to Germany, and French Foreign Minister Georges Bonnet and Monsignor Valerio Valeri.

As seen in the news reports and editorials of the *New York Times* during the war years, contemporary evidence shows everyone knew the Pope was speaking about the Jews in his numerous condemnations of Nazi policies. It was clear the Pope was speaking about their situation and trials, but in religious terms. He spoke on a higher moral level than merely condemning individual actions. The condemnations were clearly understood by his contemporaries.

The efforts to save the Jews by Popes Pius XI and Pius XII and by the Catholic hierarchies of Europe were only part of a greater good the Church tried to accomplish: the protection of all human persons. This was threatened by the enslavement by totalitarian governments of all peoples of the world. The attempted extermination of the Jews and of the Church by the Nazi government was very real. The Church's work was to uphold and defend the truth that the human person is the image of God.

Stalin's cynical question about the Pope's power was an important one: "How many divisions has the Pope?" Stalin was correct: The Pope may condemn moral wrongs in the world, but he has no military might to support his words. Pius XII did strongly and clearly condemn the Nazi and Fascist government extermination of the European Jewish community. But he had only words and prayers in his armory. Hitler was moved by neither; he respected only guns and armies. None but Hitler and the Allied forces could stop the killing. Hitler refused; the Allies arrived too late.

How can one claim that Pius XII was guilty of not doing more to stop the slaughter without holding other world leaders equally culpable for the deaths of millions? Did the German cardinals, bishops, and clergy speak out against Nazis? Indeed, they did.

Bishop von Preysing's pastoral letter indicates that the Catholic Church and Nazi leaders were at odds in the Reich. It was read in all churches of his diocese: "War imposes reserve upon all Germans. The enemies of the church are taking advantage of this fact to deal it blow after blow, but all the faithful know that the Saviour is master of history and the sole protector of the church."[119]

The specific complaint was the expropriation of ecclesiastical property in St. Edwige Parish, ordered under decrees of 1933 relating to possessions of "Communist elements hostile to the State." Bishop von Preysing protested with indignation against linking the Church to Communism and submitted formal protests to the Nazi government about the broken promises of the state to protect the Church, the restriction of worship and religious education, the expropriation of Church property, and the expulsion and internment of priests for no other crime than the practice of their faith. The document shows with irrefutable logic that this assault is only part of a broader attack on all human rights, human freedom, and the human spirit.

Writing for the *Times,* Anne O'Hare McCormick stated: "There is nothing new in the story of the Nazi campaign to stamp out religion, or in the heroic resistance of the church leaders to the systematic attempt to destroy the last vestiges of religious freedom....The Bishops have taken the unusual step of circulating among the people the official protest they have addressed to the Government. This document is a detailed disclosure of the conflict, described by the Bishops as an 'internal war,' a 'fatal struggle,' that lies like an incubus on the German people. This confirms that the Catholic Church has succeeded the Jews as the scapegoat of the Nazis. No one who reads their brave defense of 'human rights' and 'personal freedom' can believe that the love of liberty is dead in Germany."[120]

Following the war, numerous tributes were made to the Pope by members of the Jewish Community worldwide. On December 1, 1944, the *Times* reported that the World Jewish Congress publicly thanked the Holy See's protection of Jews, especially in Hungary; in October, 1945, the World Jewish Congress made a financial gift to the Vatican in recognition of the Vatican's work to save the Jews; on May 26, 1955, the Israeli Philharmonic gave a command performance of Beethoven's Seventh Symphony at the Vatican as a gesture of thanks to the Pope for his services to Jews during the war. Delighted with the magnificent performance, the Pontiff was photographed in the midst of the Israeli orchestra, gave his blessing, and afterward granted an audience to the musicians.

At the Pope's death, numerous tributes were made, so many that the *Times* could list only the names of their authors in the October 9, 10, and 11 issues. For example, in the October 9, 1958, issue: Bernard Baruch; Rabbi Theodore L. Adams, president of the Synagogue Council of America; Irving M. Engel, president of the American Jewish Committee, and Jacob Blaustein and Joseph M. Proshauer, honorary presidents; Rabbi Joachim Prinz, president of the American Jewish Congress; Dr. Israel Goldstein, chairman of the Western Hemisphere Executive of the World Jewish Congress; Rabbi Alan Steinech, president of the New York Board of Rabbis; Mrs. Moise S. Cahn, president of the National Council of Jewish Women; Rabbi Jacob P. Rudin, president of the Central Conference of American Rabbis.[121] The October 10, 1958, issue included: Rabbi Emmanuel Rockman, president of the Rabbinical Council of America; Isaac H. Herzog.[122] Among the tributes in the October 11, 1958, issue was one by the Jewish Labor Committee.[123] All referred to the work the Pope and the Vatican had done to save the Jews during the Second World War. In the October 12, 1958, number the *Times* reported the numerous memorial services for the late Pope in the synagogues of New York City.[124] On October 10, 1958, the *Times* reported that Leonard Bernstein began the performance of the New York Philharmonic the previous evening with a tribute by Harold C. Schonberg, and by Mr. Bernstein asking the audience to stand in silence for one minute, in tribute to Pius XII.[125] Among the very many tributes to Pope Pius XII, there was only one negative statement.

It came from Paris. *L'Humanité* was the official organ of the Communists, who accused the late Pope of allowing his doctrinal condemnation of Marxist atheism "to be transformed into an arm of anti-Soviet policy in Europe and the world." While the Pope had spoken out against the arms race, the Communist paper contended, criticism should be made against the Pope "for not having taken a stand against the Nazi concentration camps during the war."[126] The false accusations that Pope Pius XII had been silent concerning the Holocaust originated in Soviet Russia. They were propaganda for Communist ends.

Chapter VIII
The Vatican Radio

1. Technological Revolution

*I*t should be noted that Vatican Radio has continued to flourish at a remarkable rate. Prior to the fifteenth century, the most effective way of communicating Christian doctrine was to copy manuscripts for storage and distribution throughout the world. Church structures served as religious teaching tools, by illustrating biblical stories on their walls and stained-glass windows. Priests and bishops were usually the only literate people of the villages and were the primary educators of the populace.

The technological revolution of the nineteenth century both simplified and complicated the propagation of the Catholic faith. By the twentieth century the Church was firmly established, thanks to the dedication and vigilance of its missionary outreach. Beginning with Pope Benedict XV during World War I, the Church has been actively involved in ecclesiastical diplomacy, and Vatican Radio has become a major channel of propagation for the survival of the universal Catholic Church. Technology created instantaneous communication throughout the world.

The Church was closely associated with the implementation of international policies and politics as well as the development of an effective communication system to support them. As political borders changed, the Vatican was prepared to meet the new challenges of international relations within a media framework. From this point on, papal diplomacy would never be the same.

Robert Graham, S.J., author of *Vatican Diplomacy: A Study of Church and State on the International Plane,*[1] defines papal diplomacy as "the system of reciprocal permanent representation which the papacy has developed through the centuries to expedite through official channels any issue requiring negotiation or consultation with [other sovereign] states." Father Graham defines ecclesiastical diplomacy as similar to civil diplomacy, with one principal difference: "the fact that the relations are not between two states but between the State and a religious authority. The relationship is, therefore, not identical on both sides, though the techniques and outward forms may be the same. Unfortunately, efforts at defining ecclesiastical diplomacy have no more succeeded than efforts in the domain of purely secular diplomacy."[2] As implied in Graham's definition, hundreds of years of political and religious change have evolved into today's concept of international relations between Church and State.

Vatican Radio has enjoyed a long history of world recognition and credibility, supporting both the sacred and secular objectives of six popes throughout seven decades of religious and political turmoil. It has been the daily "voice" of the Pontiffs—a bridge uniting the Shepherd with his flock. It not only broadcasts the teachings of the Roman Pontiff, but it also gives information on the activities of the Holy See, reports on Catholic life throughout the world, and indicates the Church's point of view on current issues and her readiness to respond to the signs of the times. Vatican Radio announces the Christian message freely and efficiently and links the center of Catholicism with the different countries of the world.

When the Papal States were invaded by the new Italian army in 1870, Pope Pius IX, the Bishop of Rome, was deprived of all temporal power and became a prisoner in the Vatican. The succeeding Popes also remained in the Vatican. In 1929, during the pontificate of Pope Pius XI, the signing of the Lateran Treaty with the Italian government was accomplished. Vatican City became an independent, sovereign state within Italy, with separate laws, currency, and postage stamps.

Among members of the ecclesiastical hierarchy was Cardinal Eugenio Pacelli, then Vatican Secretary of State, who sought ways to strengthen the Vatican's power against the growing pressures applied by the secular state. Pacelli suggested that the Holy See investigate the possibilities of incorporating a new medium, "radio," into Church evangelization. With "airwaves" of broadcast technology, no Pope could ever be driven into isolation again; geographic and political borders had become virtually meaningless. Pius XI listened intently to Pacelli's arguments and later supported his proposal to build a transnational system for the Church. Pacelli began negotiations with inventor

Guglielmo Marconi to create a powerful shortwave radio system for Vatican use.

2. Transnational Broadcasting

As early as 1925, the future first director, Jesuit physicist Giuseppe Gianfranceschi,[3] wrote a letter recommending the creation of a Vatican broadcasting center. By June 1929, only four days after the Lateran Concordat entered into force, Pius XI entrusted the setting up of Vatican Radio to Marconi. On November 8, 1929, a Vatican-Italy accord stipulated the regulations for Holy See communications. Its inauguration took place in the Vatican gardens, February 12, 1931.

Pius XI's dream of transnational broadcasting was realized mainly because of the strong friendship between Cardinal Eugenio Pacelli and Guglielmo Marconi. In 1930 Pacelli approached Marconi to help him modernize the Vatican Secretariat by introducing an efficient telephone system as well as a powerful shortwave radio station. Marconi readily agreed. Construction of the Vatican radio facility went quickly and smoothly. Within months of Marconi's original discussions with Cardinal Pacelli, Pope Pius XI blessed the world's first transnational radio system. For the first time the Roman Pontiff's live voice was heard simultaneously across the planet.

Marconi introduced the Pope at the inaugural ceremonies: "It is my very great honor and privilege to announce to you that within a few moments the Supreme Pontiff, His Holiness Pius XI, will inaugurate the radio station of the State of Vatican City. The electric waves will carry his august words of peace and benediction throughout the world.

"For nearly twenty centuries the Roman Pontiffs have given their inspired messages to all people, but this is the first time in history that the living voice of the Pope will have been heard simultaneously in all parts of the globe. With the help of Almighty God, who places such mysterious forces of nature at mankind's disposal, I have been able to prepare this instrument that will give to the faithful throughout the world the consolation of hearing the voice of the Holy Father.

"Holy Father, I have today the happiness of consigning to Your Holiness the work entrusted to me. Its completion is now consecrated by your august presence. Be pleased, Holy Father, I pray you, to let your voice be heard all over the world."

Following Marconi's inaugural comments, Pius XI prayed for God's blessings on this new and powerful medium. "To God let our first words be 'Glory to God in the highest and on earth peace to men of good will.' Glory to God who in our days hath given such power to men that their words should reach in very truth to the ends of the earth, and peace on earth where we are the ambassador of that Divine Redeemer, Jesus...."

Listeners were amazed at the technical clarity of his message on shortwave. Pius XI was delighted. Vatican Radio became a significant force in Church propagation, programming much of its content to diverse audiences in many languages. The Holy Father instituted a "Catholic Information Service" via Vatican Radio airwaves. This program attempted to clarify the Pope's position as Church leader and was created solely to attack the atheistic propaganda coming from Germany, Italy, Japan, and Russia. Radio became a primary medium for the pontiff's anti-Communist message.

For the second anniversary of the Lateran Treaty between Italy and the Vatican State, within moments of its first broadcast, Radio Vaticana was received enthusiastically throughout the world. It focused mainly on international missionary activity, Church teachings, commentary on various Catholic lay groups, and religious-oriented newscasts. Despite a few reception problems, the Pope's first address was heralded as a great success.

3. Propagating the Faith

Thus began a long history of propagating the Catholic faith by the airwaves. The mission of Vatican Radio was seemingly uncomplicated. The Jesuits were charged with programming the station: "[to spread] the Gospel, in its specific religious meaning as the revealed word of God and in its wider meaning of the Christian view of the whole of reality and all aspects of human life." However, since the station's inception, the original goals and objectives of both papacy and papal radio have become more complicated by social change, propaganda usage, and evolving models of faith. Vatican Radio's historical growth has been phenomenal.

The Pope had remained true to the institutional goals of the Church: to try to protect his clergy and to seek any means possible to propagate the Word of God. Diplomatic alliances were seen as only temporary, especially when compared to his obligation to protect the Church. The 1933 Concordat with Germany and those with several other countries, including Austria, Yugoslavia, and Prussia, were attempts to protect the Catholic Church.

His Holiness asserted the rights of Catholicism against the attacks of international Communism and German National Socialism. He proclaimed the Church's neutrality and reiterated her unwavering support of the principles of social justice and international morality.

The first papal message was broadcast for Christmas in 1936. Confronted with increasing appeals from Germany and Latin America to respond to Nazi and Soviet propaganda, Jesuit director Father Filippo Soccorso augmented the radio's transmissions in German and other languages as well as Italian. At the same time, the Radio's equipment was updated with a new transmission tower, which German technicians nicknamed the "Papstfinger" (Pope's finger).

The Church's institutional strength had brought hope and inner peace to its faithful followers through periods of political conflict and economic turmoil. Toward the end of his pontificate, Pius XI was aware that his successor would need to possess a broad world view of diplomatic issues as well as a strong awareness of media as a means of propagating Church doctrine. He prayed that Cardinal Eugenio Pacelli, who possessed the diplomatic experience and media knowledge necessary for the challenges of World War II, would be his successor. When Pope Pius XI passed away on February 10, 1939, Vatican Radio was the first to announce the news.

4. Pius XII's Election

Vatican Radio (station HVJ)[4] announced Pius XII's election to the papal throne, March 2, 1939. Ten days later, Cardinal Eugenio Pacelli became Pope Pius XII, the new Bishop of Rome. Station HVJ aired the entire ceremony, reaching a large portion of the world's three hundred million Catholics. The "Pope's Voice" was to play a significant role throughout World War II. Pius XII recruited Vatican Radio's help to transmit his spiritual and temporal messages. He reemphasized the Catholic Church's position of supranationality and universality. On August 24, 1939, before war commenced, he made an urgent appeal for peace via Vatican Radio: "Nothing is lost by peace; everything can be lost by war."

On January 21, 1940, Vatican Radio denounced Nazi atrocities in Poland and, two days later, condemned the existence of concentration camps. Pius XII clearly and unequivocally condemned the Nazi persecution of the Jews. He understood the importance of radio to disseminate his messages to vast territories instantaneously and reach greater numbers of people within a shorter period of time than any other medium. He understood that this was the most efficacious source to communicate to the world emotionally, dramatically, and persuasively. While maintaining neutrality during the war years, the Pope emphasized the Roman Catholic Church's traditional position of supramorality and universality. However, during 1940 and 1941, when the power of the Axis seemed to increase, Vatican Radio became the object of a constant struggle between the London Foreign Office and the Berlin Government.

How can one forget the work of the Vatican Radio during World War II? In Germany, listening to Vatican Radio in 1938 was a criminal offense. Within days of the German invasion of Poland on September 1, 1939, Pope Pius XII ordered Vatican Radio to begin its broadcasts as an independent, autonomous entity and not as an organ of the Holy See. The British propagandistic versions of the Vatican Radio were bitterly denounced by the Germans in their repeated diplomatic protests. Not only were the "manipulated" broadcasts vilified, censored, and jammed, but the Germans also retaliated. Goebbels swore to reduce Vatican Radio to silence. Catholics and non-Catholics, in Germany and elsewhere, were imprisoned for listening to the "voice of the Pope." Reaction to Vatican Radio was so severe that people were condemned for listening to its transmissions and, in some cases, there were death sentences. German law prohibited the use of Vatican transmissions declaring that its "propagandistic information could undermine the resistance of the Germans."

5. Persecutions in Poland

A communiqué, repeated with slight modifications in other languages, was intended for America and broadcast on the night of January 21–22, 1940:

"While the Apostolic Nuncio to Poland is busy at Bucharest alleviating the distress of thousands of war refugees, Monsignor Alfredo Pacini, Counsellor at the same Nunciature, was received during this week in private audience by the Holy Father, prior to his departure for Angers in France, where the Polish Government is now established. It is no longer a secret that His Holiness has been profoundly pained by reports lately received at the Vatican, and all too completely confirmed, on the martyr's fate reserved once more for his dear Poland, in whose inevitable resurrection he continues to count with such confidence.

"In his much-published discourse delivered at Castelgandolfo on September 30th to the Polish pilgrims, led into the Father's presence by their Ambassador and their Cardinal Primate, one month after the outbreak of war, millions of Polish Catholics in America, along with all sensitive souls everywhere, were heartened at these words of Pius XII: 'We will also hope, notwithstanding many reasons to fear, reasons caused by the too well known designs of the enemies of God, that Catholic life will be able to continue abundantly faithful; that you will be able to carry on your religious services, those manifestations of devotion to the Holy Eucharist and homage to the kingship of Christ of which your cities and the entire country recently gave such magnificent evidence; that the Catholic press, institutions of charity, social works, and the teaching of religion will enjoy the liberty which is their right.'

"These modest hopes of the Holy Father for the Polish people he tenderly loves have been grossly deceived, we regret to announce, and the misgivings which accompanied them abundantly justified. The new year with its frail but refreshing promise of peace brings us from Warsaw and Cracow, from Pomerania, Poznania and Silesia almost daily the tale of destitution and destruction and infamy of all descriptions, which one is loath to credit until it is established by the unimpeachable testimony of eye-witnesses to the horror and inexcusable excesses committed upon a helpless and homeless people, as peaceful and unpretentious as any in Europe, and not confined to the sections of the country under Russian occupation, heartrending as news from that quarter has been. Even more violent and persistent is the assault upon elementary justice and decency in that part of prostrate Poland which has fallen to German administration. The richest part of Western Poland is being unceremoniously stolen from the Poles and deeded over to the Germans, as the real proprietors are packed off in foul-smelling trains to the war-torn region of Warsaw, which the Holy Father only last week described as 'a desert where once the smiling harvest waved.'

"A system of interior deportation and zoning is being organized, in the depth of one of Europe's severest winters, on principles and by methods that can be described only as brutal; and stark hunger stares 70% of Poland's population in the face, as its reserves of foodstuffs and tools are shipped to Germany to replenish the granaries of the metropole. Jews and Poles are being herded into separate 'ghettos,' hermetically sealed and pitifully inadequate for the economic subsistence of the millions destined to live there.

"But the crowning iniquity in an administration that has never ceased to claim it had no claims against religion lies in the cynical suppression of all but the merest suggestion of religious worship in the lives of this most pious and devotional of the peoples of Europe. An administrative decree, applied with varying effectiveness throughout the General Government Protectorate, restricts public religious services to a bare two hours on Sunday. The thousands of churches in Poland, second homes for old and young from morning till sunset ever since the nation was born and baptized in the Catholic faith, are deserted and closed for six and a half days of the week, separating an afflicted people from the altar of its hopes and sacrifices.

"It adds up to a fearful total and a tremendous responsibility: one more grievous affront to the moral conscience of mankind; one more contemptuous insult to the law of nations; one more open thrust at the heart of the Father of the Christian family, who grieves with his dear Poland, and begs for peace with decency and justice from the throne of grace."

6. The Church in Poland

Robert Graham, S.J., described Vatican Radio's heroic role in *Civiltà Cattolica* (January 17, 1976, pp. 132–50): "Diligent research into the broadcasts during the crucial period 1940–1941 reveals a notably massive denunciation of persecutions and oppressions in Germany and in the territories occupied by German troops....Some of the most important of them were due to the initiative of Pius XII....A note from Monsignor Giovanni Battista Montini (the future Pope Paul VI), substitute in the Secretariat of State, refers to the start of this campaign." Vatican Radio explicitly named Germany as the perpetrator of these war crimes and specifically named Jews and Polish Catholics as their victims.

From the beginning of the war, German propaganda falsely asserted that the position of the Catholic Church in Poland had improved. The Vatican Radio categorically denied the statement and stressed the fact that the brutal persecutions of the Church and the Polish people continued.

In fact, Vatican Radio broadcasts in various languages on November 16–17, 1940, denied the reports of some Spanish journalists, inspired by German sources, according to which the situation of the Catholic Church in the districts of Poland occupied by the Germans had undergone a change for the better. The Radio asserted that in those districts, inhabited by many millions of Catholics, their religious life continued to be brutally restricted. Among other things, in the course of the last four months (from the middle of July to the middle of November 1940) at least four hundred clergy had been deported from those districts to Germany.

On November 29, 1940, the Vatican Radio issued a further communiqué, rendered in French, on this subject. It said: "A statement which has appeared in one of the Breslau journals must be corrected. It referred to signs of the revival of religious life in Poland, and to the protection which the faithful in that country enjoy in the performance of religious practices. The German journal mentions the close relations alleged to exist between Catholic associations and the Polish Red Cross on the one hand and the German State authorities on the other. But the author did not mention that a large part of five dioceses is situated in Polish territories unceremoniously incorporated with the Reich. In view of this, the author's conclusions cannot be recognized as a criterion of the general development of religious life in Poland, but can only refer to the General Gouvernement. Undoubtedly the churches in this part of Poland are filled to overflowing with the faithful, but the Catholic associations in the General Gouvernement also have been dissolved, the Catholic educational institutions have been closed down, and the Catholic professors and teachers have been reduced to a state of extreme need, or have been sent to concentration camps. The Catholic press has been rendered impotent.

"That is the real situation in that part of Poland which is the most favourably treated by the Germans. The Breslau journal makes no mention of what is happening in other parts of Poland. In the part incorporated with the Reich, and especially in Poznania, the representatives of the Catholic priests and orders have been shut up in concentration camps. The number of priests sent to camps from the Poznan area alone exceeds 200. Certain of them have died in these camps. In other dioceses the priests have been put in prison. Entire areas of the country have been deprived of all spiritual ministrations, and the church seminaries have been dispersed."

7. Arrests and Killings

The noted journalist Friedrich von Lama, one of the "martyrs of Vatican Radio," was arrested on January 14, 1941, on suspicion of having transcribed Vatican transmissions. He died in prison, probably assassinated.[5] Other martyrs included Alfons Wachsmann, a priest who defied the Nazis and was condemned to death in Stettino on February 24, 1944. He was accused of encouraging his friends and students to listen to Vatican Radio.[6] Carl Lampert, a priest from Tyrol, was accused of providing information to Vatican Radio. He was sent to Dachau and condemned to death.[7] For the same reason Johannes Neuhäusler, Auxiliary Bishop of Monaco, was arrested and sent to Dachau along with the Franciscan Odilo Gerhardt who was accused of having been the source of Vatican transmissions on Poland.[8]

In a booklet distributed clandestinely, Bishop Stanislao Adamski of Katowice, wrote: "During the first months of the war, every day Vatican Radio cited the assassinations, the arrests, the reprisals against the Polish people, especially in the concentration camps."[9] After its publication, the Bishop stopped revealing the tragic situation. Why?

The Vatican soon learned that priests and religious were maltreated and suffered worse cruelties because of the revelations. Prisoners were told: "This is compensation since your pope and your cardinal have again condemned us."[10] Every time a program aired, a number of prisoners lost their lives, and others contracted serious illnesses. The *Nouvelle Revue Théologique*[11] stated: "In Belgium, the *Osservatore Romano* rarely arrived and listening to the Vatican Radio was considered a crime comparable to listening to the BBC."

Vatican Radio was soon forced to refrain from further broadcasts. Contrary to the directives and the will of the Holy See, for sixteen months BBC had misused Vatican transmissions against the interests of the faithful in certain lands. Of course, the British press then regretted the "silence" of the Vatican. Meanwhile, Sir Alec Randall commented: "The Vatican Radio has been very useful for our propaganda and we have used it to our advantage. No other neutral power would have persisted so long in providing us with useful material and risking the criticism of other powers with whom they had normal diplomatic relationships."[12]

In Italy, the government refused Italian Radio the right to broadcast Pius XII's messages. However, in occupied France, the French Resistance transcribed and circulated Vatican Radio bulletins.

8. Vatican Information Office

Between 1940 and 1946, the bells of the Basilica of Saint Peter resounded and penetrated everywhere, as Vatican Radio united the faithful. Expressing words of comfort, encouragement, and hope, Pope Pius XII's voice reached hundreds of thousands of listeners. Vatican Radio also collaborated with the Vatican Information Office, transmitting almost 1,240,000 shortwave messages to locate prisoners of war and other missing persons in order to reunite war-torn families and friends.

The Pope established this Office so that families could contact prisoners. The Office had access to station HVJ and thereby facilitated its appeals for help. These shortwave messages helped locate prisoners of war and other missing persons. Later, Vatican Radio combined its information services with the International Refugee Organization, forming a team "Tracing Service" to reunite war-torn families and friends.

Although the process was slow, it raised the hopes of tortured families by transmitting brief messages. To avoid misunderstandings, names were spelled out with the letters of each name given the initial of famous Italian cities, since it was neither possible to repeat nor to clarify a conversation. Thus names, regardless of race or religion, were announced in response to the sighs and prayers of countless grieving mothers and wives. Indeed, Vatican Radio's service for tracing missing persons, both civil and military, helped compensate for the lack of normal communication.

Vatican Radio's broadcasts concerning the atrocities that were taking place in Poland countered the false claims put out by Axis leaders. Cardinal August Hlond, exiled in Rome, delivered a broadcast on

September 28, 1939, in which he condemned aggression against his country: "Martyred Poland, you have fallen to violence while you fought for the sacred cause of freedom....On these radio waves...I cry to you. Poland, you are not beaten."[13]

According to a letter from Bishop Carl Mario Splett of Danzig to Pius XII, this protest resulted in the arrest and execution of priests and teachers. Vatican Radio's response—to Hitler's proposal for a "new order," with a federation of European states under the control of Germany and Italy—was: "It is a world order which is as dry as the desert, an order which is the same order as the order of the desert. It is being achieved by the exploitation of human life. What these falsehoods call life is no life. It is dissolution—it is death."[14]

With four shortwave bands to areas that were the focus of German propaganda, Vatican Radio was able to refute the Germans' claim when it reached Spain that National Socialism was compatible with Christianity. Vatican Radio reduced the number of English broadcasts and increased Spanish broadcasts to report about the religious conditions in Poland, Austria, and Germany. On November 20, 1940, Vatican Radio responded to an editorial in the Madrid newspaper *Alcazar* that stated: "National Socialism is primarily a religious movement based on Christian principles."[15]

Vatican Radio reviewed Nazi attacks on Christianity, the Catholic Church, religious leaders, Church doctrine, religious education, and discussed other matters such as the closing of monasteries in Austria and the confiscation of religious property. The broadcast also noted the deportation of priests in Poland and the refusal to recognize the validity of Church wedding services.

Some of the most courageous broadcasts aired by station HVJ at this time were those that unveiled the horrors of the Jewish Holocaust at the hands of the Nazis. On January 20, 1940, an American Jesuit became the first announcer in world radio to report the imprisonment of Jewish and Polish prisoners in "sealed ghettos." From that point on, Vatican Radio continued to report on concentration camps and other Nazi torture chambers.

In response to German news reports concerning the Church in Poland, on October 25, 1940, Vatican Radio revealed that 115 parishes had been deprived of their clergy, 200 clergy from the Poznan diocese had been placed in concentration camps, the cathedrals of Poznan and

Gniezno had been closed, most larger seminaries had been taken over, and the Catholic University of Lublin had been closed.[16] On November 2, the Nazis filed a protest with the Vatican, complaining that recent transmissions were "against Hitler, against Nazism" and "in contrast with neutrality."[17] There were frequent protests from Mussolini and the German Ambassador to the Holy See against Vatican Radio broadcasts. Documentation shows that Pius XII personally not only gave directives regarding the content of broadcasts but also authored many of the anti-German statements beamed around the world.

9. Catholic Resistance

On March 30, 1941, Vatican Radio directed its words to the Catholic resistance inside Nazi Germany: "The threat of a national religion is looming increasingly over all religious life. This national religion is based solely on the Führer's will, and is the only one wanted by him. In the countries which have been incorporated into the Reich, as for instance in Slovakia, a national church has been formed. These tendencies have been forced to the extreme in Alsace, Austria, and in Sudenten Germany. These countries are to be made an example for the spiritual structure of the others. What we demand is that Catholic Germany wakes up and sees clearly the pagan tendencies which are spreading everywhere."

In Germany, when Bishop Rarkowski—a pro-Nazi army prelate—published a pastoral supporting the German war effort on the first anniversary of the outbreak of war, Vatican Radio immediately broadcast a response pointing out the discrepancy between his position and that of the Holy See. Vatican Radio also reported that "Hitler's war unfortunately is not a just war" and that "God's blessing therefore cannot be upon it."[18]

On December 24, 1941, Pius XII pleaded for the safety of "those expelled from their native land and deported to foreign lands." He stated that in the interests of the common good the rights of the smaller states should be respected—"rights to political freedom, to economic development and to the adequate use of that neutrality which is theirs according to the natural, as well as international, law. In this way, and in this way only, will they be able to obtain a fitting share of the common good, and assure the material and spiritual welfare of their people."

On May 12, 1942, the twenty-fifth anniversary of his episcopal consecration, Pius XII addressed the world by Vatican Radio, reaffirming his hope for peace. In the summer of 1942, after France's Catholic bishops publicly condemned the Nazi persecution and deportation of Jews, the Pope not only had these protests reprinted in *L'Osservatore Romano* but ordered Vatican Radio to broadcast the most powerful of them (by Cardinal Saliége) twice—and make comments on it for six consecutive days.

In his radio message for Christmas Eve 1942, Pius XII again denounced the war and emphasized reconciliation and a new internal order among the various nations. He urged the faithful to pray for peace. The Holy Father expressed hope for peace among men and spoke about a "sad succession of acts at variance with the human and Christian sense." Pius XII invited "magnanimous and upright people to gather together in a solemn vow not to rest" until society is brought back to its "center of gravity, which is the Law of God." He stated: "Humanity owes this vow to the innumerable exiles, torn from their motherland by the hurricane of war and scattered on foreign soil, who might join in the lament of the prophet: 'Our inheritance is turned to aliens, our houses to strangers.'

"Humanity owes this vow to the hundreds of thousands of people who, through no fault of their own, sometimes only owing to nationality or descent, are doomed to death or to slow decline. Humanity owes this vow to the many thousands of non-combatants…to the endless stream of tears and bitterness, to the mountains of suffering and torment, which are the results of the destructive madness of the widespread conflict which cry out to heaven, invoking the descent of the Spirit for the liberation of the world from the spreading of violence and terror."

The Pope's frequent Vatican Radio messages were in many languages. On February 19, 1943, speaking in French, he invoked "the curse of God" on whomever abuses the liberty of men. Broadcasting in German in April 1943, he protested a long list of horrors, including "an unprecedented enslavement of human freedom, the deportation of thousands for forced labor, and the killing of innocent and guilty alike."

Radio Vatican's policy began as one of neutrality. When aggression became more severe and global battle seemed to be inevitable, diplomatic neutrality was not an easy policy to maintain. For example, when Italy declared war on France and Great Britain, both Allied representatives moved to the Vatican. Ironically, when the tides of war began to favor the Allied forces, Pius XII found himself obligated to offer the same protection to the Axis countries. Amid this backdrop, personnel at Vatican Radio were asked to do many things that involved humanitarian assistance.

The *New York Times* stated that Vatican Radio denounced the racial laws of the totalitarian states in a broadcast directed to France which was recorded by the Columbia Broadcasting System: "As long as men make differences in the treatment of members of the human family, the peace of the world, order and justice will be at stake."[19]

10. Pius XII's Directives

On January 19, 1940, after a special meeting with the cardinals belonging to the Congregation for Extraordinary Ecclesiastical Affairs, Monsignor Montini wrote Pius XII's directive: "*Ex audientia Sanctissimi:* To give Vatican Radio, for its German broadcast, information regarding the conditions of the Church in Poland." Two days later, during the first report in German, the announcer stated: "Conditions of religious, political, and economic life have thrown the Polish people, especially in those areas occupied by Germany, into a state of terror, of degradation and, we dare say, of barbarism, much akin to what the communists imposed on Spain in 1936....The Germans employ the same methods, perhaps even worse, as those used by the Soviets."[20]

On January 23, 1940, in England, the *Manchester Guardian* reported: "Tortured Poland has found a powerful advocate in Rome....Vatican Radio has warned all who care for civilization that Europe is in mortal danger." The January 26 English-language broadcast declared that Jews and Poles were herded into separate ghettos and that the outrages committed against the Polish people were not limited to Soviet territory. In fact, the *New York Times* headline was: "Vatican Denounces Atrocities in Poland; Germans Called Even Worse than Russians." Soon after, a separate story reported that a Soviet newspaper had labeled Pius XII the "tool of Great Britain and France." It confirmed that "the horror and inexcusable excesses committed on a helpless and a homeless people have been established by the unimpeachable testimony of eye-witnesses." Pius XII ordered the publication of these eyewitness accounts of the German efforts to crush the Church.

Under instructions from the Pope, Vatican Radio regularly reported on the atrocities: "Still more violent and constant are the attacks upon justice and the most elementary decency in sections of Poland that have fallen under German control." German reaction came on January 27, 1940, when Fritz Menshausen, the Counselor of the German Embassy, told Monsignor Montini that he was instructed to inform the Holy See of the inopportuneness of the recent broadcast on Vatican Radio. It was provoking an anti-German attitude in the world press and in public opinion, and this could lead to "disagreeable repercussions."

The Vatican understood the veiled threat of reprisals and, two days later, Monsignor Montini informed Menshausen that Vatican Radio would suspend any broadcasts about the sad conditions in Poland. In June, Germany's ambassador sent a note from his government declaring that, in view of the hostile and anti-German attitude of the Vatican's press and radio, priests and religious would not be allowed to leave Poland. For fear of having letters intercepted by the Germans or by the Russians, the Pope and the bishops were extremely cautious when drafting letters. Political questions and obvious allusions to the terrible treatment of the population were rarely mentioned.

The October 15, 1940, transmission describing the German police in Alsace-Lorraine as inhumane and barbarian became the object of a grievance from the German Embassy. Fritz Menshausen began to justify the Reich's policy, which he called restrained and respectful of the rights of the Church. Cardinal Maglione reminded him that the Nazi police had expelled the Bishop of Metz from his See, giving him only two hours to prepare for his departure; they had forbidden the Bishop of Strasbourg from returning to that city; at Innsbruck the Gestapo had raided the Capuchins, laying hands on all they found—papers, money, and even the meal that had been prepared for the community—and had expelled these religious, also giving them only two hours during which to prepare their departure.

11. Allied Propaganda

In his book *Pius XII and the Second World War* (1999), historian Pierre Blet states: "On 25 October Menshausen returned to the Secretariat of State and said that ten days ago he had asked for the text of the incriminating broadcast; yet he had received nothing. Tardini's reply was that the director of Vatican Radio had sent not the exact text but rather the news aired in English on 15 October, namely, that in Alsace-Lorraine schools had been shut down, seminaries closed, and priests were no longer permitted to impart religious instruction in schools. All this was true. The only piece of news that could not be confirmed was the closing of the cathedral in Strasbourg. Menshausen became very angry when he found out that he was being refused the text asked for by his government. Then he took out of his briefcase a piece of paper from which he read several sentences, the text of the broadcast as recorded by the Germans: in Alsace-Lorraine national-socialism exercises its 'pernicious influence'; the 'immoral principles of Nazism' are being spread there.

"And now becoming more and more angry, the diplomat stated that for a long time the German press and radio had refrained from attacking the Vatican and that Vatican Radio, on the other hand, was taking a hostile stance toward Germany, that the so-called autonomy of Vatican Radio was not admissible, that the Holy See was the most totalitarian of all regimes and that the Secretariat of State should use all possible means to curb the radio, and that, if things should continue in this manner, the Vatican must expect Germany to reply most strongly. Tardini, remaining calm, answered that he completely agreed that Vatican Radio should refrain from broadcasting inexact information, especially since there existed so much accurate news to point out the religious persecution taking place in Germany. Menshausen tried to defend himself but without great conviction, noted Tardini, since he could not deny the facts."

Allied propaganda had profited from the Vatican Radio news and commentaries. Sometimes the press mixed inexact details with this information. On January 25, 1940, the director of Vatican Radio, Father Filippo Soccorsi, complained to Monsignor Montini and sent him the text of a broadcast, adding: "I inform you that broadcasts from England have often cited and made reference to this while on its own adding things we have not said." Two days later, Father Soccorsi was told to limit broadcasts to news that was well verified. Nazi propaganda took advantage of the situation and presented the Pope as Germany's enemy. Pius XII directed that Vatican Radio be perfectly objective and decided to suspend any broadcasts regarding Germany. The British, who had found these anti-Nazi broadcasts advantageous to their cause, protested against this silence.

In November 1940 Lord Halifax instructed Sir d'Arcy Osborne to send the Secretariat of State a memorandum concerning the attitude of European Catholics who were being confronted with National Socialism. The answer, on November 22, began by rejecting the English pretense of having the Holy See issue a statement that would be the equivalent of taking a political position: "The Holy See cannot forget that too often there has been a desire to attribute a purely political meaning to doctrinal and religious actions; by its very nature it is not certain that such a statement will dispel the confusion that is of such concern to His Majesty's legation."

However, a circular letter, personally reviewed and corrected by Pius XII, signed by the Cardinal Secretary of State and dated February 18, 1941, was sent to the Holy See's representatives in France, Switzerland, Spain, Argentina, Brazil, and the United States. Describing the Church's situation in regions under Nazi control, Germany itself, and the occupied countries (especially Poland), it mentioned in detail that Catholic schools and churches were closed, religious houses were invaded and searched, priests were arrested, bishops were kept far from their flocks, and religious teaching and worship were impeded in a thousand ways.

In response to Sir d'Arcy Osborne's comments, Pius XII replied that there was no agreement between the Holy See and the Axis powers and that it had not been stated that no one could speak, day after day, about what was happening in Germany. The Pope further replied that he was not unaware that some broadcasts were exposing German Catholics and religious to harsh reprisals.

In formulating their criticisms, apparently the British Legation had forgotten how the Holy Father had freely denounced crimes perpetrated against the rights of religion and how he had alerted the faithful about the evils threatening them.

Regarding Vatican Radio, Father Pierre Blet concludes that broadcasts were retransmitted or published in reports "obviously altered in form and denatured in substance." Extracts were circulated; taken out of context, they contained many and serious inexactitudes "on exceptionally complex and delicate matters," offering Nazi propaganda a perfect pretext for which to attack the Holy See, its independence, and its impartiality.

12. Mystici Corporis Christi

The Vatican expressly repudiated forcible conversions in a memorandum, dated January 25, 1942, from the Vatican Secretariat of State to the Legation of Yugoslavia to the Holy See (addressing conversions in Croatia). Furthermore, Pius XII not only publicly condemned these forced conversions, but did so in one of the highest forms of papal teaching—the encyclical, *Mystici Corporis Christi,* issued June 29, 1943, during the very height of the brutalities against the Serbs. In paragraph 103 of that encyclical, the Pope declared: "The 'faith without which it is impossible to please God' is a wholly free submission of intellect and will. Therefore, whenever it happens, despite the invariable teaching of the Apostolic See, that anyone against his will is compelled to embrace the Catholic faith, our sense of duty demands that we condemn the act." This encyclical explicitly defended and praised the Jewish people (paragraph 110) and also declared: "Our paternal love embraces all peoples, whatever their nationality or race."

The June 2, 1943, reference was clear on Vatican Radio. Pius XII spoke of those "who guide the fate of nations. They should not forget that, in the words of the Scriptures, he who bears the sword is not therefore the master over the life and death of men, unless it be according to the divine law, from whence all power derives." He also mentioned his unsuccessful negotiations on behalf of the persecuted victims.

On June 21, 1943, Vatican Radio broadcast in German a long text on the rights of Jews under natural law, and a few days later broadcast to Germany a defense of Yugoslav Jews: "Every man bears the stamp of God." On July 28, 1943, Vatican Radio further reported on the Pope's denunciation of totalitarianism and support for constitutional democracy: "The life and activities of all must be protected against arbitrary human action. This means that no man has any right on the life and freedom of other men. Authority cannot be at the service of any arbitrary power. Herein lies the essential differences between tyranny and true usefulness. The Pope condemns those who dare to place the fortunes of whole nations in the hands of one man alone, a man who as such is the prey of passions, errors, and dreams." The meaning of these words was lost on no one—least of all their intended targets: Hitler and Mussolini. There was no doubt to whom the Pope was referring.

Pius XII, in his 1943 Christmas message, declared: "We see, indeed, only a conflict which is degenerating into that form of warfare which excludes all restriction and restraint....It is a form of warfare which proceeds without intermission on its terrible way, and piles up slaughter of such a kind that the most bloodstained pages of history pale in comparison with it....Every human sentiment is crushed and the light of reason eclipsed so that the words of wisdom are fulfilled: 'They were all found together with one chain of darkness.'"

In a letter to the editor of *Inside the Vatican,*[21] Italo DePra, an eye-witness in Rome (1941–44), described how the Nazis took control of Rome on September 8, 1943. They were so enraged that, as a warning to Pius XII, they bombed the Vatican Radio station. Father DePra also described the Nazis' contingency plan to seize the Pope and take over all papal territory because they considered Pius XII's words "too political" and were convinced that he was siding with the Allies.

After World War II, as Vatican Radio returned to its prewar programming schedule, broadcasting in many languages throughout the world, the Cold War brought with it a renewed commitment to boost the Church's radio service. Underground radio had become one of the only ways to communicate with countries such as Hungary and Poland—largely Catholic populations that had been placed behind the Iron Curtain of the USSR.

In 1950, to combat the atheistic propaganda being poured into the Iron Curtain countries, Vatican Radio officials asked for contributions from the faithful to expand the transnational system's facilities. With this money, Pius XII proposed to use Vatican Radio vigilantly, broadcasting twenty-four hours a day, in at least twenty-eight languages. The "free world" responded to his announcement, contributing almost two and one-half million dollars to the cause. The new facilities took almost six years to build. In 1957, Radio HVJ introduced its high-powered station to the world, reaching new areas in North and South America and much of Asia.

Vatican Radio's transmitter is on the highest point in Vatican City. During World War II, its steel tower became a symbol of hope. Pius XII's commitment to Vatican Radio and its broadcast policy was firmly established by the late 1950s. In October 1958, station HVJ had the unhappy task of broadcasting the last days of his life. Indeed, Eugenio Pacelli had led the Catholic Church through a major global war as well as through a dramatically changing technological, theological, and diplomatic world for almost twenty years.

It is interesting to note that coupled with the new production facilities for film and television (created in 1955), as well as the establishment of a Pontifical Commission for Cinematography, Radio, and Television, the Holy See has clearly confirmed its commitment to transnational media propagation. *Palazzo Pio,* named after Pope Pius XII, has been Vatican Radio's production headquarters since 1970.[22] Its programs included world news copy from seven wire services, religious services, religious and political interviews and commentary, as well as sacred and classical music.[23] Its staff is made up of over 200 journalists from 60 different nations and some 150 technicians. Service is universal and free to the entire world. There is no advertising income. Its operating costs amount to a considerable sum ($22 million in 1995), though lower than those of other international radio stations.

Until Italian physicist Guglielmo Marconi overcame the obstacles of geography by his development of wireless telegraphy, communication with papal representatives throughout the world had been difficult. The Holy See station now broadcasts on five channels and in five continents on short- and medium-wave frequencies by 24 transmitters with a total power of nearly 4,000 kilowatts to reach millions of listeners in 37 different languages for a total of 388 hours weekly.

Pope John Paul II's numerous apostolic visits have intensified the Vatican Radio staff's personal contact with people from around the world. Special attention has been given to eastern Europe and the Soviet Union. Program exchanges are now possible. For example, Poland receives Vatican Radio's Polish news report on its national network. These programs focus on the Pope, the activities of the Holy See, the local churches and the socio-economic-cultural situation seen from a Christian point of view. Other programs focus on religious culture and catechetic information, liturgies in various rites, music for the Rome area, and live broadcasts of ceremonies presided over by the Holy Father.

Pius XII's efforts to establish Vatican Radio have not been in vain. Vatican Radio is a member of the European Broadcasting Union (EBU), the International Catholic Association for Radio and Television (UNDA), the International Radio and Television University (URTI), and the Union of African National Radio and Television (URTNA). Vatican Radio collaborates with other member radio stations throughout the world. The International Relations Office, charged with overseeing these complicated interrelationships, provided technical and editorial assistance to journalists and technicians on assignment abroad, or offered international exchanges of both live and recorded radio programs—religious, cultural, news, or musical (such as the New Year's Concert broadcast live from Vienna).

On January 1, 1993, Vatican Radio entered the era of broadcasting via satellite, covering the continent of Europe through services offered by World Radio Network Ltd. (London), which sends the signal of Vatican Radio's European programs to one of the satellites of the EUTELSAT system (13° east) for a total of over fifteen hours a day. This offered the possibility to many broadcasting stations to receive Vatican Radio's signal very easily and economically and to retransmit it on their own frequencies to their listeners, by prior agreement with the General Direction of the pontifical broadcasting station.

There is now in Europe a wide network of radio stations that rebroadcast Vatican Radio's programs in different European countries, in their respective languages. They include, among others, the national radios of Poland, Lithuania, and Albania; scores of Catholic stations in Italy and in France; other Catholic or commercial stations in Poland, Spain, Slovakia, Hungary, and Lebanon. The rebroadcasting is generally on medium wave or on FM. Another step forward in the satellite era is the construction of two earth-fixed stations with parabolic antennae of 7.5 meters in diameter, through which Vatican Radio is in the position to transmit its signals directly to two satellites of the INTELSAT system, placed respectively above the Atlantic Ocean (325.5° east and over the Indian Ocean (66° east), covering the greater part of the inhabited world. The possibility of increasing the number of listeners in Latin America and Africa is enormous, and the service provided by the pontifical station is gradually being integrated with these local stations, bringing the voice of the Pope and the life of the Catholic Church worldwide.[24]

In *Pius XII Was Not Silent,* Jenö Levai wrote in the prologue that Robert M. Kempner—a German-born lawyer on the American prosecution team who was Chief of Division responsible for preparing the cases against the defendants at the Nuremberg trials—testified that there were many Vatican protests: direct and indirect, diplomatic and public, secret and open. Catholics during the war were motivated by the words and protests of Pope Pius XII. Statements by the bishops condemning anti-Semitism and the Nazi persecutions always cited the words of Pope Pius XII.[25]

On February 9, 1944, there were two successive stories in the *New York Times* about the Vatican's heroic actions during the German occupation of Rome: "The Vatican Radio, commenting on the Fascist raid on St. Paul's Basilica last Thursday in which 64 Italian officers and Jews who had received sanctuary there were arrested, said tonight that the Church would never yield in offering charity to everyone." Entitled "Pope Lodges Strong Protest," the second story reveals the Pope's concern: "Pope Pius XII has protested energetically against a German interpretation of a clause in the Vatican's Lateran Treaty with Italy, fearing that it may foreshadow further German searches in Rome."

After Italy declared war against the Allies, ambassadors from France, Great Britain, Poland, and Belgium moved into Vatican City. In June 1944, when Italy joined the Allies, the French, British, Polish, and Belgian representatives returned to their embassies in Rome, and the German ambassador to Italy moved into the Vatican. Indeed, during World War II, the Vatican became a refuge for all refugees. After Rome had been liberated from the German occupation, Pius XII, fearing for the fate of Jewish prisoners still in Nazi-Fascist hands in northern Italy and Germany itself, made one of his most fervent pleas for tolerance: "For centuries, Jews have been unjustly treated and despised. It is time they were treated with justice and humanity. God wills it and the Church wills it. St. Paul tells us that the Jews are our brothers. They should be welcomed as friends."[26]

Chapter IX
L'Osservatore Romano

1. Vatican Newspaper

After the Nazis invaded the Low Countries in the spring of 1940, Pius XII immediately ordered *L'Osservatore Romano* to explicitly condemn the aggression. It was reported in *The Tablet* of London (May 25, 1940, p. 530): "Today Germany crossed the frontiers of Holland, Belgium and Luxemburg as she crossed the frontiers of Denmark and Norway....The German move has not a semblance of justification. States are occupied against their will and turned into bloody battle-fields; peace, prosperity and lives are thrown to the winds. War bursts the dams, and submerges countries with floods of fire and blood. It is dreadful! The deepest feelings of humanity, Christian charity, Christian brotherhood of nations, are stung, and protest in pain.

"Once more, at this dreadful hour, let us be on the side of him who represents the Prince of Peace, of the Lord of the Gospel and its laws; who in his Christmas address declared to the irreconcilable with either the positive principles and rights of nature, or with the principles of humanity, facts such as we are witnessing today and whose victims are those 'small, hard-working and peaceful nations,' who proclaimed the inviolability of 'the right to independence and life of all nations, whether big or small, powerful or weak,' because 'one nation's desire to live should never carry another nation's condemnation to die.'"

L'Osservatore Romano, the official Vatican newspaper, has been published daily since 1861. It is the main source of information concerning the Holy See and reports on the life of the universal Church and of Catholics in the various countries and continents. Two other editions are published in Italian: *L'Osservatore Romano,* Sunday edition, and *L'Osservatore Romano,* weekly edition.

196

In 1946, after the Second World War, a weekly edition of
L'Osservatore Romano began publication in French. Following
many requests for the teachings of the Pope to be translated and published in other languages too, a series of weekly editions was introduced: in English (1968), in Spanish (1969), in Portuguese (1970),
in German (1971), and the monthly one in Polish (1980). The aim of
these editions is to spread the words of the Pope, the documents of
the Offices of the Holy See, and news on the life of the Catholic
Church throughout the world. The entire collection of the Italian
daily edition of the Vatican newspaper has been transferred from
microfilm to CD-ROM. The collection contains all issues from July
1, 1861, to December 31, 1996.

L'Osservatore Romano became the most widely read source of
news in Italy during World War II. The newspaper was criticized by the
Nazis and the Fascists, who placed a ban on its sale; both vendors and
purchasers were harassed. Roberto Farinacci, editor of *Regime
Fascista,* charged that it was the "evident mouthpiece of the Jews," that
its primary readers were Jews and Masons, and that it, like the Vatican,
had "joined the cause of the Allies."[1]

In his book, *Pius XII: Pope of Peace* (New York: Robert M.
McBride and Company, 1939, pp. 198–202), Joseph Dineen writes
of the 1930s: "The voices of the Pope [Pius XI] and Pacelli—the
Vatican—had been as loud in protest as that of the democracies and
rest of the civilized nations." Speaking of the Vatican newspaper, he
states: "*L'Osservatore Romano* had been forthright and downright in
its denunciation of Hitler for his excesses against the Jews, his sterilization law, his restrictions upon the freedom of speech and assem-
bly and freedom of religious worship. This little newspaper,
published within the Vatican state, was one of the few remaining in
Europe that dared to criticize Hitler or Mussolini. Even the French
press had become respectable toward Hitler, and in Poland, Norway,
Sweden, Denmark, the Netherlands, Finland, Hungary, Romania,
Yugoslavia, and Czechoslovakia, newspapers were silent on Hitler.
His name did not appear in Lithuania. But the Vatican newspaper
fulminated and poured its criticism upon his head, even while he was
in Italy. The newspaper had been just as persistent in its attacks upon
Mussolini."

2. *Circulation*

Both the Vatican newspaper and Vatican Radio reported and condemned Hitler's barbarous crimes and spoke about the Nazi atrocities against Jews and non-Jews in Poland. When war was declared in 1939, The *New York Times* reported that Hitler immediately imposed a news blackout on the Nazi invasion and war activities.

The Catholic resistance inside Nazi Germany continued to circulate *L'Osservatore Romano,* even though Catholics caught reading it were subject to punishment. In its issue for December 12, 1940, the Vatican newspaper published an article on German-occupied Poland: "The printing establishment of Antonio Corsetti at Ceprano has printed a brochure entitled, *Germans and the Catholic Faith in Poland,* which is now being extensively distributed. The brochure maintains that the authorities have not taken and will not take any initiative to restrict Poles' religious activities, that the churches are open from early morning till late in the evening, that owing to the friendliness of the civil administration, which has financed and provided building material gratis, certain churches have been rebuilt.

"This brochure calls for a few words of explanation, since the impression it may leave—we have to say it regretfully—is not in accordance with the reality.

"First and foremost we note that the publication does not give the name of the author and that, while using the name of 'Poland,' it does not have in mind the whole of the territory which constitutes the Republic of Poland at the beginning of the German-Polish conflict, but only a part of it. It is well known that Poland is partly occupied by Germany and partly by Soviet Russia. The territory held by the Germans, approximately half of the Republic of Poland, was further divided into two parts—namely, the Western Provinces and the rest, called the General Gouvernement, administered by a Governor residing at Cracow.

"The Western Provinces embrace the Archbishoprics of Poznan and Gniezno, parts of those of Warsaw and Cracow, the dioceses of Katowice, Chelmno, Wloclawek, and Plock, and part of the dioceses of Lomza, Lodz, Czestochowa, and Kielce. The General Gouvernement includes mainly parts of the archbishoprics of Warsaw and Cracow, the dioceses of Siedlce, Lublin, Tarnow, Sandomierz, and part of those of Przemysl, Czestochowa, Kielce, Lodz, and Lomza.

"The brochure published at Ceprano has only the General Gouvernement in mind when it speaks of Poland, although there also, to tell the truth, the situation is not so good as it would seem on reading this publication. The bishop of one of the dioceses, and possibly others also, has been exiled from the area of his jurisdiction, while his suffragan has been held in Germany in a concentration camp. Numerous members of the clergy, most of all monks, are in prison; many restrictions hinder the normal functioning of training colleges and orders.

"The religious press, which once was flourishing, has been subjected to very severe restrictions: many publications of prayerbooks are prohibited and suspended, and the monthly *Messenger of the Sacred Heart,* which the author maintains is being published just as it was before the war, is suspended, and was suspended in October, when this brochure was published. Only a few diocesan bulletins are published, subject to censorship.

"The Catholic University in Lublin has been closed, and, for that matter, all secondary and higher schools conducted by orders and religious congregations have been closed. The Polish Catholic Agency can no longer function.

"In the brochure we read: 'The German Catholics, of whom there are millions, living both in the old and in the new provinces of the Reich, live in complete freedom of religious observance.'

"If among these new provinces the districts of Western Poland are also included, and if, as we have said, it is a question of the two archbishoprics and several dioceses, that statement is not in accordance with the reality even in regard to the German Catholics, who, at least in certain areas, have been forbidden to take part in services conducted by Polish priests.

"These areas are inhabited by millions of Catholics, who are living in the worst of religious conditions. A certain number of churches, including the cathedrals, have been closed. The entrance of the faithful to many other churches is allowed only during a few hours of holy days and on very few ordinary days. Hundreds of priests, monks, and nuns have been sent into exile and shut away in concentration camps, where not a few of them have died. Many parishes are deprived of clergy; the priests who are left have insufficient means of existence, as they do not receive the salary which they formerly received from the Republic of Poland. Almost all the training colleges are closed. The diocesan authorities have not got the necessary freedom to govern the faithful; certain bishops have been refused permission to return to their dioceses, other bishops are interned or exiled.

"From the foregoing brief information it is evident to what extent the religious life of the Poles is not taking such a normal course as one would like to believe. The Polish Catholics to a large extent need rather the prayers of Catholics all over the world, that they may endure the test to which they are subjected."

3. Teaching the Truth

L'Osservatore Romano had the courage to oppose the great evils of the twentieth century: Fascism, Nazism, and Communism. It helped educate and inform Catholics throughout the world. It offered examples of persons who were champions of the faith during this tragic century. The Vatican declared: "Belonging to the National Socialist Party of Hitler is irreconcilable with the Catholic conscience."[2] In fact, in his book, *Who Voted for Hitler?*[3] Richard Hamilton proves that in 1932, when the Nazis were beginning their climb to power, German Catholics voted overwhelmingly—more than 85 percent—against Hitler's National Socialism.

News items from *L'Osservatore Romano* were regularly reported by *New York Times* correspondents. The *Times* printed the following: "The *Osservatore Romano*, Vatican organ, joins issue with Chancellor Adolf Hitler today for his statement to the Reichstag that there is no religious persecution in Germany. If by persecution is meant persecution unleashed with fire and sword, Herr Hitler may be considered rigorously correct, but nobody can deny that a subtler and perhaps deadlier form of persecution is at present carried on against the Catholic Church in Germany."[4] Everything was done in Germany to keep youth away from religion. The clergy was exposed to public scorn by means of scandalous trials, the parish priest's mission was suspected, watched and hindered, legislation contrary to Christian marriage was in force, confessional institutions abolished and religious instruction reduced to teaching those things that do not oppose National Socialist principles and doctrines.

The German press, according to *L'Osservatore Romano*, carried on an antireligious campaign that "spares neither God nor the

Redeemer nor the Gospel nor the Church. In this same press, the Pope is dragged with the bishops and clergy, with the sacraments and religious services, through a sea of insults and immoral caricatures on pages that concede the right of asylum to every most incredible audacity....Nor is this all."

L'Osservatore Romano continued. "The anti-religious campaign is carried on also by means of street posters that are even more harmful, because such posters are seen by every one, even children. Propaganda is carried on everywhere in offices, factories, schools and clubs so as to give any one who resists it the impression that he [the Pope] is an anachronism and relic of a bygone age. Sinister symptoms have not been lacking to warn that the propaganda of hate may finally explode in sanguinary episodes."

The *New York Times* reported on September 16, 1939, that the Vatican disputed the Italian explanation of the closing of churches in the Reich. The Stefani News Agency dispatched a message regarding stories printed in the foreign press about anti-Catholic measures of the Reich: "Recently a certain number of churches have been closed in Germany. These are buildings which, being far from habitations, do not offer a possibility, in case of aerial alarms, for the faithful to reach refuges in time. So far as the Catholic press is concerned, restrictions have been adopted because of the scarcity of paper. The number of Catholic reviews and periodicals, therefore, has been reduced to five. All these measures anyway are likewise applied to the Evangelical Church."[5]

In response, *L'Osservatore Romano* noted that German anti-Catholic measures were not confined to closing churches and reducing the number of Catholic periodicals. It pointed out that isolated churches would not be targets for bombs and hence would not constitute places so dangerous that they needed to be kept permanently closed. As for the periodicals, it noted that there were 30,000,000 Catholics in Germany and the reduction to five publications could not be justified even by the necessity for restricting the consumption of paper. The Vatican condemned the Catholic persecution in Germany and permitted its official organ to comment critically on a dispatch from Berlin excusing German measures.

When an attempt to assassinate Hitler did not succeed, *L'Osservatore Romano*[6] cautioned the German press not to seize upon the attempt to disseminate hatred among the people against another power, meaning Britain, by charging the latter with organizing the assassination attempt. Caution should especially be exercised after the Communist International's manifesto, which the newspaper terms "a cynical world appeal" showing the hatred of Communism for Germany and the democracies alike. The German charges are "the exasperation of tension harbored by two hostile sides. Unfortunately, in all frantic times, and especially under the nightmare of war, similar mad effects of collective psychosis always occur."

On November 10, 1939, Abel Nicolas Leger, Haitian Minister to the Vatican, presented his credentials to Pius XII. The following day, *New York Times* correspondent Herbert L. Matthews wrote: "The Pope suggested today the formation after the war of 'a stable and fruitful international organization.' …It is significant as the first indication that he has something to propose when peace comes. His speech contained another condemnation of 'the cult of force employed against law' which is considered to be his third indirect attack against Germany in two weeks. His encyclical and his sermon at St. Peter's on October 29 were also taken as attacks against Nazism.…As he did in his encyclical, the Pontiff again today stressed 'the unity of the great human family.…' Vatican circles say that when the Pope makes such remarks he intends them to be a reproach against racism, which does not recognize human unity or the equality of those converted to Christianity. Today's reference is considered particularly significant because the Pope was speaking to a representative of a predominantly Negro State.…

"There is grave anxiety at the Vatican regarding the threat to the neutrality of the Netherlands and Belgium, and it seems certain that the Pope's animosity toward German procedure would be greatly increased if the Reich violated either of those frontiers. On the juridical side an article in *Osservatore Romano* gives what is considered the official Vatican viewpoint. It says: 'The difficulties placed on the commerce of a neutral country do not justify remonstrances from another belligerent toward that neutral State. The Netherlands is a neutral country and remains so in so far as she leaves nothing undone to defend her neutrality. Nobody can accuse the Netherland Government of neglecting any of those means of procedures that a neutral government can employ in its defense against the demands of belligerents.'"[7]

At the end of the war there were many demonstrations of thanks and gratitude from the Jews saved through the assistance of Church institutions. Abramo Giacobbe Isaia Levi, a man of renowned intellect and a Senator of the Kingdom of Italy until the promulgation of the racial laws, was hidden in a convent during the Nazi occupation of Rome. He and his wife later converted to Christianity. He died in 1949 and, in his will, left a large sum of money to help elderly and impoverished Italian Jews. His beautiful estate in the center of Rome, Villa Levi, was renamed Villa Giorgina, in memory of his young daughter who died prematurely. In his will he donated it to Pope Pius XII because he had been "preserved from the dangers of evil racial persecution, overthrower of every relationship of human life" and was "grateful for the protection that was provided me in that turbulent period by the Sisters of the Infant Mary."

The fact that Pius XII saved thousands of Jews from the gas chambers cannot be obliterated by revisionists. Nor can the fact that the Jewish Community praised the Pope's efforts during and after the Holocaust be denied. Apparently, posterity wishes to ignore these facts. This is the real "silence."

Voices of hindsight are judging the Pope's "silence" without considering the consequences of "speaking out." Those critics do not recall that the Pope had been advised by Jewish leaders and by the bishops in occupied countries not to protest publicly against the Nazi atrocities. However, Pius XII frequently invoked "God's vengeance" on the persecutors. His words were the brave words of a diplomat who put focus on "those who are responsible."

Why is it that Pope Pius XII's numerous protests have been and are ignored by the world press? His messages and addresses have been and are available in the records of both the Vatican Radio and the Vatican newspaper, *L'Osservatore Romano.*

"The Church did not submit to Germany," wrote Paolo Vincentin in an article that appeared in *L'Osservatore Romano* in 1965. "We who were members of the German Embassy, although we judged the situation differently, were in complete accord on one point: a solemn protest by Pius XII against the persecution of the Jews probably would have exposed him and the Roman Curia to great danger and certainly then, in the autumn of 1943, he would not have been able to save the life of a single Jew."

L'Osservatore Romano (August 6, 1967) justly observed: "Who can count the languages of the Vatican Information Service? Every living, universal, local language,[8] even dead languages. Also Latin, the language of the Church, a language that became fire as a perpetual Pentecost warming the will and the heart of individuals in the midst of warfare. *Tu es Petrus,* in sixty-two languages."

An article, in *L'Osservatore Romano,* November 1, 1998, by the Honorable Herbert Schambeck, President of the Parliament of the Federal Republic of Austria, stated: "The total number of Jews who, also thanks to Christian assistance, survived Hitler in that part of Europe occupied by the Nazis, and leaving Russia apart, was about 945,000. Officially the number of Jews to whose salvation the Catholic Church contributed is given as 700,00 but probably their number should be 800,000."[9] Schambeck also quoted impressive Jewish testimony from Rabbi André Ungar and the Chief Rabbi of Rome, Elio Toaff.

In his allocution to the cardinals,[10] Pius XII clearly referred to the Jews: "Do not be astonished....There are those who, because of their nationality or their descent, are pursued by mounting misfortune and increasing suffering and extermination." The Germans and Italians were so astonished that they suppressed this section from all their reports of what the Pope had said. But the Vatican wireless broadcasted it to Germany.

Similar facts are documented by Jesse Lynch, an American citizen known as Mother Mary St. Luke, who worked in the Vatican during World War II. In her diary, *Inside Rome with the Germans,*[11] published under the pen name of Jane Scrivener, she depicts the role of Pope Pius XII and the Vatican with great spontaneity—a vivid and authentic eyewitness account about Pope Pius XII's rescue efforts and those of others in consonance with him.

The author describes the months of suspense, hope, and despair as food was scarce and the city of Rome was overcrowded with refugees and escaped war prisoners. Many details about the Allied bombings and other historic events taking place in Rome are included. In her entry for December 3, 1943, she mentions the work of women in the Church: "The nuns here have been magnificent in the midst of bombardments, evacuations and many other tragic circumstances of war. With superhuman strength of mind and body, in the teeth of chaos they have organized, and in the teeth of famine they have fed the hungry and harboured the shelterless. Indeed mute and inglorious they have been and are. Individuality is hidden beneath the uniforms they wear; they are not out for medals or ribbons or recognition; but if people in the Allied countries salute women in uniform, they certainly ought to salute women wearing the religious dress, when they get here, at last. The salute will have been earned."

Significantly, the entry includes reference to the courage of the Catholic newspaper *L'Osservatore Romano:* "Today the Vatican daily, *L'Osservatore Romano,* published a strong protest against the treatment of Jews; it is called forth by the new directions issued by the 'Republic' to the heads of the Provinces, to the effect that all Jews must be sent to concentration camps. The order was issued obviously at the instigation of the Germans."

L'Osservatore pointed out: "It is unreasonable, unchristian and inhuman. Times are bad enough, it says, without our creating fresh sources of suffering and anxiety; we are sorely in need of God's help, which we can gain by exercising charity toward His creatures, and all of us, nations as well as individuals, are in need of that today. Let us take care to be just and merciful, it concludes, and to pay our own debts so that God may remit ours with both justice and mercy."[12]

The *New York Times* noted the gratitude of Jews who universally praised Pope Pius XII for his humanitarian efforts. According to the renowned journalist Herbert I. Matthews: "Much could be written on the Pontiff's encouragement of the Vatican's important work for refugees and war prisoners and of the support he gave to the Vatican's campaign to save Italian art and cultural treasures from destruction. No Pope could have done more along the simple lines of charity and helpfulness than Pius XII....The Vatican's population grew, for in that period under the Pope's direction the Holy See did an extraordinary job of sheltering and championing the victims of the Nazi-Fascist regime. I have spoken to dozens of Jews, who owe their liberty and perhaps their lives to the protection of the church....Through all the worldly strife, and the new and difficult burdens laid upon him by this war the Pope's role has remained what it always has been and what he chose that it should be—that of peacemaker and conciliator...."[13]

Pius XII's words were an indictment of Hitler's war crimes. He warned the world about the consequences of Nazi policies and responded as best he could to suffering people throughout Europe. Despite the wealth of evidence proving Pius XII's innocence and heroism, one of the biggest lies of our time—that the Pope was "silent" about Hitler's efforts to exterminate the Jewish people—continues.

Professor Ronald Rychlak provides convincing evidence as he addresses three of the major twentieth-century topics in his book *Hitler, the War, and the Pope.*[14] He refutes those who present Pope Pius XII as anti-Semitic, passive, and silent in the face of the Holocaust. With the expertise of a "legal" historian, his arguments are clear and concise as he destroys John Cornwell's defamatory book: *Hitler's Pope: The Secret History of Pius XII.*

In a lengthy epilogue, Rychlak takes Cornwell to task in his analysis of the author's inaccuracies and misrepresentations regarding Pius XII's words and actions. It is a comprehensive defense that offers readers a clear exposition of facts and documents that contradict Cornwell's theses. Indeed, it is a balanced exposition that must be considered in any discussion of this contemporary and much-debated topic.

The Vatican sent countless protests to the Nazis. Did Pius XII do the best he could for those who were being persecuted? He definitely did more than any other world leader. He could not do more publicly. In a conflict of unprecedented violence, Pius XII proved to be a man of extraordinary compassion. The Catholic Church, with its international network under the central direction of Pius XII, saved the lives of hundreds of thousands.

Pius XII is not the real target, but John Paul II and the very future of the papacy are at stake. Rychlak's research took him to the Vatican archives, where he reviewed the same documents that John Cornwell had used; yet the results are different. Historian John Jay Hughes called *Hitler, the War, and the Pope* "a massive refutation of the black legend depicting Pius XII as passive and silent in the face of the Holocaust out of fear, cynicism, and anti-Semitism." Professor Robert George of Princeton University observed that "the myth is buried under an avalanche of facts and demonstrates that Pacelli's reputation deserves to be what it was during the war."

More than once the *New York Times* praised Pius XII as "a lonely voice crying out of the silence of a continent." Who can refute Golda Meir's observation that "the Pope raised his voice to condemn the persecutors and to commiserate with their victims?" The strained relations between the Catholic Church and Hitler's Third Reich as well as the efforts of Pope Pius XII to protect Jews and other victims of the Nazis need to be examined.

Only by looking at Pius XII's actions, inactions, silence, and statements in the context of their time can one explain the Pope's position. Rychlak wrote: "Pius was well aware of the Church's vulnerability with regard to the Italian Fascist state, which could violate the Lateran Treaty at any time, treat the Vatican as a subordinate state rather than an equal, and establish national Catholic churches apart from the Vatican. He was especially concerned about the ability of the Holy See to provide for the needs of the Church and the people if the Vatican were under the control of a Fascist government."[15]

According to Michael O'Carroll, Pius XII wrote to German Bishop von Preysing and refrained from "speaking out" to protect the persecuted: "We are leaving to the pastors, according to each location, the care of evaluating if, and in what measure, the danger of reprisals and pressure, as well as perhaps other circumstances due to the length and psychology of war, warrant restraint—despite the reasons for intervening—so as to avoid greater evils. This is one of the reasons for which We ourselves are imposing limits in Our declarations."[16]

The Pope's compassion is reflected in his personal letter of April 30, 1943, as he explains to Bishop von Preysing, the difficult situation of the Holy See. He describes the aerial attacks and his efforts to make the aerial war more human. He speaks of the Vatican Information Bureau for prisoners of war. He refers to the German veto on news of prisoners; information requested in Russia was also refused. The Pope approves the very clear sermons of the Bishop; he sees positive results of these declarations for the future. He approves of the help given to non-Aryans. He expresses his sympathy for Monsignor Lichtenberg and his concern for preserving the youth from the pernicious conception of the times. For him the liturgical question passes to the second place.

Other considerations are: whether the reprisals one fears render possible or not the public declarations of the Church; motives for the reserve of the Pope; measures taken against the Church, particularly against the Poles, above all in "Warthegau," and against the priests in concentration camps. Pope Pius XII refers to the memorandum of the German episcopate sent to the government. He describes the assistance of the Holy See to the non-Aryans and the limitations of this assistance.

He appreciates the fidelity of German Catholics and stresses his particular concern for the youth.

L'Osservatore Romano found it necessary to recapitulate the long record of papal condemnations of Nazi and Fascist persecution of the Jews (*The Tablet,* July 30, 1955). This was in reply to certain Israeli newspapers which had been reporting that the Pope could have done more than he did to stop it. One newspaper, *Hakol,* an organ of the Orthodox Jews, stated that it was not clear "why the Pope had not published an Encyclical to raise the alarm among Christians about the Nazi excesses." Yet *Hakol* acknowledged with gratitude "the immense work of humane assistance undertaken by the Pontiff to save a great number of Jews during the Second World War." *L'Osservatore Romano* also quoted the following statement from another newspaper, *Maariv:* "During the Hitlerite massacres, the Catholic Church has shown herself most humane, and we know that many Christians have saved great numbers of Jewish lives....However, it does not seem that the Pope sufficiently manifested his indignation over the massacres of millions of Jews."

To refresh memories, and not without sharp comment, *L'Osservatore* therefore quoted at length what the Pope said on this topic on repeated occasions during the war, recalling also that at a Congress of Refugees held in Italy in 1945 the delegates asked for "the honor of expressing personally their thanks to the Pope for his generosity towards the victims of Nazi and Fascist persecution."

Ralph McInerny warned in his editorial (*Catholic Dossier,* January-February 2001): "There is something diabolical about the campaign to portray the Church of Christ as the enemy of mankind, an obstacle to progress and happiness. Diabolical, but not really new. From the account in Genesis and throughout the Bible, Satan has been portrayed principally as a liar. The truth is not in him. It is under his banner that march those who would portray good as evil, truth as falsity, and Pius XII, the greatest friend the Jewish people ever had, as their enemy."

In the lead book review of *The Tablet* of London (June 30, 2001), Owen Chadwick, a well-respected British historian, responded to Susan Zuccotti's *Under His Very Windows: The Vatican and the Holocaust in Italy:* "At times it looks as though this excellent narrative is told not for its own sake but to prove that the Vatican did nothing to help. Susan Zuccotti believes that 'the myth of papal involvement in the rescue of the Jews continues to grow' and must be diminished. She keeps emphasising that these courageous and life-risking endeavours were carried on without any instruction, order, encouragement, from the Vatican. But why should they have been? The most fanatical bull-on-the-breakfast-table papalist does not demand an order from the Pope before a Christian needs to behave like a decent person when faced by murder....Historians need to let facts speak for themselves. There are sentences here which tire the reader, preaching that far more could have been said, that this letter or utterance was grossly inadequate to the occasion....If the author were not a historian, one might suspect that she had an obsession about any document coming out of the Vatican....All this is not history but guesswork."

Part IV
The Discussion Continues

Chapter X
Feeding the Controversy

---

1. The Controversy

No modern pope has generated as much controversy as Pius XII, and few modern leaders have had the vision and have influenced society as he did in all fields of activity. He was indeed a leader for all times. He prepared the way for Vatican Council II, which was later implemented by Pope John XXIII and succeeding popes.

Why does the media focus attention on Pope Pius XII's presumed silence? While Pius XII was a leading spiritual figure, he was not a political entity. Why is he on trial? The record shows that the Vatican not only sent numerous papal protests to the German government, but also saved hundreds of thousands of lives. What protests were sent from Washington or from London? Did these governments listen to Pius XII's pleas for peace before the outbreak of World War II? How often did the United States and Great Britain denounce the Holocaust? Present-day critics and journalists continue to demonstrate their hostility to Catholicism when they state that Pius XII was "silent." Contrary to the charges of critics, he was consistently anti-Nazi in words and actions, both before and after he became Pope. Indeed, Pius XII spoke about the Holocaust, but in a way that would not compromise the practical commitment to fight the Nazis. Under his courageous and compassionate leadership, the Catholic Church saved hundreds of thousands of Jews. These facts are supported by eleven volumes of more than five thousand documents.[1]

Critics completely ignore this evidence and perpetuate the spurious claims based solely on speculation and on the distortion of truth. John Cornwell's book, *Hitler's Pope: The Secret History of Pius* XII, damns and vilifies Pope Pius XII more than any previous volume.[2] It appeared in late September 1999, in American and European book-stores promoted by extraordinary radio, TV, and media ballyhoo. The media repeated the book's falsehoods, misrepresentations, and exaggerations. Cornwell himself toured America to focus on his book's two main themes—the villainy of Pius XII and the need to destroy the papacy. *Hitler's Pope* is a vicious character assassination of Pope Pius XII, replete with inaccuracies and omissions. It is indeed an attack on the Catholic Church and its Magisterium.

Reading Cornwell's book, as well as his promotional materials, and listening, on radio and TV, as he cleverly and glibly dodges criticisms in order to attack Pius XII, John Paul II, and the Church has been a painful experience for me. Even thirty years of passively enduring endless attacks on Catholicism by the dominant media hardly prepared me for the insidiously clever ways Cornwell presented himself and his half-truths and falsehoods.

Unfortunately, Cornwell has included just enough plausible history and carefully selected quotations, dressed up by a fistful of footnotes from previous Pius XII critics, to hoodwink the average reader into thinking this book is a serious work of historical scholarship. Nothing is further from the truth. The book is an accomplished work of historical revisionism, whose claims are so extreme and camouflaged with such flimsy evidence that they would be more suitable to a work of fantasy than a work of supposed historical scholarship.

2. The Crusades

The article "The Crusades, Even Now" by Karen Armstrong in the magazine section of the *New York Sunday Times* (September 19, 1999) charged that the Crusades caused anti-Semitism: "It was after all the murderous anti-Semitism of Europe, first unleashed by the Crusades, that made the State of Israel a necessary haven for the Jewish people. It was also the ferocity of the Crusader attacks that shaped for Muslims of the region a lasting impression of persistent Western aggression."

However, Karen Armstrong's history lesson is biased and misleading. Robert H. Goldsborough[3] explains that the Crusades responded to Islamic and Jewish assaults on Christianity and Christian nations. The First Crusade began in November 1095, when Pope Urban II called forth the Knights of Europe to aid the Orthodox Christians of Byzantium and to free part of Anatolia, which had recently been conquered by Islamic tribes. Goldsborough quotes the historian Philip Hughes: "The new successful Catholic offensive against Islam [was] an offensive undertaken in Spain, and also in those Eastern lands whence Islam had first issued forth to destroy a whole Christian empire....."[4]

Goldsborough writes: "For nearly eight centuries, until the reign of Queen Isabella, the Muslims inflicted torture, death, and destruction on the Spanish Christians. Christian churches were used as mosques; Christian children were kidnapped, sold into slavery, and raised as Muslims. To the devout Crusader, the destruction of the Christian faith was a far greater evil than the taking of a human life. The lost soul passes into eternal damnation, whereas the lost life (especially in defense of the Faith) can be the passage to eternal life in Christ."

Isabella, the Crusader, who believed that as Queen it was her sacred duty to protect the faithful, proclaimed on March 31, 1492, that certain Jews must live separately from Christians because those Jews "have demonstrated that they would always endeavor by all possible ways and manners to subvert and draw away faithful Christians from our Holy Catholic Faith....."

Four centuries later, Rabbi Louis Israel Newman published an extensive compendium on the influence of Judaism and the Talmud in shaping the many heresies that attempt to undermine Christianity. The article ends by apologizing to the Jews and asking "forgiveness for past Catholic transgressions. We await a response from Jewish leaders apologizing for the centuries of devastation that Jews, in alliance with the Muslims, inflicted upon Christians."

3. Martin Luther

According to Andrea Tornielli's article, Hitler's followers executed the program found in Luther's book *Von den Juden und ihren Lugen* (1543), translated from German into Latin by Justus Jonas. This volume was unknown to the Italian reader until 1998, when it was published with a commentary by Attilio Agnoletto, a professor of the history of Christianity at the University of Milan. Although unknown in Italy, it had been much appreciated in Hitler's Germany. In 1936, it was circulated in a version edited by the evangelical theologian Dr. Linden.

"Special attention was given to the seven points of *Salutaria con-silia*—executive recommendations—some of which are: forced labor and the destruction of synagogues which were followed literally by the Nazis. Luther's 'salutary advice to get rid of the blasphemous Jewish doctrine' appears in fact like a definite plan for *Kristallnacht* and the persecution of Jews.

"'First of all,' writes the Father of the Protestant Reformation, 'it is useful to burn their synagogues and sweep away their blasphemous doctrine. Secondly, their private homes should be destroyed. Meanwhile you can throw them in stables or huts with their wives and children.' After intimating that they should be 'deprived of their prayerbooks,' Luther advises that 'under pain of death the Rabbis should not be allowed to teach and Jews should be denied the public trust and safe-conduct.'"

Everything should be sequestered: "With very strict laws, usury should be forbidden and all their money, gold, and silver sequestered." Finally Martin Luther states that "work should be imposed on all young and robust Jews, men and women, so that they will earn their bread with the sweat of their brow." That the Nazi hierarchy would find in these words the legitimization of the concentration camps, is not difficult to imagine. "Certainly," writes Tornielli, "no one wants to blame the Protestants for anti-Semitism. The Catholic Church, with the Shoah document, *We Remember,* has asked pardon for the sins of Christians. But it is strange that during the commemoration of *Kristallnacht,* the one to be accused has been Pope Pius XII. In fact, he is the only one, at least in this case, who cannot be blamed. Instead, not a word about the Lutheran theologians who applauded and reprinted the ferocious anti-Jewish libel."

4. The Concordat

Hitler requested a concordat. If Pius XI had refused the negotiations, Hitler could have said that he extended a hand of peace, but it was summarily rejected. The persecution of the Catholic Church, which existed already on local levels, could have become a national government-sanctioned persecution. Totally false is the assertion by Cornwell that the Concordat only impeded political and social activities on the part of Catholics. It was agreed that priests and religious should not engage in "party" politics. No such restriction was applied to laypeople. Bishops and priests were granted permission to announce freely the Catholic doctrine on faith and morals. They made use of this permission without violating the Concordat. Cornwell repeats the totally incorrect and eventually totally debunked hoax that Pacelli was instrumental in the autodissolution of the Christian Center party (Zentrum).

In the Nuremberg trials, the Minister of Foreign Affairs, Joachim von Ribbentrop, admitted that Secretary of State Pacelli had sent scores of protests about infractions of the Concordat but that these were nearly always ignored by the Nazis. Finally in 1937 there came the encyclical letter *Mit brennender Sorge.* Pacelli was the main author of this powerful protest. Cornwell plays down or downright ignores the sharp condemnations of Nazism made by Papal Legate Pacelli at Lourdes, Lisieux, Paris, and Budapest.

It is true that neither Hitler nor Nazism were mentioned by name in the encyclical, but everybody understood against whom these condemnations were directed. Cornwell should have read newspapers (USA, England, France, Holland, etc.), as well as Nazi publications. Every objection against the tyranny of the Nazis imperiled Catholics in Germany (just as later happened in the countries occupied by the Nazis).

Cornwell belittles the serious efforts Pius XII made to prevent World War II and ridicules Pius XII's first encyclical, *Summi Pontificatus.* In fact, if this encyclical letter was so insignificant, as Cornwell wishes us to believe, why then did the Allies airdrop eighty-eight thousand copies of this letter over Germany, where it could not have been published?

There is evidence that Pius XII was deadly opposed both to National Socialism and to Communism. He thought, perhaps, that in the long run Communism was the greater danger for the world and for Christianity. Prime Minister Churchill never shared the optimism of President Roosevelt, who was convinced that the Russian Communists would change their ideology and their hostile attitude to religious communities. These facts are well known to all serious authors, but Cornwell avoids mentioning them.

Cornwell acknowledges the saintly life of Pius XII: "I believed that Pacelli's evident holiness was proof of his good faith."[5] After noting the Pope's "good faith," how could Cornwell deceitfully imply that Pius XII was pro-Nazi by using a provocative photograph of an ordinary ceremonial accorded Pacelli, years before Hitler came to power, for the jacket of his book?

Pacelli repeatedly went on record saying that Hitler's victory in World War II would mean the end of the Catholic Church in Europe. If he was indeed "Hitler's Pope," why did he transmit to the English government the proposal of a group of anti-Nazi German generals, who asked whether England would make peace with Germany, if they (the group of German generals) succeeded in arresting Hitler and removing him from government?

Incidentally, it was not a low-ranking officer, Colonel Oster, who was responsible for this proposal, but Colonel-General (four-star general) Ludwig Beck. The latter had been the chief of the German General Staff, but in 1938 resigned from this new post since he had become convinced that Hitler was a criminal who against all promises and treaties would attack other nations. Pacelli had known Beck when he was Nuncio in Berlin and highly esteemed his honesty and integrity. If Pius XII had been "Hitler's Pope," he would never have risked the dangers of passing on this anti-Hitler communication.

Cornwell contends that Pacelli's negotiations for the Concordat led to the demise of the Catholic Center party: "The principal condition imposed by Hitler in 1933 was to be nothing less than voluntary withdrawal of German Catholics from social and political action as Catholics, including the voluntary disbanding of the Center Party."[6] Contrary to these allegation by Cornwell, Pacelli did everything in his power to preserve Germany's Catholic Center party. In fact, the Vatican agreed to the Concordat with Germany only after Hitler's reign of terror forced the Catholic party to dissolve itself.

When the extermination of Jews began, the Dutch bishops issued a statement that unfortunately stirred the Nazis in the summer of 1942 to accelerate their roundup of Jews. Newspapers spoke of "deportation of 40,000 Jews of the Lowlands." That number included Jews, priests, and religious throughout the entire region. Cornwell disputes Pius XII's reported statement that there were forty thousand Jews, by calling this figure exaggerated.[7] However, everyone knew that the deportation was not limited to the Jews of Holland.

5. Critics

The Italian journalist Andrea Tornielli pointed out: "It is ironic that Meir Lau, Israel's Chief Rabbi, denounced the silence of Pope Pius XII after *Kristallnacht* on November 9, 1938." The Rabbi questioned: "Where was Pius XII in November of 1938." "Why didn't he denounce the violence of that night?" Tornielli writes: "Eugenio Pacelli was not yet Pope. He was in Rome, Secretary of State to Pius XI who did not hesitate to condemn racial hatred during an audience, stating: Spiritually we are all Semites." [The Rabbi seems to have forgotten that Eugenio Pacelli had not yet been elected to the Chair of Peter, which took place on March 2, 1939.]

What was Eugenio Pacelli doing in the Vatican? Even before *Kristallnacht,* he was assisting the Pontiff in writing the encyclical *Mit brennender Sorge* (March 14, 1937), with which the Catholic Church condemned Nazism. This was a denunciation that provoked Hitler's anger. It was written in German because the Vatican wanted it read in all the churches in Germany on Palm Sunday, March 21, 1937. In fact, the following day, the National Socialist party newspaper *Volkischer Beobachter* published a very poisonous counterattack to the "Jewish God and his Vicar in Rome."

Tornielli belongs to a group of Jewish and Christian writers who want to spread the truth. However, the difficulty lies with the fact that prejudice regarding the "silence" of the Pontiff is a very popular theme. Apparently, the media refuses to acknowledge the truth. Yet, the facts cannot be denied. Over sixty years ago on *Kristallnacht,* the Nazis destroyed fourteen hundred synagogues and stores belonging to Jewish citizens in Germany and Austria. German newspapers published statements by Lutheran theologians who, far from condemning the violence, were pleased that the persecution began on Martin Luther's birthday.

6. Fosse Ardeatine

It should be noted that the Salesians [members of the Society of St. Francis de Sales] were in charge of the Catacombs of St. Callixtus on the Appian Way. The Nazis knew the Salesians sheltered and fed some 376 Jews hidden in the catacombs, but they could not invade the property because it was extraterritorial, belonging to the Holy See and not legally part of Italy.

On March 24, 1944, the Nazis massacred 335 civilian hostages at the Fosse Ardeatine. Pius XII could not intervene with the Nazis as he had on so many other occasions because he knew nothing about the massacre until it was over. The reprisal, completed within twenty-four hours, was carried out in secrecy. After the execution, the Caves were sealed with explosives. A few days later, a group of seminarians discovered the bodies near the Catacombs of St. Callixtus.

Cornwell accuses Pius XII of having had prior knowledge of plans for the March 24, 1944, Rome massacre. This is an old lie, which has long ago been disproved. He states that Pius XII's sister and nephew sued perpetrators of this lie in a Roman court. It was not the Pope's sister and nephew who brought this to court; it was his niece! It was Elena Rossignani Pacelli who brought suit for defamation against film producer Carlo Ponti, author Robert Katz (*Death in Rome,* 1967) and director George Pan Cosmatos.[8]

After the trial and appeals, the producer, author, and director were found guilty of calumny against Pope Pius XII. Cornwell totally twisted the court's decision in this famous case and falsely reported the verdict. To quote from *Hitler's Pope:* "The Pacellis lost, but appealed, and the case was eventually judged inconclusive."[9] The truth is that on February 7, 1981, the Italian court found that Pope Pius XII had been falsely accused.

Many more examples could be cited. Cornwell portrays Cardinal Henri de Lubac—the great French Catholic anti-Nazi theologian—as being progressive and totally opposed to Pius XII (pp. 274–79). The truth is, however, that de Lubac was a great admirer of Pius XII and wrote a book of wartime memoirs, *Christian Resistance to Anti-Semitism: Memories from 1940–1944,*[10] in which he discusses Pius XII's influence on Catholic rescuers of Jews. Nowhere does Cornwell mention this book.

Cornwell also quotes Cardinal Tisserant out of context on page 262, to suggest that Tisserant denounced Pius XII in a private letter to Cardinal Suhard.[11] In fact, in "Interview," *Informations Catholiques Internationales,*[12] as well as in other Catholic papers, Cardinal Tisserant clearly stated that he was not criticizing Pius XII, whom he admired, but criticizing members of the Curia for not carrying out the Pope's policies.

Concerning Pius XII, Cardinal Tisserant said: "The Pope's attitude was beyond discussion. My remarks did not involve his person, but certain members of the Curia....If the consequences of a protest were to fall on himself alone, Pius XII would not have been in the slightest way concerned. Everyone knows that he was ready to go to a concentration camp. But he weighed before all else the mortal risks to which the victims of Nazism could be exposed in the case of a protest...."[13]

7. Nikolaus Kunkel

On January 24, 2001, *L'Osservatore Romano* carried the testimony of a witness to Pius XII's actions to save Roman Jews during the Second World War. In an interview with German Catholic News Agency (KNA), Nikolaus Kunkel, a lieutenant at the headquarters of the military governor of Rome in 1943, directly witnessed the SS roundup of the Jews. He remembers those dramatic days, when the SS wanted to take advantage of the transition of power from Mussolini to Badoglio to carry out "the final solution to the Jewish question."

When asked if he thought that a more vigorous protest from Pope Pius XII would have saved more Jews in Rome, the rest of Italy, and occupied Europe, Kunkel stated: "At the time I spoke about this with my immediate superior, Major Böhm, a Protestant from Hamburg. We were both of the opinion that, faced with Hitler's unpredictability, any action directed to world public opinion by the Pope would have been harmful....Pius XII was in a most difficult political situation. Considering the circumstances, no one can reproach him for his actions."

The SS unit's task was to deport all the Jews in Rome. According to Kunkel, "...when the rumor of the raid proved to be true, Major General Rainer Stahel summoned and informed the officers of divisions 1A, 1B and 1C saying that he was totally opposed to the operation."

Roman Jews were rounded up on October 16, 1943. That same day the rector of Santa Maria dell'Anima, Bishop Alois Hudal, and Father Pancrazio Pfeiffer called on General Stahel, informing him that the Pope would turn to world public opinion if the roundup was not immediately stopped. The next day the order came from SS Chief Heinrich Himmler to stop.

Kunkel recalled that "most Roman Jews had got wind of the imminent SS action because of delays in the preparations and so many of them were saved....We considered it a success that only 1,000 of the 8,000 or 9,000 or so Jews were arrested by the SS. Today, of course, one looks above all at the 1,000 victims....By the way, a few days after the roundup and despite his poor health, General Stahel—a Catholic— was transferred to the Eastern front."

Again during a March 1, 2001, interview with the German News agency KNA, Kunkel confirmed that the Vatican played a decisive role in stopping the Nazi roundup of Rome's Jews. He reiterated that, having been informed of a papal protest in favor of the Jews, General Stahel immediately contacted SS Chief Heinrich Himmler, who ordered SS Lieutenant Colonel Herbert Kappler, Chief of the German security police in Rome, to end further roundups.

Nikolaus Kunkel's testimony and Eichmann's revelations in his memoirs decisively refute Susan Zuccotti's claim in *Under His Very Windows* (p. 169), regarding "no evidence" that Pope Pius XII helped save Roman Jews.

8. The Spin Master

Why does Cornwell spin this tale? Today any competent scholar can obtain access to the Vatican archives without saying anything about being "favorable" or "unfavorable" to any pontiff or ecclesiastic. Further, what honest scholar approaches his or her subject with a closed mind? The only side a real scholar is on is the side of truth. What does Cornwell get by presenting himself as the honest spy in the Vatican? It is a self-serving gimmick that assumes Vatican vice.

Almost everything about Cornwell's description of his research in the archives is fiction. He writes: "For months on end I ransacked Pacelli's files, which dated back to 1912, in a windowless dungeon beneath the Borgia Tower in Vatican City...."[14] What have we here? The heroic detective working in a dungeon, feverishly rifling through top secret files, just a few feet below the room where the Borgias committed unspeakable crimes. But the fact is, the archive is not a dungeon, just an ordinary underground vault where files are stored.

Cornwell is cleverly vague about the files he was examining, saying they "dated back to 1912." This gives the impression that the files went from 1912 to 1958 without explaining that the available archives' files stop in 1922. He "ransacked" only files from 1912 through 1922!

Cornwell also misleads us about the length of time spent in the archives. He says it was "months on end." But the Vatican reports that he used the archives for three weeks. "Months on end" is not three weeks. For the period of Cornwell's research the reports state: "In that archive precise annotations are made about the purpose of the day, and the period of time (hours and minutes) that each person employs to carry out his consultation. From these data, it is deduced that Mr. Cornwell was admitted to the archive from May 12 to June 2 of 1997....Mr. Cornwell did not come every day; and on the days he did come, often his stay was for very brief periods of time"[15]

One more example of Cornwell's exaggerated, spy-thriller style of writing: "By the middle of 1997," he says, "I was in a state of moral shock. The material I had gathered amounted not to an exoneration but to an indictment...." What caused his "moral shock"? In his own words: "Long buried Vatican files reveal a new and shocking indictment of World War II's Pope Pius XII: that in pursuit of absolute power he helped Adolf Hitler destroy German Catholic political opposition, betrayed the Jews of Europe, and sealed a deeply cynical pact with a 20th-century devil."[16]

This is ridiculous. It is complete fiction—the work of a mystery writer fictionalizing a dungeon where he discovered buried documents that cast light on one of the greatest tragedies in recorded history and reveal a secret pact with the devil himself. The truth is that the documentary evidence that Cornwell quotes was not "buried." It was available to any scholar in the world, and in fact what Cornwell cites as his most important document, a 1919 letter, had already been published in 1992 by an Italian scholar Professor Emma Fattorini in *Germany and the Holy See: The Pacelli Nunciature between the Great War and the Weimar Republic.*[17]

And what of Pius XII's supposed pact with Hitler? Cornwell discovered nothing. He did not even have access to archival material after 1922. His research was limited to two series of documents: Bavaria (1918–21) and Austria (Serbia, Belgrade: 1913–15). Thus, the "long-buried files" concerned matters prior to 1922. Cornwell did have access to documents concerned with Pius's possible canonization. But these are not "long-buried files."

One of the most respected authorities for the history of the Catholic Church and the Second World War is Peter Gumpel, S.J., a church historian, who is the Relator (by papal appointment, the investigative judge) of the cause for Pope Pius XII's beatification. In light of the controversy provoked by *Hitler's Pope,* Peter Gumpel's rebuttal takes on special significance.

9. Cornwell Ignores Facts

One wonders whether Cornwell knew of the famous Jewish surgeon Guido Mendes, who was a schoolmate of Eugenio Pacelli. Young Eugenio and Guido visited each other's homes and remained in touch over the years. When the Fascists began to threaten Jews in Italy, Secretary of State Pacelli helped the Mendes family flee to Jerusalem. Why would not such a historian as Cornwell have known about this friendship? How could he delve into Pius XII's relationship with the Jews without mentioning it? How can he suggest that Pacelli was an antiblack racist? Rather, he was an outspoken champion of blacks and explicitly condemned segregation. In fact, upon his election as Pope, he elevated African priests to the episcopacy. Cornwell accuses Pacelli of delivering a speech in Hungary that was a thinly veiled attack upon the Jews, while the speech was actually an attack upon the Nazis. It later inspired eminent Jewish historian Jenö Levai to write his book *Pius XII Was Not Silent* (London: Sands and Co., 1968).

Cornwell ignores the Vatican documents of 1916 and 1928 that condemn anti-Semitism. As Secretary of State, Pacelli issued a statement (October 11, 1930): "Belonging to the National Socialist Party of Hitler is irreconcilable with the Catholic conscience." In 1934, after the first Nazi massacre in Germany, Pacelli published three articles against the movement. In 1935, in an open letter of March 12 to Cardinal Schulte of Cologne, he attacked the Nazis "as false prophets" for attempting to create a "mendacious antinomy between faithfulness to the Church and to the Fatherland."

John Cornwell refers to Sister Pascalina Lehnert's memoirs, *Ich durfte ihm dienen: Erinnerungen an Papst Pius XII* (1982), which he claims to have consulted. This book explicitly states that Eugenio Pacelli warned the Germans against Adolf Hitler in 1929, four years before the dictator came into power on January 30, 1933. When asked if Hitler could perhaps help the German people, Pacelli shook his head and said: "Who among these has at least read his horrifying book, *Mein Kampf*? I would be very much mistaken in thinking that all this could end well." The future Pope Pius XII could not understand why even highly competent Germans did not share his totally negative judgment. Either Cornwell did not read Sister Pascalina's book or he purposefully omitted this statement and other similar easily ascertainable statements of Pacelli simply because they do not tally with his destructive tendencies.

10. Notes

Unlike Cornwell, Jewish historian Pinchas Lapide, a practicing Jew, strongly defended Pope Pius XII. Why? "If fairness and historical justice are keystones of Jewish morality, then keeping silent in view of slanderous attacks on a benefactor is an injustice....Far more than two million Jews did indeed survive, thanks to the help of the Church, bishops, priests, laymen....The Talmud teaches us 'whoever saves a life receives as much credit as if he had saved an entire world.' If this is true—and it is just as true as the most typical of all Jewish principles: that of the holiness of human life—then a Jew must also defend loudly a great saver of Jewish life."[18]

But the real object of the controversy is not Pius XII. It is the Chair of Peter. Destroying Pius XII's reputation is only a means to an end, destroying the papacy and the Church as we know it. By denigrating Pius XII, depicted as authoritarian, traditional, and Roman, by painting John Paul II with the same brush, some writers are contributing to the goal of many confused Catholics—changing the Church into a social institution.

To quote, in part, a 1999 resolution passed by the Board of Directors of the Society of Catholic Social Scientists: "It is time to restore the truth as to the role of Pope Pius XII during World War II and the Holocaust and to address also the unjust attacks upon his proved, unequalled, and historic efforts in this regard, and upon his good, virtuous character. It is ironic, and should be a source of serious concern, that since the issuance of the Vatican document on the Shoah, these attacks have grown in frequency and vituperation. They have appeared in such major publications as the *New York Times* and *Atlantic Monthly*, and have also been carried on by spokesmen from major organizations."

This matter has taken on a particular urgency, however, with the publication of *Hitler's Pope*. Interestingly, reviews in *Time* magazine, the *New York Times,* the *Washington Post,* and other leading American publications are in contrast to the book's reception in Europe, where perhaps people have a firmer historical sense about the period. It also strongly underscores the need to set the record straight about the facts in the United States, where the apparent lack of this historical knowledge is making people prey to deliberate and careless distortions.

Repeatedly Pius XII protested against the unjust treatment of the occupied countries. However, especially the Polish bishops—except those who had fled Poland and lived abroad in safety, such as Cardinal Hlond and Bishop Radonski—begged the Pope not to protest, for such action would only aggravate the situation of oppression and persecution. Some writers are totally unaware of the situation and, therefore, a great many of their judgments and appraisals are completely unrealistic, utopian, and anachronistic. From a historical point of view, one must be able to understand the situation as it was then and not judge it with the hindsight from today's situation in free countries.

Prior to the appointment of Hitler as Chancellor, the German bishops had been warned against the Nazis and their pagan ideology. When Hitler became the legitimately appointed Chancellor of the Reich, a modus vivendi had to be found. It was then not clear to the bishops, the German politicians, and many German Jews how Hitler would act once he had obtained the government. However, the bishops did not approve his ideology. They increasingly protested against his actions. A public protest would have aggravated the persecution both of Jews and of Catholics. Moreover it would have impeded the very extensive silent action of helping Jews in every possible manner.

John Cornwell makes much of an interview that U.S. diplomat Harold Tittman had with Pope Pius XII. He says that this interview took place on October 18, 1943, thus a few days after the rounding-up of a thousand Jews. He accuses Pius XII of being so little concerned with the fate of the Jews that he did not even mention them. The whole argument falls flat. In fact, the dispatch of Tittman, in which he says to have had an interview with Pius XII "today," is dated not October 18, but October 19. Even the date "19" is wrong. The interview took place on October "14." This results from the very accurate lists of interviews granted to diplomats by Pius XII. The fact that this interview took place on October "14" is registered in two distinct volumes of the *Acts and Documents,* which Cornwell quotes and did not find it worth his time to check the date of this audience in *L'Osservatore Romano*. In this easily accessible newspaper he would have seen that the audience took place on October 14, 1943, that is, two days before the roundup of the Jews in the early hours of October 16, 1943.

According to protocol, a newly elected Pope informs all the governments with which the Holy See has diplomatic relations that this election has taken place. A personal note of Pius XII to Hitler was therefore necessary. The tone is moderate. The encyclical *Mit brennender Sorge* had declared in the clearest and sharpest possible way that Hitler was not trustworthy and that a treaty signed by him was worthless. And then in 1938, a year later, there was the ill-fated Munich Conference (England, France, Italy, Germany). Mr. Neville Chamberlain and Mr. Daladier thought that now there would be "Peace for our times, and peace forever!"

Little is said about the great encyclicals of Pius XII, namely *Mystici Corporis* (On the Church), *Divino afflante Spiritu* (On Advanced Scripture Studies), *Mediator Dei* (the liturgy's Magna Charta), as well as his numerous other encyclicals or speeches, which covered all modern problems. Cornwell has the impudence to make negative remarks on those important activities without which the Second Vatican Council would not have been possible. In fact, after Sacred Scripture, the Council's documents cite no single author as frequently as Pius XII. Cornwell attacks Pius XII on the document *Humani generis* without even realizing that there were, at that time, some tendencies of theological relativism emerging which needed to be corrected.

Today judgments on this whole question are far more just and balanced than they were then. Cornwell also refers to the question of the priest-workers. Pius XII appreciated the generosity of so many priest-workers, but felt it necessary to safeguard their priestly life by reducing the hours as workers in lay occupations. It was John XXIII, former Nuncio in Paris, who forbade radically the institute of priest-workers, which Paul VI restarted, while insisting on a severe selection and accurate formation and supervision.

Cornwell calls Pius XII ambitious and insinuates that he was a careerist. This is not true. The young Pacelli made rapid progress in his career because he was brilliant, conscientious, and hardworking. It was only in obedience to higher authority that he entered the diplomatic service of the Holy See. When in 1929, his task as Apostolic Nuncio had come to an end, he desired to become a diocesan Bishop and do pastoral work. When elected Pope, he did not accept his election immediately, but insisted on another ballot. When this was overwhelmingly in his favor, he accepted the election as a sign of God's will, but *"in signum crucis,"* as a heavy cross. Cornwell speaks of Pius XII's "narcissism." This cannot be substantiated.

During his reign Pius XII received many millions of people in public audiences. These audiences were different from those of later times. Pius XII went into the midst of people, talked to them, even heard confessions. Cornwell mocks Pius XII, claiming that he had his hands doused but forgets to say that in shaking so many hands, his own hands were frequently bruised and scratched. Undoubtedly people reacted to these audiences and saw in Pius a humble, charitable, saintly person.

John Cornwell ignores the scores of scientific and highly documented volumes of the Kommission für Zeitgeschichte, which now number well over forty volumes. He certainly knew about Jenö Levai's book. The prologue and epilogue of this book written by Dr. Robert Kempner—Chief Assistant Prosecutor of the United States of America at the Nuremberg trials—refute the attacks against Pius XII. Cornwell does not mention these judgments, which are in contrast with his thesis that Pius XII was "Hitler's Pope." He does not give importance to the fact that the International Red Cross (with headquarters in neutral Switzerland) came to exactly the same appraisal of the situation as Pius XII and equally refrained from loud protests so as not to jeopardize secret and silent actions helping Jews. The same applies to the then nascent Ecumenical Council of Christian Churches (also situated in neutral Switzerland). He quotes the work of Klaus Scholder, which has been severely criticized because of his anti-Catholic bias. Cornwell prefers Scholder to Volk, because this suits his negative thesis with regard to Pacelli. Obviously, he is also totally unaware of the fact that Scholder's book was severely criticized by German scholars.

He seems to have blind faith in what is published in the memoirs of the late Dr. Brüning. The latter was Chancellor of Germany in the desperate years 1930–1932 (i.e., after "Black Friday"—the 1929 New York Stock Market crash—the recall of loans made to Germany by foreign countries was followed by the unemployment of millions and the bankruptcy of numerous German banks and businesses). Brüning made serious economic mistakes. Qualified experts have rightly challenged the objective truth of his memoirs. John Cornwell quotes these memoirs and also claims to have studied all the *Acts* of the canonical inquiry made with regard to the beatification of Pius XII. He totally omits the nearly 100 percent of positive judgments of all these witnesses. This is not honest.

11. Propaganda

As a follow-up to Alessandra Stanley's review[19] of John Cornwell's book, *Hitler's Pope: The Secret History of Pius XII,* it is important to point out that she did not address the issue of Pius XII's "silence" during the Holocaust. She refers to the Christmas 1942 papal message but neglects the *New York Times* Christmas 1941 editorial that praised Pius XII for having "put himself squarely against Hitlerism." She ignores the fact that *L'Osservatore Romano* explicitly condemned "the immoral principles of Nazism";[20] that *The Tablet* of London reported that Nazi leader Goebbels condemned Pius XII as a "pro-Jewish Pope";[21] that the London *Times* praised Pius XII: "There is no room for doubt. He condemns the worship of force…and the persecution of the Jewish race."[22] And how can one ignore the countless survivors of the Holocaust who confirmed the fact that Pius XII frequently spoke out against the Nazis?

Cathy Lynn Grossman's piece in *USA Today* (September 7, 1999) on John Cornwell's excerpts from his book promotes clever, sensational propaganda. The *Vanity Fair* excerpts attack Pope Pius XII as "anti-Jewish," a "hypocrite," and "an ideal Pope for the Nazis' *Final Solution.*" Where is Cornwell's documentation for these statements?

Linda Massarella writes in the *New York Post:* "Cornwell says that when Eugenio Pacelli came to power in 1939, he knew about Hitler's plans for a *Final Solution.*" But where is Cornwell's documentation for this statement? Hitler's extermination program was not finalized and implemented until several years later. The debate on this continues. Some consider mid-1941 as the earliest date for the "finalization" of the scheme. However, according to Louis Snyder in the *Encyclopedia of the Third Reich,* the decision to adopt the Final Solution took place at the Wannsee Conference in January 1942.

The indictment against the Catholic Church and, in particular, against Pius XII in *Hitler's Pope* is an injustice. Cornwell may well have done a good deal of research, but he has not made one new discovery that helps us understand a very complex man and a very complex time. His achievement is a partial interpretation of documents that need to be interpreted by trained scholars who are completely dedicated to the truth, not to wild exaggerations.

12. Constantine's Sword

James Carroll, an ex-priest and columnist who has authored nine novels and a collection of poems, is relentless in his attacks on the Catholic Church. For him, the Church is the cause of every social evil: poverty and overpopulation in the Third World; violence throughout the world; the oppression of women; historic persecution of pagans, Jews, and Muslims; and even the rise of Nazism! His willingness to malign the reputations of those who are no longer able to defend themselves is disturbing. Carroll willingly advances antipapal accounts of a supposed deathbed condemnation of Pius XII by Pope John XXIII. Archbishop Loris Francesco Capovilla, his private secretary, was with him when he died and has emphatically called this account "a lie."

Carroll's new book, *Constantine's Sword: The Church and the Jews: A History,* shows no change in his thinking. He unfairly reconstructs the story of the Church's conflicts during the past two thousand years, from the Gospel accounts of the death of Jesus on the cross, to Constantine's transformation of the cross into a sword, to the rise of blood libels, scapegoating, and modern anti-Semitism. The author fails to deal fairly with the issues.

Carroll had previously mentioned in his autobiography that he had incurred the penalty of excommunication, yet he continues to identify himself as a member of the Catholic Church. In an effort to achieve celebrity and professional standing, he is subservient to the dominant secular culture. He makes a point of Pius XII's refusal to publicly announce Hitler's excommunication. In *An American Requiem,* writing about his own excommunication, Carroll made clear that this punishment had virtually no meaning to him. Would it have mattered more to Hitler?

Despite his self-identification as a Catholic, Carroll is a vicious anti-Catholic bigot. This book is not a work of history. It is driven by theological "animus" reflecting his personal opinions and padded with hatred toward Christianity as well as irrelevant material from his own life. He joins other writers who unjustly blame Christianity and Pope Pius XII for the Holocaust.

Carroll shares anti-Catholic techniques with John Cornwell, Susan Zuccotti, Garry Wills, Michael Phayer and others who ignore the massive historical evidence that defeats their agenda. Interspersed with speculation, these writers manipulate bits and pieces of historical facts to support their preconceived conclusions as to what the Catholic Church and Pius XII did or did not do in respect to the Jewish victims of Nazi oppression.

13. Pack of Thieves

There were "wild" assertions in *U.S. News & World Report* made by senior correspondent Richard Z. Chesnoff on November 15, 1999. In his provocative new book, *Pack of Thieves,*[23] Chesnoff apparently accepts "impressive" documents, like notes stemming from the "communication of a trustworthy Roman informant." Those who genuinely trust such statements should read what Robert A. Graham wrote about the exploits of the informant Scattolini, who made a living by circulating "information" made up in his own mind and transmitting it to all the Roman embassies, including that of the USA, which duly relayed the "information" to the State Department.

The reputable historian Pierre Blet stated (*Civiltà Cattolica,* March 21, 1998): "The claim that the Vatican helped Nazi criminals escape to South America is not a new one. Of course, we cannot exclude the possibility that some Roman ecclesiastic used his position to aid the flight of a Nazi. The sympathies of the Rector of the German national Church in Rome, Bishop Hudal, for the Reich are known....

"Some authors have a rather lofty idea of the forgiveness practiced by the Pope's entourage if they imagine a large number of Nazis were received into the Vatican and conducted to Argentina, protected by Peron's dictatorship, and from there sent to Brazil, to Chile, to Paraguay, to save what could be saved of the Third Reich in the hope of bringing about a Fourth Reich in the pampas." They do not distinguish between history and fiction.

14. Robert S. Wistrich

In his article, "The Pope, the Church, and the Jews," Robert Wistrich repeats misrepresentations and deep-rooted prejudices about the role of Pope Pius XII and the Catholic Church. The author speaks of the Church's "less than felicitous handling" of Holocaust issues and "a lack of sensitivity to Jewish feelings, let alone to the separate integrity of Jewish history, no less disappointing has been the Church's effort to come to terms with its own actions." Catholic leaders "lent their moral authority to the Nazi regime and thereby became complicit to a degree in its crimes."

The article questions Pius XII's opposition to National Socialism and discusses the moral and historical worth of *We Remember.* Wistrich admits the Pontiff did some good by opening "buildings within Vatican City to offer refuge to those who managed to escape the manhunt." He then adds: "What cannot be sustained, however, is the unconvincing and inflated claim in *We Remember* that Pius XII and his representatives saved hundreds of thousands of Jewish lives."[24]

The author asks "whether Pius XII did in fact do everything he might have done to resist a genocidal campaign...." He concludes: "The answer, clearly, is that he did not." He mentions his "one public reference to the Shoah," stating that "Pius XII's chief concern was less with the ongoing annihilation of the Jews than with the interests of the Church."[25] Finally, the article mentions "the imperfections of *We Remember*—especially as compared with the more candid statements on the Shoah issued in recent years by the bishops of Germany and France."[26]

When Pius XII declared that many were killed only because of their race and nationality, it was plain to everyone that he was referring to the Poles, Jews and all hostages. He explained that when talking of atrocities he could not name the Nazis without mentioning at the same time the Bolsheviks, and this, he thought, might not be wholly pleasing to the Allies.[27] Would those who now condemn Pius XII wish that he had publicly condemned the Western alliance with the Soviet Union and excommunicated any Catholic who participated in it? If not, why not, considering the millions of innocent civilians brutally murdered by the Soviet authorities?

In 1940 the British bombed German cities with the intention of killing as many civilians as possible so as to persuade Hitler to surrender. Should Pius have denounced these tactics and forbidden Catholics from participating in them on pain of excommunication? One strongly suspects that few of those who condemn the Pope for failing to denounce the Nazis by name for the killing of civilians would countenance any such criticism of the Western alliance. Is it fair to condemn Pius XII, who placed his own life and the lives of all working with him in danger? The Pope's approach was to seek peace and an end to the killing by all parties.

Peter Novick endeavors to explain the Nazi concentration camp and extermination system in *The Holocaust in American Life*.[28] He states that despite Nazi attempts to keep secret what went on in concentration camps in the thirties, their horrors were known in the West. Until late 1938, among those imprisoned, tortured, and murdered in the camps there were few Jews. The victims were Communists, Socialists, Trade Unionists, and other political opponents of the Hitler regime.

In fact, from early 1933 to late 1942—more than three-quarters of the twelve years of Hitler's Thousand-Year Reich—Jews were seen as among but by no means as the only victims of the Nazi regime. By the time the news of the mass murder of Jews emerged in the middle of the war, those who had been following the crimes of the Nazis for ten years readily and naturally concluded it to be part of the already-existing framework.[29] Even when reports of atrocities against the Jews began to accumulate in 1942, the numbers were contradictory. All this is extremely important in understanding the wartime statements of Pius XII, who was concerned in his many public statements with the overall carnage of the war, which involved the killing of many millions of civilians.

There are pros and cons on many issues of World War II. Among the writers who help supply the "bits and pieces" is George Kendall with a balanced and significant statement reviewing Peter Novick's book: "It is time to transcend the use of the Holocaust as a tool of religious and ethnic conflict. Understood in universal terms as a tragedy suffered by all mankind, Jew and Gentile alike, it can be a powerful symbol for mobilizing human activity to overcome totalitarian ideologies and work for a civilization of life, a civilization that respects the dignity of the human person."

What is perhaps of some importance is that insofar as the word *holocaust* was employed during the war, it was almost always applied to the totality of the destruction wrought by the Axis, not to the special fate of the Jews. To speak of "the Holocaust" in different ways is to introduce an anachronism that stands in the way of understanding contemporary responses.[30]

To accuse Pius XII of failing to speak out against the Holocaust is meaningless since no such event existed in the consciousness of the time. He spoke out frequently against the carnage of the war itself, and the references he did make to the wrongness of racial killing should thus be seen not as inadequate but as unusually telling, given the perceptions of the 1940s.

15. Opinions

To put the matter to rest, perhaps it is necessary to record various issues by the media, as well as to respond to the general public's opinion. Invited to address a group of Freemasons on March 21, 2000, my topic was about justice to the memory of Pope Pius XII. Soon after, Jack Soroka of Union, New Jersey, wrote: "As a Jewish Freemason, I was moved by your research on the Holocaust and the work of Pope Pius XII. Indeed, he was one of the greatest men of his age and is to be enshrined in the hearts of all Americans, especially those of the Jewish religion."[31]

In a letter to the editor of *The Homiletic & Pastoral Review,* Stanley Smolenski wrote: "A great debt of gratitude is owed to Margherita Marchione for her valiant defense of Pope Pius XII, as manifested in her April article 'The Nun versus the Spin Master.' I have also acquired videos of her two-hour EWTN presentation on *The Abundant Life* series. May I express my 'musings' on this subject?

"A few years ago a nun who attended a conference on Polish-Jewish relations told me of a question asked of a participating Jewish historian: 'Why is it that in some discussions about the Shoah/Holocaust, Germany is hardly ever mentioned anymore?' His answer was that Germany has become a great financial benefactor to Israel. If that be true, then someone else has to be targeted for the anger over that genocidal crime. But why a Pope? Could it be that this 'papal bashing' is actually a subconscious reaction against God who allowed that suffering? And thus equating papal 'silence' with God's 'silence' during the time of that affliction? Is there a greater visible religious figure, representing God as it were, than the Pope? In other words is this attack on Pope Pius XII a type of unconscious psychological transferral (of anger) to a symbol (of God)?"[32]

A letter from Joseph H. Wade states: *"Pope Pius XII: Architect for Peace* certainly gives the lie to those who insist Pius XII remained silent during World War II especially in his opposition to Hitler and his alleged lack of assistance to the Jews. The criticism appears to come mainly from the left which erroneously concludes since the Church is against Communism it is, therefore, in favor of Fascism. This view is found when reading histories of the Spanish Civil War, and when reading or listening to today's media which are hardly objective. Moreover, there is the factor of the 'Big Lie' as it pertains to Pius XII in particular or to the Catholic Church in general—undermine the Church by denigrating her Pontiffs. Your efforts demonstrate the real role Pius XII played in World War II and in helping the Jews."[33]

The Most Reverend Thomas G. Doran, Bishop of Rockford, Illinois wrote on October 27, 2000: "I read Cornwell's book for the first time last week and was disgusted. Mr. Cornwell may be a brilliant journalist, but he is no logician....When one looks over the pontificate of Pope Pius XII, it is obvious to all but the most ardent advocate of special pleading that the Church was very fortunate to have as its visible head a pastor who was truly angelic."

16. Among the Heroes

The Holocaust was an unspeakable tragedy beyond comprehension that cannot be forgotten. The International Red Cross, the World Council of Churches, and the Vatican worked quietly to save Jews. Some individuals betrayed Jews, but there were many other Christians of all denominations who performed heroic acts of mercy. Among countless heroes, were Father Maximilian Kolbe (Saint Maximilian)[34] and Corrie ten Boom, who are examples of true compassion and love of neighbor.

Kolbe was a combination of mystic, intellectual genius, and theologian. A Polish Franciscan who volunteered to die in place of a fellow prisoner at Auschwitz, he heroically accepted a martyr's death. Corrie ten Boom, with John and Elizabeth Sherrill, wrote *The Hiding Place,*[35] an everlasting testimony of heroic individuals during the Holocaust.

Recently the German Bishops Conference investigated the issue of "forced labor" by Hitler's "slaves." The services of these laborers were used for charitable purposes, including care of the sick, elderly, handicapped, etcetera. Diocesan archives were destroyed during the

1943 and 1945 bombings in Berlin. However, several Gestapo reports revealed that Catholic priests had the courage to openly protest the conditions of life endured by forced laborers. Historian Christoph Koster said that "many of them [the priests] ended up in prison or even in concentration camps." The SS archives also contain harsh letters against the Archdiocese of Berlin, because of its protests against the conditions of forced laborers. Koster affirms: "In almost all the sources to which we have access, the Catholic Church, rather than being a 'beneficiary' of forced laborers, appears as an institution that tried to defend them."

17. Architect for Peace

My earlier book, *Pius XII: Architect for Peace*[36] has already provided arguments and facts to counter the attack launched by Cornwell—a British journalist, novelist, and nominal Catholic with a long history of distaste for Catholicism. His brother, John LeCarré, happens to be the noted master spinner of thrilling spy mysteries that incorporate reality. *Hitler's Pope* is, above all, a book that also cleverly combines fact and fiction. It very much depends on creating a sense of mystery, rumor, intrigue, false clues, baffling conflicts, double agents, sleaziness, and betrayal—all grounded in a network of a Vatican manipulated by an almost monomaniacal, clerical monster at the time of the cataclysmic horrors of World War I and II. *Hitler's Pope* bears comparison to Malachi Martin's imaginative novels of the Church's being subverted by sinister Masonic and secular powers that have infiltrated the Vatican. Cornwell would have done well to have followed his fictional bent all the way and not pretended to produce a work of historical accuracy and objectivity.

It is useful for any reader to know something of an author's history; in Cornwell's case such knowledge is absolutely necessary. For Cornwell is an ex-seminarian who says in earlier writings that he delighted in baiting and shocking his fellow seminarians as well as his instructors by attacks on the faith. Even today he is ambiguous and evasive when speaking of his Catholicism. In one interview, when an interviewer asked him what members of his parish church would think of *Hitler's Pope,* he had no response. He mumbled something about not going to church very often and went on to talk about priest friends who disagree with one another. Cornwell has previously reported himself a former Catholic, an agnostic, but on the publication of this book he claims to be a Catholic scholar who seldom goes to church.

In order to understand Cornwell's attitude toward Pius XII, one has also to go back to the 1980s, when he persuaded Vatican officials to grant him access to confidential files to study the death of John Paul I. These officials were very willing to do so because another accusatory writer, David Yallop, had just made a bizarre allegation about the Vatican, an attack not unlike the accusations Cornwell himself would come to make. Yallop claimed that John Paul I had been murdered by someone inside the Vatican! Vatican officials opened the files to Cornwell hoping he would set the record straight. The book that Cornwell wrote, *The Thief in the Night: The Mysterious Death of Pope John Paul I,* evinced no respect for the truth—that the Pope had not been murdered. It went on to blame the Pope's death on the Vatican because, Cornwell said, the Pope had died, isolated and alone, in the heart of a cynical and uncaring power structure. Cornwell had corrected one falsehood only to promote another completely insupportable but more subtle lie. He also filled his book with snide descriptions of ecclesial foibles, follies, and sins.[37]

Cornwell assumes a role of importance in the unfolding of *Hitler's Pope.* He goes out of his way to present himself as the honest researcher who set out to write a pro-Vatican, pro-Pope book, only to end up having to write a scathing denunciation because of some amazing discovery he uncovered. He tells us that when he began studying Pius XII he was "convinced of his innocence" and had wanted "to write a new defense of his reputation for a younger generation.....I applied for access to archival material in the Vatican reassuring those who had charge of crucial documents that I was on the side of my subject."[38]

18. Vatican Documents

There are more than one hundred pages of documents taken from the Vatican archives in *Pope Pius XII: Architect for Peace* (2000): correspondence between the Holy See and world leaders; the Pope and national hierarchies; the Vatican Secretariat of State and the papal nuncios around the world. These documents show the esteem in which the Pope was held by government officials and how clearly they understood his concern for peace and for the saving of human lives, including and even especially those of Jews. It also contains an annotated bibliography of selected works, which consists mainly of books and articles by scholars who support the role of Pope Pius XII. They confirm the truth about the commendable record of the Church; the humanity and compassion of Pope Pius XII; and the rescue by Catholics of countless European Jews and other targeted victims of the Nazis.

Karol Jozef Gajewski reviewed *Pope Pius XII: Architect for Peace*.[39] Gajewski points out: "For a number of years throughout the war, indeed until the early 1960s, Pius XII was generally hailed as a towering moral hero in the face of cataclysmic terror: a man who worked tirelessly for peace, and was solicitous on behalf of Jews and Gentiles alike. In examining the cultural and ideological shifts that took place in Western society in the 1960s, Marchione arrives at conclusions which even hardened detractors of Pius XII will have to consider.

"With regard to Rolf Hochhuth's 1963 play *Der Stellvertreter* (The Deputy) she examines the testimony of those 'who were there' and offers a veritable mountain of evidence to the contrary, provided by witnesses to the actual events of World War II.

"Further, those who criticize the Holy See for its 'secret archives' should take time to read and ponder the implications of the documents presented here. Take, for instance, the response of Allied governments to increasingly desperate queries from Rome as to the fate of prisoners of war, whether in allied or Axis hands. In May 1941, British Foreign Secretary Anthony Eden declined to provide copy-typists so that lists of prisoners could be forwarded to the Vatican Information Service.

"As one reads through the appendix, it is hard not to be moved by the human tragedies lying behind diplomatic statements. A typical example were the thousands of Polish deportees who had disappeared into the vast interior of the Soviet Union after 1939. In spite of strenuous Vatican efforts to find out more, evidence suggests that the USA was reluctant to press its ally further on the matter. Was President Roosevelt keener on maintaining cordial relations with the man he called 'Uncle Joe' than in humanitarian efforts?

"The author considers the controversial question: Did Pius do enough to help the Jews? Did anyone else do as much? *Pius XII: Architect for Peace* seeks not just to recommend Pius and defend him against unjust accusation, but acts as a plea for future toleration between faiths."[40]

19. Father Gumpel Speaks

During a presentation in Rome of the book *The Jews, Pius XII and The Black Legend* (1999), by Italian journalist and writer Antonio Gaspari, Father Gumpel concluded: "After reading over 100,000 pages of the documents related to the process of beatification, I am more and more convinced that Pius XII was a saint." ZENIT News Agency has made the full text of Gumpel's remarks available to the general public. Excerpts taken from his presentation follow: "The cover of John Cornwell's book depicts Archbishop Pacelli leaving a German government building, guarded by two soldiers. This official visit took place not later than 1929, that is, four years before Hitler came into power (January 30, 1933). Since Pacelli left Germany in 1929 and never returned there, using this photograph is misleading and tendentious. The fact that Cornwell uses this photo on the cover of his book reveals from the outset his intention to denigrate Pope Pius XII.

"In his book, Cornwell includes a list of archives which he claims to have consulted. It is an extremely meager list and scores of archives which could and should have been consulted are simply ignored: German, Italian, U.S. archives, the Acts of the Nuremberg Trials, etc. Even those archives which are mentioned are certainly neither fully explored nor used. Most sources cited by Cornwell are secondary sources. Cornwell deals at length with the situation of the Catholic Church in Germany, but rarely mentions the standard work of Dr. Heinz Hürten whose extremely well-documented scholarship reveals the situation of the German Catholics between 1918–1945.

"Other standard works dealing with this topic are also overlooked by the author. Instead of solid documentation, one finds conjectures, suppositions, insinuations. Cornwell deals at length with concordats, totally ignoring their primary pastoral importance, and suggesting that the only purpose of the Holy See is to fortify its power and in particular to hold secure its right to appoint bishops of its own choosing. He does not mention such abuses as Josephinism, popular in Austria and to a certain extent even in Bavaria. He speaks about modernism without even mentioning its real dangers (Loisy, Tyrrell), rather concentrating on the witch hunt which ensued, but in which Pacelli never participated."

The information Cornwell offers is based principally on a letter Nuncio Pacelli supposedly wrote on April 18, 1919—before Hitler began his political career—and sent to Rome from Munich. According to Cornwell this letter reveals Nuncio Pacelli's "antipathy toward the Jews" in "a more blatantly anti-Semitic fashion" than in previous correspondence. But Vatican scholar Pierre Blet, S.J., denies that Nuncio Pacelli actually wrote the letter.

This letter is not "blatantly anti-Semitic" as Cornwell would have it. The crucial lines Cornwell cites describe a group of Bolshevik revolutionaries occupying a particular palace on a particular day. The leaders of these revolutionaries were Bolshevik Jews, sent to Germany to foment revolution. Cornwell finds unflattering descriptions of the Bolsheviks and cites the use of the word *Jew* three times in one paragraph as proof of Pacelli's anti-Semitism, writing: "This association of Jewishness with Bolshevism confirms that Pacelli, from his early 40s, nourished a suspicion and contempt for the Jews for political reasons."[41]

But the letter merely reports a fact. Were there a number of Jews among the revolutionaries or were there not? Were they threatening, frightening, unpleasant, or were they not? Cornwell doesn't deny the accuracy of the letter. The outstanding British historian Ian Kershaw, in his highly praised biography, *Hitler, 1889–1936: Hubris,*[42] describing the same Munich revolution, identifies three of the leaders as Jewish— within the space of four lines.

The letter in question highlights the uprising in 1919. In his report to the Secretary of State, the then Nuncio Pacelli's noting that the leaders of these terrorists were Jews sent from Russia is a historical fact. Such mention has absolutely nothing to do with anti-Semitism, as Cornwell wrongly implies. It was necessary to mention who the terrorist leaders in Munich were so that Pacelli's superior would learn that the Russian Communists were seeking to extend their power in various Western countries. Indeed, has any Jewish author spoken favorably about the criminal activities of the terrorists who led the revolution in Munich?

Cornwell has to be aware that this letter is a report by Pacelli's assistant, Monsignor Schioppa, who felt helpless before the armed revolutionaries. Weighing the language of the letter, one has to consider the terrifying circumstances Schioppa faced. His letter is antirevolutionary, which one should expect. Cornwell's description makes for good drama: "The letter has lain in the Vatican secret archive like a time bomb until now."[43] This is not true. Not only was the letter known to serious scholars, but Cornwell does not adequately explain the motive or the circumstances.

20. In Defense of Pius XII

After Rolf Hochhuth produced his play *The Deputy* in 1963, Giovanni Battista Cardinal Montini (later Paul VI) wrote a strong letter in defense of Pius XII, a few days before he himself was elected Pope. This letter was published in *The Tablet* of London a few days after Montini's election to the papacy. It was also published in *La Civiltà Cattolica* and elsewhere. John XXIII had always expressed his highest esteem for Pius XII. In his latest trip to Africa, Pope John Paul II called him a great Pope. Cornwell either ignores or plays down such statements, just as he does not duly appreciate the fact that in the document *We Remember* there is a long footnote in defense of Pius XII.

Contrary to what critics state, in the United States an article by Rabbi Lazaron of the Baltimore Hebrew Congregation, entitled "Holy See Is Eager to Rescue Hebrews" tells of the arrest of Roman Jews, the concern of the Vatican, and the Pope's offer of gold to ransom Jewish hostages. Speaking of Pius XII as a prisoner in the Vatican, the Rabbi appeals for prayers on his behalf, declaring: "The Pope has condemned anti-Semitism and all its works. Bishops of the Church have appeared in the streets of Antwerp, Brussels, The Hague, and Paris with the Star of David on their arms. Humble priests…have joined with Protestant ministers in protecting Jews…at the risk of their own lives."[44]

Robert A. Graham's response to the BBC television documentary *Pius XII and the Jews* is an important defense of the Pope. It was published on February 4 and March 11, 1995, in *The Tablet* of London and has been included in *Yours Is a Precious Witness: Memoirs of Jews and Catholics in Wartime Italy.*

21. Rabbi Eric Yoffie

There is no doubt about tensions between Jews and the Roman Catholic Church. It has been noted that some American Jews continue to condemn the Catholic Church and are divided in their opinion of Pius XII. Are they solely interested in keeping this agenda alive in order to have a unifying element among the various Jewish organizations?

According to Rabbi Eric Yoffie, "the issues in dispute vary, but many are related to Catholic attitudes about the Holocaust and the conduct of Pope Pius XII during World War II. Other controversies include decisions of the Church about who should be declared a saint, relations between the Church and the Palestinians, and Israeli policy toward Christian holy places....

"I regret in particular a pattern that has developed in responding to important Church statements. For example, let us look at what occurred when the Church put out *We Remember: A Reflection on the Shoah*—a document that appeared in March of 1998 in which the Church asked for forgiveness for the sins of passivity of its sons and daughters during the Holocaust. The document is in fact quite an extraordinary one, containing sentiments that not long ago would have been impossible to imagine as coming from the Vatican. The Jewish reaction in most cases was to issue a litany of complaints about what the statement failed to say, very nearly creating the impression that the omissions were more important than the affirmations.

"This pattern repeated itself with the Pope's historic March 12, 2000, public apology in St. Peter's Basilica, asking for forgiveness for the sins of the Church over two millennia, and with the issuance of *Memory and Reconciliation*....

"Jewish representatives should have welcomed the recent statements as an important step forward in the developing relationship between Catholicism and Judaism, encouraged those who produced the statements and noted the importance of ongoing deliberations between the two groups to explore fully the implications of what has been said.

"More fundamentally, I do not believe that the attitude conveyed by Jewish responses of this sort are in any way broadly representative of the sentiments toward the Church which exist in the Jewish community. I am the president of the largest grass-roots Jewish organization in North America, with almost 900 synagogues and more than 1.25 million members. My experience is that grass-roots Catholic-Jewish relations differ considerably from place to place.

"I would emphasize three points: First, I believe that the masses of American Jews view with understanding and appreciation the steps taken by the Church to revive and redefine Catholic-Jewish relations, and that the hurtful tone that some have used in pursuing this dialogue does not reflect majority feeling in the Jewish community. There are issues that divide Catholics and Jews, of course, but our community understands that confronting these issues is appropriately seen as part of the process of renewal. Second, I believe that at least some of the

Jewish organizational voices that have been so outspoken in recent years have minimal claim to speak in the name of the community. And third, I believe that the major religious movements must recognize their responsibility to assume a greater role in the dialogue with the Church. I refer in particular to Reform and Conservative Judaism, which are mass-membership religious groupings that are moderate, mainstream and firmly rooted in community life....

"Pope John Paul II has written eloquently and powerfully on 'the unspeakable iniquity of the Shoah,' and the 1998 Vatican document proclaimed that 'the spoiled seeds of anti-Judaism and anti-Semitism must never again be allowed to take root in any heart.' What then is the source of disagreement? The major Jewish criticism has been that the Church, as an institution, has not acknowledged any wrongdoing during the Holocaust, ascribing blame only to individual Catholics. Jewish representatives have also condemned what they have seen as the silence of Pope Pius XII during the Nazi era. The Church has found no merit in either argument.

"It is not my intention to review all of the arguments on both sides of these questions. Our starting point needs to be the simple recognition by both of our religious communities that there exists little possibility for us to reach agreement on many of the difficult historical and religious issues surrounding the Shoah....

"I am familiar with the history of the war and the pressures to which the Church was subjected. But what remains with me are certain uncontested historical facts: Pius XII never condemned either Hitler or the Nazis by name. He never mentioned specifically the suffering of the Jews, though many people, both clergy and lay diplomats, pleaded with him to issue a public condemnation....

"And so where do we go from here?...I am interested in discussing ethics and redemption and sin. I would like to read the Hebrew Bible with you. And I want to do this not because I expect to win your agreement or elicit your approval, but because I want you to understand Judaism as a living and dynamic religion.

"We may read the Bible somewhat differently, but I think that we can agree that there is a biblical mandate for a just society. I think that we can agree that religion without a passion for justice is a failed mission, a contradiction in terms. I think we can agree that in the future social action will be primarily interreligious, reaching across the chasms of race, faith and culture.

"Finally, let me mention the desperate need for a joint campaign of positive religious education. This means that the Catholics need to educate Catholics about Jews, and the Jews need to educate Jews about Catholics. I believe that the Church is far ahead of the Jewish community in this area. I pledge, therefore, that the Union of American Hebrew Congregations will immediately undertake to produce textbooks for its religious schools that will portray accurately and sympathetically the evolving position of the Church on the Jews and Judaism."[45]

Chapter XI
The New Commission and Its Questions

---

1. Judeo-Catholic Commission

*I*n the last thirty years, especially with the pontificate of John Paul II, giant steps have been made toward progress in dialogue between Jews and Catholics. To prepare a serious scholarly analysis of Pius XII's actions, several scholars were called to participate in the Judeo-Catholic Commission in order to examine the Vatican documents of the Holy See during the Second World War. This group's assignment as scholars was to analyze documents already published. The group consisted of three Catholics: Eva Fleischner, Gerald Fogarty, and John Morley; and three Jews: Michael Marrus, Bernard Suchecky, and Robert Wistrich.

During three days of meetings in October 2000 in Rome, members of the Commission presented a report entitled: "The Vatican and the Holocaust: A Preliminary Report Submitted to the Holy See's Commission for Religious Relations with the Jews and the International Jewish Committee for Interreligious Consultations by the International Catholic-Jewish Historical Commission."

The report consisted of forty-seven questions, some of them concerning alleged papal indifference toward Jewish victims of the Nazis. The general thrust of several questions was that the Commission was seeking evidence of the failures of Pius XII and the Catholic Church during the period of the Shoah. These questions, submitted to the International Catholic-Jewish Liaison Committee, were grouped into three categories: the first, of a very specific character arising from particular documents in the collection; the second, of a more general character, involving themes that appear in one or more of the volumes; and the third, general questions.

245

A. Questions arising from particular documents:

1. Eugenio Pacelli, then Secretary of State, and German cardinals played a central role in drafting the 1937 encyclical *Mit brennender Sorge* (With Burning Concern), which was a forceful condemnation of National Socialism. Soon after he was elected Pope, Pacelli met with the same group of German cardinals to discuss how they should deal with Nazism. In order to understand Pacelli's evolving policies as Secretary of State and as pope, can we see the drafts of *Mit brennender Sorge,* or any other relevant material pertaining to that encyclical or his meeting in 1939 with the German cardinals after his election?[1]

2. In 1938, after the *Kristallnacht* pogrom, only one prominent German prelate, Bernhard Lichtenberg, rector of Saint Hedwig's cathedral in Berlin,[2] had the courage to condemn the outrages publicly. Pacelli was given a detailed report by the papal nuncio in Berlin but there appears to have been no official reaction by the Vatican. This issue is especially important because Archbishop Amleto Cicognani, Apostolic Delegate to the United States, certainly informed the Vatican of the public broadcast of the American bishops' condemnation of *Kristallnacht.* Do the archives reveal internal discussions among Vatican officials, including Pacelli, about the appropriate reaction to this pogrom?

3. In June 1938 Pope Pius XI commissioned Father John LaFarge S.J. to draft an encyclical on racism and antisemitism. The editors of the *ADSS* affirmed that nothing was found in the Vatican archives on this subject.[3] However, in an article that appeared in the *Osservatore Romano* in 1973, Father Burkhart Schneider, one of the *ADSS* editors, stated that "the texts prepared, as well as many on other topics, have ended up in the silence of the archives."[4] May we review the drafts and materials relating to that document from the archives?

4. A substantial part of Volume 6 is devoted to the aborted efforts to obtain Brazilian visas for Catholics of Jewish origin. Numerous questions have been raised concerning the failure of this project. In addition, it is known that a part of the money destined for the refugees came from funds raised by the United Jewish Appeal in the United States.[5] Is there further documentation as to why this money was allocated to the attempted rescue of converted Jews rather than to Jews?

5. From the outbreak of the war, appeals rained down upon the Vatican for help on behalf of the population of Poland, brutally victimized in a cruel and bloodthirsty occupation. And from the earliest days of the fighting, observers, ranging from the exiled Polish government to the British and French ambassadors to the Vatican, recounted the opinion of many Catholic Poles, both inside and outside Poland, that the Church had betrayed them and that Rome was silent in the face of their national ordeal.[6] Is there any further documentation beyond what is already in the volumes concerning deliberations within the Vatican with regard to these insistent appeals on behalf of the Poles?

6. On November 23, 1940, Mario Besson, Bishop of Lausanne, Fribourg, and Geneva, sent a letter to Pope Pius XII expressing deep concern at the grave conditions of thousands of prisoners, including Jews, in concentration camps in southwest France.[7] In his report he pressed for a public appeal by the Pope against the persecutions and a more active Catholic defense of the rights of all the victims. We know that it must have been taken seriously by the Vatican, especially since its observations were confirmed by the papal nuncio to Switzerland, Archbishop Filippo Bernardini, who forwarded Besson's message to the Pope.[8] The subsequent responses by Luigi Maglione, Secretary of State, also indicate that he considered it worthy of attention, and he certainly would have discussed it with the Holy Father.[9] Is there any evidence that Pius XII, Maglione or any other high Vatican official considered, then or subsequently, responding in the manner requested by Besson?

7. In August 1941 the French head of state, Marshal Philippe Pétain, asked the French ambassador to the Holy See, Léon Bérard, to ascertain the views of the Vatican on the collaborationist Vichy government's efforts to restrict the Jews through anti-Jewish legislation. The response came, reportedly from Giovanni Montini, substitute Secretary of State, and Domenico Tardini, Secretary of the Congregation of Extraordinary Ecclesiastical Affairs, who stated that there was no objection to these restrictions so long as they were administered with justice and charity and did not restrict the prerogatives of the Church.[10] Was the Pope consulted on this matter? Are there any additional materials in the archives regarding this issue that are not contained in the *ADSS*?

8. In Romania, where Catholics were a small but significant minority, both the local Catholic authorities and the Vatican clung to the concordat of 1929 as defining the relationship between the Church and the dictatorial regime of Marshal Ion Antonescu. During 1940 and 1941, as persecution of the Jews intensified, the Vatican received a stream of communications from the nuncio, Archbishop Andrea Cassulo, relaying the strain that the anti-Jewish laws put upon what the Church saw as its prerogatives—among others, the protection of the civil and religious rights of Catholics who had converted from Judaism. Cassulo repeatedly reported on his efforts to secure the "freedom of the Church" by insisting upon the need to exempt converts from anti-Jewish laws, their rights to attend schools and vocational institutions.[11] Did Cassulo or his interlocutors in the Vatican view these interventions as the only practical means by which a blanket of protection, or at least some protection, might be extended to Jews who were not converts? Are there any further documents to elucidate this issue?

9. Cassulo had very good relations with Jewish leaders in the core Romanian provinces of Moldavia and Wallachia. He appealed directly to Antonescu to limit deportations planned for the summer of 1942.[12] He toured Transnistria in the spring of 1943, visiting one of the principal killing grounds for Jews during the Holocaust. Cassulo reported extensively on his activities to Maglione.[13] He traveled to Rome in the fall of 1942 and was received by the Pope. Do any documents record what transpired during that visit? Were his actions approved by the Holy See?

10. At the end of August 1942, the Greek Catholic Metropolitan of Lviv (Lwow), Andrzeyj Szeptyckyj, wrote to the Pope and described with stark clarity the atrocities and mass murder being carried out against the Jews and the local population.[14] No other high-ranking Catholic Churchman, to the best of our knowledge, provided such direct eye-witness testimony and expressed concern for Jews qua Jews (and as primary targets of German bestiality) in the same way. Moreover, he indicated to the Pope that he had protested to Himmler himself. Finally, he publicly denounced the massacres of Jews in circumstances in which some Ukrainian Catholics themselves were collaborating with the Germans in these murders. Is there evidence of a discussion or a reply to Szeptyckyj's plea?

11. The Cardinal Archbishop of Krakow, Adam Sapieha, in a letter of February 1942 to the Pope, vividly described the horrors of the Nazi occupation, including the concentration camps that destroyed thousands of Poles.[15] However, neither in this nor in any other communication to Rome, of which we are aware, did Sapieha make any specific reference to the Jews. Nor, to the best of our knowledge, did the Vatican ever request any information on the subject from him. Yet Sapieha undoubtedly knew what was happening in Auschwitz, which was within his archdiocese. Was there any unpublished communication of Sapieha to Rome in which he alluded to the fate of the Jews? Can the archives tell us more regarding the interaction on this and related matters between the Vatican and Polish church leaders?

12. On 18 May 1941, Pope Pius XII received the head of the Croatian fascist state, Ante Pavelic. While the Vatican had received Pavelic as an individual Catholic, not as head of state, there were political implications as a result of this reception. Before his reception, the Yugoslav minister to the Holy See brought to the Vatican's attention Pavelic's involvement in committing atrocities against the Serbs and protested the reception of Pavelic in any capacity because he was the head of an "illegitimate" puppet state.[16] Subsequently, Pavelic's regime was responsible for the massacre of hundreds of thousands of Serbs, Jews, Gypsies, and partisans. It is not known how the Pope reacted to these atrocities. Are there any archival materials that can illuminate this issue?

13. Many unanswered questions also surround the Archbishop of Zagreb, Aloysius Stepinac, beatified in 1999. While in 1941 he initially welcomed the creation of a Croatian state, he subsequently condemned atrocities against Serbs and Jews and established an organization to rescue Jews. Are there any archival documents or materials from the beatification process that can illuminate this matter?

14. On several occasions Konrad von Preysing, Bishop of Berlin, had vainly appealed to the Pope to protest specific Nazi actions, including those directed at the Jews. On 17 January 1941 he wrote to Pius XII, noting that "Your Holiness is certainly informed about the situation of the Jews in Germany and the neighboring countries. I wish to mention that I have been asked both from the

Catholic and Protestant side if the Holy See could not do something on this subject, issue an appeal in favor of these unfortunates."[17] This was a direct appeal to the Pope, which bypassed the nuncio. What impression did von Preysing's words make on Pius XII; what discussions, if any, took place about making such a public appeal as the German bishop requested, and was any further information about Nazi anti-Jewish policy sought?

15. On 6 March 1943, von Preysing asked Pius XII to try and save the Jews still in the Reich capital, who were facing imminent deportation which, as he indicated, would lead to certain death: "The new wave of deportations of the Jews, which began just before 1 March, affects us particularly here in Berlin even more bitterly. Several thousands are involved: Your Holiness has alluded to their probable fate in your Christmas Radio Broadcast. Among the deportees are also many Catholics. Is it not possible for Your Holiness again to intervene for the many unfortunate innocents? It is the last hope for many and the profound wish of all right-thinking people."[18] On 30 April 1943, the Pope indicated to von Preysing that local bishops had the discretion to determine when to be silent and when to speak out in the face of the danger of reprisals and pressures.[19] Although he felt that he had to exercise great prudence in his actions as Pope, he made it clear that he felt comforted that Catholics, particularly in Berlin, had helped the "so-called non-Aryans" (sogenannten Nichtarier). He particularly singled out for "fatherly recognition" Father Lichtenberg, who had been imprisoned by the Nazis and who would die shortly afterwards. Are there earlier examples in the archives of the Pope's solicitude for Father Lichtenberg or any reference to the bishops' stand against the persecution of the Jews going back to 1938? Is there any evidence of discussion in the Vatican regarding the deportations from Berlin?

16. Apart from von Preysing's direct observation of the Nazi deportations of Jews from Berlin, and what was reported to him, we know that he had been kept informed about the persecution through his frequent contact with Helmut James Graf von Moltke (the driving force of the anti-Nazi Kreisau Circle). Did the Pope receive other information from von Preysing about the Holocaust? Do the archives contain any additional information regarding von Preysing's and other German bishops' interaction with the Vatican about the persecution and murder of Jews?

17. The Pope's reply to von Preysing did not give a specific commitment to make any public appeal for the Jews. But on 2 June 1943, just over a month later, the Pope in a speech to the Sacred College of Cardinals did elusively refer to those "destined sometimes, even without guilt on their part, to exterminatory measures."[20] This was the second and last occasion on which Pope Pius XII would make any (indirect) reference to the Holocaust during the war years. Its proximity in time to his reply on 30 April 1943 to von Preysing suggests that there may have been a connection, though once again only a closer investigation of the Vatican archives could reveal whether this was the case. What unpublished documents regarding the Pope's speech and his reply to von Preysing do the archives contain?

18. In a letter to von Preysing in March 1944, the Pope stated: "Before me lie your eight letters of 1943 and five letters of 1944."[21] Do these letters exist in the archives and can we see them?

19. Astonishingly detailed accounts of killings are reported in Volume 8. In one striking instance, on 7 October 1942, the Vatican received information on the massacres of Jews compiled by an Italian hospital train chaplain, Father Pirro Scavizzi, reporting two million deaths by that point.[22] It has been suggested that Scavizzi had four audiences with the Pope—two of which go unmentioned in the eleven volumes.[23] Relaying the views of Cardinal Innitzer of Vienna, Scavizzi deplored the timorous reactions of Archbishop Cesare Orsenigo, nuncio to Germany, to matters such as this, writing directly to the Pope in May 1942.[24] Were reports such as these ever discussed within the offices of the Secretary of State? Did the Pope himself refer to such accounts at meetings or in other conversations within the Vatican? Is there material from other Italian military chaplains in the archives?

20. In August and September 1942, there were vigorous protests against the deportations of Jews from France by Archbishop Saliège of Toulouse, Bishop Théas of Montauban, and Cardinal Gerlier of Lyons.[25] According to The *New York Times,* in an article published 10 September 1942, the Pope "sent to Marshal Pétain a personal message in which he intimated his approval of the initiative of the French Cardinals and Bishops on behalf of the Jews and foreigners being handed over to the Germans. It is understood the

Pope asked the French Chief of State to intervene."[26] Is there confirmation in the Vatican archives of this news account?

21. Casimir Papée, the Polish ambassador to the Holy See, on 28 April 1943, sent Maglione an extract from a Zurich newspaper, describing the martyrdom of many Polish priests interned at Dachau. He reminded the Cardinal of the sentiments awakened among all civilized and Christian nations by German cruelty in the occupied territories adding: "My colleagues and I never failed to draw Your Eminence's attention to these painful facts." In concluding his letter, Papée asked what the Holy See had been able to do "to save lives precious to the Church," and which measures it proposed to take "in the face of so much injustice."[27] There is no evidence of a reply in the *ADSS*, though the grievances of the Poles were noted on several occasions.[28] Appeals such as these had been coming to the Vatican since 1939. Are there any materials in the archives regarding internal discussions as to how the Vatican was to respond?

22. There are letters from the bishops of Northeast Italy to the Holy See between 1943 and 1945 (for example, Giuseppe Nogara, bishop of Udine, Antonio Santin, bishop of Trieste, and other bishops).[29] They provide a detailed picture of the political-religious situation in those dioceses, such as the persecution of the Jews, the shooting of hostages, the dangers posed by the partisans, and the suffering of the Italians. Are there more such letters from these and other Italian bishops in the archives?

23. Early in 1944, the World Jewish Congress appealed to the Holy See through Archbishop Cicognani in Washington to intervene with Hungarian authorities, and to accept and assist Jews from Poland. During this period, Hungary was seen as a place of refuge for Jews. Maglione informed Angelo Rotta, nuncio to Hungary, of this appeal and instructed him to take whatever steps he thought "possible and opportune."[30] Other appeals came to the nuncios and delegates from various Jewish groups.[31] The nuncios then sent telegraphic summaries of these appeals. May we see the original documents to determine how closely they are reflected in the summaries?

24. In February 1944, the Pontifical Commission for the Vatican City State (Pontificio Commissione per lo Stato della Città del Vaticano), the administrative agency of Vatican City, recorded the presence of Jews and others who were given refuge within the Vatican.[32] Are Pontifical Commission records and communiqués

available with respect to the housing of refugees? Are there records of other people finding refuge in pontifical institutions, for example, the papal villa at Castelgandolfo?

25. In April 1944, on the eve of the deportations of the Jews from Hungary, Rotta reported that the head of the Hungarian government assured him that he wanted to maintain cordial relations between the Holy See and Hungary. These assurances came after new anti-Jewish laws had been enacted under German influence. A note at the bottom of Rotta's report indicates that it had been seen by the Pope, but such notation is missing from most other such documents.[33] Is there any record of which reports the Pope actually saw? What was his reaction to Rotta's reports? Were there any discussions regarding the papal relationship with the Hungarian government?

26. Rotta was the only nuncio to cooperate with the diplomatic representatives of neutral states, Spain, Portugal, Sweden and Switzerland. On three occasions in late 1944, he and his diplomatic colleagues submitted protests to the Hungarian government in defense of Jews and took active measures to save them.[34] The Vatican expressed its approval of Rotta's actions at this juncture.[35] Is there evidence of earlier Vatican approval or encouragement of Rotta's activities?

27. In 1933, Edith Stein wrote to Pius XI asking him to issue an encyclical condemning antisemitism.[36] This may have been the first of many appeals made to the Vatican for intervention on behalf of the Jews. Though the date falls beyond the parameters of our mandate, the document is relevant because of its content. How was this letter received? Is the letter itself in the archives, and if so may we see it?

B. Questions arising from themes in one or more volumes:

28. Pius XII's spirituality was shaped by the times and circumstances in which he lived, and profoundly affected his outlook on such matters as the Jews and other victims of the war (such as Poles, Serbs, Gypsies, German civilians, Italian POWs and others). For example, in his letters to the bishops of Hamburg and other places, his theology of suffering deeply influenced how he responded to reports of persecution, bombing and other attacks on

civilian populations. Are there other unpublished letters and documents that would shed further light on how the Pope viewed the
Church's role during the war?

29. Under the Secretariat of State, the Congregation of Extraordinary Ecclesiastic Affairs dealt with relations between states.
Meetings of the Congregation would discuss reports from nuncios
and delegates and the Congregation's drafts of instructions to
them. Minutes of these meetings would provide valuable information about the Vatican's reaction to activities of the Church within
Nazi dominated Europe. Are there minutes of these meetings covering the war period? If so, could we have access to them?

30. Finances are occasionally mentioned in the context of the
relief of civilian suffering.[37] For example, an accounting of the dis-
bursement of funds is given in cases where Jewish organizations
donated funds to the Vatican for relief and rescue. However, the
volumes contain no documents regarding the Vatican's own financial transactions relating to such efforts. Is there any archival evidence to indicate how the Vatican collected and disbursed its own
or other funds in carrying out such activities, such as the annual
Peter's Pence collection?

31. During the war the Vatican followed its traditional policy that
Jews who had converted to Catholicism were full members of the
Church, and therefore entitled to its protection. This protection
was sometimes guaranteed by concordats, thereby according to
the Church the means by which to intervene in specific and general cases. Was the recourse to such interventions derived purely
from considerations of efficacy or were there moral or other considerations that were discussed among Vatican officials? Was
there a broad strategy, policy guidelines, or theological discussions among Vatican officials to determine what principles should
be applied to such interventions on behalf of converted Jews?

32. In the repeated interventions against the application of racial
laws and appeals on behalf of some of the deportees that appear in
these volumes, the emphasis upon "non-Aryan Catholics" or converted Jews is striking to the contemporary reader. This is all the
more so because of the lasting resentment, among Jews, of the
Church's promotion and encouragement of such conversions. From
the standpoint of the Vatican, of course, the purported reasons for
this emphasis are threefold: first, what the Church understood as its

responsibility to look after its own; second, that the Vatican did not believe that Jewish organizations took care of Jewish converts to Catholicism; and third, the claim that it was only in the cases of this particular class of "Jews" that the Vatican had locus standi with aggressive and dictatorial regimes—and hence some prospect of success. To what degree was the latter a rationale for inattention to Jews qua Jews? And how accurate was it to refer, as many regularly do, to interventions on behalf of "Jews" when that term frequently connoted baptized Jews? Are there any documents that would clarify this ambiguous use of terminology?

33. Almost alone of the Vatican diplomats, Mgr. Domenico Tardini, principal assistant to Maglione, wrote memoranda and office notes on a wide variety of topics, many of which are published in the *ADSS*. Did he write other notes relating to the fate of the Jews not published in the *ADSS?*

34. On March 18, 1942, Gerhart Riegner of the World Jewish Congress and Richard Lichtheim, representing the Jewish Agency for Palestine, sent a remarkably comprehensive memorandum on the fate of Jews in Central and Eastern Europe to Archbishop Filippo Bernardini, the nuncio in Switzerland, and a day later Bernardini forwarded the document to Maglione himself. While the report gave no clear sense of a European-wide "final solution," it left little to the imagination in its description of horrors organized on a continental scale.[38] Is there any indication in the archives about what response, if any, was made to this report? For example, did the Holy See notify hierarchies or its diplomatic representatives regarding the contents of the report?

35. There is evidence that the Holy See was well-informed by mid-1942 of the accelerating mass murder of Jews. Questions continue to be asked about the reception of this news, and what attention was given to it. How thoroughly informed was the Vatican regarding details of Nazi persecution and extermination? What was the Holy See's reaction, and what discussions followed the reports that flowed in describing evidence of the "Final Solution?" What, more specifically, were the steps leading up to the Pope's Christmas message of 1942? Are there drafts of this message?

36. In light of the above, in September 1942 there were requests for a papal statement from the British, Belgian, Polish, Brazilian and American diplomatic representatives to the Holy See. In Volume 5

of the *ADSS,* only the response to Myron Taylor, the American representative to the Pope, is published. Might the responses to the other representatives be made available?

37. Questions have been raised regarding the attitude of the Vatican toward a Jewish national home in Palestine during the Holocaust period. Maglione generally responded to requests for assistance in sending Jews to Palestine by reminding appellants of all that the Holy See had done to help the Jews, and of its readiness to continue to do so. But in internal notes published in the volumes, meant only for Vatican representatives, the Secretary of State and his aides explicitly reaffirmed the Vatican's opposition to significant Jewish immigration to Palestine, stating that "the Holy See has never approved of the project of making Palestine a Jewish home...Palestine is by now holier for Catholics than for Jews."[39] The documents also reveal that Angelo Roncalli (the future Pope John XXIII), apostolic delegate to Istanbul, aided Jews to reach Palestine notwithstanding his uneasiness concerning Jewish political aspirations there.[40] Is there documentation regarding guidelines for rescue efforts and their implications concerning the Vatican policy with regard to Palestine?

38. On March 12, 1943, a consortium of rabbis in North America sent a passionate appeal to Maglione, describing the horrors in Poland and the liquidation of the Warsaw Ghetto, and asking for help from Rome.[41] It is curious that there are no references in the volumes to the Warsaw Ghetto uprising. Are there any documents relating to this event in the archives?

39. The Vatican chargé d'affaires in La Paz (Bolivia) wrote about the "invasive" and "cynically exploitative" character of the Jews—allegedly engaged in "dishonest dealings, violence, immorality, and even disrespect for religion."[42] His highly charged account may have negatively influenced Maglione, especially since he received similar reports from some other nuncios, such as Aldo Laghi, in Santiago (Chile). This nuncio claimed that Jewish immigration to Chile had already created "a serious problem." The Jews, he claimed, instead of becoming farmers as promised, had turned to small commerce and trade, provoking popular protests from secular and clerical circles in Chile. The nuncio, in advising against the immigration of "non-Aryan" Catholics, took into account the violent mood triggered by what he called "the

invasion of the Jews."[43] If other reports of this kind exist in the Vatican archives, could we see them? What internal discussions did they provoke and did they influence policy on the "Jewish question" at a time of pervasive antisemitism?

40.   How regularly did Maglione, Tardini and Montini brief the Pope on wartime events, the activities of papal nuncios, and the policies they were handling? Are there notes of these discussions? Did Pius XII or his aides maintain diaries which alluded to these discussions?

41.   The Vatican radio from time to time addressed issues relating to Nazi persecution, and extracts from these broadcasts appeared in the London *Tablet*. It is said that Pius XII may have written or edited the texts for some of these broadcasts. Is there any documentary evidence regarding Pius XII's role and are the original broadcast transcripts available?

C. General questions:

42.   The case has repeatedly been made that the Vatican's fear of communism prompted it to mute and limit its criticism of Nazi atrocities and occupation policies. We are struck by the paucity of evidence to this effect and to the subject of communism in general. Indeed, our reading of the volumes presents a different picture, especially with regard to the Vatican promotion of the American bishops' support for the alliance between the United States and the Soviet Union in order to oppose Nazism.[44] Is there further evidence on this question?

43.   In several of the volumes, the editors cite hundreds of documents which are not themselves published. For example, in Volume 10 alone the editors list 700 such documents. In some cases, the documents are briefly summarized or quoted. It would be helpful if these documents could be made available.

44.   The Poles were major victims of the Nazis. Members of the Polish Government in Exile in London and some Polish bishops were often very vocal in their criticism of Pius XII's role. It has been reported that the Vatican commissioned the Jesuits to prepare a defense of its Polish policy.[45] Is this correct and, if so, may we see the report? More generally, the subject of Vatican-Polish relations is

an essential element for understanding the role of the Holy See during the Holocaust period and deserves further investigation in the Vatican archives. Is there other pertinent information on this subject in the archives that is not in the volumes, and may we see it?

45. The volumes contain urgent appeals to the Vatican for assistance, articulated by desperate Jewish petitioners. These petitions frequently are couched in language of effusive praise as well as gratitude for actions already undertaken.[46] Yet the volumes contain few examples of the assistance already given that gave rise to such expressions of praise and gratitude. What information can be obtained from either the archives or other sources concerning the concrete assistance already given which gave rise to these expressions of gratitude?

46. In countries in which Vatican representatives clashed with the local authorities over the application of racial laws, there are repeated references to conversions. Governments, occupation authorities, nuncios, the Secretariat, and local Churches all raised questions about the sincerity of these conversions. Were such conversions a means to avoid the disabilities of discriminatory laws, regulations, and even worse, deportation and murder? To anyone familiar with the wartime persecution of the Jews—and this must include Vatican officials whose voices are represented here—such questions may appear cruel, or at best naïve. In light of certain Church officials issuing false identity papers to unconverted Jews, were such Vatican expressions of concern that conversions be "sincere" intended to hold persecuting and even murderous officials at bay? Or were these rather a genuine reflection of the priorities of the Church jealously guarding the integrity of its sacramental life, especially baptism, and unhesitatingly promoting, even in the midst of the Holocaust, what it felt to be its apostolic mission for the souls put in its care? Are there any documents that could shed light on this issue?

47. Did Pope Pius XII have serious doubts about the wisdom or correctness of his policy of "impartiality," whether it related to Jews, Poles or any other victims of the Nazis? The published documents unfortunately provide little evidence, although Volume 2 gives us a valuable insight into his thinking during the wartime period, especially about the German Church, to which he felt particularly close.[47] In his diary, Roncalli reports of an audience on 11

October 1941 with the Pope who asked whether his "silence" concerning Nazism would be badly judged.[48] Are there any personal papers of Pius XII or records of his discussions with leading advisers, diplomats or important foreign visitors that would illuminate this issue, and, if so, could we see them?

2. Commentary

The preliminary report reveals that the panel members felt it would be necessary to see more documents before arriving at any final judgment. They attempted to persuade the Vatican[49] to open its archives so that they could determine if all vital documents had been included in the *ADSS (Actes et Documents du Saint-Siège relatifs à la Seconde Guerre Mondiale)*.

This request raises the question whether much valuable evidence of the Pope's conduct is being hidden or is missing still. One member of the Commission,[50] Michael Marrus, revealed this fear in two separate interviews on the subject.

Marrus was interviewed by Paolo Mastrolilli, an Italian journalist. "We must not fall into the error of evaluating facts that occurred more than 50 years ago with today's sensitivity," Marrus stated. "Vatican Council II has enormously changed relations between Jews and Catholics, and therefore now certain attitudes may seem strange. During the period of Pius XII, the reality of the times was different."

Yet, in the *Los Angeles Times* (March 4, 2001) book review of *Under His Very Windows* by Susan Zuccotti and *The Catholic Church and the Holocaust* by Michael Phayer, Marrus affirms: "Both authors present a much more detailed and sophisticated assessment of the official Catholic outlook of the time than most previous works while remaining quite critical of the Church's leadership. They paint a portrait of a papacy obsessed with its fears of Nazi retaliation and relentless other wartime threats to the Church's existence, with the result that other concerns were pushed to the periphery. The result is less a story in black and white, and rather a more tangled account replete with shortsightedness, miscalculations, sporadic indifference, half-hearted efforts and failure of the imagination."

While admitting that the Pope regularly expressed his concerns for suffering humanity and the victimization of innocent civilians,

Marrus states: "Both books make the case that the Vatican was far from the model of benevolence suggested by its defenders, including some Jews who embraced such a view of the Holy See immediately after the war. There is no convincing indication, as Zuccotti energetically documents, that the Vatican ever urged clerics in Italy or elsewhere in Europe specifically to shelter Jews....Cautious, balanced and preoccupied with what he believed was possible to achieve, the Pope and his emissaries energetically defended the prerogatives of the Church, strove mightily to spare Italy and in particular Rome from the ravages of war and championed the cause of Catholics throughout Europe. Jews who appealed to the Holy See were received politely but usually came away disappointed."

A more balanced analysis of what the archives would or would not hold was given by another member of the Commission, Gerald Fogarty. "Pius XII believed more in diplomacy than in public declarations and he behaved himself accordingly. His priority was to stop Nazism and for this reason he also accepted in silence the alliance with Russia, reserving for himself the fight against Communism at a later date. The American Secret Services have documents that judge in a very positive way the actions of the Vatican during the war, but until now they have remained secret. The Holy See was careful to preserve its neutrality, but there exist proofs of the help offered to several German generals, who in the Spring of 1940 had planned a plot to free themselves of Hitler: therefore, what counts more, the public words of the Pope, or the acts accomplished to stop Nazism?" There are no documents in the Vatican archives that refer to the attempted coup; yet documents have been found in British archives. Fogarty also said that "the panel has still not succeeded in overcoming the widespread myth in Anglo-Saxon culture which believes that there are important unpublished documents in the Vatican archives. If such files existed, other proofs of those documents would have been found in the studies I have carried out in archives all over Europe. The opening of the Vatican archives does not answer these questions definitively."

Fogarty's statement underscores that in 1943 and 1944, there was no guarantee that the Nazis would have respected the Vatican's neutrality. One can readily understand that when the Nazis occupied Rome and when the SS and the Gestapo were searching for Jews throughout the Rome area, it was necessary to destroy whatever documentation might have placed the Vatican in peril.

3. Research

Obviously, the Commission members could not research all the existing material that would have answered, at least in part, some of the forty-seven questions. Additional information may be found in archives other than the Vatican's. The Commission requested more documentation from the Vatican archives than would be found in the *ADSS* collection. But much of what they would likely want to find may already be found. A typical example is number 44. It reads: "The Poles were major victims of the Nazis. Members of the Polish Government in Exile in London and some Polish bishops were often very vocal in their criticism of Pius XII's role. It has been reported that the Vatican commissioned the Jesuits to prepare a defense of its Polish policy. Is this correct and, if so, may we see the report? More generally, the subject of Vatican-Polish relations is an essential element for understanding the role of the Holy See during the Holocaust period and deserves further investigation in the Vatican archives. Is there other pertinent information on this subject in the archives that is not in the volumes, and may we see it?"

One source for information about Vatican-Polish relations is the New York Public Library. Thus, for example, in response to question 21, it has available the document "Pope Pius and Poland," published by America Press. With the imprimatur of Cardinal Francis J. Spellman, Archbishop of New York, this documentary outline of papal pronouncements and relief efforts in behalf of Poland since March 1939 was published in 1942 and made available at ten cents per copy.

In the foreword, Francis X. Talbot, S.J., editor-in-chief, states: "To those who love and seek the truth, here is the truth. History will record the truth that Pope Pius XII stands united with Poland, as Poland and the Polish people everywhere are united with the Pope." This pamphlet is a schematic outline of the evidence available that shows the fatherly affection and deep understanding which His Holiness revealed toward the Polish people. It is based on what has been published in newspapers and other periodicals or announced on the radio.[51] The day after his election, March 3, 1939, Pius XII pleaded for peace and diplomatic efforts to prevent the outbreak of hostilities.[52] Other statements to the Sacred College of Cardinals followed on Easter Sunday and on June 2, 1939.[53]

In his radio appeal on August 29, 1939, Pius XII pleaded: "Humanity craves justice, bread and liberty, not the sword that kills and destroys. Christ is with us; for brotherly love was made by Him a solemn and fundamental commandment...."[54]

On August 31, 1939, the Pope called the ambassadors of Germany, France, Italy, and Poland to his study, and the Cardinal Secretary of State distributed to each a copy of his pontifical message: "The Holy Father is unwilling to abandon the hope that the present negotiations may issue in a just and peaceful solution such as the whole world continues to implore. In the name of God, therefore, His Holiness exhorts the Governments of Germany and Poland to do everything possible to avoid incidents of every kind and to forego every measure that might aggravate the present tension. He begs the Governments of England, France and Italy to second this request."[55]

Already on September 30, 1939, many Polish cities were burning and the country was bathed in blood and tears. The Pope received a group of Polish refugees at Castelgandolfo and tried to comfort them, pointing out that the fatherly providence of God was the fundamental guarantee of the indestructibility of the nation and of its rebirth after the passing calamities of the moment. "Christ...one day will reward the tears you shed over your beloved dead, and over a Poland that shall never perish."[56]

Cardinal Hinsley, Archbishop of Westminster, wrote the preface to *The Persecution of the Catholic Church in German-Occupied Poland.*[57] This book contains reports presented by Cardinal Hlond, Primate of Poland, to Pope Pius XII, as well as Vatican broadcasts and other reliable evidence. It definitely confirms the fact that Vatican Radio broke the news of Nazi atrocities in Poland against Jews and Catholics.[58]

Regarding question 2 on *Kristallnacht* (The night of the broken glass), the Commission raised the issue of the role of Pope Pius XII. But Eugenio Pacelli was not yet Pope. He was Secretary of State.[59] During this period, he had much control over Vatican media and undoubtedly approved the articles in the Vatican newspaper, *L'Osservatore Romano,* reporting on the anti-Jewish atrocities committed on *Kristallnacht.* This newspaper described the crimes on November 13, 1938, with headlines,

"Dopo le manifestazioni antisemite in Germania" (After the Anti-Semitic Demonstrations in Germany) and two days later, "La ripercussione delle manifestazioni antisemite in Germania" (The Repercussion after the Anti-Semitic Demonstrations in Germany).[60]

Pope Pius XI was the reigning Pope during these anti-Jewish atrocities. His condemnation had preceded *Kristallnacht*. On October 21, 1938, the Pontiff personally attacked Hitler, likening him to Julian the Apostate (Roman Emperor Flavius Claudius Julianus), who attempted to "saddle the Christians with responsibility for the persecution he had unleashed against them." That same month the Pope officially filed a protest against the racial laws in Italy that had increased in severity after the "law for the defense of the Italian race" was passed.

In its report, the Judeo-Catholic Commission requested in question 13 materials from the beatification process of Archbishop Aloysius Stepinac of Zagreb. Since there have been recent charges that the Archbishop and Catholic leaders in Croatia supported the government's brutality toward the Serbs, historian Ronald Rychlak responded to this accusation: "There is no credible evidence that the Pope or the Vatican behaved inappropriately....In August 1942, the Grand Rabbi of Zagreb, Dr. Miroslav Freiberger, wrote to Pius XII expressing his 'most profound gratitude' for the 'limitless goodness that the representatives of the Holy See and the leaders of the Church showed to our poor brothers.'" (*Actes et Documents,* vol. 8, no. 441. See also, no. 473, which describes Vatican efforts to find sanctuary for Croatian Jews in Italy; no. 537, on Vatican efforts to "alleviate the sad conditions of the Croatian Jews"; no. 557, which reports Vatican insistence on "a benevolent treatment toward the Jews.") In October, a message went out from the Vatican to its representatives in Zagreb regarding the "painful situation that spills out against the Jews in Croatia" and instructing them to petition the government for "a more benevolent treatment of those unfortunates." In December 1942, Dr. Freiberger wrote again, expressing his confidence "in the support of the Holy See."

Notes by the Cardinal Secretary of State reflect that Vatican petitions were successful in getting a suspension of "dispatches of Jews from Croatia" by January 1943, but Germany was applying pressure for "an attitude more firm against the Jews." Cardinal Maglione then outlined steps that could be taken by the Vatican to help the Jews and, on March 6, 1943, he instructed its unofficial representatives in Zagreb to work on behalf of the Jews. On September 24, 1943, Alex Easterman, the British representative of the World Jewish Congress, contacted Monsignor William Godfrey, the Apostolic Delegate in London, and informed him that about four thousand Jewish refugees from Croatia were safely evacuated to an island in the Adriatic Sea. "I feel sure that efforts of your Grace and of the Holy See have brought about this fortunate result," wrote Easterman.

Sir Francis D'Arcy, British Minister to the Holy See during the war years, wrote that Archbishop Stepinac always acted according to the "well-intended dictates of his conscience." In a speech on October 24, 1942, the Archbishop refuted Nazi theory: "All men and all races are children of God; all without distinction. Those who are Gypsies, Black, European, or Aryan all have the same rights....For this reason, the Catholic Church had always condemned, and continues to condemn, all injustice and all violence committed in the name of theories of class, race, or nationality. It is not permissible to persecute Gypsies or Jews because they are thought to be an inferior race." The Associated Press reported that by 1942, Archbishop Stepinac had become "a harsh critic" of that Nazi puppet regime, condemning its "genocidal policies, which killed tens of thousands of Serbs, Jews, Gypsies and Croats."

Question 17 states that the Pope, addressing "the Sacred College of Cardinals on 2 June 1943, did elusively refer to those 'destined sometimes, even without guilt on their part, to exterminatory measures.' This was the second and last occasion on which Pope Pius XII would make any (indirect) reference to the Holocaust during the war years. Its proximity in time to his reply on 30 April 1943 to von Preysing suggests that there may have been a connection, though once again only a closer investigation of the Vatican archives could reveal whether this was the case. What unpublished documents regarding the Pope's speech and his reply to von Preysing do the archives contain?"

By stating, "second and last occasion," what do the members of the Commission mean? That same month the Pope issued an encyclical, *Mystici Corporis Christi,* which was an obvious attack on the theoretical basis of National Socialism, and Vatican Radio followed up with a broadcast that expressly stated there was no distinction between Jews and other men. On July 28, 1943, another broadcast reported on the Pope's denunciation of totalitarian forms of government and support for democratic ideals: "The life and activities of all must be protected against arbitrary human action. This means that no man has any right on the life and freedom of other men....The Pope condemns those who dare to place the fortunes of whole nations in the hands of one man alone, a man who as such, is the prey of passions, error and dreams." There was no doubt to whom the Pope was referring.

Pius XII appealed to Catholics "to look to the Vicar of Jesus Christ as the loving Father of them all, who...takes upon himself with all his strength the defense of truth, justice and charity." He explained, "Our paternal love embraces all peoples, whatever their nationality or race," and made an appeal for all to "follow our peaceful King who taught us to love not only those who are of a different nation or race, but even our enemies." Pinchas E. Lapide, the Israeli consul in Italy, wrote: "Pius XII chose mystical theology as a cloak for a message which no cleric or educated Christian could possibly misunderstand."

Question 18 reads: "In a letter of March 1944 to Cardinal Konrad Graf von Preysing, Bishop of Berlin (1880–1950), the Pope stated 'Before me lie your eight letters of 1943 and five letters of 1944.' Do these letters exist in the archives and can we see them?" All letters from Pius XII to the German bishops are available in volume 2 of the *ADSS*. The Commission mentions letter number 105, dated April 30, 1943. Here Pius XII explains that he must consider whether the reprisals he fears render public declarations possible or not. He further describes his motives for reserve: the measures taken against the Church, particularly against the Poles in "Warthegau," and the retaliation toward priests in concentration camps.

In his earlier letter of September 25, 1939, to the archbishops and bishops of Germany, Pius XII had already expressed his concern. A summary of this letter is indicative of some of the topics discussed throughout his correspondence with the German hierarchy.

After thanking the German archbishops and bishops for their words of gratitude, he praises them for the close union maintained among the bishops with the Holy See. He is distressed because of the present situation and reminds them that faithfulness to the papacy is the guarantee and the assurance against all dangers to the Church. He states that the tiara of the Pope became a crown of thorns and that from the beginning of his pontificate all efforts were made to preserve peace. He reminds them of his radio message of the month of August. Despite that message war became a reality. The Pontiff expresses his compassion for the universal misfortune. Among other statements, the Pope recognizes the difficult situation of the Church in Germany, where the attacks against her were becoming increasingly violent. The Church is now persecuted and calumniated. His Holiness speaks about the particular danger for the youth of Germany and the necessity for prayer. He exhorts the bishops toward generous charity and makes a special recommendation for their apostolate to the soldiers. He encourages close rapport between the pastors and the faithful and offers praise for the nursing sisters. He ends with a final prayer for God's protection.

The Commission questions whether or not letters, other than the April 30, 1943, letter, exist in the Vatican archives. Regarding such letters, it should be noted that volume 2 contains eighteen letters from Pius XII to Cardinal Preysing—from April 9, 1939, to March 21, 1944. These letters, written in German or Latin, should be consulted.

In general, the Judeo-Catholic Commission's report, issued after a year-long study, said that some of the kinds of documents it would still like to see include "the records of day-to-day administration of the Church and the Holy See. In addition, there are the internal communications that every administration leaves behind—diaries, appointment books, minutes of meetings, memoranda, draft documents, and so forth that detail the process of how the Vatican arrived at the decisions it made."

The Commission members, however, often revealed individually their personal convictions that Pius XII did not speak out forcefully enough against the Nazis. A Jewish member of the International Commission, Bernard Suchecky, research director at the Free University of Brussels, Belgium, expressed satisfaction with the cooperation established among the six historians. He also commented during a press conference, prompted in part by a news leak by the French newspaper *Le Monde:* "Pius XII was especially concerned about the fate of German Catholics, a posture nourished by his personal historical appreciation, according to which there was a Communism that had to be ended, and a Nazism that was considered a passing trial."

A Catholic member of the Commission, professor emerita Eva Fleischner, Montclair University, New Jersey, volunteered her opinion on Pius XII: "The expectations on the role he could play against Nazism are very high, higher than for any other leader. In addition, Pope Pacelli believed in the role of diplomacy, which also has its rules and limitations.

"Perhaps he did not understand that to stop the lethal destructive machine of Nazism something more was needed in addition to prayer and diplomacy," she added. "In this connection I maintain that he was more of a diplomat than a prophet."

A Jewish member, Michael Marrus, University of Toronto Dean of Graduate Studies, an expert in Holocaust studies, called for a distinction between "information and conscience: the news on the Nazi crimes was in the possession of the Vatican as it was in that of other governments, but conscience needs more time."

But the Vatican has taken the questions posed by the Commission very seriously. In response to the *Le Monde* report, Vatican spokesman Joaquin Navarro-Valls said: "The Commission's report expresses positive appreciation for the documentation that has been made available by the archives and indicates, succinctly, the lines on which future research will be based. The report also contains a series of questions that, according to the experts of the group, would need further documentation for more profound study."

4. Some Reflections on the Shortcomings of the Forty-seven Questions

Father Peter Gumpel, S.J., relator of the beatification cause of Pius XII and a noted German historian, eager to exchange information with his fellow historians, had prepared forty-seven separate dossiers containing documentation—declarations, letters, books, essays, and dispatches—in an effort to respond fully to the questions. However, in the time allotted to him, he could respond to only ten of the forty-seven questions. He offered to meet at any other time in order to reply to the remaining questions.

When interviewed, Gumpel complained: "I find the conduct of the Commission…academically unacceptable.…By what right have they circulated the Preliminary Report…without having even heard the answers to the questions they themselves posed?" Apparently, the Preliminary Report was leaked to the press and published in its entirety on the Internet site of the Jewish International B'nai B'rith Association. It was also leaked to the French newspaper *Le Monde*—a full-page article with long citations and aggressive quotations from a member of the Commission.

Unfortunately, Gumpel's complete answers to the forty-seven questions have not been published. Why not publish these fully documented answers? In the same vein, Andrea Ricciardi, professor of contemporary history and author of *The Church of Rome during the Resistance* (1976), warns that "there must be respect for pluralism, but there cannot be sensationalism as practiced by John Cornwell....We are faced with a historiographical debate at the international level imposed in a manic way in regard to Pius XII. Considered in life as one of the highest interpreters of the needs and aspirations of his time, Pope Pacelli has been the object of attacks that have caused arguments over his political action and the value of his entire spiritual magisterium."

Fuller education and discussion is the only answer to these polemics, not statements as printed in the Israeli newspaper *Ha'aretz* (August 4, 2000), claiming that the Commission had already reached an agreement on Pius XII's moral shortcomings and that "Jewish activists and European leaders have seen the preliminary report."

During the International Catholic-Jewish Liaison Committee meeting in 1992, on behalf of the Congregation for Catholic Education, Dr. Remi Hoeckman, O.P., stated: "Intuition, discovery, and vision have met with positive response in both our communities. They have laid bare wrong approaches, mentalities and attitudes, and principles which had been forgotten or obscured. They have produced guidelines for change and made suggestions for implementation. The objective now is to make the contents of those principles and guidelines really affect, by means of education, the wider community, and therefore, in the first place, the educators of the wider community, i.e., our theologians and priests, teachers and catechists. This means not just adding units on Judaism to the old curricula, or footnotes to the old texts, but also to revise the existing curricula and courses in the light of the results of scholarly research, greater sensitivity, and, on the part of the Church, in the light of the Church's teaching."[61]

The Vatican archival policy compares very favorably with that of other states around the world. The accusation that the Church is concealing documents is a very serious matter.

But, on the contrary, in an effort to educate the public about the Vatican documents, Father Pierre Blet, S.J., the last surviving member of the team of Jesuit editors for the *ADSS (Actes et Documents du Saint-Siège relatifs à la Seconde Guerre Mondiale),* published a synthesis of the Vatican archival material dating between 1965 and 1981, in *Pius XII and the Second World War* (Mawah, N.J.: Paulist Press, 1999). He rejected the accusation that Pope Pius XII was anti-Semitic and defended him vigorously.

And as part of the process of education, there can be no doubt about the gratitude of the Jews. In 1955, when Italy celebrated the tenth anniversary of its liberation, Italian Jewry proclaimed April 17 as a "Day of Gratitude." Among the thousands of Jewish people who made a pilgrimage to the Vatican to express appreciation for the Pope's wartime assistance was the Israeli Philharmonic Orchestra.

According to the *Jerusalem Post,* "Conductor Paul Klecki had requested that the Orchestra on its first visit to Italy play for the Pope as a gesture of gratitude for the help his Church had given to all those persecuted by Nazi Fascism."[62]

Before the celebration, Monsignor Montini, who later became Pope Paul VI, was asked to accept an award for his work on behalf of Jews. Though visibly touched by the honor, he declined: "All I did was my duty," he said. "I only acted upon orders from the Holy Father." When Archbishop Angelo Roncalli, the future Pope John XXIII, was thanked for his work on behalf of Jewish refugees in Istanbul, he too explained that he was carrying out the Pope's orders.

Pius XII was honest, holy, and charitable. In conformity with Catholic social doctrine of subsidiarity, he encouraged and inspired others to help suffering humanity. Indeed, there was a great deal of papal involvement in Jewish rescue operations. One finds a mountain of testimony from rescuers, victims, Germans, Jews, priests, nuns, seven cardinals and two Popes.

Pope Pius XII alone had the authority to open buildings to outsiders. Many witnesses have testified under oath that he directly assisted the Jews and other refugees. The Pope not only gave orders to open Vatican buildings to shelter them, but authorized convents and monasteries to welcome them, and provided funds and food to care for them. He also authored many of the intensely anti-Nazi statements that were beamed around the world by Vatican Radio. The Nazis called Vatican Radio the "Voice of the Pope."

Finally, to return to the hidden suspicion that much evidence is still hidden in Vatican Archives, Ronald Rychlak, author of *Hitler, the War, and the Pope,* confronted Susan Zuccotti during a debate cosponsored by

Trinity College[63] on February 26, 2001. Zuccotti failed to mention the reaction provoked in Nazi ranks whenever Pius XII protested. She suggested that the only versions of Vatican Radio available to researchers today are the rebroadcasts of the BBC which, she says, are unreliable. But besides the BBC broadcasts themselves, there are other lines of evidence that support the need to destroy records or make very indirect references in Vatican communications.

It was extremely dangerous to keep any records related to anti-Nazi efforts. In fact, even Susan Zuccotti, in her 1987 book, *The Italians and the Holocaust,* wrote: "Any direct personal order would have had to be kept very quiet to protect those who were actually sheltered."

Arguments based on the lack of an existing written order from the Pope to protect Jews severely underestimate the danger of life in a Nazi-controlled nation. Undoubtedly recipients of Vatican papers were careful to destroy them. Evidence refutes Zuccotti's argument regarding an alleged lack of papal involvement. In his opening statement at the Eichmann trial, Israeli Attorney General Gideon Hausner said: "The Pope himself intervened personally in support of the Jews of Rome." Heinrich Grober, a Protestant minister, testified that Pius XII helped him save Jews. Documents introduced in that trial also show Vatican efforts for a halt to the arrests of Roman Jews.

Zuccotti is unfair and inconsistent in measuring evidence. By insisting that there are no documents regarding Jews in the Pope's handwriting, she is advancing an argument that was made by Holocaust denier David Irving. He once offered a reward for anyone who could find a document from Adolf Hitler linking him to the extermination of Jews. Serious historians rightfully reject this argument.

In *Yad Vashem Studies,* volume 15, John Conway, a leading authority on the Vatican and the Holocaust, states that the archival material "confirms the picture already drawn by such Jewish authors as Livia Rothkirchen and Pinchas Lapide. Where the Nuncios were alert, and the governments susceptible to Papal remonstrances, then the interventions succeeded in delaying or reducing…the deportations and other acts of persecution towards the Jews."

From documents of the Vatican archives contained in the *Actes* volumes, it is clear that the Vatican, through its nuncios in Germany, Italy, and the occupied countries, received information regarding Nazi atrocities in Poland and other occupied countries, including deportations of

Jewish victims. Through Vatican Radio the Pope was aware of the assistance the Church was able to give them (considerably more than any other person, nation, or agency). Documentation, news reports and newspaper editorials in the United States and Britain prove that this information was passed on to Jewish agencies and led to diplomatic and public protests and condemnations against Nazi atrocities inflicted upon Jewish victims.

*   *   *

On July 23, 2001, Associated Press International announced that the committee of Jewish and Catholic historians, who were appointed by their respective groups to examine Pope Pius XII's wartime actions, suspended its work. Initially the historians had agreed to the project without a Vatican pledge to open the archives.

Prior to this action, in a letter of June 21, 2001, Cardinal Walter Kasper, president of the Commission for Religious Relations with the Jews, said the Vatican's archives dating after 1923 were not accessible for "technical reasons." He explained that documents not yet catalogued are released as they become ready. He also suggested that in the meantime archives elsewhere could help answer questions. It should be noted that

1. The "general thrust" of the forty-seven questions unmistakably conveyed the unfair implication that there may be hidden evidence of the so-called failure on the part of Pius XII to help the Jewish victims of the war. At that time the Associated Press called the Committee's document "explosive"; the *New York Times* said it expressed the dissatisfaction of the six panel members with Vatican records. *Le Monde* of Paris and, in substance, many other newspapers said it pointed to failures of the Pope and the Church. Accusatory questions and negative insinuations abounded in the "leaked" portion of the Committee report; but no positive findings about the Vatican documents or the Pope were reported.

2. In the previous report, the six members of the Committee agreed that the four Jesuit scholars who spent more than fifteen years in meticulously assembling the twelve volumes of the *Actes,* "had done an excellent job and had approached their task with admirable scholarly objectivity" in reporting documents which they deemed relevant, as to the wartime activities of the Pope and the Catholic Church, in rescuing

many thousands of Jewish victims of the Nazi horrors. Apparently, this positive note was not "leaked."

3. After the damage was done, the attempt to shift the blame to those who have justifiably criticized the form and lack of scholarship of the said questions was not very persuasive. In view of this "unleaked" statement, it appeared inconsistent to continue to push aggressively for the complete opening of the archives. One must assume, from the deserved compliment, that the Committee had given full credence to Father Blet's answer to the recent revisionist critics that there was no attempt, on the part of the Jesuit team, to intentionally hide anything of a negative nature relating to the actions of the Vatican or the Pope; that in the event of the remote possibility that the scholars may have missed any such negative materials, they would have been discovered in the archives of the many countries that had diplomatic relations with the Vatican at the time, or other relevant materials. Father Blet justly resented the implications that reflected upon the integrity of this group of Jesuit scholars, of which he is the last surviving member.

4. The Committee chose to issue an unnecessary "interim report," which was improperly and unfairly "leaked" by a member of the Committee. Neither the coordinators nor the Committee took on any responsibility in connection with the severe damage caused by the "leak." No attempt was made by anyone concerned to initiate appropriate public actions calculated to make amends for what had occurred.

5. This resulted in giving further impetus to "the big lie": the technique of constant repetition of a variety of baseless charges and implications in derogation of Pius XII and the Catholic Church; false propaganda, which had its origin in Communist Russia just before the end of World War II and, resurrected in 1963, has been repeated relentlessly. The statement that the Committee read all the volumes of the *Actes* is not supported by the evidence which indicates that, had members read the *Actes* "painstakingly," they would have found many of the answers to questions they raised.

Only if dialogue between Jewish and Catholic scholars is conducted in a spirit of mutual respect and trust can historical research bear fruit. Every scholar knows that no archive can be consulted if the documents are not catalogued and classified. Cardinal Jorge Maria Mejìa, Vatican archivist, explained that there are more than three million pages of post-1922 documents that will be made available to all scholars as soon as the work is completed.

Ultimately, the Catholic-Jewish voices of reason and truth will prevail, and the true role of Pius XII toward the Jewish victims of World War II will be restored. The time has come to eliminate myths, stereotypes, and prejudices. Jews and Christians must move ahead in common witness to their shared religious values and moral principles. St. Paul's letter to the Romans sets the tone for true brotherhood: "Here there is no difference between Jew and Greek; all have the same Lord, rich in mercy toward all who call upon him. 'Everyone who calls on the name of the Lord will be saved.'"

In *Pius XII and the Second World War* (1997), Pierre Blet wrote that Pius XII returned to the years of fire and sword in a speech to nurses given in May 1952. "He asked the question: 'What should we have done that we have not done?' The Pope was saying that he was conscious of what he had accomplished to prevent the war, to alleviate its sufferings, to reduce the number of its victims—everything he thought he could do. The documents [the *Actes*], in so far as they allow one to probe the human heart, come to the same conclusion. As for results, to affirm that the Pope himself or some other person in his place might have been able to do more is to depart from the field of history in order to venture into the undergrowth of suppositions and dreams."

Pope John Paul II has extended an invitation for all, Jews and Gentiles, to be united spiritually: "I hope that at the dawn of the third millennium sincere dialogue between Christians and Jews will help create a new civilization founded on the one, holy and merciful God, and fostering a humanity reconciled in love."[64]

Ours should be a common fight against anti-Semitism, anti-Catholicism, and all other forms of bigotry. Our common message should be one of renewed hope for all humanity.

Chapter XII
Pope John Paul II

1. The Efforts of John Paul II

*R*epeatedly, Pope John Paul II has defended Pope Pius XII. Speaking to a group of Jewish leaders in Miami in 1987, John Paul II stated that documents "reveal ever more clearly and convincingly how deeply Pius XII felt the tragedy of the Jewish people, and how hard and effectively he worked to assist them."

Some Jewish organizations objected to John Paul II's support of Pius XII in the March 16, 1998, document, *We Remember: A Reflection on the Shoah*. They strongly criticized the statement that the Pope personally or through his representatives had contributed to saving hundreds of thousands of Jewish lives.

"Peace" was the first word John Paul II spoke when he arrived in Amman, Jordan, March 20, 2000, and this was the clear message he gave on March 25, 2000, the last day of his stay in Jerusalem: "In this place of memories, the mind and heart and soul feel an extreme need for silence. Silence in which to remember. Silence in which to try to make some sense of the memories which come flooding back. Silence because there are no words strong enough to deplore the terrible tragedy of the Shoah.

"My own personal memories are of all that happened when the Nazis occupied Poland during the war. I remember my Jewish friends and neighbors, some of whom perished, while others survived. I have come to Yad Vashem to pay homage to the millions of Jewish people who, stripped of everything, especially of human dignity, were murdered in the Holocaust. More than half a century has passed, but the memories remain.

"Here, as at Auschwitz and many other places in Europe, we are overcome by the echo of the heart-rending laments of so many. Men, women, and children cry out to us from the depths of the horror that they knew. How can we fail to heed their cry? No one can forget or ignore what happened. No one can diminish its scale.

"We wish to remember. But we wish to remember for a purpose, namely to ensure that never again will evil prevail, as it did for the millions of innocent victims of Nazism.

"How could man have such utter contempt for man? Because he had reached the point of contempt for God. Only a godless ideology could plan and carry out the extermination of a whole people.

"The honor given to the 'just Gentiles' by the state of Israel at Yad Vashem for having acted heroically to save Jews, sometimes to the point of giving their own lives, is a recognition that not even in the darkest hour is every light extinguished. That is why the Psalms and the entire Bible, though well aware of the human capacity for evil, also proclaim that evil will not have the last word.

"Jews and Christians share an immense spiritual patrimony, flowing from God's self-revelation. Our religious teachings and our spiritual experience demand that we overcome evil with good. We remember, but not with any desire for vengeance or as an incentive to hatred. For us, to remember is to pray for peace and justice, and to commit ourselves to their cause. Only a world at peace, with justice for all, can avoid repeating the mistakes and terrible crimes of the past."

The Church rejects racism in any form as a denial of the image of the Creator inherent in every human being. The Pontiff assured the Jewish people that the Catholic Church was motivated by the Gospel law of truth and love, and was deeply saddened by the displays of anti-Semitism.

It was also fitting that, during the Jubilee Year 2000, on March 7, 2000, Vatican officials should release the nineteen-thousand-word document titled "Memory and Reconciliation: The Church and the Faults of the Past," which examined several difficult theological questions and tried to correct mistaken perceptions about the apology movement. This was not a political but a religious act, addressed first of all to God.

Joseph Cardinal Ratzinger, head of the International Theological Commission, who prepared the document, said the Church was not setting itself up as a tribunal to judge the actions of past Christians. The aim was to "know ourselves and open ourselves to the purification of memories of Christ's death. Sin is...always personal, even though it wounds the entire church."

Pope John Paul II called for "genuine brotherhood" between Christians and Jews, telling Jewish people: "We are deeply saddened by the behavior of those who in the course of history have caused these children of yours to suffer." His expression of repentance on behalf of Catholics should stir the conscience of others to recognize the truth that all human beings are sinners and that we bear equally the guilt of man's inhumanity to man during the past centuries.

On March 14, 2000, the *New York Times* editorial, "The Pope's Apology," stated that John Paul II's words fell short of candidly acknowledging Pius XII's failure "to speak out against the Nazi genocide." This pointed accusation implies that Pius XII bears the responsibility for the cruelties inflicted by the Nazis.

Whenever newspapers reported that Pius XII spoke against Nazi doctrines and atrocities, everyone understood what he denounced. The Nazi media called him "the mouthpiece of the Jews." The soundness of style of his judgment is supported by ample documentary proof, including testimony at the Nuremberg trials. Pius XII's manner of denunciation was calculated to save lives. His heroic, compassionate efforts avoided the inevitable recriminations.

At Yad Vashem Holocaust Memorial, March 23, 2000, the present Pontiff personally addressed the Jewish people: "The words of the ancient Psalm rise from our hearts: 'I have become like a broken vessel. I hear the whispering of many—terror on every side—as they scheme together against me, as they plot to take my life. But I trust in you, O Lord: I say, *you are my God'* (Psalms 31: 13–15)....In this place of solemn remembrance, I fervently pray that our sorrow for the tragedy which the Jewish people suffered in the twentieth century will lead to a new relationship between Christians and Jews. Let us build a new future in which there will be no more anti-Jewish feeling among Christians or anti-Christian feeling among Jews, but rather the mutual respect required of those who adore the one Creator and Lord, and look to Abraham as our common father in faith. The world must heed the warning that comes to us from the victims of the Holocaust, and from the testimony of the survivors. Here at Yad Vashem the memory lives on....."

During the historic "Day of Forgiveness" service at St. Peter's Basilica, Pope John Paul II asked forgiveness for the sins Catholics have committed over the ages. Church leaders and members have wronged women, Jews, Gypsies, other Christians, and Catholics themselves. As the Pope's message spread quickly around the world, non-Catholic leaders who had pressed the one-billion-member Church for redress responded with mixed reactions.

Among those who reacted was Israel's chief rabbi, Meir Lau. He expected more in the way of an apology and described himself as "deeply frustrated." Reference was made to the past history of the Church with regard to the burning of heretics at the stake during the Inquisition; the slaughter of Muslim armies during the Crusades; and the silence of some Catholics who stood silent in the face of Nazi genocide during the Holocaust. However, the Pontiff had not been specific in his mention of wrongs nor had he mentioned names or provided a full list of groups.

Repentance is a personal mission for Pope John Paul II, who in recent years has sought to cleanse the Church's conscience for a fresh start in its third millennium. During his twenty-two-year pontificate, he has held lengthy discussions on the Holocaust and the Inquisition. But in scope and prominence, this liturgical petition for forgiveness was unlike anything in the history of the Church. The Pope said during his homily: "We are asking pardon for the divisions among Christians, for the use of violence that some have committed in the service of truth, and for attitudes of mistrust and hostility assumed toward followers of other religions."

Next in the service came a series of seven prayed petitions, delivered by five cardinals and two bishops. The Pope responded to each of their petitions: "Have mercy on your sinful children." Though worded generally, the petitions cited the mistreatment of women, "who are all too often humiliated and marginalized," the "contempt for cultures and religious traditions," the "sins committed in the service of the truth," and "the sins committed by not a few against the people of the Covenant."

The Jewish leaders expressed the same hope and disappointment as earlier over their efforts to elicit a direct apology from the Church for its record during the Holocaust. The March 1998 Vatican document titled *We Remember: A Reflection on the Shoah*—issued by the Commission for Religious Relations with the Jews—had disappointed many Jewish leaders because it did not ascribe direct responsibility for the Holocaust to the Church and it defended wartime Pope Pius XII.

A panel of Vatican-appointed theologians prepared a thirty-page document expanding the philosophical and theological basis for the Pope's apologies and repentance. Mentioned by name was the Roma group, also known as Gypsies, consisting of many of the least structured members of society. Also mentioned were the sins of abortion, mistreatment of children, and of "those who abuse the promise of biotechnology." While the theologians hope that their plea will improve relations with Jews, Eastern Christians, Protestants, minorities, and other groups, their document leaves no doubt that this churchwide confession is addressed to God.

With an introduction by Pope John Paul II, the document *We Remember* apologized for the role certain members of the Church played not only in the destruction of European Jewry, but also for their role in events over the two thousand years of Christendom. To the surprise and chagrin of many Catholics, this document was rejected by many in the Jewish community, as well as by many liberal Catholics. According to a *New York Times* editorial, *We Remember* was a rationalization, a whitewash—too little, too late. The insults of Rolf Hochhuth's play *The Deputy* were repeated as well as charges of further outrages attributed to the Pontiff.

However, the caring actions of the Holy See—sheltering Jews in the Vatican and in the papal summer home in Castelgandolfo; ordering that convents, monasteries, hospitals, and schools shelter Jews; the issuing of false baptismal certificates and false identity papers and providing money for ransom—must never be underestimated. It should be noted that these actions, in addition to Pius XII's hundreds of private appeals to Italian and German authorities on behalf of particular Jews and Jewish communities, are acknowledged by many authorities.

Critics of Pius XII say he should have been much more outspoken in his condemnation of the Holocaust; in particular, that he should have publicly excommunicated Hitler and Mussolini. In fact, for their violence and apostasy, these ungodly leaders incurred automatic excommunication under canon law then in force. Hitler was an anti-Catholic. Would a papal declaration of excommunication have done some good? "No," said Don Luigi Sturzo, founder of the Christian Democratic movement in wartime Italy. Sturzo did not think so. He pointed out that the last times a nominal excommunication was pronounced against a head of state, like Queen Elizabeth I and Napoleon, neither monarch changed policy. And there is reason to believe that violent retaliation, the loss of many more Jewish lives, and an intensification of the persecution of Catholics would have immediately followed such provocation.

Today critics fail to remember that when the Pope and his bishops condemn abortion and suggest that Catholic politicians who seek to promote abortion "rights" are automatically excommunicated, these same critics are outraged. According to these critics, this is interference by the Church in the affairs of state: The separation of Church and State is at risk; or, it is said, "We will have to look closely at the tax-exempt status of the Church." Other critics want the Church to intervene only when their favorite causes are at risk.

It is also alleged that Pius XII did not adequately "speak out." Very often people are censured for being all talk. Is Pope Pius attacked for not being all action? A kind of moral selectivity thus distorts decisions made (and not made) by Pius XII. On October 20, 1999, a document was discovered in the U.S. National Archives, which contains the impressions of Harold Tittman, the American envoy to the Vatican in 1942. In December of that year, Tittman had a private meeting with Pius XII, who expressed great surprise that anyone would think that he had not clearly condemned the Nazis in his Christmas message.

So the accusation is not that the Pope did nothing, but that he didn't do enough. As six million Jews perished at the hands of Hitler, it is not hard to make a case that not enough was done. The question is, did the Pope do as much as he could do? The answer is, "Yes, he did!"

On March 31, 2000, following the Israeli Papal visit, I was asked to appear on NBC's Channel 4 special forum *Journey to the Holy Land.* The focus of the discussion was on Pope John Paul II' s visit to the Holy Land. Also appearing on the program were Father James Loughran, Director of the Ecumenical Commission of the Archdiocese of New York, Imam Izak El Pasha of the Malcom Shabazz Mosque, Rabbi David Woznica, Director of the Bronfman Center, of the 92nd Street Y, and Reverend Eileen Lindner, Associate General Secretary of the National Council of Churches. Other members of the panel were Abe Foxman of the Anti-Defamation League and Dr. Hani Awadallah of the Arab-American Association. Hosts were Chuck Scarborough, Lynda Baquero, Gabe Pressman, and Ralph Penza.

During this hour-long town meeting held at the Y's Kaufman Concert Hall in New York, I tried to set the record straight. I defended Pope Pius XII and reminded my copanelists of the important papal decree on anti-Semitism issued March 25, 1928, long before World War II: "The Holy See...condemns unreservedly hatred against the people once chosen by God; the hatred that commonly goes by the name of anti-Semitism."

Indeed, a link to the 1928 decree is Pope John Paul II's visit to Israel in 2000 that symbolized another historic movement to promote better relations and understanding in the Jewish world. He fulfilled his spiritual pilgrimage in order to link the Old and New Testaments. The interreligious services in the Holy Land included Muslims, Palestinians, Israeli. He repeated that we are all sons and daughters of the same God. He wanted all Catholics to rekindle their faith in the Eucharist. The pilgrim Pope was leading his people to affirmation and repentance with the hope of preserving the Christian heritage and presence in the Holy Land. He spoke about love of God that translates into love of neighbor and is manifested by our actions. His message transcended all political aims. At Yad Vashem he further prayed for unity, understanding, forgiveness. He invited all men and women to follow his example. He insisted that anti-Semitism is not condoned by the Catholic Church.

While in Jerusalem the Pope also visited the "Wailing Wall"—the western wall built by Herod to enclose the Temple's courtyard. It is a sacred place for Jews where they pray and weep in memory of the ancient splendor of Jerusalem and the Temple, once the center of all Jewish life, definitively destroyed in 70 A.D. by the Romans. They place small votive messages in the crevices of the slabs of stone. Pope John Paul's petition for forgiveness was the prayer he had read in Rome on March 12, 2000—a commitment to genuine fraternity with the people of the Covenant. It was a very emotional moment: the Pontiff walked up to the Wall alone, prayed there for a few moments, and placed a piece of paper with his signature in one of the crevices. He then placed his right hand on the Wall, before blessing himself.

The Pope's final words were: "Only a world at peace, with justice for all, can avoid repeating the mistakes and terrible crimes of the past. Let us build a new future...." In his official response, Prime Minister Barak praised John Paul II, saying, "You have done more than anyone else to bring about the historic change in the attitude of the Church toward the Jewish people, and to dress the gaping wounds that festered over many bitter centuries."

Among this Pope's previous actions were: In 1979 he visited the Auschwitz concentration camp near Cracow, in Poland; in 1990 he endorsed the Prague statement that declared anti-Semitism a sin against God and humanity and one for which Christians should repent; in 1993 he announced full diplomatic relations with Israel. These commitments and the heartfelt words spoken at Yad Vashem have comforted many Jews. Some wonderful expressions of gratitude arrived in response. The following headline appeared in Rome's Sunday edition of the newspaper *Avvenire* (March 26, 2000): "Today I, an Elder Brother, Feel Like Wojtyla's Son."

Paolo Alazraki stated: "I am a Jew, but over the last weeks, I wish I had been a Christian. To have such a religious father, so majestic in his simplicity, so powerful in his humility, so wise in his strength to combat and overcome, with the gentleness and enormous force of faith, the resistances that he met within his 'circle' to the petition to 'forgive us,' first made to himself, then to his faithful, and finally to the entire world, and to his sublime words of strength and charity spoken in Palestine."

Alazraki emphasized that the Pope had spoken in Israel, land of Canaan, land of the Patriarchs and also land "of our deepest self, in the ancient roads of the salt and silk caravans, the birthplace of extraordinary civilizations. Those who forgive are not weak; those who ask forgiveness are strong. My Rabbis and a great part of Israeli Judaism have acted wrongly in not understanding, not interpreting, not rejoicing over this immense gesture of reconciliation which opens new, extraordinary possibilities in favor of mutual respect among peoples and, therefore, a better life for them and among themselves, and also greater economic development because it will allow, especially in the Middle East, but not only there, the freeing of those creative, mercantile and intellectual forces that for dozens of centuries have characterized the mind of Jews and Arabs."

All the foregoing has "positive influences also for Europe," according to this Jewish writer. "This young, shaky but serene old man, who is conscious of the importance of his actions and the steps he is taking, reflected in his face, has sublimated, gone beyond, made the suspicious, uncomfortable postures of the Rabbis and Muftis, probably pressured by political authorities, look almost ridiculous. What did they want with the condemnation of Pius XII, the humiliation of their younger brothers?"

Alazraki congratulated the Jewish people and Prime Minister Barak, "an angel of peace with a good face who has given the Holy Sepulcher as a 'present' to the Vatican." Behind this news were five years of struggles and mutual recriminations over the administration of the Holy Places. "Praised be the Lord, whoever he is and wherever he is. Praised be this Pope," the writer states, overwhelmed with gratitude to the Holy Father, and not knowing how to thank him. "Perhaps, giving him, but only for this Jubilee year, something of my religious being, which is what matters most to me in the world. This year, with my Jewish friends, I myself will try to meet Christians again, as they did during the first three centuries of this era, when they prayed together in the same synagogues and only after Constantine's reign, sadly, went on different roads.

"Dear Wojtyla, this is my gift for a year. And the promise to become a promoter of a huge forest of new trees, right there, on the border (which I hope will soon disappear forever) between Gaza and Israel, in your name, with our names, but also our hearts, engraved. What you have done for all is immense. Like faith, like love. Extraordinary things that are often lost, re-found, and lost again."

The writer ends his article: "This is my present for the Jubilee. I have no debts and no credits. Therefore, I can celebrate it worthily, in my deepest interior and with all Jews and Christians who have understood your gesture. So be it! So be it!"

Another expression of gratitude: On March 23, 2000, with reference to Pope John Paul II's statement at Israel Yad Vashem Holocaust Memorial, Rabbi Eric Yoffie, President of the Union of American Hebrew Congregations, stated: "I believe that Jews everywhere were touched by the ceremony and by his words, which so clearly came from his heart."[1]

Still another account touches our hearts. During World War II, Jewish and Catholic families struggled for survival in Poland. The Hillers lived in the Cracow ghetto and begged their childless gentile friends, the Yachowitches, to care for their two-year-old son, Shachne. This the Catholic couple did at great risk to their own lives. In an emotional parting, Helen Hiller handed over her only child to her Christian friends along with several crucial letters.

One was addressed to the child, telling of his parents' great love for him and how this love had prompted them to leave him alone with the Yachowitches. It also informed him of his Jewishness and expressed the hope that he would grow up to be proud of his Jewish heritage. Another, addressed to relatives in Montreal and Washington, D.C., informed them of the child's whereabouts and asked that they rear the boy if anything happened to his parents. The last letter was to the Yachowitches. It asked that the boy be reared a Jew and returned to his people if his parents perished. Tragically, the Hillers were consumed by the Holocaust.

These were perilous times for everyone. Fleeing the dreaded Gestapo, the Yachowitches often hid out in barns and haystacks with Shachne and became attached to the child, whom they decided to have baptized and reared as their own. One day Mrs. Yachowitch approached a young, newly ordained priest in Cracow and, revealing to him her secret about the true identity of the little boy, she asked that Shachne be baptized a Christian.

"What were the parents' wishes when they entrusted their only child to you and your husband?" the young priest asked. When the priest heard about the letters and Helen Hiller's last request that the boy be brought up a Jew, he shook his head, refusing to perform the ceremony.

"It would not be fair," the priest said that day in 1946. Soon after, when he was nine, Shachne was taken in by relatives in Montreal. When he was twelve years old, he was adopted by a great aunt in Washington, D.C., where he graduated from college, became a very successful businessman, and remained an observant Jew.

However, the story takes one more warm, dramatic turn and borders on the miraculous. The young priest who refused to baptize young Shachne Hiller a Catholic in Cracow in 1946 was Pope John Paul II, a worthy successor of Pope Pius XII.[2]

2. Vatican Update

March 25, 2000, was a historic day for Jews and Catholics. The *Vatican Update* on EWTN (Eternal Word Television Network) described the Pope's visit to the Holocaust Memorial in Jerusalem. In an emotional appearance at Yad Vashem, John Paul II emphasized that the Catholic Church "is deeply saddened by the hatred, acts of persecution and displays of anti-Semitism directed against the Jews by Christians at any time and in any place."

Vatican documents explained that the Church is holy and cannot sin, but that its members have sinned through the ages. Acknowledging these faults can foster renewal and reconciliation in the present, the document insisted. It rejected any notion of collective guilt by Christians.

In their reports on John Paul II's message at Yad Vashem, newspapers repeated that the Pope failed to apologize for Pius XII's silence. They implied that the wartime Pope failed to do all that he could have done, in preventing the Nazi atrocities inflicted upon the Jewish people.

The Pope chose silent action and shared his hesitations and his doubts in letters to the German bishops. On March 3, 1944, he wrote: "Frequently it is with pain and difficulty that a decision is made as to what the situation demands; prudent reserve and silence or, on the contrary, candid speech and vigorous action." He had no illusions and took into consideration not the regime and its leaders, but the German Catholics.

Historian Pierre Blet writes: "Pius XII had to consider that a public statement on his part would have furnished ammunition to Nazi propaganda, which would in turn have presented the Pope as an enemy of Germany." Pius XII knew that every word of his public addresses "had to be considered and weighed with a deep seriousness in the interest of those who are suffering."

Until the arrival of the Allies in 1945, the Vatican was totally dependent for its survival on the Fascists and the Nazis. Would the Fascist and Nazi governments have continued to supply utilities and food for the thousands of refugees living in the Vatican? The media's evaluation of Pius XII's record is unfair.

With regard to the Holocaust in central and eastern Europe during World War II, what else could Pope Pius XII do? Were the Swiss Guards supposed to liberate the millions of Jews, political prisoners, and others condemned to Nazi concentration camps? If the Pope had spoken out forthrightly against the Holocaust, would the thousands hidden in the Vatican and in Europe be saved?

The Pope's only choice was to save as many Holocaust victims as possible from deportation to the labor camps for enslavement and death. By the end of the war, he saved 85 percent of Italy's Jews by harboring them in churches and monasteries in Rome and elsewhere across Europe. Now he is painted as an anti-Semite who was publicly and selfishly silent on the Holocaust in order to protect the Catholic Church.

Some claim that the reason for smearing the Catholic Church is to deflect attention from the fact that leading Zionists were not prepared to help the vast majority of Jews from eastern Europe during the Holocaust years. Rescue of Holocaust victims was definitely a secondary agenda for these Zionists. Theirs was an implied strategy of keeping as silent as possible on the matter of Holocaust victims.

Yizhak Gruenbaum was head of the Rescue Committee for European Jewry based in Palestine. In February 1943, he spoke in Tel Aviv: "For the rescue of the Jews of the Diaspora, we should consolidate our excess strength and the surplus of powers that we have. When they come to us with two plans—the rescue of the masses of Jews in Europe or the redemption of the land—I vote, without a second thought, for the redemption of the land. The more said about the slaughter of our people, the greater the minimization of our efforts to strengthen and promote the Hebraicization of the land. If there would be a possibility today of buying packages of food with the money of the United Jewish Appeal to send it through Lisbon, would we do such a thing? No! And once again, No!"

Rabbi Moshe Shonfeld commented: "The rescue committee of the Jewish Agency falsely bore the name 'rescue.' It would be more appropriate to call it the 'Committee for Covering Up, Ignoring and Silencing.'"[3] The libel trial of 1953–54, involving Rudolf Kastner (later assassinated, some claim by the Israeli Secret Service) makes similar points about the attitude of leading Zionists to the Holocaust. Rabbi Shonfeld added: "Today, all have regrets: the past Nazis, the good Germans, the merciful Catholics, the very democratic British and Americans, and even the Jewish secular leaders."[4]

Pope John Paul's condemnation of the anti-Semitism and anti-Jewish acts by Catholics "at any time and in any place" did not satisfy some Jews. Efraim Zuroff, head of the Israeli office of the Simon Wiesenthal Center in Los Angeles, said the Pontiff's speech "left a lot to be desired." Such statements appear to be part of an anti-Catholic crusade.

Part V
Conclusion

Chapter XIII
The Catholic Church

1. The Church and the Holocaust

*T*he Vatican was not responsible for the Holocaust. Germany was. The Catholic Church was interested in saving people everywhere in Europe and the world. Never did the Church compromise the teaching of Christ and respect for human life. Pius XII is responsible for minimizing the suffering and for helping wherever he could during the Holocaust. Compare his statements with those of Churchill, Roosevelt, and some Jewish leaders!

Who is responsible for the Holocaust? The discussion began when the former member of the Nazi Youth Organization, Rolf Hochhuth, placed the guilt of the Holocaust on the Catholic Church even though Germany was primarily Lutheran. The Holocaust is a German problem, not a Catholic Church problem. Catholics in Germany were in the minority as compared with Lutherans and other Protestant denominations.

The Catholic Church was persecuted during the twelve years of Hitler's regime. Why should the focus be on German Catholics? What was the position of the German Lutherans, the Protestants? They were often partisan Nazis. In the state of Hessen, Germany, 388 men of the clergy had to undergo denazification at the end of World War II. Of those, only two were Catholics. The others were Lutherans who followed the teaching of Martin Luther and not only attacked the Pope's encyclicals but also supported the Holocaust.

According to Lutheran Bishop Sasse's book, "Martin Luther was the leading anti-Semite of his times and maybe of all times." Karl Barth, the leading Protestant theologian of the '30s and '40s, wrote an

289

article in 1939 stating that the devastation and extermination by Hitler would not have been possible without Luther's teaching on anti-Semitism. One must remember:

1. Hitler came into power legally in 1933. After he started his anti-Semite campaign, Cardinal Pacelli sent his first diplomatic protest on April 10, 1933.

The majority of Lutherans voted for Hitler and Catholics voted against him. In the Reichstag elections of November 1932—the last fully free elections of the Weimar Republic—Ian Kershaw states that the Nazi party had "failed to make inroads into the big left-wing and Catholic voting blocks."[1] In spite of increased Nazi pressure, intimidation and blackmail after January 1933, the Catholic votes held up remarkably.

2. The Lutheran World Council of New York and the Ecumenical Movement in Geneva organized protests against Hitler in 1933. Yet this is what German Lutherans wrote to the Lutherans in New York: "There is no persecution of Jews. This is a semitic campaign by Jews against Germany. Nothing is happening."

Did the Lutherans protest the infamous T4 extermination program? In Bavaria there was a Lutheran asylum where people were killed. Organized by the state, Lutherans decided that no Jews could be baptized under any circumstances. Baptized Jews who had been members for generations were excluded from participation.

3. When Hitler passed the racial laws, the Catholic Church sent fifty-five protests between 1933 and 1939 signed by Secretary of State Cardinal Pacelli. Cardinal Bertram sent a major protest that the laws were totally unacceptable. Other bishops protested. German bishops opposed Hitler and protested against his persecution of the Catholic Church. Some Catholic bishops, who respected Hitler merely as the Head of State, are quoted out of context. However, Cardinal Faulhaber, Cardinal Galen, and others issued denunciations regarding the deportations of Jews. They strongly protested against the racial policies and insisted on respect for natural law and the laws of the Catholic Church.

Some questions need to be answered: How can the *New York Times* deny its own World War II editorial vision? What did the Allies do? What did the Protestants in Europe do? What did the Jews in America do? Did any of these groups do more than the Vatican? Is there any individual whose work on behalf of the Jews can be compared with the work of Pope Pius XII? The evidence in favor of the Catholic Church is provided by the wartime media. The Pope was not silent!

Bishops throughout Europe followed the example of Pius XI and Pius XII and spoke out against the racist and anti-Semitic policies of the Nazi government. The German bishops' protests, in the form of pastoral letters from Fulda in 1941 and 1942, were based on papal encyclicals. They vehemently condemned Hitler's interference in Church affairs and education, and strongly protested against "all violations of personal freedom."

The media is simply uninformed. Who can deny the historical fact that world Jewish leaders commended Pius XII before, during, and after the war? Were they wrong? Why did they express their gratitude? Why was *Hitler's Pope* given the attention of the media and Pierre Blet's book, *Pius XII and the Second World War,* dealing with the eleven volumes of Vatican documents, ignored?

In spite of all obstacles the Holy See persevered in its noble purpose to make the war more humane, to alleviate its evils, to assist and console its victims. "Pius XII's attention," writes Father Blet, "extended to the war in all its breadth and under all its aspects. Countries under military occupation, countries suffering from starvation, the civilian population, the elderly, the women and the children who perished by the thousands during the bombing of German cities, the Poles who were destroyed, the Jews who were deported and murdered, the combatants who fell on the first line of battle on both sides of the front, prisoners separated from their spouses and children, mothers, married couples, and children separated from these captives—all were the objects of his concern and, insofar as he could do something for them, of his tender care. To all these evils Pius XII wanted to bring the remedy of peace."

Pius XII spoke out many times against Nazi atrocities, without mentioning names. But the whole world knew to whom he was referring. The soundness of his judgment, in not publicly and stridently condemning the Nazi leadership by name, is supported by ample evidence, including testimony at the Nuremberg trials. The wartime German Ambassador to the Vatican, Ernst von Weizsäcker, and Robert Kempner, a leading member of the prosecution, are in agreement that it avoided certain recriminations and further tragedies. Pius XII's judgment was not questioned then and should be respected now. His judgment was calculated to save lives; he was not cowardly or indifferent.

Some people have been misled by the negative propaganda about Pope Pius XII. To educate and restore peace and love, there is need to inform the general public in order to help them understand the truth. Pius XII was not a "silent" Pope. The wisdom of his words and actions is supported by the evidence.

At a press conference on February 16, 2001, Italian author and journalist Antonio Gaspari presented his book, *Gli ebrei salvati da Pio XII* (The Jews Saved by Pius XII), published by Logos Editions. Elio Toaff, Rome's chief rabbi, explained that he came out of deference to an old friend, a Catholic priest who had saved his family from the Nazis during World War II. "Friendship can save lives," he remarked.

Recorded in this book are the sentiments expressed by founders of the state of Israel, leaders of Jewish associations, and survivors of concentration camps. Among them is Gideon Hausner, Israeli General Prosecutor at Adolf Eichmann's trial (October 18, 1961): "The Italian clergy helped numerous Jews and hid them in monasteries, and the Pope intervened personally in support of those arrested by the Nazis." Gaspari's book offers a staunch defense of Pius XII against the allegations that he remained indifferent to the plight of Jews.

The Holy See's collaboration with the nuncios and the leaders of Jewish organizations is eloquent witness that Pius XII did carry out his humanitarian mission. The Vatican documents are a testimony to the care of the Pope on behalf of humanity. Coordinating his efforts with the International Red Cross and with many Jewish organizations, he remained conscious of the humanitarian and religious mission of the Catholic Church, as he extended his charitable work to all—regardless of nationality, race, religion, or political party. To say otherwise is to do violence to the historical record.

It is impossible to reconstruct the whole picture of events from the documents. Professor Burkhart Schneider in his introductory remarks to volume 9 of the *Actes,* stated: "What is preserved in writing and transmitted is often only a pale shadow of the reality. And if that is true in general, it applies all the more in the field of charitable activities, which the Church tried to develop. For charity and its initiatives pass unnoticed, to a fair extent, when it is a question of a scientific collection of data, which is necessarily dry and detached."

On March 23, 2000, John Paul II met with Israeli President Ezer Weizman to discuss the peace process and, accompanied by Israel's

Prime Minister Ehud Barak, the Pope also met with a number of Holocaust survivors. Among the several hundred people present for the occasion was Jerzy Klüger, a Jewish childhood friend. The Pope praised the Christians—recognized in Yad Vashem as the "Righteous Gentiles"—who had helped to rescue Jews from the Holocaust. Many of the spectators wept freely as the Pope made his remarks.

Failure and lack of success do not detract from the merit of Pius XII. Most appropriately, Pinchas Lapide, a Jewish diplomat and historian, wrote: "When an armed force ruled well-nigh omnipotent, and morality was at its lowest ebb, Pius XII commanded none of the former and could only appeal to the latter, in confronting, with bare hands, the full might of evil. A sounding protest, which might turn out to be self-thwarting—or, quiet piecemeal rescue? Loud words or prudent deeds? The dilemma must have been sheer agony, for whatever course he chose, horrible consequences were inevitable. Unable to cure the sickness of an entire civilization, and unwilling to bear the brunt of Hitler's fury, the Pope, unlike many far mightier than he, alleviated, relieved, retrieved, appealed, petitioned and saved as best he could by his own lights.…."[2]

Pius XII realized that both Nazism and Communism had to be defeated. He was aware of the infamous Nazi-Soviet Pact of 1939 to carve up Roman Catholic Poland. In an article, "Pius XII and the Nazis: An Analysis of the Latest Charges that the Pope was a 'Friend' of the Axis," published in the December 5, 1964, issue of *America* (pp. 742–43), Father Robert A. Graham[3] responded to the accusation that Pius XII sympathized with the Axis: (1) Pope Pius XII willingly aided the anti-Nazi German resistance that plotted to abolish Hitler and his regime; (2) despite Axis pressure, the Pope sturdily refused to hail the mid-1941 Nazi attack on Russia as a "crusade"; (3) he also supported Roosevelt's desire to extend the Lend-Lease program to Russia.

Pope Pius XII had to deal with Adolf Hitler and the Holocaust, Benito Mussolini and Fascism, the occupation of Rome by the Nazis, the development of atomic warfare, and the spread of Communism across eastern Europe.

After serious consideration of the consequences, Pius XII decided to use pastoral action instead of political posturing. All evidence shows that he believed his approach would best serve Jewish victims of the Nazis. This is what most Jewish leaders advised, as well as Polish

Archbishop Adam Sapieha, almost all German religious leaders, the International Red Cross, and many Jewish rescue organizations.

The 1943–44 *American Jewish Yearbook* reported that Pius XII "took an unequivocal stand against the oppression of Jews throughout Europe." The head of the Italian Jewish Assistance Committee, Dr. Raffael Cantoni, reported: "The Church and the papacy have saved Jews as much and in as far as they could save Christians....Six million of my co-religionists have been murdered by the Nazis, but there could have been many more victims, had it not been for the efficacious intervention of Pius XII."

Dr. Robert Kempner wrote: "Every propaganda move of the Catholic Church against Hitler's Reich would have been not only 'provoking suicide'...but would have hastened the execution of still more Jews and Priests."

The *New York Times* reported in 1944: "Under the Pope's direction the Holy See did an exemplary job of sheltering and championing the victims of the Nazi-Fascist regime."

Undoubtedly, Pius XII deserves "that forest in the Judean hills which kindly people in Israel proposed for him in October 1958. A memorial forest, like those planted for Winston Churchill, King Peter of Yugoslavia and Count Bernadotte of Sweden with 860,000 trees."

In conclusion, it is also important to recall the contribution of Pius XII to the theological preparation of the Second Vatican Council as regards the doctrine on the Church, the first liturgical reforms, the fresh drive given to biblical studies, and the great attention devoted to the problems of the contemporary world.

2. Franz Werfel

In fulfillment of a vow, Jewish novelist Franz Werfel wrote a personal preface in May 1941, to *The Song of Bernadette:*[4] "In the last days of June 1940, in flight from our mortal enemies after the collapse of France, we reached the city of Lourdes. The two of us, my wife and I, had hoped to be able to elude them in time to cross the Spanish frontier to Portugal."

Werfel described how he and his wife hid for several weeks in the Pyrenean city: "It was a time of great dread. The British radio announced that I had been murdered by the National Socialists....But it was also a time of great significance for me, for I became acquainted with the wondrous history of the girl Bernadette Soubirous and also with the wondrous facts concerning the healings of Lourdes."

In response to the skeptical reader, Werfel added: "All the memorable happenings which constitute the substance of this book took place in the world of reality. Since their beginning dates back no longer than eighty years, there beats upon them the bright light of modern history and their truth has been confirmed by friend and foe and by cool observers through faithful testimonies. My story makes no changes in this body of truth."

Werfel states that he wrote to "magnify the divine mystery and the holiness of man—careless of a period which has turned away with scorn and rage and indifference from these ultimate values of our mortal lot."

3. Four Hundred Visas for Jews

More recent evidence with regard to papal representatives who followed the Pope's instructions comes from Maussane-les-Alpilles, France. Monsignor Giovanni Ferrofino gives us a marvelous glimpse into the way Pius XII worked to help the persecuted Jews.[5]

Among the papal representatives was Archbishop Maurilio Silvani (1882–1946)—titular Archbishop of Lepanto—who was named Nuncio to the Dominican Republic by Pius XII, May 23, 1942.

"This is my personal testimony," writes Ferrofino. "During the war, I was at Port-au-Prince as secretary to Silvani who had collaborated with Pacelli in Bavaria when he was Secretary of State and during negotiations on the Concordat with Germany. In 1943, instructions came to Nuncio Silvani from Pius XII telling him to ask General Rafael Leonida Trujillo, dictator of the Dominican Republic, to grant four hundred visas to Jews. It was subsequently learned that these refugees had been refused admittance to the United States.

"Nuncio Silvani immediately consulted the Dominican ambassador in Port-au-Prince. The ambassador said: 'Trujillo will never say *No* to the Pope. But it is well known that the only way one can ask for such a favor is *in person*.'

"The capital of Santo Domingo was an overnight trip of some 80 difficult kilometers across rocky Haitian territory and then another 350 kilometers of rugged Dominican roads under a blazing sun. And the Nuncio was not well, but he set out at once."

Ferrofino writes: "I remember that trip like yesterday. It was traumatic. It would have been difficult at any time but with the Nuncio's illness, an illness that would eventually lead to his death, every hour was torture. When we arrived in the capital, the Foreign Minister very kindly offered use of an official car. We traced Trujillo down and found him on horseback inspecting the sugarcane plantations, the *cañaverales*. He was wearing his *Panama*. As he tipped his hat to us, he made a move to dismount. But the Nuncio shouted: 'Oh, no, General, remain on your horse. You already know why I am here.'"

Trujiled smiled, nodded and replied that he could not refuse the Pope. But he had conditions that Ferrofino describes. "He told us: 'None of the four hundred can remain in the capital. They must live on the frontier and protect us from the clandestine immigration of Haitians. They will have land, houses, everything that is needed for a well-organized colony.'

"We sent this information to the Vatican, and returned to Haiti. A few weeks later, the four hundred Jews arrived in Santo Domingo. It was not long after they were settled that a taxi from the Dominican capital came to the Nuncio's residence in Port-au-Prince. A couple stepped out of the taxi, identified themselves as two of the refugees, and asked to see Nuncio Silvani."

Ferrofino describes the meeting: "They thanked us and begged us to help them remain in Port-au-Prince. The wife was an attractive blond, ex-ballerina from the Vienna Opera House. 'What would such a couple do in the capital,' asked the Nuncio? 'Start a ballerina school,' came the reply. The Nuncio said: 'I am not the most qualified person to tell you how to appeal to Trujillo for help to start a classical ballet School. Furthermore, as everyone knows, you must first win him over personally or by paying taxes. Trujillo never just gives anything to beautiful women.'

"I observed the two of them. There was no reaction from either the husband or the wife. They seemed stunned. They thanked us and left. But three years later, the Diplomatic Corps and all the members of the upper crust were invited to the opening of a new ballet school named after Trujillo's daughter, *Flor de Oro*.

"As for others in the group of four hundred, one night, after having obtained passports from Mexico, they left clandestinely for Cuba and from that country, after a short stay there, they crossed the Mexican border and arrived safely in the United States, the land that had originally denied their entrance. All this happened, thanks to Pius XII."

It is also interesting to note that on September 19, 1942, Monsignor Paolo Bertoli, Chargé d'Affaires at Port-au-Prince, wrote to Cardinal Luigi Maglione, Vatican Secretary of State, informing him that General Trujillo was ready to offer hospitality to 3,500 Jewish children in France between the ages of three to fourteen. General Trujillo would organize the group and take care of expenses for their voyage. Again, thanks to Pius XII's intercession.

4. Pope Pius XII

During World War II, Pius XII did more than any other world leader. In fact, the Church had an international network under the central direction of the Pope. The record of the Allies during the war in relation to the Pope's rescue operations leaves something to be desired. Government officials in London, Moscow, and Washington had important information about the extermination camps. What did they do to save the Jews from the Holocaust?

Pius XII was almost universally regarded as a saintly man, a scholar, a man of peace, a tower of strength, and a defender and protector of all victims of the war and genocide in Europe. At the end of the war, Western nations paid tribute to his compassionate efforts toward the oppressed. Pius XII died on October 9, 1958. Jews heaped praise on him for his help and were among the first to express sorrow and gratitude for his solicitude during the Holocaust.

Instead of questioning the "silence" of Pope Pius XII, why not consider the fact that the entire world was deaf to his words before the war: "Everything can be saved with peace; nothing can be gained with war." His was the outstanding religious voice that openly and consistently defied the Nazis. While some individuals betrayed their Jewish friends by revealing their destinations, the Pope's so-called "silence" saved lives. Had he spoken out, would not many more lives have been destroyed? The Pope provided food and other necessities to the thousands of victims hidden in convents and monasteries. It is foolish to think that the assistance given Jews, in the Vatican and in Rome alone, would have been successful without his knowledge.

Critics who judge Pius XII's honesty and loyalty must consider his *forma mentis*. He lived profoundly the spiritual drama of the victims. The dialogue between the German bishops and the Pope was filial and devoted. With paternal spontaneity he encouraged them in his pastoral letters. He was a modern man; he anticipated the needs of today; he introduced the native tongue in the liturgy; he served the cause of religion, defended the rights of humanity, invoked and defended peace and freedom for all; he was an indefatigable pastor, a teacher of justice, honor, loyalty; he provided money, ships, food; he placed his radio, his diplomacy, his convents, at the disposal of the refugees. What would survivors have preferred—words or actions? If he had condemned Hitler or Mussolini, would they have survived?

5. Opposition to Revisionists

Jews and Catholics should stand for the moral law and be united in their opposition to the revisionists! Not only Jews but also Catholics suffered and many were exterminated. Why should Catholics who risked their lives be branded with collective guilt for the Holocaust? Obviously, the Holocaust is being used as a tool for attacking Christianity and, in particular, the Catholic Church.

Robert M. Kempner, in the prologue of *Pius XII Was Not Silent* by Jenö Levai, compared those who defame Pius XII with revisionists who deny the full reality of the Holocaust: "In the last few years there has been no lack of farfetched or malicious attempts to obscure, falsify or interpret perversely this historical fact. We do not need to argue with those who are unteachable and even today try to diminish or even completely deny the monstrous deeds of the third Reich....

"We are concerned here with another deliberate or, at the very least negligently applied, method which aims at reducing the guilt of those who were really responsible. This is done by focusing the guilt for the Holocaust not on Hitler as the central figure for the liquidation system but on Pope Pius XII; by propagating in print and in the theatre a new theory which runs as follows: Pope Pius XII never made an energetic protest against Hitler's 'Final Solution of the Jewish Problem,' and that is how the catastrophe came to reach the proportions it did. Both the premise and the conclusion drawn from it are equally untenable."

On March 1, 2000, the Israeli government released the Adolf Eichmann *Diary,* describing the extermination of Jews by the Nazi regime and the actions taken by Pope Pius XII when Jews in Rome were deported on October 16, 1943. Eichmann clearly states that the Vatican "vigorously protested" the arrest and deportation of Jews. These memoirs reveal the truth.

Jewish military chaplains have confirmed that the Italian Catholic people, inspired by papal instruction, did much to rescue and shelter the Jewish victims of Nazi persecution, even providing false passports for them under Italian names. This is a historic source that cannot be ignored.

On June 22, 1944, Rabbi André Zaoui expressed gratitude "for the immense good and incomparable charity that Your Holiness extended generously to the Jews of Italy and especially the children, women and elderly of the community of Rome." Rabbi David de Sola Pool, Chairman of the National Jewish Welfare Board, wrote to the Pope: "We have received reports from our army chaplains in Italy of the aid and protection given to so many Italian Jews by the Vatican and by priests and institutions of the Church during the Nazi occupation of the country....."

Some Jews have claimed that the Church's statements on the Holocaust in recent years have not gone far enough. Nothing could be further from the truth. Jews who have been critical of Pope Pius XII were certainly not aware of the facts. Otherwise, how could they have deliberately ignored the truth?

No one can deny that, during the period of the Holocaust, Pius XII performed acts to stop the evils of Nazism. It is a delusion to think that by threatening excommunication, the Pope could have stopped Hitler, who violated the 1933 Concordat with the Vatican. How can anyone claim that Cardinal Pacelli "said and did nothing" when there were so many Vatican dispatches to Berlin protesting against Adolf Hitler's treatment of the Jews before and during World War II?

Michel Riquet, S.J., who survived Dachau and rescued six Jews, wrote: "Pius XII has spoken; Pius XII has condemned; Pius XII has acted. . . throughout those years of horror, when we listened to Radio Vaticana and to the Pope's messages, we felt in communion with the Pope, in helping persecuted Jews and in fighting against Nazi violence."[6]

Despite allegations to the contrary, historical evidence confirms that Pius XII was not silent. In 1935, as Vatican Secretary of State, he met with anti-Nazi Dietrich von Hildebrand, and declared that "there can be no possible reconciliation" between Christianity and Nazi racism. He also wrote an open letter to the Bishop of Cologne, calling the Nazis "false prophets with the pride of Lucifer." During this same period, he stated to Sister Pascalina, his longtime Secretary: "Hitler is completely obsessed. All that is not of use to him, he destroys;…this man is capable of trampling on corpses."

Journalist Cragg Hines' outrageous articles on the editorial page of the *Houston Chronicle*[7] have been added to the media's numerous attacks on the Catholic Church. Bishop Joseph A. Fiorenza, Diocese of Galveston-Houston, responded on June 8, 2001: "Hines went into dangerous waters when he repeated the canard that Pius XII did little or nothing to protest the Nazi treatment of Jews and when he ignored the historical record of witnesses and relied on the highly suspicious credibility of Zuccotti's book.

"Pope Pius XII was not silent about Hitler's massacre of Jews— his many interventions were significant and effective. Many Jews alive today owe their existence to parents or grandparents who were saved from death by Pius XII. Could he have done more, as some have suggested? Perhaps.

"But we must remember that he was in a duel with a madman who proved capable of perpetrating the greatest evil yet known to the world. It is neither fair nor historically accurate to judge people and events of 50 years ago by today's criteria.

"But whatever standard is used, Pius XII prevented Hitler from succeeding with his demonic plan to eliminate all European Jews, and for that he deserves history's praise and the world's admiration."

Catholics and Jews have also rejected the recent attacks on Pius XII in *Hitler's Pope, Under His Very Windows, Papal Sin* and *Constantine's Sword.* Rabbi David G. Dalin writes that in these books "the parallel comes clear: [Pope] John Paul's traditionalism is of a piece with Pius XII's alleged anti-Semitism; the Vatican's current stand on papal authority is in a direct line with complicity in the Nazis' extermination of the Jews. Faced with such monstrous moral equivalence and misuse of the Holocaust, how can we not object?"

I have attempted to describe the misunderstandings that continue to stall the peace process between Catholics and Jews. While I have provided primary sources, I am fully aware that my book could not possibly describe all the tensions, the hostilities, and the anti-Catholic criticism that exist in the media. I have simply gathered information that might enlighten others. Posterity will then evaluate and judge that Pope Pius XII spoke out many times in a strong "lonely voice" in language the whole world understood, condemning the ideologies of the Nazis and the Fascists and their cruelties toward the Jews. With the Church, Pius XII did all in his power and worked more effectively than any other agency or government, saving thousands of Jewish lives.

From Santiago, Chile, the sentiments of Jews and Catholics throughout the world were adequately expressed on October 3, 1943, in *El Diario ilustrado:* "In these tragic days, our minds recall the elevated figure of the Supreme Pontiff, His Holiness Pius XII, proven defender of the cause of the persecuted, especially our millions of European brothers and sisters who are innocent victims of inhuman massacres and cruelties. We remember with indignation that those who inflict, at this present time, untold sufferings on our Holy Father, are the same forces of evil who flaunt their unspeakable attempt to imprison behind the walls of Vatican City the irrepressible winds of the immense spiritual force emanating from the Chair of Saint Peter."

During World War II, Pius XII's goodness and spirituality deeply impressed the visitors who appreciated his intellect and his extraordinary capacity to understand the sufferings and the dangers of people everywhere. He was a Pope who radiated an inner peace and beauty that inspired everyone. He was a truly exceptional and holy person—a symbol of compassion, of hope and of love during a period of lies, despair, and hatred.

David J. Crotta, Jr., of the New Haven Bar Association responded to "The Case of Pius XII," an article by Judith Shulevitz in the April 8, 2001, issue of the *New York Times.* His "unpublished" letter to the editor stated: "Ms. Shulevitz does not answer the important question, 'By what standard are we allowed to judge a man for what he failed to do rather than for what he did?' Shulevitz notes that Pius XII's papacy continues to polarize minds on either side of a great ideological divide, but she fails to acknowledge that ideology itself provides no standard for judging another's conduct, particularly where, as here, the accused has become a symbol of something wholly beyond himself or his conduct. Indeed, the ex-seminarian Cornwell admits to being motivated more by a desire to influence the next conclave than by a need to explicate Pius' errors.

"How should Pius XII then be judged? Shulevitz suggests the answer: by reference to the judgments of his contemporaries, such as this paper itself and others, like Golda Meir, who heaped praise on the pope after his death. Was not Mrs. Meir better able to judge Pius' actions (and his motivations) than a cabal of ideologues bent on influencing the next conclave? Judges hear and examine evidence. In Pius' case there is abundant documentary and testimonial evidence establishing the case in his favor....

"Justice demands that judges examine the evidence presented by the accused, setting aside the passions of ideology in their deliberations. Were this standard followed in the case against Pius XII, he would be fully exonerated, and the bickering which Shulevitz rightly laments would peaceably end."

The Israeli press became enthusiastic when Pope John Paul II visited the Memorial to the Holocaust in Yad Vashem during the millennium celebrations. People learned the truth about Christianity that had been misinterpreted or eliminated in school textbooks. Hopefully, inappropriate comments on Christianity in history books will be reviewed and corrected.

Christians must be a bridge to reconciliation and recognize the great dignity of Jews and Muslims. The Pope asked that the spiritual message of the Bible be rediscovered and that the promises of Abraham and their fulfillment in Jesus Christ be acknowledged. He spoke about brotherhood, love, and peace among all groups in the Holy Land. His message was: "Be not afraid, have courage in faith, and preach the Ten Commandments and the Eight Beatitudes."

This, too, was the message of Pius XII who comforted Christians and Jews alike during World War II. He was an inspiration, a saintly messenger who tried to unite and bring peace to the world. His words of wisdom and untiring deeds translated like few others the message of Christ to his time—a time of spiritual poverty and material destruction of epic proportions. The people of Rome called Pope Pius XII *Defensor Civitatis*. His contemporaries acclaimed him *Pastor Angelicus*.

Part VI
Appendices

1. Documents

World War II documents may be found in the *Actes et documents du Saint-Siège relatifs à la Seconde Guerre Mondiale,* published from 1965 to 1981. As Jews and Catholics strive for brotherhood during the third millennium, the five thousand documents will serve to enlighten them about Pope Pius XII's activities and help spread the truth about the Catholic Church.

The following list is from *Pius XII: Architect for Peace* (Mahwah, N.J.: Paulist Press, 2000, pp. 227–330), with brief introductions translated from the French that will help readers understand the injustice toward the memory of Pius XII.

Volume 1, Le Saint-Siège et la guerre en Europe *[The Holy See and the War in Europe, March 1939–August 1940] 1970, 558 pp.*

Rome, May 6, 1939
Britain's first response to Pius XII's peace conference proposal.

Washington, May 15, 1939
The Pope wishes to inform President [Franklin D.] Roosevelt of the steps taken toward peace talks.

Rome, July 11, 1939
The Apostolic Delegate communicates with Secretary of State Sumner Welles on the international situation.

Vatican, August 16, 1939
Consists of alleged Press information, sent by Great Britain's Minister. The Internuncio of Holland wired the same information.

305

Rome, August 26, 1939

Great Britain's minister wishes to transmit personally to the Pope, Lord Halifax's thanks for the message of peace.

Rome, August 26, 1939

From London, the following proposal was suggested: Make Danzig and Corridor a free city, protected by the other Powers.

Washington, February 14, 1940

Roosevelt thanks the Pope for receiving Myron Taylor, serving as intermediary to work toward peace and harmony among peoples.

Volume 5, Le Saint-Siège et la guerre mondiale *[The Holy See and the World War, July 1941–October 1942] 1969, 795 pp.*

Vatican, September 19, 1942

The United States will fight until total victory; the Pope must not be carried away by Axis propaganda in favor of a peace compromise.

Vatican, September 22, 1942

The Pope is not disposed toward a peace compromise that would consist of oppression of the rights and consciences of certain nations.

Vatican, September 22, 1942

Collaboration with British will introduce religious tolerance in Russia.

Vatican, September 22, 1942

Deportation of Jews in France and the examination of measures to be taken to protect them.

Vatican, September 26, 1942

Pope's intervention on behalf of civilians exposed to bombings.

Vatican, September 26, 1942

Regarding the condition of prisoners in Russia.

Vatican, September 26, 1942

Pope's appeal to provide information service to prisoners.

Vatican, September 26, 1942

Report on religion in Russia.

***Volume 6, Le Saint-Siège et les victimes de la guerre [The Holy See
and the Victims of the War, March 1939–December 1940] 1972, 559 pp.***

Jerusalem, May 1, 1939
Request for Papal Audience.

Vatican, May 13, 1939
The Chief Rabbi will be received by the Cardinal Secretary of State.

Rome, September 13, 1939
News about the bombing of the Germans in Poland.

Vatican, December 31, 1939
Thanks for the gift offered to the Pope by the American Jewish organizations.

Vatican, March 21, 1940
*Thanks for the gift offered to Cardinal Hlond by the Americans and a request
to continue the help.*

Vatican, April 26, 1940
Information on the work of papal assistance to Poland.

Jerusalem, May 12, 1940
*The Grand Rabbi asks the intervention of the Holy See for the Polish Jews in
Lithuania.*

Armagh, May 14, 1940
The Cardinal sends a telegram from Chief Rabbi Herzog.

Vatican, June 5, 1940
*Request for information about the Poles arrested and deported by the
Russians.*

Rome, July 15, 1940
Recognition of the efforts of the Holy See in Poland.

Rome, October 6, 1940
*The United States can do nothing for the Poles residing in territory occupied
by the Russians.*

Volume 7, **Le Saint-Siège et la guerre mondiale** *[The Holy See and the World War, November 1942–December 1943] 1973, 767 pp.*

Washington, June 16, 1943
Roosevelt appreciates Pius XII's efforts regarding Italy and promises that the air attacks will be limited to military objectives.

Washington, June 29, 1943
The President promised that Italy would be able to choose its own government. Meanwhile the United States must continue the war, but had no intention of damaging Rome's artistic and cultural patrimony.

Vatican, July 7, 1943
Prime Minister Eden rejects the idea to declare Rome an open city. The English will bomb the city if necessary.

Vatican, July 20, 1943
Message following the bombing of Rome. As a neutral State, the Holy See wishes that the homes of the poor be spared. The Pope witnessed the destruction in Rome, and deplores the bombing of cities. He hopes Rome will be spared new attacks.

Washington, September 15, 1943
Disappointment created among American Catholics by the aerial bombardments of Rome, and the present difficult situation. Responsibility of the government; measures to be taken.

Vatican, November 7, 1943
The British government always promised that the Vatican would be carefully spared.

Vatican, November 8, 1943
The American government will search for those responsible for the bombing of the Vatican.

Volume 8, **Le Saint-Siège et les victimes de la guerre** *[The Holy See and the Victims of the War, January 1941–December 1942] 1974, 807 pp.*

Vatican, March 31, 1941
Request to facilitate the work of the Information Service for Prisoners of War.

Vatican, April 23, 1941
The help asked for Belgium will only aid the Germans and prolong the war.

Vatican, May 12, 1941
The English Government will facilitate visits by papal representatives to prison camps.

Vatican, May 19, 1941
Renewed efforts to obtain lists of prisoners of war.

Vatican, September 25, 1941
Request for intervention in order to obtain information about prisoners of war in Russia.

London, September 26, 1941
Request for intervention in favor of Belgians condemned to death by the Germans.

Vatican, September 29, 1941
Assistance to Poles deported to Russia.

Rome, November 26, 1941
The United States cannot help the Poles and Lithuanians in Russia.

Vatican, January 30, 1942
Information on the prisoners of war in Russia.

Vatican, February 2, 1942
8,000 tons of grain will be transported to Greece, but this does not release the occupying Government of its responsibility.

Vatican, February 19, 1942
The United States did not obtain any information on the prisoners of war in Russia; general information on the organization of the Central Bureau of Information in the United States.

Vatican, March 18, 1942
Urgent request to intervene for Poles interned in Spain.

Vatican, March 25, 1942
For the exchange of wounded prisoners of war, the good offices of the Holy See are no longer needed.

Vatican, April 15, 1942
Request to intervene for Dutch interned in Spain.

Vatican, April 27, 1942
Regarding assistance to prisoners of war given by the English Government.

Vatican, June 10, 1942
Request to intervene for Roman Jews condemned to forced labor.

Vatican, June 19, 1942
Information on the Holy See's efforts for Polish internees and others in Spain.

Vatican, August 19, 1942
Request to intervene for Polish internees in Spain.

Vatican, August 27, 1942
Renewed insistence for liberation of Polish internees in Spain.

Vatican, October 3, 1942
News on the famine in Greece; severe warning to the Italians who are responsible for the fate of the population.

Vatican, October 5, 1942
Internment of British prisoner who fled from an Italian camp and took refuge in the Vatican.

London, November 6, 1942
Request to stop reprisals against prisoners of war.

London, December 23, 1942
Request to intervene for Jews in Eastern Europe threatened with annihilation.

Vatican, December 29, 1942
Joint Declaration of the Allies regarding the persecution of the Jews by the Germans.

Volume 9, Le Saint-Siège et les victimes de la guerre *[The Holy See and the Victims of the War, January–December 1943] 1975, 689 pp.*

Vatican, January 7, 1943
The Holy See and Poland (partial translation).

Vatican, January 7, 1943
New request for the Holy See's intervention in favor of the persecuted Jews.

Vatican, February 15, 1943

Request to facilitate the work of the Vatican Information Service, particularly in Northern Africa.

Vatican, March 1, 1943

Vatican assistance to war victims in Greece. Assistance to the Poles. Vatican activities on behalf of refugees, especially Jews. Memorandum on Vatican efforts to promote the exchange of sick and maimed prisoners. Solicitude for prisoners of war and internees. Activities on behalf of prisoners in Russia and Russian prisoners elsewhere. Difficulties met by the Information Service. Statistics of activities. Information on prisoners of war transported to the United States.

Washington, August 13, 1943

Request to facilitate the work of the Vatican Information Service.

Maison-Carreé (Algiers), November 13, 1943

Report on activities of the Information Service established in Algiers, and on the situation in general.

Madrid, December 14, 1943

Report on activities on communications with Sicily and Southern Italy, on the Information Service for prisoners of war, and on visits to prison camps.

Volume 10,* Le Saint-Siège et les victimes de la guerre *[The Holy See and the Victims of the War, January 1944–July 1945] 1980, 684 pp.

New York, February 18, 1944

Acknowledgment to the Pope for his interventions on behalf of the persecuted Jews in Europe.

Vatican, April 1, 1944

Request for intervention on behalf of Hungarian Jews.

Washington, June 13, 1944

Solidarity of North American Bishops with Bishops of France; they insist that the authorities protect religious monuments and works of art.

Vatican, June 24, 1944

The "War Refugee Board" reports on the imminent massacre of Jews in Hungary, and requests the intervention of the Holy Father.

London, July 3, 1944
Request for intervention on behalf of Hungarian Jews.

New York, July 21, 1944
Acknowledgment of Pope's efforts on behalf of Italian Jews.

London, July 21, 1944
Thanking the Holy See for its intervention in Hungary, a final appeal to Regent Horthy is requested.

Vatican, August 7, 1944
Intervention on behalf of civilian internees in Egypt.

Rome, August 12, 1944
Recommendation of the Under-Secretary to the Minister of War Patterson and suggestions for an audience.

Istanbul, August 18, 1944
Information on charitable work of Delegation on behalf of Jews.

Vatican, September 15, 1944
Request for information on prisoners of war and internees.

Vatican, October 4, 1944
The Pope supports and encourages the North American Agency for the help given to the Italians.

London, October 14, 1944
Request for intervention on behalf of Hungarian Jews.

Vatican, October 18, 1944
Intervention for foreign Jews in Slovakia.

Rome, November 15, 1944
The Holy See's efforts on behalf of the Jews.

Vatican, November 17, 1944
Request on behalf of Italian prisoners interned by the Allies in Italy.

Vatican, December 14, 1944
The Holy See's efforts on behalf of Slovak Jews.

Rome, February 1, 1945
Request for Pope's intervention on behalf of Jews.

Vatican, March 2, 1945

Return of Italian civilians from Albania.

Vatican, March 3, 1945

The Holy See's attitude regarding the post-war situation.

Washington, March 9, 1945

Report on the conditions of Poland occupied by the Russians.

Vatican, April 16, 1945

Assistance offered to the Pope by American Catholics to support his charitable works.

Vatican, April 19, 1945

Request on behalf of the Italian internees in Germany.

Vatican, April 23, 1945

The Pope acknowledges the offering from the Diocese of Boston for war victims.

Vatican, May 3, 1945

Acknowledgment of the Pope for assistance given by the Catholics of the United States.

List of documents from *Pio XII: Architetto di pace* (Editoriale Pantheon, Rome, 2000, pp. 197–395) follows:

Volume 1*, Le Saint-Siège et la guerre en Europe *[The Holy See and the War in Europe, March 1939–August 1940] 1970, 558 pp.

Vatican, March 3, 1939

Discourse to Catholics and non-Catholics, with special prayers for peace.

Vatican, May 3, 1939

The papal nuncios must question their Governments on the possibility of a peace conference.

Rome, May 6, 1939

The first response to Pius XII's proposal for a peace conference was from Great Britain.

Washington, May 15, 1939
The Pope wishes to inform President [Franklin D.] Roosevelt of the steps taken toward peace talks.

Vatican, August 16, 1939
The Polish Ambassador spoke to Cardinal Maglione about the protests exchanged between Poland and Germany. According to the Ambassador, the Danzig question is a pretext for Germany to assault Poland. The Cardinal received information that confirms these facts, as well as the fact that Russia is in agreement about the partition of Poland.

Vatican, August 31, 1939
Pope Pius XII's last appeal for peace.

Paris, September 2, 1939
The French nunzio states that the Pope's appeal made a favorable impression. The Government prepares for war: censure, evacuation from Paris, etc.

Vatican, September 13, 1939
Pope Pius XII does everything possible to stop the conflict.

Zaleszczyky, September 17, 1939
The resistance of the Polish troops. The Cardinal Primate leaves for Rome.

Rome, September 28, 1939
Nunzio Borgongini-Duca thanks Count Ciano for his peace efforts. The Nuncio is assured that Italy will not enter the war.

Washington, October 27, 1939
Apostolic Delegate transmits Spellman's report and confirms Roosevelt's intentions to have a representative in the Vatican.

Brussels, November 8, 1939
Rulers of Belgium and Holland make offers for peace treaties.

Vatican, November 13, 1939
More precise information on steps taken in August 1939 regarding peace with the Polish Government.

Vatican, December 16, 1939
Great Britain does not accept a truce, and the French Government confirms the refusal.

Vatican, December 24, 1939

Pius XII recalls the last message of his predecessor. He mentions the horrors of the war, the violations of human rights, and his own peace efforts. He can only alleviate the sufferings of people and prepare for the return of peace. The norms for future peace are: 1) Respect for the independence of nations. 2) Mutual disarmament. 3) Reconstruct international institutions. 4) Respect the just requests of ethnic minorities. 5) The sense of responsibility. It is necessary to promote justice instead of the spirit of revenge and one must return to Christ, the Prince of peace. The Pope added news about President Franklin D. Roosevelt's representative to the Vatican and his collaboration toward peace efforts.

Vatican, March 11, 1940

Report by Monsignor Sericano about Cardinal Maglione's conversation with Ribbentrop.

Vatican, May 10, 1940

The British Minister brings the Vatican Secretary of State notes similar to those of the French Ambassador.

Vatican, May 10, 1940

Cardinal Maglione and Monsignor Tardini send messages to the three countries invaded by Germany. The Holy See expresses its sorrow to these neutral countries and deplores the violation of international rights.

Vatican, May 13, 1940

The Pope receives the Italian Ambassador who complains about the telegrams sent to Belgium, Holland and Luxemburg. The Pontiff responded vigorously that he had the liberty to send them and that he had the right to speak. He added he would also like to speak out about what is happening in Poland, but he refrains to do so for fear of worsening the situation of the victims.

Volume 5, Le Saint-Siège et la guerre mondiale *[The Holy See and the World War, July 1941–October 1942] 1969, 795 pp.*

London, July 9, 1941

Great Britain had foreseen Hitler's invasion of Russia; an Anglo-Russian agreement against Germany is possible. The Holy Father's discourse. Difficulty in obtaining a list of prisoners of war.

Vatican, July 11, 1941
The Holy See's thoughts on the recognition of new States during the war.

Belgrade, July 24, 1941
The Archbishop of Belgrade requests that the Pope send a Prelate to bring back information on the persecution of Orthodox Serbs to the Holy See.

Vatican, July 25, 1941
Abbot Marcone goes to Croatia to take note of the religious situation and to report to the Holy See. Possibility to have contact with the Government.

Vichy, July 25, 1941
Limits imposed on the circulation of the Holy Father's discourses. People are moved by the Pope's affection toward the occupied regions.

Rome, July 26, 1941
Reasons why the Italian government praised the Yugoslav Minister to the Holy See. Respect for the spirit of the Lateran Pact.

Vatican, July 31, 1941
The Yugoslave Minister to the Holy See was expelled from Italian territory; the Italian government refused to reveal the accusations against him.

Berlin, August 2, 1941
The Nuncio transmits Cardinal von Galen's sermons and gives information about those who are reacting.

Zagreb, August 5, 1941
Abbot Marcone contacts the authorities in Zagreb.

Vatican, September 6, 1941
Information given to the Italian Ambassador on the Bishop of Münster's sermons.

Berlin, September 10, 1941
Success of Cardinal von Galen's sermons; the closing of religious institutions suspended; the anti-religious campaign of the Nazis continues.

London, September 19, 1941
British public opinion, favorable to Russia and against Italy, appreciates the independence of the Holy See which is opposed to the politics of the Axis.

Rome, September 22, 1941
The situation between Croatia and Italy is tense; there are incidents on the borders.

Vatican, September 27, 1941
Conversation between Monsignor Montini and Minister Osborne: the British Government is reserved regarding the bombing of Rome.

Vatican, September 27, 1941
The British Minister asks for confirmation regarding the refusal of the Holy See to associate itself with the anti-Bolshevik campaign.

Vichy, September 30, 1941
Hitler considers Pius XII as his personal enemy.

Washington, October 7, 1941
The President of the United States hopes that Russia will grant religious liberty.

Vatican, October 21, 1941
Only schismatic priests are authorized to enter Russian territory.

Rome, October 25, 1941
The Nunzio's conversation with Ciano. If Hitler would offer some proposals, England would not accept them; landing on the English coast would be very difficult for Hitler.

Berlin, November 12, 1941
Monsignor Lichtenberg, Protonotary of the Cathedral Chapter of Berlin, was arrested.

Lisbon, November 25, 1941
Informed of German reprisals, the Yugoslav Minister asks the Vatican to intervene.

Vatican, November 27, 1941
Reasons why the Holy See rejects the Reich's request regarding episcopal nominations. The Pope refuses to speak about the anti-Bolschevic crusade. Persecutions continue; the Vatican tries to keep Catholics of other countries informed.

Budapest, December 4, 1941
Cardinal Serédi asks the Pope to prevent Great Britain's declaration of war with Hungary.

Vatican, December 16, 1941
Monsignor Montini speaks with Great Britain's Minister about the Italian missionaries in East Africa.

Washington, January 5, 1942
The Bishops of the United States approve the politics of the President and the Allies.

Washington, January 15, 1942
The unfavorable reaction to the media and the need to deny the information.

London, February 14, 1942
Insinuations against the Vatican in the media and in the movies. The Apostolic Delegate protests.

Vatican, February 23, 1942
The Italian Ambassador denies the anticlerical statements attributed to Mussolini.

Rome, February 25, 1942
It is said that Rosenberg and Goebbels will receive the doctorate honoris causa at the University of Padova. Ciano and Bottai know nothing about this matter.

Rome, March 8, 1942
Farinacci published articles against the Vatican. Ciano promised to intervene; but it is appropriate to repeat the Italian Ambassador's protest.

Washington, March 18, 1942
Attitude of the American Bishops regarding Vatican diplomacy with Japan.

Vatican, March 27, 1942
Maglione communicated to the Italian Ambassador that the Holy See will respond affirmatively to China's and Finland's request to establish diplomatic reports.

Vatican, March 29, 1942
China appoints a Representative to the Holy See; the appointment of a Nuncio is delayed.

Rome, April 8, 1942
Objections of the Japanese Government regarding diplomatic relations of the Vatican with China.

La Paz, April 17, 1942

Explanation by the Nuncio on the matter of his encounter with the President of the Republic and of the proposals exchanged.

London, May 19, 1942

The media's reaction to the Pope's May 13th message on the radio.

Vatican, May 22, 1942

Cardinal Maglione's conversation with Baron Lersner, who is asking the Holy See's mediation with regard to peace.

Vatican, May 22, 1942

Baron Lersner's plans for the Holy See's peace mediation.

Vatican, June 12, 1942

Approval of the Delegate's actions.

Vatican, June 16, 1942

The appointment of Apostolic Delegate in Egypt is transmitted to Father Hughes.

Vatican, July 18, 1942

The British authorities have interned Italian missionaries.

Vatican, July 28 1942

Clarification given to Monsignor Hudal on the religious situation in the Reich and in occupied territories.

Vatican, August 8, 1942

Reflections on the assurances given regarding religious liberty in Russia.

Vatican, August 21, 1942

Monsignor Tardini's conversation with Minister Osborne about the British Government's attitude toward the missionaries and representatives of the Holy See.

Vatican, September 1, 1942

Agreement between the Vatican and Italy about Myron Taylor's mission.

Vatican, October 3, 1942

Osborne is against the concession of an audience to Pavelic.

Volume 6, **Le Saint-Siège et les victimes de la guerre *[The Holy See and the Victims of the War, March 1939–December 1940] 1972, 559 pp.***

Vatican, March 6, 1939

Errors published in the Italian magazine, "La difesa della razza."

Vatican, March 7, 1939

Protest against the anti-religious magazine "La difesa della razza"; errors in it are indicated in this Memorandum.

Budapest, April 2, 1939

Proposal of the racial law and opposition of the Bishops.

Vatican, June 6, 1939

Request for 3,000 immigration visas.

Berne, June 12, 1939

Precarious situation of Jewish refugees in Switzerland and the almost insurmountable difficulties regarding their emigration to countries in Latin America.

Vatican, June 23, 1939

The concession of 3,000 Brazilian visas is communicated to Cardinal Faulhaber.

Brussels, July 9, 1939

The Nuncio favors the Jewish refugees in Belgium.

Vatican, July 12, 1939

The Pope blesses the work of mercy given to Jewish refugees.

Rome, July 13, 1939

To avoid confusion, the Holy See would declare that the "Raphaelsverein" will be the only organization to distribute the 3,000 Brazilian visas.

Vatican, July 27, 1939

Doctor M. Kirschberg's proposal for mass immigration of the Jews to the Portuguese colony of Angola is judged inopportune.

Vatican, August 7, 1939

Request for information regarding the racial law of July 13, 1939.

Vatican, September 22, 1939

The Information Bureau must be established immediately.

Berlin, October 9, 1939

Report on Polish refugees and prisoners; proposal to send an Apostolic Delegate to Poland.

Vatican, October 14, 1939

Charity toward the Polish refugees is recommended.

Washington, October 20, 1939

The Poles in the United States are ready to assist their country provided the Polish Bishops, supported by the words of the Pope, have recourse to the American hierarchy.

London, November 3, 1939

A committee to help Polish refugees in Great Britain is formed.

Vatican, November 6, 1939

Approval of the Nuncio's agreement with the Red Cross. The Bishop of Freiburg will be appointed to direct the work of the Swiss Catholic Missions.

Berlin, November 6, 1939

Report on activities of the "Gildemeester-Aktion" on behalf of the Jews.

Vatican, November 8, 1939

Having seen the extreme misery in Poland, the Nuncio must find a way for the Holy See to distribute material assistance and help the Polish people.

Vatican, November 21, 1939

Responses from interested Governments to the proposal for a truce from aerial attacks on Sundays were too vague. The Nuncio must no longer insist.

Vatican, December 22, 1939

Father Tacchi Venturi is appointed to interevene once again on behalf of the Jews.

Vatican, January 11, 1940

Regarding Kirschberg's proposal for mass immigration of the Jews to the Portuguese colony of Angola.

Vatican, January 30, 1940
The German Government is opposed to the help of the Holy See on behalf of Poland.

Vatican, February 3, 1940
The Nuncio must intervene on behalf of the 17 professors of the University of Cracovia imprisoned by the Germans.

Berlin, February 10, 1940
The Nuncio's request on behalf of the Polish professors was unsuccessful.

Vatican, March 6, 1940
Report on the Holy See's endeavors to assist the Polish people.

Washington, March 15, 1940
Gift of the American dioceses to help the Poles.

Volume 7, Le Saint-Siège et la guerre mondiale *[The Holy See and the World War, November 1942–December 1943] 1973, 767 pp.*

Vatican, November 11, 1942
The Vatican regrets London's refusal regarding Monsignor Pacini's mission.

Vatican, December 2, 1942
The words of the Substitute Secretary are not directed personally to Osborne.

Vatican, December 3, 1942
The Delegate repeats to the American Government that the Pope will publicly protest the bombing of Rome.

Washington, December 4, 1942
The Delegate told the Secretary of State in Washington that the bombing of Rome would be advantageous to the Axis.

Rome, December 4, 1942
The Cardinal Secretary of State informs the Italian Embassy that the Holy See has insisted with the Allies to avoid the bombing of Rome. The British Government insists that all military objectives be removed.

Vatican, December 7, 1942
Count Sforza seems incapable of forming a Government to replace Mussolini's.

Vatican, December 11, 1942
Intervention of the Archbishop of Westminster regarding the bombing of Rome.

Vatican, December 11, 1942
Italian participation in the bombing of London, according to the British, was not important.

Vatican, December 24, 1942
Appeal for action. Reference to the principles of the dignity of the human person; of the meaning of family; of the dignity of work; of law and order; of the Christian concept of the State; of the renewal of society.

Vatican, March 8, 1943
Religious situation of the Poles in Russia.

London, March 10, 1943
Wishes on the Pope's anniversary. Hope of humanity in the magisterium of the Holy See.

Vatican, March 13, 1943
The pope thanks President Raczkiewiez and prays for the suffering Polish people.

Berlin, March 13, 1943
Letter of Cardinal Faulhaber: the bombing and actions against the Church.

Istanbul, May 20, 1943
Monsignor Spellman's visit to Istanbul.

Vatican, May 22, 1943
With the threat of imminent bombing, the Secretariat of State insists on the removal of all military objectives from Rome.

Vatican, May 29, 1943
Prospects for a concordat with Slovakia.

Rome, June 17, 1943
The Nuncio recalls the possibility of an intervention during his audience with the King who does not seem ready for action.

Vatican, July 25, 1943

Alberto De Stefani describes the meeting of the Fascist Grand Council. Situation at the end of the kingdom. It is necessary for the Holy See to intervene in order to know the dispositions of the Allies and make Italy return to neutrality. The Substitute responds that it is necessary for the Italian Government to make the request.

Vatican, July 27, 1943

Mussolini and his family's personal status. Conjectures on Farinacci and Hitler. Meeting with Weizsäcker on Italy and the Holy See's action.

Volume 8, Le Saint-Siège et les victimes de la guerre *[The Holy See and the Victims of the War, January 1941–December 1942] 1974, 807 pp.*

Rome, October 18, 1941

Request on behalf of the non-Aryan Croatians.

Vatican, October 21, 1941

A new request to obtain free navigation for Greece from the British.

Berlin, November 26, 1941

It is forbidden to transmit messages to the prisoners of war in Germany.

Beyoglu, January 17, 1942

The blockade on behalf of Greece is suspended by the British.

Zara, January 18, 1942

Information on the situation in Dalmatia and Cardinal Maglione's request to stop the reprisals.

Rome, January 20, 1942

Request on behalf of Jewish orphans in Croatia will be unsuccessful.

Vatican, January 25, 1942

Information on the deportation of Jews in Czechoslovakia. Information on the Russian prisoners of war.

Vatican, April 12, 1941

Request for protection of the civilian population in Ethiopia.

Vatican, May 12, 1941
British Government will facilitate visits of papal representatives to prison camps.

Rome, May 16, 1941
Conditions to guarantee the sincerity of conversion of Jews to the Catholic religion.

Athens, June 14, 1941
Report of assistance given to prisoners of war in Greece and on the new prospectives of activity after the changes of the military situation.

Vatican, July 19, 1941
It is recommended that assistance be given to the families of French prisoners of war.

Jerusalem, October 18, 1941
Report on assistance given to prisoners of war.

Zagreb, August 4, 1942
Acknowledgment of help given to Jews by the bishops and representatives of the Holy See. Request for intervention on behalf of women and children in concentration camps.

Vatican, October 5, 1942
British prisoners who escaped from Italian camps take refuge in the Vatican.

Laeken, November 3, 1942
Request to intervene on behalf of political prisoners.

Berlin, November 6, 1942
Proposal on behalf of the Jews.

Volume 9, Le Saint-Siège et les victimes de la guerre *[The Holy See and the Victims of the War, January–December 1943] 1975, 689 pp.*

Vichy, January 24, 1943
Assurance of spiritual assistance to prisoners of war in Germany.

London, January 24, 1943
Report on the charitable activities of the Apostolic Delegation and on the visits of the Delegate to prison and internee camps.

Vatican, February 5, 1943
Plan for the exchange of prisoners of war who are disabled and sick.

Vatican, February 13, 1943
Request to intervene on behalf of Croatian Jews who have taken refuge in Split.

London, February 26, 1943
Request to intervene on behalf of Czechs interned in Italy.

Budapest, February 26, 1943
Request to intervene on behalf of Jewish Slavs threatened with deportation.

Presbourg, March 11, 1943
Information on the situation of Jews in Slovakia.

Sidney, March 11, 1943
Repatriation of Italian prisoners of war.

New York, March 12, 1943
Request of an investigation on behalf of Jews in Poland threatened with extermination.

Rome, March 13, 1943
Transmission of false information on Russian prisoners of war.

Zagreb, March 13, 1943
Request on behalf of Croatian Jews.

Washington, March 28, 1943
The matter of obtaining information on prisoners of war in Russia by the United States government was not successful.

Vatican, April 18, 1943
Assurance that Germans will not use deadly gas.

Vatican, April 20, 1943
The Russian Government sent the list of prisoners of war to Great Britain.

Vatican, April 22, 1943
Request to intervene on behalf of the Yugoslav internees.

Vatican, May 11, 1943
Difficulty in obtaining information on prisoners of war in Northern Africa.

[...]

Il credente ha un diritto inalienabile di professare la sua fede e di praticarla in quella forma che ad essa conviene. Quelle leggi che sopprimono o rendono difficile la professione e la pratica di questa fede sono in contrasto col diritto naturale.

I genitori coscienziosi e consapevoli della loro missione educativa hanno prima ed ogni altro il diritto essenziale all'educazione dei figli, loro donati da Dio, secondo lo spirito della vera fede e in accordo con i suoi principi e le sue prescrizioni. Leggi, o altre misure le quali non tengono conto nella questione scolastica della volontà dei genitori, che hanno un diritto naturale sull'educazione della prole, sono non quaote in contrasto e nella loro intima essenza immorali.

La Chiesa, la cui missione è di custodire ed esporre il diritto naturale, inaaiato nell'uomo da Dio, non può fare altro che dichiarare essere effetto di violenza, e quindi vuote di ogni carattere legale, le iscrizioni scolastiche avvenute in un recente passato in un'atmosfera di notoria mancanza di libertà.

Alla gioventù

Rappresentante di Colui che nell'Evangelo disse ad un giovane "Se vuoi entrare nella vita eterna, osserva i comandamenti" (Matt.19,17), Noi indirizziamo una parola particolarmente paterna alla gioventù.

Da mille bocche viene oggi ripetuto al vostro orecchio un Evangelo che non è stato rivelato dal Padre celeste; migliaia di penne scrivono a servizio di una larva di cristianesimo, che non è il Cristianesimo di Cristo. Tipografia e radio vi inondano giornalmente con produzioni di contenuto avverso alla fede e alla Chiesa, e , senza alcun riguardo

in favore della scuola confessionale. E perciò non Ci stancheremo neanche nell'avvenire di rinfacciare francamente alle autorità responsabili l'illegalità delle misure violente prese finora, e il dovere di permettere la libera manifestazione della volontà. Intanto non vi dimentichente di ciò: nessuna potestà terrena può sciogliervi dal vincolo di responsabilità voluto da Dio, che unisce a voi con i vostri figli. Nessuno di quelli che oggi invadono il vostro diritto all'educazione e pretendono scioglierti dai vostri doveri di educatori, potrà rispondere al vostro posto al giudice eterno, quando egli vi rivolgerà la domanda: dove sono coloro che io mi ho dati?-Possa ciascuno di voi potere risponderli: non ho perduto alcuno di quelli che mi hai dati (Giov.18,9).

--- o O o ---

Venerabili Fratelli! Siamo certi che le parole, che Noi rivolgiamo a voi, e per mezzo vostro ai cattolici del Reich germanico, in quest'ora decisiva troveranno nel cuore e nelle azioni dei Nostri fedeli figliuoli quella eco corrispondente alla sollecitudine amorosa del Padre Comune. Se v'è cosa che Noi imploriamo dal Signore con particolare intensa essa è che le Nostre parole pervengano anche all'orecchio e al cuore di quelli che hanno già cominciato a lasciarsi prendere dalle lusinghe e dalle minacce dei nemici di Cristo e del suo santo Vangelo, e li facciano riflettere.

Abbiamo pesato ogni parola di questa Enciclica sulla bilancia della verità e insieme dell'amore. Non volevamo con silenzio inopportuno esser colpevoli di non aver chiarita la situazione, né con rigore eccessivo di aver indurito qualcuno di quelli che, essendo sottoposti alla Nostra responsabilità pastorale, continuare ad essere oggetto del

---

Pages from the Italian version of the encyclical *Mit brennender Sorge.*

German Foreign Minister Joachim von Ribbentrop visits Pope Pius XII who accused the Nazis of "religious persecution, [and] also came to the defense of the Jews" (*New York Times,* March 14, 1940).

Rally for peace, Vatican, 1940.

From every country in the world, requests about prisoners of war were answered by the staff of the Vatican Information Bureau.

Pius XII gives his blessing at the end of a radio message
during the tragic years, 1943–44.

Pius XII blesses the crowd during the
Allied bombing of Rome in 1943.

Former Chief Rabbi Israel Zolli after his conversion to Catholicism. When baptized, he took the name Eugenio, in gratitude to Pius XII for having saved thousands of Jews during the German occupation of Rome.

Feeding refugees at Montecassino.

The Pope meets with wounded Italian soldiers at the Vatican in August, 1942.

Berlin, May 11, 1943
Intervention on behalf of non-Germans is unsuccessful.

Tokyo, May 11, 1943
Difficulty in the distribution of funds to Americans only.

Scutari, May 31, 1943
Request to intervene on behalf of Jews in Albania.

Vatican, June 2, 1943
Request for information on the fate of Slovak Jews.

Vatican, June 2, 1943
Request to intervene on behalf of a group of Jews.

Vatican, June 3, 1943
Assistance sent to Polish dioceses.

Presbourg, June 4, 1943
Information on measures taken against the Jews.

Vatican, June 30, 1943
Request for intervention on behalf of three Polish children taken from the group of Rumanian Jews detained by the Germans.

Berlin, June 30, 1943
Information on the results of various requests on behalf of those condemned to death.

Vatican, August 24, 1943
The request on behalf of Slovaks and Croatians interned in Italy was not totally successful.

Vatican, August 24, 1943
Gift of the Pope for the reconstruction of churches destroyed by bombs.

Vatican, December 13, 1943
Christmas message of the Pope to prisoners of war and internees.

Vatican, December 14, 1943
Provisions for the clergy, religious institutions and their dependents in Rome.

Vatican, December 29, 1943
Review of measures taken on behalf of Jews.

Vatican, December 29, 1943
Request for information on deported Jews.

Vatican, December 29, 1943
Relief for the Italians interned in Poland.

Rome, December 30, 1943
Acknowledgment of help given to Jews.

Vatican, December 31, 1943
Request to take an interest in the Polish Jews who fled to France.

Berne, December 31, 1943
The fate of Jews who had obtained immigration visas declared invalid in Latin-American countries; request to intervene on their behalf.

Volume 10, Le Saint-Siège et les victimes de la guerre *[The Holy See and Victims of the the War, January 1944–July 1945] 1980, 684 pp.*

Ankara, February 28, 1944
Rabbi Herzog thanks the Apostolic Delegate for help given to Jews.

Madrid, February 29, 1944
Concerning communications between the Vatican and Northern Africa.

Vatican, March 1, 1944
Acknowledgments of a political refugee saved in a convent in Rome.

Washington, March 25, 1944
Requests for research on behalf of Jews in Hungary and in Rumania.

London, July 3, 1944
Request for intervention on behalf of Hungarian Jews.

Vatican, July 18, 1944
The Grand Rabbi of Rome Zolli's acknowledgment and request for Papal Audience.

Vatican, July 18, 1944
Information on the results of intervention on behalf of Hungarian Jews.

Berlin, July 21, 1944
The Nuncio's request on behalf of prisoners in concentration camps.

New York, July 21, 1944
Acknowledgment of the Pope's efforts on behalf of Italian Jews.

London, July 21, 1944
The Holy See is thanked for its intervention in Hungary and is requested to intercede with Regent Horthy.

Vatican, August 4, 1944
The Vatican requests the safety and protection of Lisieux.

Presbourg, August 4, 1944
Information on those interned in a concentration camp where almost all are Jews.

Rome, August 5, 1944
Acknowledgment of the Pope's efforts on behalf of Jews in Rome.

Washington, August 31, 1944
A special committee for the assistance of Jews begs the Holy Father's intervention.

Vatican, September 1, 1944
The text of the appeal by the women of Warsaw is transmitted to Taylor.

Washington, September 14, 1944
In Germany there is word about the reprisals by the Allies.

Presbourg, September 15, 1944
Information on the renewed persecutions of Jews.

Vatican, September 20, 1944
Request on behalf of the Slovak Jews.

Vatican, September 26, 1944
Request to stop the massacre of prisoners in the Auschwitz concentration camp.

Vatican, September 28, 1944
Information on help given to Jews in Slovakia.

Vatican, September 30, 1944
Efforts to protect the tombs of German soldiers in Italy.

Washington, September 30, 1944
Request on behalf of prisoners in the concentration camp of Auschwitz.

Cairo, September 30, 1944
Meeting with the Grand Rabbi of Palestine; new requests on behalf of Jews in Slovakia.

Bucarest, October 2, 1944
Acknowledgment by Rumanian Jews for the Nuncio's intervention on their behalf.

Vatican, October 2, 1944
Request on behalf of prisoners in Auschwitz.

Vatican, October 4, 1944
The Pope approves and encourages the work of North-American agencies who are distributing help to the Italians.

Rome, October 4, 1944
Information on the expected extermination of prisoners in the Brzezinka concentration camp.

Rome, October 5, 1944
Report on the disastrous situation of the people of Warsaw.

Vatican, October 5, 1944
Warning of the President of Slovakia with regard to the Jews.

Vatican, December 14, 1944
Request on behalf of French internees in Germany.

Vatican, December 14, 1944
Efforts of the Holy See on behalf of the Slovak Jews.

Bucarest, December 14, 1944
Information on the situation of Jews in Rumania under the new Government.

Vatican, February 6, 1945
Jewish leaders ask the intervention of the Holy See. Response.

Washington, March 18, 1945
Request for an appeal on behalf of Jews in Germany, threatened with extermination.

List of documents selected from Volume 2, **Actes et Documents du Saint-Siège relatifs à la Seconde Guerre Mondiale** *[Lettres de Pie XII aux Allemands (1939–1944),* **1993, 2nd edition]:**

Vatican, July 20, 1939

To the German Archbishops and Bishops: Importance of the Peace Conference; the need for union among the Bishops; assurance of remembrance in prayer; although efforts have been made toward a compromise with the State, measures against the Church have increased: we see its destruction; regardless of all this we must preserve peaceful arrangements, but without abandoning the principles of natural law and of revelation; praise for the fidelity and the devotion of the faithful; a look back on the years spent in Germany; the participation at the conference of the entire Episcopate is desirable.

Castelgandolfo, July 25, 1939

Thanks the Cardinal-Archbishop of Vienna; expression of sympathy on the occasion of the serious affronts to which the Cardinal and the faithful were subjected; the nunciature will protest.

Castelgandolfo, September 25, 1939

Thanks the German Archbishops and Bishops for the words of gratitude; praise for the close union maintained among the bishops with the Holy See; distress of the present period; faithfulness to the papacy is the guarantee and the assurance against all dangers; gratitude for the good wishes sent on the occasion of the papal election; the tiara of the Pope becomes a crown of thorns; from the beginning of the pontificate all efforts have been made to preserve peace; reminder of the radio message of the month of August; despite that message war is now a reality; compassion of the Pope for the universal misfortune; the possibilities that remain are the lessening of the evils of war and the measures toward peace; the difficult situation of the Church in Germany; the attacks against her become increasingly violent; the Church, that has wished only good for Germany, is now persecuted and calumniated; the propaganda campaign against the Church in all sectors of public life; particular danger for the youth; every possibility of defense is taken from the Church; necessity for always greater confidence and for prayer; the sufferings endured with patience are convincing evidence in favor of the Church; exhortation toward generous charity during the war itself; recommendation for the apostolate to the soldiers; close rapport between the pastors and the faithful; praise for the nursing sisters; recommendation for God's protection and that of the holy Virgin and of the German Saints.

Castelgandolfo, September 25, 1939

Thanks the Bishop of Meissen for the information transmitted; anxiety because of the suppression of Catholic schools; the threat against religious instruction; religious teaching outside of the school; close relations with the diocese.

Vatican, November 27, 1939

The Pope thanks the Cardinal-Archbishop of Breslau for the minutes of the episcopal conference of Fulda; he regrets the impossibility of sending a common pastoral letter; the battle against the Church; unity between the Pope and the bishops; efforts of the Pope for peace.

Vatican, June 21, 1940

Pius XII praises the Archbishop of Fribourg for his pastoral zeal; memorandum presented by the Archbishop to the Ministry of Reichsverteidigung; strict neutrality of the Pope; his efforts for peace; his sermon of the last day of the year and the pastoral letter of the Archbishop; attitude of the clergy; fear; concern for the recruitment of good priests.

Vatican, August 6, 1940

The Pope explains the tasks of the Church in times of war to the Archbishops and Bishops of Germany; the topics to be discussed; he recalls his own activities in Germany; his efforts to stop the battle against the Church; different interpretations of the situation and the concern caused by the contradictory declarations of competent authority. The Pope insists on the unity and constancy of action by the episcopacy. The accusations without foundation against the Church and its mission at this time. The principles of the Holy See that determine its approach. The impartiality of the Pope does not mean insensitivity. To maintain the principles of justice is an essential part of the Church's mission of truth. The declaration of the Pope at the time of the invasion of Belgium; the conditions of a just peace. The task of the Pope is laden with responsibilities; he multiplies his efforts to find the proper approach; praises the German Catholics; their fidelity to the Church is manifested during the persecution; dangers for dogma and the life of faith; necessity of personal piety; exhortation to the clergy.

Vatican, September 29, 1940

Pius XII thanks the Archbishops and Bishops of Germany for their letter, which manifests their loyalty toward the Holy See, their unity and their zeal; the Pope lauds all their resolutions; he recommends to them in the first place the defense against the errors of the times and the care for the integrity of Christian doctrine and its practical fulfillment in life; the primary importance of the apostolate among the youth, in school and out of school; the necessity to encourage the faithful to receive the Eucharist frequently; the usefulness of spiritual exercises; the special concern for Christian family living and for the formation of priests. The Pope recalls his years in the nunciature in Germany and praises the apostolic zeal and the loyalty toward the Church, which does not exclude love for country; exhortation to be firm.

Vatican, December 8, 1940

Pius XII thanks the Cardinal-Archbishop of Breslau for the information received about the episcopal conference of Fulda and expresses his happiness to have received a visit in Rome by two German bishops. Despite the worsening of the situation of the Church in Germany, the Pope does not want to ignore any occasion to arrive at an honorable agreement. The attitude of the Holy See during the war. The Pope encourages the new forms of apostolate and the spiritual concern for the soldiers, the youth and the "Wandernde Kirche." Directives regarding the formation of the clergy; the liturgical movement and the language of the liturgy; concern of the Pope about religious conditions in Poland.

Vatican, December 15, 1940

Pius XII emphasizes to the Bishop of Berlin the importance of the information received and thanks him for the reports sent on the debates during the episcopal conference of Fulda. The Pope recalls the contents of his letter to Cardinal Bertram: No "peace at all price" of the Church with the regime; isolated cases of attacks against the Church; the fight against religious publications; declaration of the Holy Office against euthanasia.

Vatican, February 11, 1941

The Pope thanks the Cardinal-Archbishop of Cologne for his Christmas greetings and repeats his joy over the relationship that exists between the Pope and the bishops. Pius XII refers to his efforts for peace. "Wandernde Kirche"; religious weeks for the youth; approval of the new apostolic methods; confidence in the future; recruitment of priests; "sentire cum Ecclesia."

Vatican, February 12, 1941

Thanks the Cardinal-Archbishop of Munich for his Christmas greetings; remembers the times spent in Munich. The day of prayer for peace. The Pope intends to work for a peace that will safeguard honor and the rights of all. In Germany the Church is exposed to attacks against the faith and against the Catholic conscience. Wishes for the return of the Cardinal's health.

Vatican, February 16, 1941
Thanks the Bishop of Münster for feastday wishes. The new trials for the Catholic Church in Germany and the de-Christianization of youth. The measures taken by the State against the ecclesiastical property in Oldenbourg. Protect among Catholics the spirit of fidelity toward the Holy See. The Pope is working to reduce the evils of war and to prepare the way to peace.

Vatican, February 16, 1941
To the Bishop of Trèves the Pope sends the nomination of a second auxiliary bishop. The Pope is happy about the fidelity manifested by the German episcopate, despite the efforts of an anti-Roman propaganda. The Pope's efforts toward a just peace. For eight years the Holy See has done everything possible to spare the German Catholics of such heavy sacrifces. The future could require these sacrifices, and the pastors must prepare for it by proclaiming the truth out loud.

Vatican, February 20, 1941
Thanks the Bishop of Limbourg for the greetings and the prayers and for the Saint Peter's Pence. Again attacks are directed against the Church in Germany, and "The New Order" wants to be a death sentence for them. The Pope exhorts them to a steadfast firmness. He himself will not cease to work for freedom and for peace, for he wants the well-being of all people without distinction.

Vatican, February 20, 1941
Thanks the Bishop of Wurtzbourg for his greetings. Testimony rendered by the bishop to the authority of the successor of Peter. A difficult situation for the Pope: he is constrained to keep silence and to inaction, when he would want to speak and to act. Confiscation of Kilianeum. The Pope is not indifferent toward the German people, nor of any people. He implores peace, peace for the Church and for all peoples, on the basis of rights and of justice.

Vatican, March 1, 1941
To the Archbishops and Bishops of Bavaria: The fidelity of the bishops and their zeal are a consolation for the Pope in the midst of his sorrows; thanks to them for letter which recognizes the Holy See's efforts for peace; praises the decisions of the conference; necessity for particular vigilance and firmness regarding religious education of the youth; its preservation against the errors of neo-paganism; special solicitude for theology students, for soldiers and for priests assigned to military service. He recalls the years spent in Germany as Nuncio; the trust and prudence of the bishops, with the zeal of the clergy and

the collaboration of the laity; thanks for the felicitations addressed on the anniversary of his coronation.

Vatican, March 7, 1941

To the Bishop of Osnabrück the Pope sends this thanks for Christmas greetings; remembrance in prayer; consecration of the diocese to Mary; recommendation for the Marian prayer; wishes for peace.

Vatican, June 10, 1941

Thanks to the Bishop of Passau for felicitations and prayers. Condition of the Church in Germany; increase of hostile measures toward the Church; efforts to compromise; limits regarding advances; views on the future; new restrictive measures in sight; prohibition of the Sunday journals; propaganda against the Pope; Pius XII insists on his impartiality; on his efforts for peace about which he recalls the fundamental conditions.

Vatican, September 8, 1941

The Pope thanks the German Archbishops and Bishops for their fidelity to the Church and for the report that was submitted. He repeats his special love for the German Catholics and his union with them. The persecutions of the Church during the course of history; a perfidious persecution is now at work in Germany; enumeration of some violent measures taken against Catholic civil servants, against the apostolate, against working with the youth, against the Catholic press, against religious orders. The Pope fears that there will be still more distress in the future; and despite all this, he invites them not to be discouraged but to maintain the resolution of steadfast fidelity. He praises them for the pastoral letter of June 26; the Pope has trust in their firmness and in the loyalty of the bishops; assurance of his prayers; firm hope also for the future. The Church is fought against but it will never be conquered; prayer for peace for the Church and for its persecutors; invitation for common prayer and trust in the intercession of Mary.

Vatican, September 30, 1941

The Pope writes to the Bishop of Berlin about the episcopal conference at Fulda and the pastoral letter of German bishops; the sermons of the Bishop of Münster; profound impression that was produced; praise of their courage; the particular difficult situation of the Holy See; the requests to the German Government remain answered; conferences of the bishops.

Vatican, February 2, 1942

Pius XII thanks the Cardinal-Archbishop of Munich for his feastday wishes; "The Catholic family spirit"; the connection of the Pope with Germany; his sorrow because of the measures directed against the Church and against human rights; one must encourage the Catholic conscience to resist; approval of the last sermons of the Cardinal; necessity for official declarations of ecclesiastical authority; Sunday Masses; military service of priests and theology students; apostolate to the soldiers; lack of priests; Christian spirit of the priests who have mobilized; news from the Eastern front; concentration camp at Dachau; solicitude for priests that are found there; propaganda against the Church; episcopal conference of Western Germany; information. "L'Osservatore Romano" and its diffusion in Germany; necessity for rapport with the Holy See; prayers for peace; audience accorded to some Germans.

Vatican, February 20, 1942

The Pope thanks the Bishop of Tréves for his greetings; difficulty of the situation of the Holy See; thanks for prayers and reciprocal assurances; the new auxiliary bishop; indults accorded to Germany; approval of the courageous attitude of the German bishops, a fruitful attitude despite possible reprisals; suppression of the seminary; lack of priests and their formation; suppression of Catholic Sunday newspapers; defense of the rights of people by the Church; publication of the principles for a just peace; the happiness of serving Christ.

Vatican, February 24, 1942

Pius XII thanks the Bishop of Limbourg for his greetings and prayers; dangers of war for the Church; amid help of the faithful; efforts toward peace; thanks for the Saint Peter's Pence; new ways for the apostolate; suppression of the nursery schools; importance of religious formation; suppression of the Abbey of Eibinger; words of consolation for the religious.

Vatican, March 1, 1942

The Pope regards the Diocese of Berlin with special sympathy and rejoices about the testimony of fidelity to the faith that is manifested there. Thanks for the letters received. The Pope intends to oppose the tentatives of those in power who want to control the choice of bishops. He praises the sermon against euthanasia by the Bishop of Berlin. The participation of the Pope in the fate of those who suffer for the faith. His Christmas message that speaks of a just peace could not be heard in Germany: however, the Pope hopes that those principles will be considered at the time of a peace settlement.

Vatican, March 1, 1942

Pius XII thanks the Archbishop of Fribourg for the greetings sent; promise of fidelity; double proof of faith: the misery of war and the trials of the Church; felicitations on the sixtieth anniversary; the Archbishop's pastoral letter. The present times recall the epoch of "Kulturkampf"; testimony of faithfulness to the Church; praise of the firmness of the episcopal declarations; the film "Ich klage an" and its nefarious influence; preservation of the youth; theologians of the Diocese of Strasbourg; anxiety about priestly vocations; priests in the sanitation department; Pope's efforts for peace; rebukes uttered against the Holy See in Germany; prayer to obtain patience and strength.

Vatican, May 25, 1942

The Pope thanks the Archbishops and Bishops of Bavaria for the material sent by the episcopal conference on the occasion of the anniversary of the coronation of the Pope and of his 25 years of episcopacy; alludes to the years passed in Munich as Nuncio; of the grave responsibility that the government of the Church imposed on him; the consciousness of the union existing between the Pope and the faithful, and reinforced by circumstances, is a consolation and a help. The desire of the Pope is to see Christian truth everywhere announced and efforts toward sanctity sustained; that we pray for peace and that our prayer is heard. Praise of the pastoral zeal and of the decisions of the episcopal conference; aggravation of the struggle against the Church, that is manifested by particular measures. The Pope blesses the work of the clergy and of the lay Catholics, exhorting parents to bring up their children in the faith: religious education in the home is the surest guarantee for the future, despite the actual struggle.

Vatican, June 5, 1942

The Pope thanks the Bishop of Mayence for the felicitations and for the pastoral letter: he approves the fundamental thoughts of the project. He explains his ideas; necessity for a certain reserve; the particular condition of the Church; the responsibility for the failure of efforts in view of a compromise; the painful way of the cross for German Catholics; the joy of the Pope because of their fidelity; alludes to his own activity in Germany.

Vatican, August 15, 1942

Pius XII thanks the Cardinal-Archbishop of Munich for his letter. The Pope sees his work and his responsibilities increase each day. He trusts in the prayers of the faithful especially on the occasion of his episcopal jubilee. His duty is a gift without reservations of all his strength and a renunciation of all relaxation; despite the urgent advice of the doctor the Pope will not go to Castelgandolfo; the place of the bishop in times of distress is in the midst of his flock. Great are the dangers of the times, but it will result also in many blessings. The bishops and the Pope must not give themselves any rest in these times. The Pope announces his full recovery after illness and thanks the Cardinal for a photo; he repeats his joy because of the confidential relationship that exists between the Pope and the bishops.

Vatican, October 15, 1942

Thanks for the reports on the episcopal conference of Fulda sent by the Capitular Vicar of Gurk. The Pope encourages the prelates to come to the defense of the occupied regions: in doing their duty as Christians, they also serve their country, where many ignore abuses committed. There is the question of the expropriation of Church property; conditions in the Slovak region. Consecration of the diocese to the Sacred Heart; blessings to look forward to.

Vatican, October 25, 1942

The Pope thanks the German Archbishops and Bishops for their letter on the episcopal conference of Fulda and for their prayers; alludes to the period he spent in Germany. The struggle against the Church increases and the particular measures against the Church are multiplied. The Pope expresses praise for the firmness and the fidelity of the bishops, the clergy and the faithful and he exhorts them to perseverance and to unity; he recommends prudence at the same time as courage. Make known to the faithful the sympathy and the solicitude of the Pope; exhortation to have trust in God and recall the times of the martyrs.

Vatican, January 3, 1943

The Pope remembers his efforts for German Catholics in order to arrive at an agreement with the Reich; one must evaluate the increase of the struggle against the Church. Compassion of the Pope toward apostates; the number of faithful has increased. Religious are destined from their youth; the task of the family; praise of Catholic youth. The Catholic Church and the German tradition. Efforts and prayers of the Pope for peace.

Vatican, January 31, 1943

Thanks the Cardinal-Archbishop of Munich for his Christmas greetings and repeats the bonds that unite him to Germany. His compassion for the victims of the aerial attacks; desire for peace; difficult situation of the Holy See, whose efforts are exposed to distrust. His "impartiality." Pius XII's special regard for Germany. His "Wednesday allocutions" to young spouses; threats that weigh on family ideals. The pontifical Christmas allocution. Priests in the sanitation department; anxiety about the recruitment of priests.

Vatican, February 24, 1943

Pius XII thanks Galen, the Bishop of Münster, for his wishes and prayers. He approves of the episcopal declarations on the dignity of man, of the family and of the Church. Joy given to the Pope by the courage of the German bishops. Christmas message of 1942: exposition of the fundamentals of a

durable peace. Measures taken against the Church in the Diocese of Münster.
Anxiety for the recruitment and the formation of the clergy; consoling
prediction for the future. The Pope rejoices at the prospect of Galen's visit to
Rome and at the thought of the constancy in the faith of German Catholics.

Vatican, April 30, 1943

Thanks to the Bishop of Berlin for wishes and prayers; difficult situation of the
Holy See. Aerial attacks and the efforts of the Pope to make the aerial war
more human; information bureau for prisoners of war; German veto on news
of prisoners; information requested from Russia refused. The Pope approves
the very clear sermons of the bishop; positive results of these declarations for
the future; approval of help given to non-aryans; sympathy for Monsignor
Lichtenberg. Concern for preserving the youth from the pernicious
conception of the times: the liturgical question passes to the second place. One
must consider if the reprisals one fears render possible or not the public decla-
rations of the Church; motives for the reserve of the Pope. Measures taken
against the Church, particularly against the Poles, above all in "Warthegau";
the priests in concentration camps. He approves the Memorandum of the Ger-
man episcopate sent to the government. He speaks of the assistance of the
Holy See to the non-aryans and the limitations of this assistance. Fidelity of
German Catholics; particular concern of the Pope for the youth.

Vatican, June 29, 1943

The Pope thanks Bishop d'Ermland for the greetings transmitted on the
occasion of the anniversary of his coronation, for the prayers and the
information sent; he mentions the precarious situation of the Holy See and
his letter for the 7th Centenary of the diocese; praises the faithful for the
increase of the number of communicants and the Bishop for his zeal.

Vatican, August 16, 1943

The Pope thanks the Bishop of Mayence for the memorandum on the liturgical
question; it will be examined with an understanding spirit. Three principal
points to be considered: not to obscure the efficacy of the grace of the
sacraments, insist on one's personal effort toward sanctity, not to close one's
eyes on the more important matters. The expression "Junge Kirche." Cities
destroyed by aerial attacks, among others Mayence. Monsignor Pacelli had
assisted at the feasts of the cathedral. Aerial attacks on Rome; reasons why the
Pope intervened for the eternal city in a special way. His sympathy for the fate
of the German people; ardent desire for peace; charitable works of the Holy
See; Information Bureau for prisoners; difficulties experienced on the part of
the German and Russian governments; lack of personal contacts of German
bishops with the Pope.

Vatican, September 5, 1943

Importance of information sent to the Pope by the Bishop of Berlin; the episcopal conference of Fulda and the joint pastoral letter. The Pope's Information Bureau for prisoners of war. Principles to observe regarding the attitude of ecclesiastical authority relative to the ordinances of the State. Words of consolation for the Catholic victims of calumnies in Poméranie and in Berlin.

Vatican, October 24, 1943

Religious conditions of the Diocese of Paderborn; the fourth year of war; compassion for the victims of bombings. The satisfaction of the Pope because of the fidelity of Catholics to their faith. Recitation of the rosary and courage of religious during the bombings. Liturgical movement and devotions of the people. Families are separated. Efforts of the Holy See for peace. Calumnies against the Pope. His words do not penetrate into Germany. Prayer for peace.

Vatican, February 9, 1944

Pius XII thanks the Bishop of Passau for his Christmas greetings. Prospects for peace are not very favorable; Pope alludes to his Christmas message and to the principles expressed to achieve peace. Grief in Rome and in Vatican City; attack on Vatican City. The city of Rome is affected by the war. There is a threat of famine. The situation is difficult for the Holy See. Its freedom of speech and of action is becoming more restrained. Impartiality. Echo of the encyclical "Mystici Corporis" in Germany. Objectives of Christmas message: unite the faithful on all fronts. The liturgical movement. Religious conditions in Germany and in the Diocese of Passau. Wishes to the Bishop on the 40th anniversary of priesthood. Hopes to see the German bishops.

Vatican, March 3, 1944

The Pope thanks the Archbishop of Cologne for Christmas wishes and expresses condolence on the death of the Archbishop's father. The encyclical "Mystici Corporis." "Sentire cum Ecclesia." Joy of belonging to the Church. Anxiety of the Holy See about the material and moral devastation of the war. Difficulty to decide if one must be silent or speak openly. Words of consolation for the diocese particularly affected by the war. The loss of clergy. Praise of German clergy. Words of consolation for Cologne and for Wuppertal. Hope in the salutary effect of suffering. Prayers and wishes for a just peace.

Vatican, March 12, 1944

Thanks to the Bishop of Trèves for Christmas greetings. The misery of the period and the lessons to be derived; the decline of culture. The heroic zeal of the faithful. Praise of the apostolate. Best wishes to the clergy. Hope in a better future.

Praise of special care of the Bishop for priestly vocations. Allocutions of the Pope to young married people. Aerial war; condolences for the Dominicans. Efforts of the Holy See for peace; the guiding principles. Felicitations for his golden sacerdotal jubilee.

Vatican, March 21, 1944

Pius XII thanks the Bishop of Berlin for the information and for his Christmas wishes; conditions in Rome; aerial attacks; efforts of the Pope to protect Rome. Necessity for the Pope to remain independent. Victims of the aerial attacks on Berlin. Praise of fidelity to the faith. Condolences on the death of the prelate Lichtenberg, of the bishop's secretary and of the Dominicans killed in the aerial attack. Proceedings against priests; execution of the Curé of Wachsmann. Joint pastoral letter of the German bishops.

2. Bibliography

Andreotti, Giulio. "Christians and Anti-Judaism," editorial in *30 Days*, no. 10 (1998): pp. 4–9. Andreotti explains that Pius XI condemned *Action Française* for its anti-Semitism in 1926. The clearest condemnation of anti-Semitism is found in a decree of March 25, 1928: "The Holy See...condemns unreservedly hatred against the people once chosen by God; the hatred that commonly goes by the name of anti-Semitism."

Angelozzi Gariboldi, Giorgio. *Pio XII, Hitler e Mussolini. Il Vaticano fra le dittature.* Milano: Mursia Editore, 1988.

————. *Il Vaticano nella seconda guerra mondiale.* Milano: Mursia Editore, 1992.

Blet, Pierre. *Pie XII et la Seconde Guerre Mondiale d'après les archives du Vatican.* Paris: Perrin, 1997. Translated by Lawrence J. Johnson. *Pius XII and the Second World War: According to the Archives of the Vatican.* New York/ Mahwah, N.J.: Paulist Press, 1999. This book summarizes Pius XII's assistance to all Nazi victims, demolishes the accusations launched at Pope Pius XII, establishes the historical record of his compassion and heroism, and documents his opposition to all totalitarian movements, especially Nazism.

————. "Controversy: Pius XII. Was There a Culpable Silence with Regard to the Holocaust?" *Inside the Vatican,* May 1998, pp. 52–57.

Bracher, Karl Dietrich. *The German Dictatorship: The Origins, Structure, and Effects of National Socialism.* Translated from the German by Jean Steinberg, New York: Holt, Rinehart and Winston, 1970. This is an important study by an eminent German historian who documents the resistance of many German Catholics and points out that Catholics voted against Hitler by and large.

Breitman, Richard. *Official Secrets: What the Nazis Planned, What the British and Americans Knew.* New York: Hill and Wang, A Division of Farrar, Straus and Giroux, 1998. This book is a broad effort to grasp the relationship between Nazi decisions, German behavior, and Western responses.

de Lubac, Henri. *Christian Resistance to Anti-Semitism: Memories from 1940–1944.* San Francisco: Ignatius Press, 1990. This book reveals the profound influence Pius XII had on the heroic French Catholics who rescued Jews.

Deutsch, Harold. *The Conspiracy Against Hitler in the Twilight War.* It unveils recent revelations concerning espionage activities against Hitler. Included is a chapter entitled, "Operation X: The Vatican Connection," which describes Pius XII's daring efforts to remove Hitler from power. New York: Random House, 1996. This book picks up and expands upon John H. Waller's *The Unseen War in Europe: Espionage and Conspiracy in the Second World War.*

Faulhaber, Michael von. *Judaism, Christianity and Germany.* Translated by G. D. Smith. New York: Macmillan, 1935. Delivered after the Nazis seized power, Cardinal Faulhaber's four Advent sermons were a courageous defense of Christianity's Jewish roots. He insisted: "The God of the New Testament is not a different God from the God of the Old Testament."

Gonella, Guido. *The Papacy and World Peace: A Study of the Christmas Messages of Pope Pius XII.* London: Helles and Carter, 1945. Gonella, an Italian humanist and scholar (who was arrested by Mussolini), examines Pius XII's Christmas messages, which unequivocally condemned the evils of Fascism, Nazism, and anti-Semitism. This book is a powerful antidote to those who assert that Pius XII was "silent" during the war. Professor Gonella proves that the Pontiff was an outspoken champion of human rights and freedom for all.

Graham, Robert A. "Pius XII and the Nazis: An Analysis of the Latest Charges that the Pope Was a 'Friend' of the Axis." *America,* December 5, 1964, pp. 742–43.

————. *The Vatican and Communism in World War II. What Really Happened?* San Francisco: Ignatius Press, 1996. This book demolishes the allegation that Pius XII harbored secret sympathy for Nazism because he saw it as a "bulwark" against Communism. In fact, Pius XII regarded Nazism just as diabolical as Soviet Communism. He saw them as twin evils dedicated to the destruction of Judeo-Christian civilization.

Hamilton, Richard. *Who Voted for Hitler?* Princeton: Princeton University Press, 1982. This book is an analysis of the voting patterns of German citizens during the rise of Hitler and proves that German Catholics voted overwhelmingly against him. Hamilton writes: "Unlike the situation in Protestant communities, where some elites or notables, if not actively supporting the National Socialists, at least vouched for them as worthy allies in the national struggle, in Catholic communities, the leaders, both lay and clerical, were overwhelmingly opposed to their aspirations." In the 1932 elections, when the Nazis gained their greatest electoral successes, more than half the non-Catholic Germans voted National Socialist; fewer than 15 percent of Catholic Germans voted National Socialist.

Is the Catholic Church Anti-Social? A Debate Between G. G. Coulton and Arnold Lunn. London: Catholic Book Club, 1947. Lunn, a Catholic scholar and apologist, debates Coulton, an anti-Catholic historian, on the historical wartime record of the Church. Following Albert Einstein's tribute to the Church, Lunn quotes Countess Waldeck, daughter of a Jewish banker in Mannheim: "There exist opponents to Hitler whose strength of soul and integrity is so great that, notwithstanding the calumnies with which the Nazis have tried to smear them, the Germans know that these men risk their lives and liberty, not for selfish interest, but for the spiritual protection of the Fatherland. For these men are Churchmen. Their every sermon and every pastoral letter is a political event in the Germany of today and no word by them is ever lost." In her book *Excellenx* the Countess pays tribute to the Catholic Bishops, "whose utterances are a remarkably frank denunciation of Nazi treatment of the Jews and conquered people and their contempt for individual rights....To all practical intents and purposes Catholic opposition to Nazism has been much more important and articulate than Protestant opposition."

Maccarone, Michele. *Il Nazionalsocialismo e la Santa Sede.* Rome: Editrice Studium, 1947. Monsignor Maccarone, a Vatican eyewitness, reports Pacelli's anti-Nazi protests. He provides information about the Concordat with Hitler and the oppression against the clergy in Germany prior to and during the war, as well as an analysis of the papal encyclical *Mit brennender Sorge* and the work of the Holy See during the war years.

Marchione, Margherita. *Yours Is a Precious Witness: Memoirs of Jews and Catholics in Wartime Italy.* New York/Mahwah, N.J.: Paulist Press, 1997. This book traces both documentary and anecdotal evidence of Pope Pius XII's efforts. His example inspired Italians to respond with countless acts of individual heroism. Convents, monasteries, and papal buildings in Italy became havens for refugees.

———. *Pius XII: Architect for Peace.* New York/Mahwah, N.J.: Paulist Press, 2000. Those who criticize the Holy See for its "secret archives" should take time to read and ponder the implications of the documents presented here. Her book seeks not just to recommend Pius XII and defend him against unjust accusation, but acts as a plea for future toleration between faiths.

Meltzer, Milton. *Rescue: The Story of How Gentiles Saved Jews in the Holocaust.* New York: Harper and Row, 1988. The various stories about rescue offer reasons for hope and for the belief in the goodness of men, women, and children who risked their lives to save Jews. These heroes and heroines made moral choices and by their courageous actions, defying the Nazi plan for extermination, they show us that one need not be passive or silent in the face of evil.

Miccoli, Giovanni. *I dilemmi e i silenzi di Pio XII.* Milano: Rizzoli, 2000.

The Persecution of the Catholic Church in German-Occupied Poland. London: Burns and Oates, 1941. Reports by Cardinal Hlond of Poland as well as translated material from Vatican Radio and *L'Osservatore Romano* that included documentary evidence on the Nazi assault against the Polish Church.

The Persecution of the Catholic Church in the Third Reich. London: Burns and Oates, 1940. Edited by W. Mariaux and published with the approval of Pope Pius XII. This is a compilation of primary source material from Nazi Germany, translated into English.

Rhodes, Anthony. *The Vatican in the Age of the Dictators 1922–1945.* New York: Holt, Rinehart and Winston, 1973. This book by a distinguished scholar is one of the first works to make use of the Vatican archives, as well as the largely unexamined state papers of the warring countries. Rhodes not only establishes the true wartime record of Pope Pius XII, but also refutes unfounded allegations that the Papacy harbored sympathy for Fascism and Nazism.

Ritter, Gerhard. "The German Opposition to Hitler," in *Contemporary Review* CLXXVII (1950): pp. 339–45.

———. *The German Resistance.* London: Ruskin House, 1958. Translated by R. T. Clark and published in America by Praeger. Ritter, a well-known German historian who was jailed by the Nazis, pays tribute to the anti-Nazi convictions of German Catholic bishops. On p. 56: "They [the bishops] declared expressly that they were obliged to enter the lists on behalf not only of religious and ecclesiastical rights but of 'human rights as such' without which culture must collapse. They therefore never shrank from an even stronger protest than that of the Evangelicals against the arbitrary confiscation of private property, against the concentration camp, against the methods of police spying, against the shooting of innocent hostages or prisoners and the abduction of foreign workers and, of course, against the extermination of the mentally afflicted."

Rychlak, Ronald J. *Hitler, the War, and the Pope.* Mississippi: Genesis Press, 2000/ Indiana: Our Sunday Visitor Press, 2000. With exacting scholarship, Rychlak gives a full exploration of the background facts, including discussions of history, religion, politics, diplomacy, and military tactics. He includes ten fundamental questions about Pope Pius XII and the Nazis that are answered with legal analysis and authoritative citation.

Scrivener, Jane. *Inside Rome with the Germans.* New York: Macmillan, 1945. In her diary, Jesse Lynch, an American citizen known as Mother Mary St. Luke, uses the pen name of Jane Scrivener. She depicts the role of Pope Pius XII and the Vatican with great spontaneity in an authentic eyewitness account about rescue efforts the Pope was directing and coordinating.

Stasiewski, Bernhard and Volk, Ludwig. *Akten Deutscher Bischofe über die Lage der Dirche, 1933–1945.* Mainz: Matthias-Grünewald, 1968–85. This publication in six volumes contains the formal statements of the German Bishops who were inspired by Pope Pius XII and Church teachings in defense of human rights and against Nazi racism and anti-Semitism.

Tornielli, Andrea. *Pio XII: Il Papa degli Ebrei.* Casale Monferrato: Piemme, 2001.

Von Hassell, Ulrich. *The Von Hassell Diaries: The Story of the Forces Against Hitler Inside Germany, 1938–1944.* San Francisco: Westview Press, 1947; reprinted 1994. The day-by-day testament of a leader of the anti-Nazi German resistance. It documents Pius XII's active assistance to the anti-Nazi cause within Germany, and the esteem in which the Pontiff was held. Talks were arranged through the Pope for the purpose of laying a foundation for the discussion of peace terms after a change in the German regime. The confidential agent for Operation X was Dr. Josef Müller. Omitted in the translation are many valuable notes and appendices.

3. Additional References

Actes et Documents du Saint-Siège relatifs à la Seconde Guerre Mondiale,
edited by Pierre Blet, Robert A. Graham, Angelo Martini, and Burkhart
Schneider, Vatican City: Libreria Editrice Vaticana, 1965–81, tomes
1–11 (tome 3 in 2 vols.).

Archives of the Vatican Radio.

Atti e discorsi di Pio XII, Vatican Press, 20 vols.

Bilan du Monde, 1, 1958; 2, 1960: Paris, Casterman.

Church and State through the Centuries, ed. S. Z. Ehler, J. B. Morrall, London, 1954.

Discorsi e panegirici 1931–1939.

Discorsi e radiomessaggi, 1940–1958, Vatican Press, 20 vols.

Documenti Diplomatici Italiani, Ottava Serie, 1935–39; *Nona Serie,* 1939–43, Rome, 1953.

Documents on British Foreign Policy, 1919–1939, ed. E. L. Woodward, R. Butler, HMSO, London, 1947.

Documents on German Foreign Policy, Series C and Series D, London, 1957–64.

Documents Pontificaux de Pie XII, 20 vols. ed. St. Augustin, St. Maurice-Paris, 1950–62.

Eugenio Pacelli, erster apostolischer Nuntius beim Deutschen Reich; Gesammelte Reden, ed. L. Kaas, Berlin, 1930.

Foreign Relations of the United States, Diplomatic Papers, 1939–43; Washington, D.C., 1956–70.

La Documentation Catholique, London, 1950.

Les Enseignements Pontificaux, ed. Monks of Solesmes, tr. *Papal Teachings,* St. Paul, Boston.

London *Times.*

L'Osservatore Romano.

Major Addresses of Pius XII, 2 vols., ed. V. A. Yzermans, St. Paul, 1861.

Nuremberg Transcript, National Archives, Washington, D.C.

The Catholic Periodical Index, Haverford, Pennsylvania.

The Church Speaks, Washington, D.C., 1954.

The Guide to Catholic Literature, W. Romig, Michigan, 1–6.

The New Catholic Encyclopaedia.

The Tablet of London.

The Wartime Correspondence between President Roosevelt and Pope Pius XII, ed. M. C. Taylor, New York, 1947.

Trials of War Criminals before the International Military Tribunal, Nuremberg: Proceedings, Documents, London, 1947.

Trials of War Criminals before the Nuremberg Military Tribunal, Washington, D.C., 1951–53 (vol. 13, *The Ministries*).

4. Pope Pius XII: Selected Documents

(National Catholic Welfare Conference, Washington, D.C., 1939–58)

1. *On the Function of the State in the Modern World,* October 20, 1939.
2. *To the Church in the United States,* November 1, 1939.
3. *Mystici Corporis,* June 29, 1943.
4. *Divino afflante Spiritu,* December 30, 1943.
5. *Christmas Message,* December 24, 1944.
6. *Papal Directives for the Woman of Today,* September 11, 1947.
7. *Mediator Dei,* November 20, 1947.
8. *Humani Generis,* August 12, 1950.
9. *Menti Nostrae,* September 23, 1950.
10. *The Dogma of the Assumption,* November 1, 1950.
11. *On Promoting Catholic Missions,* June 2, 1951.
12. *Counsel to Teaching Sisters,* September 15, 1951.
13. *Moral Questions Affecting Married Life* (two addresses), October 29, 1951, and November 26, 1951.
14. *Proofs for the Existence of God,* November 22, 1951.
15. *The Function of Art,* April 8, 1952.
16. *On Sacred Art,* June 30, 1952.
17. *The Moral Limits of Medical Research and Treatment,* September 14, 1952.
18. *On the Eucharistic Fast,* January 6, 1953.
19. *On Psychotherapy and Religion,* April 13, 1953.
20. *On the Marian Year and the Dogma of the Immaculate Conception,* September 8, 1953.
21. *On Holy Virginity,* March 25, 1954.
22. *On the Queenship of Mary,* October 11, 1954.
23. *On Sacred Music,* December 25, 1955.
24. *On Devotion to the Sacred Heart,* May 15, 1956.
25. *On Laws of Fasting and the Evening Mass,* March 19, 1957.

26. *On Motion Pictures, Radio and Television,* September 8, 1957.
27. *Guiding Principles of the Lay Apostolate,* October 5, 1957.
28. *The States of Perfection,* December 12, 1957.
29. *Applied Psychology,* April 10, 1958.
30. *Sacred Music and the Sacred Liturgy,* September 3, 1958.

Part VII
Notes

PART I: PROLOGUE
CHAPTER I: THE CONSENSUS AND THE CONTROVERSY

1. January 22, 1939.
2. *Mit brennender Sorge* appeared in the March 1962 issue of *Stimman der Zeit.* The German text: "Es ist bezeichnend, dass der erste Schritt, den der Hl. Stuhl bei der neuen Regierung in Berlin tat, dem Schutz der Juden in Deutschland galt. Schon am 4. April 1933, zehn Tage nach dem Ermächtigungsgesetz, wurde der Apostolische Nuntius in Berlin beauftragt, sich bei der Reichsregierung für die Juden zu verwenden und auf alle Gefahren einer antisemitischen Politik aufmerksam zu machen." The Italian translation of the German text follows: È degno di nota il fatto che il primo passo compiuto dalla Santa Sede presso il nuovo governo di Berlino[a] si riferì alla protezione degli ebrei in Germania. Già il 4 aprile 1933, cioè dieci giorni dopo la legge sui pieni poteri,[b] il Nunzio Apostolico a Berlino fu incaricato di adoperarsi presso il governo del Reich a favore degli ebrei e di attirare la sua attenzione su tutti i pericoli di una politica antisemita. [[a]Si tratta del governo di Hitler che venne al potere il 30 gennaio 1933. [b]Si tratta della legge con la quale il Parlamento tedesco conferì pieni poteri al governo di Hitler, e cioè poteri che andavano ben al di là dei poteri che la Costituzione Tedesca concedeva al Cancelliere del Reich, dando così mano libera a Hitler praticamente in tutto.]
3. Pinchas Lapide, *Three Popes and the Jews* (New York: Hawthorn Press, 1967), pp.103–4.
4. Op. cit.
5. *First Things,* August-September 2000, pp. 20–22. Michael Novak holds the George Frederick Jewett Chair in Religion and Public Policy at the American Enterprise Institute.
6. Both published by Paulist Press, Mahwah, N.J. These books are also published in Italian by Editoriale Pantheon: *Pio XII e gli Ebrei* (1999) and *Pius XII: Architetto di Pace* (2000).
7. Berlin, 1930.
8. Città del Vaticano: Tipografia Poliglotta, 1939.
9. Città del Vaticano: Tipografia Poliglotta, 1940–59.
10. Rome: Edizioni Paoline, 1940–59.
11. Vatican City: Libreria Editrice Vaticana, 1965–81, tomes 1–11 (tome 3 in 2 vols.).
12. London: Burns & Oates, 1940, edited by W. Mariaux and published with the approval of Pope Pius XII.
13. *Hungarian Jewry and the Papacy: Pius XII Was Not Silent* (London: Sands and Company, 1968).
14. According to the *Encyclopaedia Britannica* ("The Vatican" 1962 edition), by 1935, "the Vatican was complaining about German non-fulfillment

of its terms and also protesting against pagan elements in the Nazi ideology, such as the doctrine of racism and the persecution of the Jews....During the Nazi reign of terror in the city [of Rome] after the overthrow of Mussolini, substantial numbers of escaped prisoners of war, Jews and leaders of democratic parties were sheltered by the ecclesiastical power."

15. Cf. *L'Osservatore Romano*, No. 174, July 2, 1933.

16. *Il Mattino*, January 14, 2001.

17. Cf. *The Jewish Standard* (N.J.), October 10, 1997.

18. Cf. Institute of the World Jewish Congress, *An Unfinished Agenda*, Policy Dispatch, n. 23, November 1997.

19. Cf. Eric J. Greenberg's article in *The Jewish Week*, May 23, 1997.

20. *Actes et Documents du Saint-Siège relatifs à la Seconde Guerre Mondiale*.

CHAPTER II: THE CAREER OF POPE PIUS XII

1. Shirer, William L., *The Rise and Fall of the Third Reich: A History of Nazi Germany* (New York: Simon and Schuster, 1959), p. 616.

2. Cf. Charles Pichon, *The Vatican and Its Role in World Affairs* (New York: E.P. Dutton and Company, 1950), p. 147.

3. Cf. *Controversial Concordats,* edited by Frank Coppa. Washington, D.C.: The Catholic University of America Press, 1999, p. 173.

4. *New York Times,* p. 6, col. 4.

5. *New York Times,* January 17, 1939, p. 1, col. 3.

6. Cf. *I dilemmi e i silenzi di Pio XII* by Giovanni Miccoli, was published by Rizzoli (Milan: 2000).

7. Torino: Ed. Saie, 1965.

8. In this sixteen-page commentary, dated May 16, 2000, and June 11, 2000, to the six members of the Vatican Commission, he adds: "The Catholic Church, with its size and international network, stands out, thanks I believe, to the central direction by Pius XII. As to the Allies, while their record during the war in relation to rescue operations leaves something to be desired, we all are deeply thankful that they won the war."

9. *New York Times,* August 2, 1942, p. 10, col. 6.

10. *First Things,* p. 22.

11. *L'Osservatore Romano,* January 5, 1946.

12. Ibid., July 30, 1944.

13. Editrice Studium, Rome, 1947.

14. The letter from Archbishop Agostino Cacciavillan also contains authorization to publish this document. Archbishop Cacciavillan served as Apostolic Pro-Nuncio to the United States from 1990 to 1998. He became

President of the Administration of the Patrimony of the Holy See and is now a Cardinal.

15. pp. 221–25.

16. Among Pius XII's letters to German Bishops in volume 2 of *Actes* (1939–44) is this document, attached to a letter dated March 17, 1940, addressed to the Cardinal-Archbishop of Breslau.

17. Libreria Editrice Vaticana, 1993, 2nd edition.

18. A.E.S. Germania 774.

19. Cf. Collect, Third Sunday after Pentecost.

20. Cf. *Acta Apostolica Sedis* XXIX (1937): pp. 149 and 171.

21. J. Derek Holmes, *The Papacy in the Modern World 1914–1978,* (New York: Crossroad, 1981), p. 101.

22. Our Sunday Visitor, 2000, pp. 18–19; see also Pinchas E. Lapide, *Three Popes and the Jews: Pope Pius XII Did Not Remain Silent* (New York: Hawthorn Books, 1967), p. 118.

23. Op. cit., Holmes, p. 101.

24. Oscar Halechi & James F. Murray, Jr., *Pius XII: Eugenio Pacelli, Pope of Peace* (New York: Farrar, Straus and Young, Inc., 1954), p. 59.

25. August 19, 1933.

26. *Documents on British Foreign Policy,* series 2, vol. 5, London, 1956, no. 342, p. 524.

PART II: REMEMBERING THE TRUTH
CHAPTER III: DEFENSE OF THE POPE

1. Boston, Houghton-Mifflin Company, 1999, p. 68.

2. Ibid., p. 28.

3. Joseph Lichten, *A Question of Judgment,* National Catholic Welfare Conference, 1963, p. 117.

4. *Three Popes and the Jews,* p. 214.

5. *Actes,* vol. 9, p. 182.

6. *Actes,* vol. 10, p. 140.

7. *Actes,* vol. 10, pp. 358–59.

8. April 22, 1945. See Lapide, pp. 225–26.

9. Michael O'Carroll, *Pius XII: Greatness Dishonoured* (Dublin: Laetare Press, 1980), p. 21.

10. *The Tablet,* London, October 25, 1958, p. 371.

11. New York: Universe Publishers, 2000.

12. Bloomington, Ind., Indiana University Press, 2000.

13. *Vita e Pensiero,* Milan, 1975.

14. *Inside the Vatican,* December 2000.

15. *Inside Rome with the Germans,* p. 39.

16. New Haven, Conn.: Yale University Press, 2001.

17. Cf. *The Tablet,* London, July 25, 1942, p. 43.

18. *Virginia Quarterly Review,* Spring, 1939, p. 167.

19. Cardinal Gasparri, Secretary of State, "Replies to the Petition of the American Jewish Committee of New York," February 9, 1916, in *Principles for Peace: Selections from Papal Documents, Leo XIII to Pius XII,* Harry C. Koenig, ed. (Washington, D.C.: National Catholic Welfare Conference, 1943), pp. 198–99.

20. Cf. *Yours Is a Precious Witness: Memoirs of Jews and Catholics in Wartime Italy,* pp. 141–45. Since Zuccotti mentions this book in her notes, she must have been aware of Cardinal Dezza's testimony.

21. *Il clero e l'occupazione di Roma* (Rome: Apes, 1995), p. 16.

22. *But for the Grace of God* (New Jersey: Delacorte Press, 1965), p. 47.

23. Center of Studies on the Shoah and Resistance. Beth Lohame Haghettaot in Western Galilee in Israel is one of the world's largest museums and centers of documentation on the Holocaust.

24. http:/www.ewtn.com.

25. See telegram Nr. 400, F.O. 371/37255; *Actes,* vol. 7, p. 62.

26. March 3, 2000, Internet edition.

27. Simon Weisenthal Center.

28. *Auschwitz and the Allies* (New York: Holt and Company, 1981).

29. Boston: Little, Brown and Company, 1970. Carlo Falconi is a notoriously anti-Pope Pius XII writer.

30. Archdiocese of Boston, October 31, 1970, pp. 1 and 16.

31. New York, October 20, 1958.

32. New York: Hill and Wang, 1998.

33. June 29, 2000.

34. July 2, 2000.

CHAPTER IV: CHURCH LEADERS VERSUS TYRANT

1. Copyright 1942, Religion News Service. Used with permission.

CHAPTER V: SURVIVORS' TESTIMONIALS

1. Warsaw: Pax Editions, 1979.

CHAPTER VI: MEETING THE CHALLENGE

1. June 28, 1964.
2. New York: Universe Publishers, 2000.
3. New York: Holt and Company, 1981.
4. New York: Holt, Rinehart and Winston, 1985.
5. *Actes,* vol. 6, pp. 49–50.
6. *New York Times,* October 11, 1945, p. 12, col. 2.
7. October 15, 1940.
8. March 30, 1941.
9. October 1, 1942.
10. October 24, 1942.
11. June 11, 2000.
12. *Newsweek,* December 20, 1999.
13. Letter to Margherita Marchione, December 5, 2000.
14. *New York Times,* March 31, 2000.
15. March 25, 2000
16. *A Thief in the Night,* 1989; *The Hiding Places of God,* 1991; *Strange Gods,* 1993; *Hitler's Pope,* 1999.
17. Winnipeg, November 6, 1958.
18. Confidential document, no. 101307.
19. *Yours Is a Precious Witness: Memoirs of Jews and Catholics in Wartime* Italy (Mahwah, N.J.: Paulist Press, 1997); *Pope Pius XII: Architect for Peace* (Mahwah, N.J.: Paulist Press, 2000); *The Fighting Nun: My Story* (Cranbury, N.J.: Cornwall Books, 2000).

PART III: THE MEDIA
CHAPTER VII: THE *NEW YORK TIMES*

1. *New York Times,* September 1, 1938, p. 10, col. 6; September 8, 1938, p. 4, col. 2; September 20, 1938, p. 10, cols. 4–6; December 25, 1938, p. 1, col. 1.
2. Ibid., July 17, 1938, p. 1, col. 1.
3. Ibid., February 13, 1939, p. 3, col. 3.
4. Ibid., March 7, 1939, p. 11, cols. 1–2.
5. Ibid., March 7, 1939, p. 1, col. 2.
6. Ibid., April 9, 1939.
7. Ibid., April 10, 1939, pp. 2–6.
8. Ibid., May 9, 1939, p. l, col. 1.
9. Foreign editor of the *Paris-Soir.*
10. *New York Times,* May 10, 1939, p. 22, col. 1.

11. Ibid., May 17, 1939, p. 4, cols. 6–7.
12. Ibid., June 7, 1939, p. 1, col. 6.
13. Ibid., August 13, 1939, p. 8, col. 6.
14. Ibid., September 16, 1939, p. 3, col. 7.
15. Ibid., October 28, 1939, p. 1, cols. 1–3.
16. Ibid., p. 14, col. 2.
17. Ibid., October 30, 1939, p. 1, col. 6.
18. Ibid., p. 16, col. 5.
19. Ibid., January 10, 1940.
20. Ibid., March 2, 1940.
21. Ibid., March 31, 1940, p. 8, col. 7.
22. Ibid., December 25, 1940, p. 26, col. 2.
23. Ibid., January 14, 1939, p. 5, col. 3.
24. Ibid., p. 4, col. 6.
25. Ibid., October 20, 1945, p. 4, cols. 2–5.
26. Ibid., May 9, 1942, p. 1, cols. 2–3; p. 5, col. 2.
27. Ibid., May 10, 1942, p. 14, col, 3.
28. Ibid., June 10, 1942, p. 20, col.5.
29. Ibid., January 23, 1943, p. 3, col. 8.
30. Ibid., May 9, 1942, p. 1, cols. 2–3; p. 5, col. 2.
31. Ibid., p. 4, cols. 1–2.
32. Ibid., June 7, 1942, p. 12, cols.1–5.
33. Ibid., June 9, 1942.
34. Ibid., p. 6, col. 2–3.
35. Ibid., p. 20, col. 5.
36. Ibid., p. 10, cols. 4–5.
37. Ibid., June 12, 1942, p. 10, col. 2.
38. Ibid., August 27, 1942, p. 3, col. 5.
39. Ibid., August 29, 1942, p. 14, col. 2.
40. Ibid., September 3, 1942, p. 5, col. 1.
41. Ibid., September 5, 1942, p. 3, col. 1.
42. Ibid., September 9, 1942, p. 9, cols. 4–5.
43. Ibid., January 10, 1943, p. 9, col. 1.
44. Ibid., September 10, 1942, p. 9, cols. 7–8.
45. Ibid., September 20, 1942, p. 25, col. 5.
46. Ibid., December 25, 1942, pp. 1, 7.
47. Ibid., December 25, 1942, p. 10, cols. 2–5.
48. Ibid., December 25, 1942, p. 16, col. 2.
49. Ibid., January 8, 1943, p. 4, col. 6.
50. Ibid., January 23, 1943, p. 3, col. 8.
51. Ibid., January 31, 1943, p. 37, col. 2.
52. Ibid., February 7, 1943, p. 29, col. 4.

53. Ibid., April 1, 1943, p. 10, col. 2.

54. Ibid., April 22, 1943, p. 7, col. 2.

55. Ibid., April 26, 1943, p. 9, col. 1.

56. Ibid., May 28, 1943, p. 4, col. 4.

57. Ibid., May 25, 1943, p. 6, col. 6.

58. Ibid., p. 4, col. 5.

59. Ibid., October 2, 1943, p. 3, col. 6.

60. Ibid., April 26, 1943, p. 6, col. 5; May 22, 1943, p. 2, col. 7.

61. Ibid., p. 4, col. 3.

62. Ibid., June 11, 1943, p. 4, col. 1.

63. Ibid., p. 4, col. 4.

64. Cf. the Church in History Information Centre, Birkenhead, England.

65. *New York Times,* June 19, 1943, p. 2, col. 5.

66. Ibid., June 27, 1943, p. 16, col. 2.

67. Ibid., p. 8, col. 3.

68. Ibid., July 6, 1943, p. 9, col.1.

69. Ibid., September 6, 1943, p. 7, col. 1.

70. Ibid., p. 4, col. 6.

71. Ibid., December 5, 1943, p. 3, col. 4.

72. Ibid., February 8, 1944, p. 7, col. 1; February 9, 1944, p. 7, col. 4; February 11, 1944, p. 3, col. 2. See also pp. 189–91, *Yours Is a Precious Witness: Memoirs of Jews and Catholics in Wartime Italy.*

73. Ibid., April 28, 1944, p. 5, col. 5.

74. Ibid., April 14, 1944, p. 15, col. 1.

75. Ibid., November 19, 1944, p. 24, col. 6.

76. Ibid., July 15, 1944, p. 12, col. 5.

77. Ibid., July 27, 1944, p. 3, col. 4.

78. Ibid., August 21, 1944, p. 14, col. 5.

79. Ibid., February 2, 1944, p. 1, col. 6.

80. Ibid., p. 11, col. 5. For over seventy years, the Communist regime persecuted the Catholic Church in Russia. After the 1917 revolution, of the more than three hundred churches, there were only two. Over twenty million faithful perished—priests, nuns, religious, and laity.

81. Ibid.

82. Ibid.

83. Ibid., p. 11, col. 6.

84. Ibid., February 4, 1944, p. 14, col. 2.

85. Ibid., February 8, 1944, p. 7, col. 1.

86. Ibid., March 19, 1944, p. 32, col. 1.

87. Ibid., February 9, 1944, p. 3, col. 8.

88. Ibid.

89. Ibid., March 8, 1944, p. 5, cols. 2–3.

90. Ibid., p. 5, col. 4.
91. Ibid., July 6, 1944, p. 7, col. 1.
92. Ibid., July 21, 1944.
93. Ibid., July 21, 1944.
94. Ibid., August 7, 1944.
95. Ibid., p. 14, col. 5.
96. Ibid., January 31, 1945, p. 3, cols. 5–6.
97. Ibid., January 3, 1945, p. 5, col. 4.
98. Ibid., February 10, 1945, p. 3, col. 5.
99. Ibid., February 13, 1945, p. 11, col. 1.
100. Ibid., February 10, 1945, p. 22, col. 6.
101. Ibid., February 28, 1945, p. 22, cols. 6–7.
102. Ibid.
103. Ibid., February 11, 1945.
104. Ibid., April 9, 1945, p. 3, col. 6.
105. Ibid., April 17, 1945, p. 5, col. 1.
106. Ibid., p. 3, cols. 2–3.
107. Ibid., June 24, 1945, p. 27, col. 7.
108. Ibid., p. 5, col. 3.
109. Ibid., p. 10, col. 4.
110. Ibid., May 14, 1945, p. 3, col. 1.
111. Ibid., May 26, 1945, p. 4, col. 5.
112. Ibid., June 3, 1945, p. 1, col. 3.
113. Ibid.
114. Ibid., p. 22.
115. Ibid.
116. Ibid.
117. Ibid.
118. Ibid., p. 1, col. 8.
119. Ibid., March 11, 1942, p. 6, col. 2.
120. Ibid., June 10, 1942, p. 20, col. 5.
121. Ibid., p. 12, col. 1.
122. Ibid., p. 12, col. 2.
123. Ibid., p. 2, col. 5.
124. Ibid., p. 5, cols. 1–2.
125. Ibid., p. 35, col. 4.
126. Ibid., October 11, 1958, p. 2, cols. 4–5.

CHAPTER VIII: THE VATICAN RADIO

1. Princeton, N.J.: Princeton University Press, 1959, p. 12.
2. Ibid., pp. 9–10.
3. President of the Pontifical Academy of Sciences and Rector of the Pontifical Gregorian University.
4. H = Holy See; V = Vatican; J = Jesus Christ. Vatican Radio played an important role in spreading the truth during World War II. Some writers dismiss its importance. In the January 21, 2002, issue of *The New Republic,* there is a long, anti-Catholic essay based on Daniel Jonah Goldhagen's controversial new book, *A Moral Reckoning: The Catholic Church during the Holocaust and Today.* Goldhagen quotes the letter Pacelli wrote in 1919 on Communist revolutionaries out of context and uses it to condemn Pacelli as an anti-Semite. But he does not quote the entire letter. He misuses it. Other errors concern historical dates on the establishment of Jewish ghettos "in Frankfurt (1460); Madrid (1480); Prague (1473); Rome (1556); Venice (1517); and Vienna (1570)." According to the *Encyclopedia Judaica* (edited by Cecil Roth), Jewish ghettos were established in Frankfurt (1462); Venice (1516); Rome (1557); and Vienna (1624). Goldhagen is mistaken by over fifty years for Vienna. On page 26, he asks rhetorically: "Why, as a moral and practical matter, did he [Pius XII] speak out publicly on behalf of the suffering of Poles, but not of Jews? No good answer....(On the instructions of Pius XII, Vatican Radio broadcast the following in January 1940: 'Conditions of religious, political, and economic life have thrown the Polish people, especially in those areas occupied by Germany, into a state of terror, of degradation, and, we dare say, of barbarism. The Germans employ the same methods, perhaps even worse, as those used by the Soviets.')"

Goldhagen deletes the word "Jews" from Vatican Radio's groundbreaking report on Nazi brutalities in Poland. He was unaware of the complete transcript and attacked the Vatican for not explicitly naming Jews as victims, when in fact they were mentioned. He tries to prove that the Vatican was only concerned about Polish Catholics and was so anti-Semitic that it could not spare a good word for Jews in Poland or anywhere else. But, according to the complete transcript, Jews are explicitly named. Goldhagen shamefully does not cite the relevant passage: "A system of interior deportation and zoning is being organized, in the depth of one of Europe's severest winters, on principles and by methods that can be described only as brutal; and stark hunger stares 70 percent of Poland's population in the face, as its reserves of foodstuffs and tools are shipped to Germany to replenish the granaries of the metropolis. Jews and Poles are being herded into separate 'ghettos,' hermetically sealed and pitifully inadequate for the economic subsistence of the millions destined to live there." [Vatican Radio Broadcast of January 21–22, 1940; official English translation. Also repeated in German, Spanish, and Portuguese; full transcript reprinted in

The Persecution of the Catholic Church in German-Occupied Poland (New York: Longmans Green, 1941), pp. 115–17].

    5. Cf. Actes, III, 431.

    6. B. M. Kempner, *Priester vor Hitlers Tribunalen* (Munich: Rütten and Loening, 1966), p. 448.

    7. Ibid., p. 209.

    8. Cf. *Actes,* vol. 2, p. 209, n. IV, p. 420.

    9. Robert A. Graham, *Civiltà Cattolica,* "La Radio Vaticana tra Londra e Berlino," p. 136.

    10. Cf. J. Warszawski, *Civiltà Cattolica,* 1965, III, p. 541; *Pio XII e la Polonia,* p. 28.

    11. March–April 1945, p. 924.

    12. FO 371/30180. (Cf. *Actes,* vol. 4, 514s. pp. 576–83.)

    13. David Alvarez and Robert Graham, *Nothing Sacred: Nazi Espionage Against the Vatican 1939–1945* (London: Frank Cass, 1997), p. 142.

    14. Cianfarra, Camille, *The Vatican and the War* (New York: E. P. Dutton, 1944), p. 256.

    15. Ibid.

    16. Pierre Blet, *Pius XII and the Second World War,* Paulist Press, 1999, chapter 5.

    17. *Actes,* vol 4, no. 140.

    18. Holmes, op. cit., p. 129.

    19. *New York Times,* January 24, 1940, p. 16, col. 2.

    20. Robert A. Graham, op. cit., p. 139

    21. *Inside the Vatican,* October 1999.

    22. January 2000.

    23. Associated Press, Agence France Press, Reuters, Spanish EFE, English-language Tass, and Italian services ANSA and AGI-AP.

    24. *Radio Vaticana* (English, Spanish, French brochure) (Vatican City: Tipografia Vaticana).

    25. London: Sands and Co., 1968, p. x.

    26. Oscar Halecki, *Eugenio Pacelli: Pope of Peace* (New York: Creative Age Press, 1951), p. 340.

CHAPTER IX: *L'OSSERVATORE ROMANO*

    1. Camille Cianfarra, *The Vatican and the War* (New York: Literary Classics, Inc., 1944, distributed by E. P. Dutton & Company), pp. 220–21.

    2. *L'Osservatore Romano,* October 11, 1930.

    3. Princeton, N.J.: Princeton University Press, 1982.

    4. February 3, 1939, p. 3, col. 8.

5. *New York Times,* p. 3, col. 7.
6. November 11, 1939, p. 2, col. 7.
7. Ibid., p. 1, col. 2.
8. Some known only to bishops and missionaries.
9. Cf. Lapide, *Three Popes and the Jews....*
10. Published that same day, June 2, 1943, in *L'Osservatore Romano.*
11. New York: Macmillan, 1945.
12. Ibid., p. 65
13. *New York Times,* October 15, 1944.
14. Columbus, Miss.: Genesis Press, 2000.
15. Ibid., p. 264.
16. Michael O'Carroll, *Pius XII: Greatness Dishonoured* (Dublin: Laetare Press, 1980), p. 89.

PART IV: THE DISCUSSION CONTINUES
CHAPTER X: FEEDING THE CONTROVERSY

1. Cf. *Pius XII and the Second World War: According to the Archives of the Vatican,* by Pierre Blet, S.J. (Mahwah, N.J.: Paulist Press, 1999).
2. New York: Viking, 1999.
3. *Catholic Family News,* November 1999.
4. Ibid.
5. *Vanity Fair,* October 1999, p. 172.
6. *Hitler's Pope,* p. 85.
7. Ibid., p. 287.
8. Ibid.
9. Ibid., p. 380.
10. San Francisco: Ignatius Press, 1990.
11. *Le Monde,* March 26, 1964.
12. April 15, 1964.
13. Ibid.
14. *Vanity Fair,* op. cit., p. 172.
15. *L'Osservatore Romano,* October 13, 1999.
16. *Vanity Fair,* op. cit., p. 172.
17. Bologna: Il Mulino, 1992, pp. 322–25.
18. *Die Welt,* July 16, 1964.
19. November 3, 1999.
20. April 5, 1941.
21. October 24, 1942.
22. October 1, 1942.
23. New York: Doubleday, 1999.

24. *Commentary,* April 1999. According to Jewish historian Pinchas Lapide's book *Three Popes and the Jews* (New York: Hawthorn Books, 1967), the figure may be 860,000.

25. For a partial list of Pius XII's actions and words against the Nazis, consult Pierre Fernessole's book, *Pie XII et la paix du monde* (Paris: Beauchesne, 1947), pp 74–99.

26. It should be noted that the French condemnation came from 30 out of a total of 120 bishops!

27. *New York Times,* October 21, 1999.

28. Boston: Houghton-Mifflin, 1999.

29. Ibid., p. 21.

30. Ibid., p. 20.

31. Letter to Margherita Marchione.

32. April 4, 2000.

33. July 13, 2000.

34. Canonized by Pope John Paul II.

35. London: Hodder and Stoughton, 1972.

36. Mahwah, N.J.: Paulist Press, 2000.

37. New York: Simon and Schuster, 1989.

38. New York: Viking, 1999.

39. Mahwah, N.J.: Paulist Press, 2000.

40. *Inside the Vatican,* May, 2000.

41. *Vanity Fair,* op. cit., p. 176.

42. New York: W. W. Norton, 1998, p. 114.

43. *Vanity Fair,* op. cit., p. 176.

44. *Catholic Review,* November 5, 1943.

45. Excerpts reprinted from *Origins,* CNS Documentary Service, April 20, 2000, vol. 29: no. 44.

CHAPTER XI: THE NEW COMMISSION AND ITS QUESTIONS

1. *ADSS,* vol. 2, appendix 1–9, pp. 385–436.

2. *ADSS,* vol. 6, appendix 4, pp. 536–37.

3. *ADSS,* vol. 2, note 12, p. 407.

4. Burkhart Schneider, "Un'enciclica mancata," *L'Osservatore Romano* (April 5, 1973).

5. *ADSS,* vol. 6, no. 60, p.137; no. 125–26, pp. 211–14; no. 131, p. 219; no. 137, pp. 224–25; no. 341, pp. 437–39 provide several examples of the discussion of these funds. Even within these documents, other reports are referred to but not published, and these letters could be of importance to historians.

6. In the *ADSS,* vol. 1, there are claims advanced that the Pope viewed events in Poland with the greatest sorrow; that he agonized over how to respond; that everything possible that could be done was being done; and that to be more forceful was certain to prompt retaliation.

7. *ADSS,* vol. 6, no. 378, pp. 477–80.

8. *ADSS,* vol. 6, no. 378, note 3, p. 479.

9. *ADSS,* vol. 6, no. 378, notes 4–5, p. 479.

10. *ADSS,* vol. 8, no. 165, pp. 295–97; no. 189, pp. 333–34.

11. *ADSS,* vol. 8, no. 581, pp. 762–63.

12. *ADSS,* vol. 8, no. 421, pp. 586–87.

13. Many of these documents appear in *ADSS,* vol. 8.

14. *ADSS,* vol. 3.2, no. 406, pp. 625–29.

15. *ADSS,* vol. 3.2, no. 357, pp. 539–41.

16. See Gerhart Riegner, "Observations on the Published Vatican Archival Material," unpublished paper, December 5, 1999, p. 6. *ADSS,* vol. 4, no. 398.

17. *ADSS,* vol. 9, no. 82, p. 170. A letter from von Preysing to the Pope, dated January 17, 1941. The original letter read: "Eure Heiligkeit sind wohl über die Lage der Juden in Deutschland und en angrenzenden Ländern orientiert. Lediglich referierend möchte anführen, dass von katholischer wie von protestantischer Seite an mich die Frage getellt worden ist, ob nicht der Heilige Stuhl in dieser Sache etwas tun könnte, einen Appell zugunsten der Unglücklichen erlassen?" Von Preysing presents this request as coming from third parties, rather than in his own name, as if he were only the messenger—though in reality it clearly was a matter of some importance to him. It is interesting that the request has a more general Christian character (not self-evident at the time, given the strength of the Catholic-Protestant divide). Most significant of all, it tends to suggest that the German bishops (or at least some of them) were keeping the Pope well informed about the condition of the Jews or they were aware that he knew about the Jewish plight in the German Reich.

18. *ADSS,* vol. 9, no. 82, p.170. See also note 9, *ADSS,* vol. 2, no. 105, p. 323.

19. *ADSS,* vol. 2, no. 105, p. 318–27.

20. *ADSS,* vol. 3, no. 510, p. 801; 7, no. 225, pp. 396–400. It is also mentioned in *ADSS,* vol. 9, no. 213, p. 327.

21. *ADSS,* vol. 2, no. 123, p. 376.

22. *ADSS,* vol. 8, no. 496, pp. 669–70. In particular, see note 4.

23. Sergio Minerbi, "Pius XII: A Reappraisal," paper presented at the symposium, "Memories, Intertwined and Divergent: Pius XII and the Holocaust," Kings College, Wilkes-Barre, Pennsylvania, April 9–11, 2000.

24. *ADSS,* vol. 8, no. 374, p. 534.

25. *ADSS,* vol. 8, no. 454, pp. 625–27; no. 463, pp. 635–36; no. 468, pp. 638–40; no. 484, p. 658.

26. *New York Times,* September 10, 1942, pp. 7, 8, 9.

27. *ADSS,* vol. 3.2, no. 497, p. 781.

28. In addition, Papée is on record as saying that not all of his memos appear in the *ADSS* volumes. What do his other letters contain? It would be important to know the contents of these communiqués in order to better understand the Polish question.

29. For example, see *ADSS,* vol. 10, no. 165, pp. 239–42; no. 463, p. 554.

30. *ADSS,* vol. 10, no. 40, p. 115.

31. For example, see *ADSS,* vol. 10, no. 127, p. 198; no. 249, p. 335; no. 253, p. 341, no. 254, p. 342, no.1; no. 260, p. 347; no. 270, p. 357, no. 3; no. 273, p. 359; no. 295, p. 378.

32. *ADSS,* vol. 10, no. 53, p. 129.

33. *ADSS,* vol. 10, no. 153, pp. 224–29; no.172, pp. 247–49.

34. See Rotta's activities as described in *ADSS,* vol. 10.

35. *ADSS,* vol. 10, no. 408, p. 497.

36. Stein herself describes her letter, stating: "I know that my letter was sealed when it was delivered to the Holy Father; some time later, I even received his blessing for myself and my loved ones. But nothing else came of it. Is it not possible that he recalled this letter on various occasions later on? My fears concerning the future of German Catholics have been gradually realized in the course of the years that followed." "Je sais que ma lettre était cachetée quand elle a été remise au Saint-Père; quelque temps plus tard, j'ai même reçu sa bénédiction pour moi-même et mes proches. Mais il n'en est rien sorti de plus. Est-il impossible que cette lettre lui soit plusieurs fois revenue à l'esprit par la suite? Mes appréhensions en ce qui concerne l'avenir des catholiques allemands se sont progressivement vérifiés au cours des années suivantes." Notes d'Edith Stein citées par Teresia Renata de Spiritu Sancto, *Edith Stein* (Nuremberg: Glock und Lutz, 1952).

37. *ADSS,* vol. 8, p. 467.

38. *ADSS,* vol. 8, no. 314, p. 466. The memorandum is reprinted in John Morley, *Vatican Diplomacy and the Jews during the Holocaust 1939–1943* (New York: KTAV, 1980), appendix B, 212. As Riegner notes, this important document was not included in the *ADSS,* only the letter of transmission by Bernardini. See Gerhart Riegner, "Observations on the Published Vatican Archival Material," unpublished paper, December 5, 1999, pp. 9–10. "I consider the omission in the Vatican documentation of [this document of March 18] and the accompanying letter of appeal to the Vatican a serious mistake," writes Gerhart Riegner. "It would have shown that important Jewish organizations had called the attention of the Vatican already in a very early stage of the

application of the final solution (six weeks after the so-called Wansee Conference) to the tragic situation of European Jewry." Ibid., 10.

39. "La Santa Sede non ha mai approvato il progetto di far della Palestine una home ebraica...La Palestina è ormai più sacra per i cattolici che...per gli ebrei." "The Holy See has never approved the project of making Palestine a Jewish homeland...Palestine is by now more sacred for Catholics than...for Jews." *ADSS,* vol. 9, no. 94, p. 184.

40. *ADSS,* vol. 9, no. 324, p. 469.

41. *ADSS,* vol. 9, no. 91, p. 182.

42. *ADSS,* vol. 6, no. 29, pp. 92–94.

43. *ADSS,* vol. 6, no.134, p. 222.

44. *ADSS,* vol. 5, no. 189, pp. 361–62.

45. See Richard Lukas, *Forgotten Holocaust: The Poles Under German Occupation 1939–1944* (Lexington: University Press of Kentucky, 1986; revised, New York: Hippocrene Books, 1997), p. 16.

46. One of many examples appears in *ADSS,* vol. 8, no. 441, p. 611, in which the chief Rabbi of Zagreb appeals to the Pope for help. See also Maglione's response in a footnote to this letter, in which he says that the Holy See "has not neglected to involve itself...in favor of the recommended persons."

47. For example, in a letter to the Bishop of Wurtzbourg, Matthias Ehrenfried, on 20 Febrary 1941, Pius writes, "There where the Pope would like to shout, he is forced to wait and keep silence; where he would act and help, he must wait patiently..." (*ADSS,* vol. 2, no. 66, p. 201); and in a letter to the Archbishop of Cologne, Joseph Frings, on March 3, 1944, Pius writes "It is painfully difficult to decide whether reserve and prudent silence, or frank speaking and forceful action are called for" (*ADSS,* vol. 2, no. 119, p. 365).

48. In a passage of Roncalli's diary concerning an audience with Pius XII of October, 10 1941. Roncalli writes that the Pope "Si diffuse a dirmi della sua larghezza di tratto coi Germani che vengono a visitarlo. Mi chiese se il suo silenzio circa il contegno del nazismo non è giudicato male." "...Continued to tell me of his generosity towards the Germans who visit him. He asked me if his silence regarding nazism was not judged badly." See Alberto Melloni, *Fra Istanbul, Atene e la guerra. La missione di A. G. Roncalli (1935–1944),* p. 240.

49. When Cardinal Edward I. Cassidy, president of the Commission for Religious Relations with the Jews, received a preliminary twenty-page document, he gave it to the Secretariat of State. However, prior to its official release by the Vatican, the Jewish group B'Nai B'rith International held a news conference stating that the researchers were asking for more information to determine what Pope Pius XII did or did not know while the Nazis tried to exterminate the Jews and why he did not speak out more.

50. The Catholics: Eva Fleischner, professor emerita, Montclair State University, New Jersey; the Jesuit Gerald Fogarty, Department of Religious

Studies, University of Virginia; and Father John Morley, a scholar on the Holocaust, Seton Hall University, New Jersey. The Jewish scholars: Michael Marrus, historian and dean of graduate studies, University of Toronto; Bernard Suchecky, researcher, Free University of Brussels; and Robert Wistrich, professor of history and Hebrew studies, University of Jerusalem.

51. Cf. *New York Times,* Vatican Radio, and *L'Osservatore Romano.*

52. Cf. *Acta Apostolicae Sedis* XXXI (1939): pp. 86, 87.

53. Cf. *L'Osservatore Romano,* June 3, 1939.

54. *Acta Apostolicae Sedis* XXXI (1939): pp. 333, 335.

55. Ibid., pp. 335–36.

56. Ibid., pp. 393–96.

57. London: Burns and Oates, 1941.

58. Cf. pp. 190–92, Vatican Radio, January 21–22, 1940; pp. 212–15, reprint of article in *L'Osservatore Romano,* December 12, 1940.

59. *Il Giornale,* November 13, 1998.

60. These anti-Semitic demonstrations in Germany continued.

61. May 4–7, 1992, Baltimore, Md.

62. May 29, 1955.

63. Hartford, Connecticut.

64. General audience of April 28, 1999.

CHAPTER XII: POPE JOHN PAUL II

1. Speaking at Assumption College, Worcester, Massachusetts, Rabbi Yoffie said: "The work of Catholic-Jewish relations is not done. Hostilities do not die overnight. But the actions of the church give us reason to hope that we are not condemned to replay them forever....There is a desperate need for a joint campaign of positive religious education. This means that the Catholics need to educate Catholics about Jews, and the Jews need to educate Jews about Catholics." He also pledged that the Union of American Hebrew Congregations will immediately undertake to produce textbooks for its religious schools that will portray accurately and sympathetically the evolving position of the Church on the Jews and Judaism.

2. This is one of eighty-nine poignant stories in Yaffa Eliach's book, *Hasidic Tales of the Holocaust.* It was the subject of an article by Tom Fox in the *Philadelphia Inquirer,* October 31, 1982.

3. *The Holocaust Victims Accuse.*

4. Ibid.

V. CONCLUSION
CHAPTER XIII: THE CATHOLIC CHURCH

1. *Hitler: Hubris* 1889–1936.
2. Lapide, *Three Popes and the Jews,* pp. 267–69.
3. Also see Robert A. Graham, S.J., *Pius XII's Defense of Jews and Others: 1944–45* (New York: Catholic League for Religious and Civil Rights, 1987), p. 44.
4. New York: Viking Press, 1942.
5. Writing to Margherita Marchione on March 19, 2001, Monsignor Giovanni Ferrofino, an eyewitness and participant, tells the story behind "Four Hundred Visas for Jews." Archbishop Maurilio Silvani was later appointed Nuncio to Chile. He sent a copy of letter no. 1261 on August 29, 1943, stating that "the President of the 'Comité representativo de la Colectividad Isreaelita de Chile' begged me, on the 27th of this month, to send to the August Pontiff the expression of their gratitude for all that His Holiness is doing in defense of the Jews in France and during the course of this war [Rapp. nr. 587/29, A.E.S. 190/43]." From Santiago, the Nuncio also sent a letter dated October 5, 1943, to Cardinal Maglione with a copy of the October 3 *El Diario ilustrado,* which he received from the President of the Committee, Samuele Goren. The article states: "...En estos trágicos dias, nuestra mente evoca la elevada figura del Sumo Pontífice, su Santidad Pio XII probado defensor de la causa de los perseguidos y en especial de millones de hermanos europeos nuestros que son víctimas inocentes de inhumanas masacres y crueles vejámenes. Recordamos con indignación que quienes inflingen en los actuales momentos incontables sufrimientos al Santo Padre son las mismas fuerzas del mal que hacen ostentación del incalificable propósito de aprisionar tras las murallas de la Ciudad del Vaticano el incontenible soplo de la inmensa fuerza espritual que emana del sitial de San Pedro..." [Rapp. nr. 3980/143 (A.E.S. 7145/43, orig.). See vol. 9, p. 498].
6. *Figaro,* January 4, 1964.
7. "John Paul's silence can be deafening," May 8, 2001, and "Back into the Breach; Pius and the Jews," May 30, 2001.

Part VIII
Index

Index

Books by Margherita Marchione

CLEMENTE REBORA:

L'imagine tesa, Edizioni di Storia e Letteratura, Rome, 1960, 300 pp.; reprinted and enlarged, 1974, 410 pp.

Lettere, vol. 1, Edizioni di Storia e Letteratura, Rome, 1976, 680 pp.; vol. 2, 1982, 450 pp.

Clemente Rebora, Twayne's World Author Series, Twayne Publishers, 1979, Boston, 183 pp.

CORRESPONDENCE OF GIOVANNI BOINE:

Carteggio Giovanni Boine-Giuseppe Prezzolini (1908–15), vol. 1, Edizioni di Storia e Letteratura, 1971, Rome, 264 pp.; reprinted, 1981.

Giovanni Boine-Emilio Cecchi (1911–17), vol. 2, 1972, 233 pp.; reprinted, 1982.

Giovanni Boine-Amici del "Rinnovamento" tome 1 (1905–10); tome 2 (1911–17), vol. 3, 1977, 1130 pp.

Giovanni Boine-Amici de "La Voce" (1904–17), vol. 4, 1979, 690 pp.

PHILIP MAZZEI:

Philip Mazzei: Jefferson's "Zealous Whig," American Institute of Italian Studies, Morristown, N.J., 1975, 352 pp.

Philip Mazzei: My Life and Wanderings, American Institute of Italian Studies, Morristown, N.J., 1980, 352 pp.

Philip Mazzei: The Comprehensive Microform Edition of His Papers, 1730–1816, nine reels and clothbound guide and index, Kraus International Publications, 1982, 172 pp.

Philip Mazzei: Selected Writings and Correspondence, Cassa di Risparmi e Depositi, Prato, 1983, vol. 1, *Virginia's Agent during the American Revolution,* XLVIII, 585 pp.; vol. 2 *Agent for the King of Poland during the French Revolution* 802 pp.; vol. 3, *World Citizen,* 623 pp.

Filippo Mazzei: Scritti Scelti e Lettere, volumes 1, 2, 3 (Italian edition, same as above, 1984).

The Constitutional Society of 1784, Center for Mazzei Studies, Morristown, N.J., 1984, 49 pp.

Istruzioni per essere liberi ed eguali, Cisalpino-Gogliardica, Milan, 1984, 160 pp.

Philip Mazzei: World Citizen (Jefferson's "Zealous Whig"), University Press of America, Lanham, Md., 1994, 158 pp.

The Adventurous Life of Philip Mazzei—La vita avventurosa di Filippo Mazzei (bilingual), University Press of America, Lanham, Md., 1995, 515 pp.

GIUSEPPE PREZZOLINI:

Giuseppe Prezzolini: Un secolo di attività, Rusconi, Milan, 1982, 160 pp.

Carteggio Cesare Angelini-Giuseppe Prezzolini, Edizioni di Storia e Letteratura, Rome, 1982, 394 pp.

Giuseppe Prezzolini: L'Ombra di Dio, Rusconi, Milan, 1984, 200 pp.

Incontriamo Prezzolini, Editrice la Scuola, Brescia, 1985, 210 pp.

Giuseppe Prezzolini: Lettere a Suor Margherita (1956–82). Introduction by Margherita Marchione, edited by Claudio Quarantotto, Edizioni di Storia e Letteratura, Rome, 1991, XXXIV, 378 pp.

Carteggio Giovanni Abbo-Giuseppe Prezzolini, Edizioni di Storia e Letteratura, Rome, 2000, 233 pp.

BIOGRAPHY:

From the Land of the Etruscans (St. Lucy Filippini), Edizioni di Storia e Letteratura, Rome, 1986, XIV, 268 pp.

Cardinal Mark Anthony Barbarigo, Religious Teachers Filippini, Rome, 1992, 220 pp.

Prophet and Witness of Charity (Tommaso Maria Fusco), edited by Margherita Marchione. Daughters of Charity, Paterson, N.J., 1993, 170 pp.

Peter and Sally Sammartino (Biographical Notes), Cornwall Books, Cranbury, N.J., 1994, 305 pp.

The Fighting Nun: My Story, Cornwall Books, Cranbury, N.J., 2000, 240 pp.

HISTORY:

A Pictorial History of St. Lucy Filippini Chapel, Edizioni del Palazzo, Prato, 1992, 130 pp.

Legacy and Mission: Religious Teachers Filippini, Villa Walsh, Morristown, N.J., 1992, 50 pp.

Yours Is a Precious Witness: Memoirs of Jews and Catholics in Wartime Italy, Paulist Press, Mahwah, N.J., 1997, 259 pp.

Pio XII e gli ebrei, Editoriale Pantheon, Rome, 1999, 288 pp. Ristampato da Edizioni Piemme, Casale Monferrato (AL), 2002.

Pope Pius XII: Architect for Peace, Paulist Press, Mahwah, N.J., 2000, 345 pp.

Pio XII: Architetto di pace, Editoriale Pantheon, Rome, 2000, 413 pp. Ristampato da Edizioni Piemme, Casale Monferrato (AL), 2002.

Consensus and Controversy: Defending Pope Pius XII, Paulist Press, Mahwah, N.J., 2002, 400 pp.

Pio XII: Attraverso le immagini, Libreria Editrice Vaticana, 2002, 200 pp.

Shepherd of Souls: A Pictorial Life of Pope Pius XII, Inside the Vatican—Libreria Editrice Vaticana, 2002, 200 pp.

POETRY:

Twentieth Century Italian Poetry: A Bilingual Anthology, Fairleigh Dickinson University, Rutherford, N.J. 1974, 302 pp.

PROFILES:

Contemporary Profiles: NIAF Awardees, National Italian American Foundation, Washington, D.C., 1993, 265 pp.

Americans of Italian Heritage, University Press of America, Lanham, Md., 1995, 39 photographs, 246 pp.